T0342417

REALM BETWEEN EMPIRES

REALM BETWEEN EMPIRES

The Second Dutch Atlantic, 1680–1815

WIM KLOOSTER AND GERT OOSTINDIE

CORNELL UNIVERSITY PRESS
ITHACA AND LONDON

First published 2018 by Cornell University Press

Printed in the United States of America

Library of Congress Cataloging-in-Publication Data

Names: Klooster, Wim, author. | Oostindie, Gert, author.
Title: Realm between empires : the second Dutch Atlantic, 1680–1815 / Wim Klooster and Gert Oostindie.
Description: Ithaca : Cornell University Press, 2018. | Includes bibliographical references and index. |
Identifiers: LCCN 2017053338 (print) | LCCN 2017058277 (ebook) | ISBN 9781501719608 (epub/mobi) | ISBN 9781501719592 (pdf) | ISBN 9781501705267 | ISBN 9781501705267 (cloth ; alk. paper)
Subjects: LCSH: Netherlands—Colonies—America—History— 18th century. | Netherlands—Colonies—Africa—History— 18th century. | Netherlands—Commerce—History—18th century. | Netherlands—History—18th century. | Caribbean Area—History— 18th century. | Africa, West—History—18th century.
Classification: LCC JV2516 (ebook) | LCC JV2516 .K56 2018 (print) | DDC 909/.0971249207—dc23
LC record available at https://lccn.loc.gov/2017053338

CONTENTS

ACKNOWLEDGMENTS

We decided to write this book in the spring of 2013, when we were both fellows at the Netherlands Institute for Advanced Study in the Humanities and Social Sciences. We thank the NIAS for providing us with this great opportunity. At the NIAS, Wim Klooster was finishing his book *The Dutch Moment*, while Gert Oostindie was concluding a project financed by the Netherlands Organisation for Scientific Research (NWO), "Dutch Atlantic Connections." With several other fellows at the NIAS, we contributed to the volume *Dutch Atlantic Connections, 1680–1800: Linking Empires, Bridging Borders* (Leiden: Brill, 2014), edited by Gert Oostindie and Jessica Vance Roitman. In writing the present book, we benefited much from the discussions that preceded the publication of that edited volume, and we thank Jessica Vance Roitman in particular.

In writing what ultimately became this book, we aimed to make a synthesis not only of the extant historiography but also of our own research over the past three decades. During this period we amassed a huge debt of gratitude to many colleagues, friends, scholarly institutions, archives, and libraries. We cannot mention them all here—the list would extend over several pages. We would like, however, to thank Henk den Heijer and Jessica Vance Roitman, who were kind enough to provide their comments on an earlier draft of the book.

We also thank the two anonymous reviewers for Cornell University Press, who helped us reorganize the manuscript, as well as Cornell's copyeditor Julia Cook, senior editor Michael McGandy, senior production editor Susan Specter, and marketing director Martyn Beeny. We also owe a debt of gratitude to the KITLV/Royal Netherlands Institute of Southeast Asian and Caribbean Studies (Leiden) for supporting the research for this book, and to the librarians of Clark University, the KITLV, and the University of Leiden. We also acknowledge the kind financial contribution of Clark University to support the publication of this book.

While we have incorporated much of what we have learned over the past decades into the present book, we have at times also used specific parts of earlier publications. Gert Oostindie borrowed from his own contributions to *Dutch Atlantic Connections, 1680–1800*, and from his chapters "Modernity and Demise of the Dutch Atlantic, 1650–1914," in *The Caribbean and the Atlantic World Economy*, edited by Adrian Leonard and David Pretel (New York: Palgrave Macmillan, 2015), 108–36, and "Intellectual Wastelands? Scholarship in and for the Dutch West Indies up to ca. 1800," in *Empire and Science in the Making: Dutch Colonial Scholarship in Comparative Global Perspective*, edited by Peter Boomgaard (New York: Palgrave Macmillan, 2013), 253–80. We thank the publishers for their kind permission to recycle this material.

REALM BETWEEN EMPIRES

Introduction

Connections within and beyond the Dutch Realm in the Long Eighteenth Century

On the eve of the Second World War, the Dutch could not imagine an end to the status of their country as a colonial power. In parliament, the idea of a parting with the Netherlands East Indies was dismissed as both fatal and unnecessary—fatal because the colonial link was perceived by many as "the cork that keeps our economy floating," without which the Netherlands, in geopolitics, would "descend unto the rank of a country such as Denmark." As it turned out, a parting was also unnecessary as, to paraphrase the words of a leading politician, the Netherlands had "been there [in the East Indies] for three hundred years and [would] remain there for three hundred more." The Indonesians, he added, appreciate the Dutch presence very much. Barely ten years later, Indonesia became an independent republic, in spite of Dutch attempts to thwart the nationalist struggle for full independence through both negotiations and brutal warfare. Suddenly the Kingdom of the Netherlands had contracted to a small state bordering the cold North Sea and some Caribbean colonies on the other side of the Atlantic.[1]

World War II and decolonization were two watersheds in modern Dutch history. While the Dutch were reluctant to accept the independence of Indonesia, they were happy to transfer sovereignty to Suriname in 1975, and it took two decades more before the Dutch grudgingly accepted that the six Antillean islands would remain part of the kingdom—not because of perceived metropolitan gains, but because these tiny islands refused the dubious gift of sovereignty. The Kingdom of the Netherlands therefore remains a transatlantic entity until this very day.

Postcolonial migrations formed another unanticipated dimension to post–World War II decolonization. Today, well over one million out of a total of 17 million Dutch citizens have colonial roots. Colonialism therefore has come home, and with it a critical reexamination of colonial history. Glorifying the colonial past is no longer de rigueur. Instead, colonialism sparks critical debates about the nation's failure to live up to its own professed ideals of democracy, liberalism, and humanism. Dutch Atlantic history today is mainly associated with the Atlantic slave trade and African slavery in the Americas, and with the resulting colonial riches converted into the stunning canal houses of old cities in Holland and Zeeland. In 2002, the National Slavery Monument was unveiled in the nation's capital Amsterdam. Both the Dutch queen and the prime minister attended the ceremony, listening attentively to solemn speeches and witnessing Afro-Caribbean rituals.[2]

This book recounts a long and crucial episode in this unfinished history: the long eighteenth century of the Dutch Atlantic. This was a period in which, unlike in the post-1815 world, the Atlantic exploits seemed as promising to the Dutch as their colonial ventures in Asia. It was also a period in which they engaged in the Atlantic slave trade, built their own plantation colonies on the "Wild Coast" of South America, and developed their Caribbean islands into commercial assets, only to suffer from overstretch and eventually irrevocable contraction during the Napoleonic wars.

This was the last period in Atlantic history in which the Dutch played a major role—a far more prominent one than might be expected bearing in mind the moderate scale of both the metropolis and its colonies. Much of the historical importance of the Dutch in the Atlantic was tied up in other Atlantic territories and ventures, as we will learn. This is not a history most Dutch are proud of today—the nation's reputation for early democracy, religious toleration, and freedom of thought compares poorly to practices of enslavement and terror, racism and bigotry, and crass exploitation. And yet there are intriguing stories here too of ethnic diversity, of cultural entanglement, and of working around the disadvantages of being a minor power by constantly forging formal and informal connections to larger nations' territories.

A key element in the recent historiography of the early modern Atlantic is the growing awareness of the interconnectedness not only of the various continents, but also of the various empires that made up this Atlantic world. This book contributes to our understanding of the deeply entangled character of the Atlantic by focusing on the Dutch Atlantic, by which we mean not just the Dutch Republic and its colonies in West Africa and the Americas, but equally the web of relations linking these nominally Dutch places and their inhabitants to a larger world dominated by the Iberian, British, and French empires. *Realm among Empires* therefore offers both a succinct analysis of a lesser-known part of Atlantic history and a contribution to our understanding of the entangled character of the wider Atlantic.

The Second Dutch Atlantic in the Historiography

While one reason for writing *Realm among Empires* was simply that this history is too often neglected in general overviews of Atlantic history, there is also a deeper motive with relevance to the wider historiography. Dutch Atlantic history illustrates how strongly the early modern Atlantic relied on the circulation of goods, people, and ideas across the lines drawn by the various metropolitan states. These entanglements have long been obscured by the tendency among historians to look at only one Atlantic domain or, if an attempt at comparison was done at all, to compare only the Spanish and British Atlantic empires.

Indeed, much of the historiography of the Dutch Atlantic has tended to look only at this slice of the colonial world, or even to focus on one of its constituent parts only. This applies to historians rooted in the Netherlands or its former Atlantic colonies, but equally to the few others who overcame the linguistic hurdles involved in studying Dutch colonial history. Traditionally, most historical studies have focused on Suriname, followed by Curaçao and the broader theme of the Dutch slave trade. Only in the last decade or two has there been more attention to the links between the various constituent parts of the Dutch Atlantic and its ties with the wider Atlantic world.

That it took a long time for Dutch Atlantic historiography to mature is not entirely surprising, even if we exclude the linguistic factor.[3] Dutch colonial history has long been associated mainly with the initial spectacular successes of the Dutch East India Company (VOC), the subsequent development and exploitation of the Dutch East Indies after 1815, and the traumatic process of decolonization in Indonesia (1945–49). The international historiography of the early modern Atlantic in turn has focused primarily on the Iberian and British empires, and to a lesser degree the French empire. For a very long time, the Dutch Atlantic fell between the cracks, perceived to have been of marginal significance to both the Dutch Republic and the emergence and functioning of the wider Atlantic. In the past prominent economic historians of the Dutch Republic and its Atlantic colonies such as Jan de Vries and Pieter Emmer indeed explicitly promoted the idea of the Dutch Atlantic as a persistent failure.[4]

In the last fifteen years or so, this interpretation has been challenged, again mainly by economic historians. The volume *Riches from Atlantic Commerce* (2003), edited by the foremost historian of the Dutch Atlantic slave trade, Johannes Postma, and the Dutch scholar Victor Enthoven, sought to highlight the substantial economic significance of the Dutch Atlantic, an argument that particularly Enthoven and historian Henk den Heijer have since defended with programmatic zeal.[5] Quantitative research done over the past decades has indeed led to upwards revisions of the volume of both the Dutch Atlantic slave trade and the bilateral trade between the Caribbean colonies and the Dutch Republic. In our own recent publications as in the present book, we also indicate that the Dutch Atlantic economy grew with leaps and bounds up to the 1780s, a growth the more remarkable as the domestic Dutch economy became stagnant for much of the eighteenth century.[6]

An even more promising line of revisionism developed in this book is the emphasis on the role Dutch Atlantic intermediaries played in the broader Atlantic world. This is the story, on the one hand, of merchants in the Dutch Republic spinning commercial networks that covered locations throughout the Atlantic, and on the other hand—and more spectacularly—of the ascent of Curaçao and St. Eustatius (or Statia) as free trade markets linking various parts of the Atlantic across imperial borders. Many contributions to the recent volume *Dutch Atlantic Connections, 1680–1800* (2014), edited by Gert Oostindie and Jessica V. Roitman, indeed testify to the role of these Dutch isles and more generally Dutch actors as lubricants of the Atlantic economy.[7] All of this confirms what De Vries has defined as the early pioneering role of the Dutch in the "soft globalization" that characterized the early phases of Atlantic history.

We use the term "realm" to denote the Dutch Atlantic of the long eighteenth century in order to distinguish it from the Dutch Moment, the period of unbridled imperial ambition that began with the founding of the West India Company (1621) and ended with the company's demise in 1674 and reestablishment as an organization without military objectives.[8] Its small size and lack of expansionism also made the Dutch Atlantic realm distinct from the domains of the other Atlantic powers of the eighteenth century. Nonetheless, Dutch markets and actors continued to play crucial roles up to the late eighteenth century across the Atlantic world.

At first sight one might not expect the eighteenth-century Dutch Atlantic to have mattered much whatsoever. By 1750, the Dutch share of the Caribbean colonial populations was less than ten percent (table 1). The relative smallness of these Dutch Caribbean populations translated into

TABLE 1. Populations of the Caribbean, ca. 1750

	White	Enslaved	Free nonwhite	Total
French	42,000	316,000	9,000	367,000
British	40,500	271,000	3,000	314,500
Spanish	166,000	46,000	78,000	290,000
Dutch	8,000	77,000	3,500	88,500
Danish	2,000	15,000	150	17,150
Swedish	150	50	–	200
Total	258,650	725,050	93,650	1,077,350

Source: Adapted from Engerman and Higman, "Demographic Structures," 48–49.
Notes: Adjustments made to allow for correct grouping of colonies under metropolitan flags as valid ca. 1750. Our rounding off of figures produced minor discrepancies (the total given by Engerman and Higman is 1,076,622). As Engerman and Higman indicate, their figures are only approximations. This also explains the discrepancy with more specific figures provided in this chapter for Dutch Atlantic populations.

a modest commercial role. The Dutch share of the Atlantic slave trade was roughly five percent, or six if limited to the period up to 1800. By the 1770s, in spite of considerable growth, the Dutch share in Atlantic imports to Europe, worth some 20 million Dutch guilders, was dwarfed by the French and British shares (worth 57 and 72 million guilders), and whereas Atlantic trade made up some 40 percent of these countries' over-all international trade, its significance to the Dutch economy was only 15 percent.[9] But as we demonstrate in this book, much of the Dutch contribution to the economic growth of the Atlantic rested elsewhere: in its indispensable auxiliary role for the Spanish, British, and French empires in legal and particularly illicit trades.

The potential of the burgeoning field of Atlantic history derives largely from its drive for a comparative, cross-imperial approach and its preference for multi- and interdisciplinary methodology. Clearly the historiography of the Dutch Atlantic has much to win by the application of these twin innovations—perhaps especially the latter, as most of the scholarly literature on the Dutch Atlantic used in wider Atlantic debates pertains to the field of economic history. Dutch Atlantic historiography has therefore been criticized as particularly conservative in its emphasis on economic rather than social and particularly cultural history[10] This criticism may be a bit overstated as over the past three decades a great number of mostly Dutch-language social historical studies on slavery and slave resistance have been published—the major exception being the work on the history of the Surinamese Maroons by the American anthropologist Richard Price (*First-Time*, 1983, and *Alabi's World*, 1990)—and these Dutch studies have been largely unheeded by English-language scholars.[11] In recent years, however, the social and cultural history of the Dutch Atlantic has come to fruition, testifying to an awareness of the wider Atlantic context and an attempt to broaden the disciplinary scope of Dutch Atlantic studies.[12]

A Singular Republic and its Decentralized Realm

The Republic of the Seven United Provinces, or the Dutch Republic for short, originated by leaps and bounds during a drawn-out war of secession against Habsburg Spain. The outcome of this Eighty Years' War

(1568–1648) was a remarkable new state, geographically confined to the northern part of what had been the Habsburg Netherlands and constitutionally exceptional because of its republican and highly decentralized character. Of the seven provinces, Holland was by far the most powerful, and within Holland the city of Amsterdam was dominant. The political history of the republic, which was proclaimed in 1581 and lasted until the French occupation in 1795, is characterized by constant bickering over the rights and obligations of the various provinces and cities. The States General, which met in The Hague, represented these entities, exercised sovereignty over the Republic, and ultimately assumed responsibility for all state matters, including international politics, warfare, and colonial affairs.

To complicate matters, the House of Orange, a family from the nation's traditional nobility, had risen to high status during the war against Spain, with a series of leaders acquiring the semi-royal position of "stadtholder." After the conclusion of the war, there was a continuous debate as to whether or not the Orange stadtholders should be allowed a major role in state affairs. The stadtholders, who had been military commanders during the independence war, would continue to represent the more belligerent factions in the republic. Their influence in Dutch politics varied enormously over time. While there were times in which the stadtholder could almost act like a traditional monarch, there were also long periods in which the House of Orange was officially excluded from high politics.

In the decades prior to and following the 1648 Peace of Westphalia that confirmed the Dutch Republic's status as a sovereign state, the state lived its "Golden Age." The Dutch enjoyed "primacy" in world trade, in Jonathan Israel's words, even attaining (following Immanuel Wallerstein) a "world-hegemonic" status. Visible in the inner cities of Amsterdam and many other Dutch port cities, this period of unprecedented economic growth was founded on both a very competitive agrarian and industrial sector and Holland's role as an international staple market.[13] This Golden Age, of course, was also the period in which the Dutch Republic excelled in urban planning, the arts, and sciences. Over time, the republic's complicated governmental structure enabled tremendous entrepreneurial drive, but also caused a lack of consistent leadership and hence stagnation. This was of particular concern as the eighteenth century progressed and the

Dutch Republic found itself no longer a match for its major European competitors, Great Britain and France. This, in the end, would lead to the republic's collapse in the late eighteenth century.

The origins of Dutch colonial history likewise date from this period. Individuals from the Habsburg Netherlands had long been involved in the Iberian ventures in Africa, Asia, and the Americas, but during the secession from Spain all of this acquired a new purpose and scale. Colonial expansion was not only driven by economic motives, but equally by the geopolitical ambition to inflict damage on the Iberian powers wherever this was possible. Overseas ventures were thus a national concern highly valued by the States General, the various provinces, and the major cities alike.

The institutional form given to these Dutch ambitions was exceptional. Rather than making overseas expansion and the establishment of colonies a state affair and therefore also a monarchical affair as it was in all other European countries, the States General decided to delegate these tasks to private companies. In 1602, the Dutch East India Company (Verenigde Oost-Indische Compagnie, VOC) was founded with its initial capital raised by a large number of private share-holders. The States General delegated all matters both economic and political to the VOC board, thus making the company a semi-state entity in the parts of the world over which it was given a monopoly: eastward from the southern tip of Africa up to East Asia.

In 1621, the States General issued a similar monopolistic permit to the Dutch West India Company (WIC), defining its operational area to West Africa and the Americas. Within a few decades, the WIC had conquered Spanish colonies in the Caribbean, Portuguese strongholds in West Africa, and parts of Portuguese Brazil, and had established new colonies in the Guianas and in Manhattan and environs (New Netherland). But unlike its Asian peer, the WIC experienced major financial problems from its very start and was bankrupted in 1674—partly because of the cost of failed military operations and partly because of its inability to enforce a monopoly for Dutch operations. A second WIC was established that would have a precarious existence until its liquidation in 1792. In 1674, the colonial Dutch Atlantic consisted of several fortresses along the coast of West Africa, of which Elmina was the most important; some nascent plantation colonies in the Guianas dominated by Suriname; and six tiny

Caribbean islands, of which Curaçao and St. Eustatius would be most prominent. This (from a comparative Atlantic perspective) modest collection of Dutch possessions would largely remain intact until the Napoleonic Wars concluded in 1815.

A highly decentralized European republic thus built an equally decentralized colonial framework, delegating governance, military matters, trade, and finance to two semi-state private companies. Each of these companies was governed by a board reflecting the character of the Dutch state, with "Chambers" representing the various provinces. Holland was always the most powerful among these, followed at a large distance by the other province bordering the North Sea, Zeeland. Within the province of Holland, several cities vied for influence, but none could hope to be a match for Amsterdam. The stadtholders, meanwhile, were ex officio members of the VOC and WIC boards, their real influence fluctuating with their overall position.

To complicate matters, the WIC lost most of its initial prerogatives during the company's first decades, although the transatlantic slave trade remained as a monopoly. Faced with the apparently unbeatable competition by domestic, predominantly Zeeland interlopers, the company relinquished its last monopolistic pretentions in the 1730s. Long before, it had accepted the consequences of the fact that it possessed neither the financial nor the military means to conquer and govern a significant number of Atlantic possessions. In the end the insular Caribbean and the fortresses along the coast of West Africa remained under the direct jurisdiction of the WIC. The Guianas, by contrast, were ruled by separate entities in which the company was only one partner along with the city of Amsterdam in particular (Sociëteit van Suriname, Sociëteit van Berbice); or in an arrangement in which the WIC's Chamber Zeeland was nominally dominant, hence inciting bickering again with Amsterdam (Essequibo).

The consequence of this institutional patchwork was that there was not one consistent Dutch interest or policy for the Atlantic, but rather many ad hoc measures and particularistic governance. Much power was thus entrusted to local assemblies headed by a "governor" or "director" representing either the WIC or one of the societies, but otherwise mainly made up by local planters and merchants. In general, they aimed for minimal metropolitan interference and taxation, but insisted on maximal military assistance in times of need. Whereas the metropolitan point of view tended towards the opposite, it is obvious that this arrangement ended up producing extremely localized variants of "Dutch" Atlantic governance. Thus each of the colonies developed its own body of rules and regulations on social order and slavery (placards), all based on Roman law but otherwise exclusively geared towards the local elites' best interest. There was no such thing as a singular governmental or legal framework valid for the entire Atlantic.

As we will later discuss in depth, migration greatly added to this diversity within the Dutch Atlantic. All early modern Atlantic societies were marked by the unprecedented phenomenon of the Atlantic slave trade—throughout this period, there were three enslaved Africans for each European crossing the ocean. The Dutch Atlantic was no different, but the resulting population mixes were highly diverse. In West Africa, the Dutch fortresses were primarily inhabited by employees of the WIC: both Europeans and, in the later eighteenth century, increasingly people—mainly men—of mixed African and European origins. More important, these enclaves harbored only small numbers of whites surrounded by infinitely larger numbers of Africans that were not in any way under Dutch control.

This was obviously different in the Dutch Americas. Colonial expansion implied the early marginalization of the indigenous population of the Guianas, and soon enslaved Africans and their descendants came to make up some 95 percent of the population in these plantation colonies. In the insular Dutch Caribbean, the Amerindian population had been marginal even at the time of the Dutch takeover from the Spanish. Again, population growth was primarily the result of the importation of enslaved Africans, but the share of slaves in the total population was much lower than in the Guianas both because of the primarily commercial function of these islands and higher levels of manumission.

While such different ethnic and legal ratios would have made for considerable diversity and hence different trajectories of creolization anyway, there was the additional factor of European heterogeneity. In the domains of both the VOC and the WIC, typically no more than half of the entire European population was of Dutch origin. As in the orbit of the VOC, European immigrants into West Africa and the Dutch Americas also hailed from Germany and Scandinavia, and to a lesser degree from a variety of other European lands. In contrast to the realm of the VOC, immigration into the Dutch Caribbean colonies also involved significant numbers of

Jews, predominantly Sephardim, but also Ashkenazim. All of this would leave deep marks on patterns of creolization in the Dutch Atlantic and help explain, as we will demonstrate, why the Dutch left less of a cultural footprint in the Americas than its major European competitors.

The Ambitions and Contents of this Book

With the present book, we present a history of the Dutch Atlantic in a comparative framework, incorporating the earliest contemporary writings up to the most recent scholarly work published by fellow historians on the early Dutch Atlantic, as well as the comparative approach characteristic of modern Atlantic studies.[14] Entanglement is a common thread in this book, as we focus on connections between actors in various locations and social positions in both the Dutch Atlantic and its wider regional context. Moreover, we attempt to move beyond both economic history and the more conventional focus on only one or two Dutch Atlantic locations. Thus we do discuss economic history, but we also engage with politics, migration and demography, and social and cultural history. While the book is not focused on the metropolis, we do look at metropolitan relations with the various colonies, but more particularly at relations between these colonies and the neighboring non-Dutch colonies.

We define the Dutch Atlantic as not only the Dutch Republic and its various colonies and settlements along the West African coast and in the Americas, but equally the network of relations entertained by Dutch actors with other parts of the Atlantic. This network certainly included (British) North America, but we do not pay specific attention to the territory formerly known as New Netherland, nor to the Dutch-speaking communities in North America. Piet Emmer and Jos Gommans have rightly argued that a Dutch settlement colony in North America might have maintained stronger links with the metropolis and displayed a more pronounced Dutch culture than the colonies that remained in Dutch America after 1664.[15] Dutchness, ironically, was stronger in the area that had once been called New Netherland than in most colonies where the Dutch flag continued to fly. The English conquest of New Netherland did not signal the start of a process of smooth assimilation of the Dutch population to English culture. On the contrary, the English takeover seems to have led to the emergence of a self-conscious Dutch identity at odds with mainstream English values.[16] The Dutch Reformed Church functioned as an anchor of Dutch identity in colonial and post-colonial New York and New Jersey. The number of congregations of the church had been 11 in 1664, but grew steadily to 78 in 1740 and 127 in 1780. These congregations, which came under the ecclesiastical authority of Amsterdam until 1772, helped shape Dutchness by systematically conforming to Calvinist orthodoxy as practiced in the Dutch Republic. Even though the ratio of ethnically Dutch men and women shrank compared to the overall population, these men and women emphasized their Dutch ways more emphatically in the eighteenth century than their forbears had done. The battle with the English language was lost eventually, but only in a process that spanned many decades. In New York City, English-language services in Dutch Reformed churches may have begun alongside those in the Dutch tongue before the American Revolution, but they were not introduced in Tappan, New Jersey, until 1835.[17] Dutchness also faded away in Albany, where the Dutch lived in a tightly-knit society prior to the revolution. Their world gradually collapsed as immigrating New Englanders began to outnumber them, and as the old communal ethos gave way to commercialization and individualism.[18]

Although the Dutch in North America valued their linguistic and religious heritage, there is no indication that this "community" had any specific link to the Dutch Atlantic, apart perhaps from the commercial links between New York on the one hand and Amsterdam and Curaçao on the other.[19] Neither do we include the Dutch Cape Colony and the Dutch commercial endeavors alongside the East African coast. Institutionally, these parts of Africa pertained to the monopoly of the VOC. More important, as historian Nigel Worden writes, the Cape Colony "shaped and was shaped by the wider Indian Ocean world" and there are no indications of significant links between these parts of Africa and the Dutch Atlantic as defined for our present purposes.[20]

The choice for a "long eighteenth century" was made because the period running roughly between 1680 and 1815 is one that may be usefully contrasted with what came before and after. Before, we have the Dutch Golden Age, an era of great imperial ambitions in the Atlantic no less than elsewhere in the world. After this "Dutch moment" had passed, the importance of the Dutch in and to the Atlantic diminished, although as we argue throughout this book their role was more significant than was long thought. Geographical contraction was offset by the economic development of both the plantation economy of the Guianas and the commercial success of Curaçao and St. Eustatius. This relative success only started to falter in the last quarter of the eighteenth century and was reversed during the Napoleonic Wars, which also saw the abolition of the slave trade and hence the progressive severing of the life line between West Africa and plantation America. In hindsight, the decline of the Dutch Atlantic was only confirmed, not initiated by, the Peace of Vienna and the establishment of the Kingdom of the Netherlands, around 1815. After this date, the Dutch Atlantic ceased to be a vital part of the Dutch colonial domain and of the Atlantic world as a whole.

We have organized the book along partly chronological, partly thematic lines. The opening chapter covers the prelude up to 1680 and then summarizes the development of the Dutch Atlantic up to the early 1780s—this chronological approach is taken up again in the closing chapter discussing the period from 1780 to 1815. We begin by outlining the early rise and subsequent contraction of a Dutch empire, placing this development in a broader geopolitical context. In spite of the vast extent of their empires in the Americas, the Iberian powers lost their early hegemony in the Atlantic in the seventeenth century. In the more dynamic Northern Atlantic, France and Great Britain emerged as the dominant powers. After its own heyday was over, the Dutch Republic's policy was dictated by the need to steer a neutral course between both powers. This policy was quite successful until the 1780s. The resulting Dutch Atlantic was defined by its deep entanglement with the rest of the Atlantic world. From an early stage, the European residents of the Dutch Atlantic were closely intertwined with foreign traders and colonies. The plantation colonies in the Guianas were as much oriented towards the British West Indies and particularly North America as they were towards the Dutch Republic. International trade was the mainstay of Curaçao and St. Eustatius, which developed into popular entrepôts for vessels from across the circum-Caribbean and from North America's eastern seaboard. All of this Dutch commerce developed in spite of British, French, and Spanish mercantilist policies, and in this way the Dutch Atlantic contributed significantly to the commercial integration of the New World.

Chapter 2 first analyzes the remarkable variety of governmental arrangements prevalent in the Dutch Atlantic, where unlike its counterpart the VOC, the WIC had neither an administrative nor a commercial monopoly. Next, we analyze the financial arrangements, including the ultimate failure of both the WIC and the other companies to adequately serve the colonies and colonial trade and to yield satisfactory financial results to its investors. The final section of this chapter summarizes the development of trade between the republic and its various colonies and settlements in Africa and the Americas, including the trade in both enslaved Africans and European and tropical commodities produced in the Dutch Guianas and in the non-Dutch Caribbean.

In the next three chapters, we move to the history of specific geographical parts of the Dutch Atlantic. Chapter 3 examines West Africa. While Dutch ships had been active along the West African coast before, the WIC's conquest of Fort Elmina from the Portuguese in 1637 made the Dutch the dominant European power during the seventeenth century, allowing for trade in enslaved Africans, gold, and ivory. Afterwards, both British competition and shifting political alliances along the coast undermined the Dutch position. Elmina and the neighboring Dutch forts were no real colonies, but rather simple trade stations, inhabited by a limited number of European males and, later on, children of mixed origins. By 1760 soldiers of mixed African and European heritage outnumbered Europeans. They were fully dependent on the immediate urban environment. Thus the main fortress of Elmina with its population of some two hundred relied on the fully African city of Elmina with its 20,000 people for the supply of food, labor, and military protection. Even if Elmina was the only major fortress on the Gold Coast, its role in the slave trade was limited. Enslaved Africans embarked from points all along the West African coast, with west-central Africa as the dominant supplier, followed by the Bight of Benin and only then the Gold Coast.

Chapter 4 discusses the development of the Dutch Guianas, particularly Suriname but also Berbice and Essequibo/Demerara. Developed from the start as plantation colonies dependent on the brutal transatlantic slave trade, the Dutch Guianas resembled the British and French sugar islands in many ways, but there were also contrasts in the system of governance (by various semi-public companies), in production (coffee was a major cash crop alongside and even above sugar), in the absence of an encompassing mercantilist framework, and in the highly diverse character of the European populations.

Chapter 5 focuses on the insular Dutch Caribbean, particularly Curaçao and St. Eustatius and to a lesser degree St. Maarten. The interimperial trade networks of these islands were far more important than those of Saba, Bonaire, and Aruba, the sparsely-populated remaining Dutch islands. In spite of their primarily trade-oriented economies, the populations of St. Eustatius and Curaçao did have slave majorities. The slave trade marked the development of Curaçao between the 1660s and 1730, most of the enslaved Africans being reexported to regional destinations. Even if the majority of the island's enslaved population worked on plantations producing provisions for the home market, a significant number was directly employed in the mercantile economy, opening up relatively good chances for manumission. Without new demographic and hence cultural influences from Africa after 1730, black Curaçaoans embraced Catholicism administered by Spanish priests from the continent. Their conversion is but one illustration of the island's close relationship with the Spanish Main. On St. Eustatius and the other northern isles, the close ties to nearby British islands enabled Methodism to flourish.

Religious toleration was a pragmatic choice all over the Dutch Atlantic. This also explains the religious liberties extended to Jews not only in Suriname, but equally in Curaçao. Yet for the gentile European population, more restrictions applied, in part because of the need for the white elite to remain united. Until the mid-eighteenth century, therefore, the Reformed Church enjoyed a privileged position, only after that date making room particularly for Lutheranism. The pragmatism evident in religious policies reflected not only economic concern, but also the need to ensure white solidarity in the omnipresent awareness of the risk of black insurrections.

Not only people and commodities circulated in the Atlantic, but also knowledge and ideas—whether by formal correspondence, publications, and research, or informally through travelers. This is the theme of chapter 6. The first section discusses the webs of communication that were spun from the very start by institutional and commercial parties and later increasingly by local gazettes and the like. As a reminder of the highly diverse character of the Dutch Atlantic, we underline that many of the resulting sources are not written in Dutch, but rather in one of the many other European or Creole languages prevalent throughout the Dutch

Atlantic. The next section discusses scholarly research and its practical uses, ranging from geography and the natural sciences through medicine and agrarian expertise to ethnography. There is every reason to assume that both practical and scholarly expertise circulated widely throughout the Atlantic. In the Dutch Atlantic, this was more a question of individual initiative than of colonial policies.

The intellectual climate in Caribbean slave societies has often been painted in starkly negative terms as a spiritual wasteland. Closer inspection of intellectual efforts in the Dutch Atlantic and particularly in Suriname cannot discard such characterizations, but we did find remarkably enlightened efforts to establish scholarly, educational, and cultural practices beyond a merely utilitarian agenda. Meanwhile the Dutch Republic managed to remain a renowned center for publications on exotic places including the Dutch Atlantic colonies well into the eighteenth century, as well as a world market that absorbed and distributed ever more tropical products to its own citizens and many more on the European continent. This prompts the question of whether the Atlantic and particularly the Dutch colonies in Africa and the Americas reverberated widely in Dutch society. Whereas it will prove difficult to arrive at firm answers to this, we cannot escape the conclusion that, unlike the British and to a lesser degree the French, the Dutch did not engage in a vibrant debate about a key issue in Atlantic history: the legitimacy of the slave trade and slavery itself.

Of course, it did not help that by the time such debates raged, particularly in Great Britain, the Dutch elites were all too concerned about the fate of their own nation and wary of engaging in experiments that might be costly, disruptive, or both. The late-eighteenth-century British takeover of Berbice, Demerara, and Essequibo, and particularly the United States' ascent in the Caribbean, sealed the fate of the Dutch Caribbean. The ensuing decline and further contraction of the Dutch Atlantic is discussed in the closing chapter. This contraction resulted from long-term geopolitical changes in Europe and particularly the rise of Great Britain. Even if the Dutch Atlantic did not matter as much to its metropolis, as was the case for all other Atlantic domains, its economic importance was increasing throughout the eighteenth century. But only as long as the stronger states tolerated the Dutch as intermediaries in a highly mercantilist world could the Dutch Atlantic thrive. From the early 1780s on, the

Dutch found that this intermediary role had only been possible as long as this suited the major European powers, particularly Great Britain. Without serious naval power and strong allies, the Dutch were at the mercy of their rivals. The demise of the Dutch Atlantic during the Fourth Anglo-Dutch War (1780–84) and the Napoleonic Wars (1795–1815) followed, culminating in the establishment of the Kingdom of the Netherlands (1815) with an Atlantic realm restricted to Suriname, the six Caribbean islands, and Elmina.

In spite of this territorial contraction, the Dutch elites including King Willem I still nurtured high hopes for Suriname as a plantation economy and Curaçao as a commercial hub. By 1830 such dreams were buried. The production of tropical staples was taken over by the Dutch East Indies, where all sorts of semi-bonded but non-slave labor arrangements proved to be immensely lucrative for the century to come, adding to the marginalization of the Dutch Caribbean colonies. Both Curaçao and St. Eustatius entered a long period of crisis. In this new era of free trade and American ascent, their services as intermediaries were no longer in demand.

This period of transition witnessed massive, even revolutionary change. The Atlantic slave trade was abolished, and the institution of slavery was bound to follow. The United States attained independence, followed by Haiti and much of Latin America. This was an era of "Creole triumphalism," but the Dutch Atlantic remained an outsider to this phenomenon. The only revolutionary spirit in the colonies was expressed by revolting slaves, most dramatically in the 1795 Curaçao slave revolt. In the colonies, like in the metropolis, there had been strong divisions between pro-British ancien régime "Orangists" and pro-French "Patriots," but no Creole nationalism nor a questioning of the slave trade or slavery.

Likewise, in the Netherlands there was broad consensus that the sole function of the colonies was to benefit the metropolis, and that in the Atlantic this implied a continuation of slavery. The abolition of the slave trade was imposed by the British, but slavery would continue until 1863. By then, the Dutch East Indies and particularly Java had become crucial to the new Kingdom of the Netherlands and the Atlantic had become a backwater in the Dutch colonial world—so much so that awareness that the Dutch Atlantic had ever mattered for the Dutch Republic and for the emergence of the early modern Atlantic at large evaporated.

In the conclusion to this book, we summarize our main findings and relate this to the broader historiography of the early modern Atlantic. We argue that the characteristics of the Dutch Atlantic as we have defined these strongly support the present emphasis among historians on the interconnectedness of the Atlantic world at large.

1

ENTANGLEMENTS

The Second Dutch Atlantic (the Dutch Atlantic world as it existed from 1680 through 1815) differed in important respects from its predecessor. The First Dutch Atlantic had taken shape from the late sixteenth century and was imbued with imperial zeal in 1621, when the war with Habsburg Spain extended across the Atlantic. In a short time, the Netherlanders wrested so many foreign colonies and trading posts from their rivals that a sizable empire emerged. Eventually, however, the Dutch were dispossessed of several key colonies.[1] The Dutch Republic lost its dominant position at home, and, compared to its predecessor, the Dutch Atlantic of the long eighteenth century was far less capacious and expansive. But as we will demonstrate in this chapter, the reorganized Dutch Atlantic realm was predicated on a multiplicity of interimperial commercial relationships and as such played a crucial role in the development of the wider Atlantic world.

Dutch interimperial trade extended, as one might expect, to areas with a strong ethnic Dutch presence, such as New York and the Danish

Caribbean islands. But trade was equally lively with places that lacked such connections. New England merchants frequented the Dutch Guiana colonies, Curaçaoan vessels conducted the bulk of their trade in Spanish colonies, and Brazilian ships routinely anchored at Elmina. Although international peace was a precondition of interimperial trade, wars offered attractive new opportunities for traders in the republic and the colonies. Some wars, however, proved very harmful to Dutch trade.

The First Dutch Atlantic

Entanglements with other empires predated Dutch expansion in the Atlantic world, which began in earnest in the last decade of the sixteenth century. If Dutch individuals and ships ventured into Atlantic waters prior to the Dutch revolt against Habsburg Spain, which began in 1568, they invariably did so to serve the commercial interests of other countries. By the 1590s, however, Dutch interests had become central to the young republic's Atlantic shipping. That decade marked the start of the First Dutch Atlantic, which lasted through 1674.

The foremost destination in the first decades of Dutch participation in Atlantic trade was the West African coast, where ships from the Dutch Republic anchored everywhere from Senegal to Benin to procure gold and ivory. In the years between 1592 and 1607, two hundred Dutch ships are estimated to have completed a West African voyage.[2] At the same time, Dutch ships in search of furs made their way to North America, while other vessels cleared the home ports to obtain tobacco, hides, and salt in the Greater Antilles and on the Spanish Main.

The sudden transatlantic activity displayed by Dutch shipowners was, at least in part, the unintended result of Spanish embargoes against Dutch shipping to the Iberian Peninsula. These measures prompted the Dutch to bypass the Iberian middlemen and sail to Spanish and Portuguese colonies in order to buy their produce directly. More important, however, was the Spanish occupation of Antwerp and the closure of the river Scheldt by the Dutch rebels in their war with Spain, which cut off Antwerp from the outside world. Antwerp was at the time not only Europe's busiest port, it was the import and redistribution center for goods from southern Europe and the Iberian empires. Individual traders and associations of merchants from Holland and Zeeland now seized the opportunity to establish direct commercial links with ports in Russia, Italy, the eastern Mediterranean, and beyond Europe.[3]

By entering the Atlantic world, the Dutch were moving into a realm still largely controlled by Spain and Portugal, the two neighbors that were united under one crown between 1580 and 1640. The Dutch challenged their Iberian foes as both privateers and smugglers. By the year 1600, Dutch privateering had become a major Atlantic pursuit. In the first seven months of that year, twenty-seven Dutch ships in Atlantic waters went on privateering expeditions, compared to fifty ships with commercial objectives.[4] Apart from seizing enemy ships, attempts were now also made to conquer Iberian colonies and trading posts, starting in 1596 with the failed attack on the Portuguese fort of São Jorge da Mina, the key to control of the Gold Coast, and the successful invasion, two years later, of the island of Principe, just off the African coast.[5] Because of the high costs of such expeditions and the Twelve-Year Truce with Spain, signed in 1609, hostilities in the Atlantic world were not resumed until 1621. The Atlantic then became a major theater of war, where the newly founded West India Company fought the hereditary enemy by fire and sword. The opening of an Atlantic front, it was expected, would bring the war at home to a happy conclusion. The company directors embarked on an overly ambitious program that was labeled "the Grand Design."

A prominent feature of the Grand Design was the invasion of Brazil, seen as a weak yet profitable link in the Habsburg imperial edifice.[6] The conquest of Brazil's capital of Salvador da Bahia was one element of the Grand Design's first stage, the other being the occupation of Luanda, Portugal's main slave trading port in Africa, from which the Dutch planned to send their own slaves to the Americas. Brimming with confidence, the WIC embarked on this ambitious program, but the Grand Design began to falter almost as soon as it was put in place. Although the occupation of Bahia was initially successful, Dutch rule ended within one year after a quick surrender to a huge Iberian fleet. By 1625, therefore, there was little to show for the WIC's enormous investments. The only bright spot was privateering. Johannes de Laet, the company's contemporary chronicler, divulged that Dutch privateers seized 547 Portuguese and Spanish ships in the period 1623–36, the proceeds of which filled the WIC treasury.[7]

On top of these proceeds came those of the Spanish treasure fleet en route from Veracruz (Mexico) to Seville in 1628. After years of preparation, a WIC fleet commanded by Lieutenant-Admiral Piet Hein seized the *flota* in the Cuban bay of Matanzas in 1628. While the event sent shockwaves around the Hispanic world and across Europe, the sudden windfall boosted the morale of the WIC, which organized a new expedition to Brazil. The new target was the sugar-rich Captaincy of Pernambuco, which was rapidly conquered. From there, Dutch forces extended the area under their control until it included half of Brazil. The colonial adventure in Brazil lasted from 1630 through 1654 and drew many critics. Founded as a trading company that had the right to wage war, the WIC had by this point largely become a military machine, but it was not obvious that it could yield profits. Unable to finance its own operations—especially those in Brazil, which soon consumed the most energy—the company turned time and again to the provinces for much-needed subsidies.

Meanwhile, the Dutch Atlantic began to resemble an empire. Instructed by the WIC, the authorities in Brazil dispatched two fleets in four years' time to conquer São Jorge da Mina (1637) and Luanda and São Tomé (1641). Both expeditions were crowned with success, allowing the Dutch to take over Portugal's main African headquarters and enabling them to get access to enslaved Africans needed to work the Brazilian plantations. Elsewhere in the Atlantic world, Dutch colonies were founded in the Guianas, in North America (New Netherland—the vast area between present-day Connecticut and Delaware), and in the Caribbean (Curaçao, St. Eustatius—which was frequently referred to as "Statia"—St. Maarten, and Tobago).

This was the "Dutch moment" in Atlantic history, a period in which the Dutch were deeply involved not only in interimperial shipping and trade to the French and English colonies but seemingly also in the process of constructing a real empire of their own that tied together North and South America as well as Africa and Brazil. Dutch rule in Brazil, the pivot of this system, was however short-lived. In 1645, a revolt broke out among the Luso-Brazilian population that reduced the area under Dutch rule and threatened the very existence of the Dutch colony. After nine miserable years, the colony was lost to a Portuguese fleet in 1654.

The long wars with the Iberians ultimately left the Dutch with few tangible results. The sugar trade from Brazil, which had been the main rationale for its conquest, only prospered for a decade. When Brazil was abandoned, New Netherland remained in the Dutch empire, an area not conquered but rather peacefully settled in 1624 in the absence of other European competitors. Its history, though, was filled with wars with indigenous neighbors of the Dutch, including Kieft's War (1640–45), named for the colony's director, during which Dutch forces killed hundreds of natives. The end of the colony in 1664 came through a military encounter, albeit one in which no shot was fired. Four English frigates sent by the Duke of York appeared off the coast of New Amsterdam, where the invaders met with little resistance. The transition from Dutch to English rule was one episode in an Atlantic-wide English offensive against the Dutch, which continued during the Second Anglo-Dutch War (1665–1667). The Dutch responded in kind. An English naval expedition that subdued many Dutch forts, lodges, and trading posts in Africa was followed by a Dutch squadron commanded by Vice-Admiral Michiel de Ruyter, reversing most English conquests and adding Fort Cormantine, the English headquarters in West Africa, to the Dutch empire. Next, the action shifted to the Caribbean. English privateers conquered the Dutch colonies of St. Eustatius, Saba, and Tobago, while the Dutch seized the English colony of Suriname. In the aftermath, warfare kept threatening the existence of the Dutch colonies and even, in 1672, the republic itself, when the outbreak of the Third Anglo-Dutch War coincided with invasions at home by the army of Louis XIV's France in the south and armies of German princes in the east. While the Dutch Republic survived its darkest hour, English troops captured the same Dutch colonies as in the previous war.[8]

France also damaged Dutch colonial interests. There was a conspicuous Atlantic rationale for the French war effort. King Louis XIV and especially his minister Jean-Baptiste Colbert aimed to free France from what they viewed as the Dutch commercial and maritime stranglehold. To end Dutch control of a good part of France's coastal and colonial commerce, privateers were dispatched in 1677–78 to seize Dutch ships and plans were developed to oust the Dutch from West Africa and the West Indies.[9] The plans did not completely succeed, but the Dutch did lose Cayenne on the South American mainland, the Caribbean island of Tobago (which had been restored to them by England), and the outpost of Goree in West Africa. Curaçao was targeted as well. To round off their expedition, the French—accompanied by hundreds of buccaneers—attempted to take the island, but never arrived there. After four days at sea, the ships were wrecked on the coral reefs of the Aves Islands, and hundreds of sailors and soldiers drowned.[10]

For all practical purposes, these dramatic events ended Dutch expansion in the Atlantic world. The Second Dutch Atlantic would be devoid of conquests and offensive wars. The West India Company, which went bankrupt in 1674, was immediately reestablished as an altogether different organization. Although the company maintained a monopoly on the African slave trade—at least until the 1730s—its chief task was governance in the three regions where the Dutch remained: West Africa, the Guianas, and the Caribbean islands.

Forging Connections, Losing Clout

During the first four decades of the new West India Company (1674–1714), the Dutch became commercially intertwined with residents of foreign empires. On the west coast of Africa, the Luso-Dutch trade prospered. In 1482, the Portuguese had built a fort called São Jorge da Mina and made it their headquarters on the "Guinea" coast. Portuguese hegemony went unchallenged until a first Dutch assault in 1596, and it was not until 1637 that the West India Company wrested control of the castle, which the Dutch dubbed "Elmina." Although the Portuguese presence in Atlantic Africa was henceforth confined to the "Angola" coast, Portuguese or rather Brazilian ships were back on the Guinea coast by the 1670s in their quest to buy slaves, ignoring the 1669 treaty with the Dutch Republic that made the Portuguese presence there illegal. The Dutch response vacillated between militancy and accommodation, with the WIC at home advocating the seizure of ships contravening the treaty and local authorities in Elmina seeking to adjust to trade and thus obtain the sweetened tobacco introduced by the Brazilians. The tobacco was consumed locally and used for exchange. This trade was informally regulated beginning most likely in the 1680s, as the Brazilians, mostly hailing from Bahia, were now obliged to purchase a trading permit in Elmina for the value of ten percent of their ship's cargo. The WIC directors did not officially consent to such trade, however, until 1714.[11]

Atlantic shipping routes never linked Suriname to Brazil. Instead, Suriname was connected to Anglo-America from the very start of Dutch colonization. Ties with the English island of Barbados were particularly close. In the days when both were still English territories, bilateral trade had begun between the mainland colony, home to a seemingly infinite supply of wood, and the island whose forests were quickly cut down during its sugar revolution. Nor did the Dutch conquest of Suriname in 1667 put an immediate end to this natural bond. Many English settlers left for Barbados, while others stayed behind, and on both ends, Jewish settlers maintained the commercial connection between the colonies. A fire that consumed eight hundred houses in Barbados's main town of Bridgetown in April 1668 reinforced the trading links, as the governor of Suriname allowed Barbadian ships to load the timber they were looking for. Although the Third Anglo-Dutch War interrupted such trade, it was resumed in 1677 to accommodate both colonies.[12] By way of Barbados, numerous products originating in North America found their way to Suriname: meat, bacon, fish, vegetables, bread, cheese, wine, and other provisions; these shipments also included metal items for sugar production such as knives, saws, pots, cauldrons, and rollers, as well as leather good such as shoes and saddles.[13]

While Suriname's plantation economy was in need of the reexported provisions Barbadians offered, the establishment of commercial contacts in North America created alternatives that the Surinamese eventually came to prefer, because they could thus buy foodstuffs directly instead of from Barbadian middlemen. The North American horse trade was another factor in the new focus of Suriname's foreign trade. The horses were used primarily to drive the mills crushing the sugar cane, but they performed other chores as well on Suriname's plantations.

The Barbadians, for their part, no longer cherished Suriname as a trading partner once they became major customers of the wood exports from New York and New England (Boston, Connecticut, and Rhode Island).[14] If anything, Suriname became Barbados's rival in trade with New England, leading the Barbadian governor to suggest in 1707 that New England's commerce with the Dutch colony should be obstructed in view of the large amounts of rum, sugar, and molasses arriving on North American ships.[15] At an earlier stage, in 1685, the same issue had led to a joint protest by ten ship captains from the Dutch Republic. They were disgruntled about the shiploads of sugar Suriname's planters sold to the North Americans in exchange for horses and provisions, at the expense of Dutch return cargoes.[16] Free international trade clashed with mercantilist systems and with the commercial interests honored by those systems. When authorities in New England, in line with the Navigation Acts, blocked horse exports to the Dutch colony, the result was a slump in sugar output, since the sugar cane could no longer be processed.[17]

A breach in mercantilist legislation took place in Amsterdam in 1704. In that year, the directors of the Sociëteit van Suriname (which ruled the colony) legalized North American trade with Suriname, provided each North American ship arrive with horses. The horse trade was, after all, the rationale for the requests to revisit the decades-old exclusion of North Americans. Colonial Dutch officials strictly upheld the rule that each ship land horses. If all horses had died during the voyage, one ship captain wrote, "the master of the vessel was obliged to preserve the ears and hoofs of the animals, and to swear, upon entering the port of Surinam, that when he embarked they were alive . . ."[18]

For the economy of St. Eustatius, trade with foreign colonies was even more important than for Suriname. It was essential for commercial reasons, but also for survival. Settled in 1636 by a Dutchman who hoped to make it a tobacco island, St. Eustatius was occupied multiple times by the neighboring English and French, but always returned to Dutch rule at war's end. Through it all, commercial ties with foreign colonies were forged. As the island largely failed as a producer of cash crops, enterprising merchants transformed it into an entrepôt. As such, it became an importer and reexporter of tropical products. By 1688, enough sugar entered the roadstead from the surrounding French and English islands to fill the holds of eight ocean-going ships leaving for Amsterdam.[19] Defying the restrictive commercial policies of England and France, St. Eustatius attracted regionally operating merchants looking for provisions and dry goods and those seeking to illegally sell sugar and coffee. Beef and salted fish from Ireland and North American flour were always available, while Dutch imports included hats, stockings, spices, paper, glassware, axes, pots, printed cotton fabric, and coarse linen from Osnabrück, Germany.[20]

Starting in the late seventeenth century, St. Eustatius also developed into a slave market. St. Eustatius provided enslaved Africans to the nearby French and English islands, where the planters were always in need of workers. During the Nine Years' War (1688–97), Dutch supplies to French customers did not pass through St. Eustatius. Since Dutch and the French were adversaries, shipments were camouflaged by the use of ships flying neutral Danish and Brandenburg flags and sailing between Danish St. Thomas and French Saint-Domingue.[21] By the early eighteenth century, though, illicit Dutch slavers—the so-called *lorredraayers* (interlopers), whose prices were twenty percent cheaper than those of the WIC—began to opt for St. Eustatius as an outlet for their human cargo because of its location close to foreign customers, but also because safe and good anchorages were available on the island's west side, far from the officials' watchful eyes. Another reason for the ascent of the *lorredraayers* was the erratic supply of slaves provided by the WIC.

Trade between settlers of Dutch America and English subjects took place in the context of a close military relationship between the respective mother countries. The alliance between the Dutch Republic and England (and later Great Britain) was based on a 1677 treaty by which both sides agreed to defend the other's territory in case of attack. The ascension to the English throne of Dutch stadholder William III in 1688 reinforced the pact between the two neighbors, who came to be seen in the rest of Europe as the maritime powers. The Dutch invasion that enabled England's Glorious Revolution was a great risk that William and his supporters took, especially since tensions with France were running high. But it also underlines the tremendous power the Dutch Republic could still wield at this juncture.[22] The subsequent close collaboration between the Dutch and the English did not serve to reduce English suspicion of the Dutch overnight, but apprehensions about Dutch commercial rivalry were eclipsed by England's concerns about France, which "became the *bête noire* of the commercial classes."[23]

Locked in fierce mercantile and industrial competition with France, the Dutch Republic sided with England in the Nine Years' War (1688–97), which had a pronounced economic dimension. Along with their English allies, the Dutch undertook a blockade of France that paralyzed most of its commerce.[24] For its part, France changed from a naval approach to a full-scale privateering war by 1695, realizing that their maritime enemies depended much more than France itself on the maintenance of overseas trade.[25] The *guerre de course*—the French war on trade—was highly destructive to the transatlantic trade of the English and the Dutch. It came on top of the occupation of St. Eustatius, ordered at the start of the war by

Louis XIV himself. The reason for his decision, as explained in a letter to the governor-general of the French West Indies, Charles de Blénac, was the island's continuing smuggling with French colonists in spite of all French attempts to root out such trade.[26] The 17 ships and 1,200 men that left Martinique under Blénac succeeded in their mission, largely because theirs was a surprise attack. The Dutch settlers surrendered and were taken to Nevis, while their slaves, horses, furniture, and merchandise were shipped to Martinique and sold.[27]

The French also showed themselves eager to engage in actions detrimental to other Dutch colonies. A French squadron failed in its attempt to invade Suriname at the start of the war, but some ships sailed further west to Berbice, where troops were landed and a few plantations destroyed. Although a ransom was agreed upon that prevented further damage, the 20,000 guilders, to be settled in letters of exchange by the Zeeland proprietors of the colony, would never be paid. Suriname's governor insisted that a few Frenchmen whom he had made prisoners of war would only be released if they destroyed the letters of exchange. That happened accordingly.[28]

The war largely bypassed Curaçao, the Dutch colony that was closely intertwined with Spanish America. It had taken more than two decades after the Dutch conquest of 1634 before the islanders established commercial ties with subjects on the nearby Spanish Main. Once supply and demand were coordinated, commerce flourished in spite of the Spanish law, which prohibited foreign trade. In 1661, the governor of Caracas, dismayed about the presence of Dutch "smugglers," counted thirty Dutch vessels on the coast. Such a Dutch presence would remain a familiar sight for many decades to come.[29] Numerous firms based in the Dutch Republic switched their operations from Cádiz, where they had freighted the *flotas* and *galeones* that maintained commercial connections between Spain and its colonies, to Curaçao.[30]

After its reestablishment in 1674–75, the West India Company declared Curaçao a free port, inviting vessels from any country or colony to trade after paying a 5 percent duty on the value of the cargo they carried. Foreign bottoms had previously been refused entrance to the port unless they produced a WIC permit. Warehouses in Curaçao's port of Willemstad were soon well stocked with European and even Asian manufactures, including silk, woolen, and linen fabrics, lace, cotton, muslins, ironware, naval supplies, brandy, and spices.[31] Besides, Curaçao was attractive to its Spanish trading partners because of the supply of enslaved Africans. For half a century, starting in 1662, the island played an official or unofficial role in virtually all monopoly contracts (*asientos*) the Spanish Crown signed with foreign merchants for the export of slaves to Spanish America, making Curaçao the largest transit port in the inter-American slave trade. The trade in enslaved Africans to the Spanish Main was not even interrupted by the War of the Spanish Succession (1702–13), during which the Dutch Republic was at war with Spain.[32] A total of 100,000 slaves found their way from Africa to Curaçao in the period 1656–1730, most of whom were reshipped to Spanish colonies. A small percentage ended up in Jamaica.[33]

Essequibo, located between Venezuela and Suriname, also regularly traded with residents of Spanish America. One significant difference was that the settlers of Essequibo—and at times those of Berbice and, in the early days, Suriname—often relied on Amerindian trading partners, in particular Caribs. Spanish officials reported in 1694 that Caribs regularly guided the Dutch on futile search missions to the mythical city of El Dorado. As in previous generations, precious metals tied the Dutch to native allies.[34] In 1711, for instance, Caribs aided Dutchmen from Suriname, Essequibo, and Berbice in an attempt to locate silver mines in Spanish Guyana. In that year, the governor of Spanish Trinidad dislodged a group of Dutchmen from Angostura, where they were about to establish themselves and build a fort in order to exploit the mines that supposedly existed in Araguacay.[35] In 1714, an expedition leaving Essequibo in search of Lake Parima, the suspected location of El Dorado, carried many axes, firearms, and machetes valued by the Amerindians.[36] A quarter century later, colonial authorities dispatched a German surgeon to find a silver mine along the Iren River. His expedition, which also aimed to locate gold, failed to meet expectations.[37]

Essequibo's trade with the native and Spanish residents at the Orinoco started in the late 1670s. Like in Curaçao two decades earlier, it was the highest-ranking Dutch official who took the initiative to conduct trade with his Spanish neighbors. At regular intervals, Essequibo's commander Abraham Beekman dispatched a canoe with a soldier to exchange axes, cutlasses, knives, and beads for annatto dye and other local produce. Beekman intended to organize such expeditions in advance of the arrival of the *galeones*, the southern Spanish fleet that would touch at Cartagena de Indias before anchoring at Portobelo for a trade fair.[38] Produced by Amerindian women, shiploads of annatto soon ended up in the Dutch colony, allowing Beekman in 1684 to send a cargo of 157 barrels of annatto dye to Middelburg.[39] It has been calculated that between 1700 and 1742, 335 tons of annatto were exported from Essequibo, for which the equivalent of almost 200,000 machetes were exchanged. As one scholar has remarked, that was "enough to supply the entire Carib nation twice over!"[40]

Commerce with Spanish colonies came under threat when the War of the Spanish Succession broke out. Dutch opposition to the French candidate in the Spanish Succession War did not really amount to a new antagonism, but derived primarily from the fear of the strengthening of French might.[41] After Spain's Habsburg King Charles II died in 1700 without leaving an heir and Louis XIV's grandson Philip of Anjou was proclaimed King Philip V, a coalition that included England and the Dutch Republic and supported Habsburg candidate Archduke Charles faced an alliance of France and Bourbon Spain that favored Philip.

Having laid the foundation for this coalition, William III did not live to see the outbreak of the war. He passed away in 1702 at the age of fifty-one, like the Habsburg King without issue. His demise was followed within a week by a declaration by the States of Holland that no new stadholder would be appointed. The second stadholderless period (1702–47), which saw the expansion of the influence of regents and the formalization of decision-making, had begun.[42]

The prospects for the Dutch Atlantic were bleak even before the war formally broke out. One immediate outcome of the Franco-Spanish alliance was the granting by Philip V of the *asiento*—the monopoly to supply slaves to Spanish America—to the French slaving company Compagnie Royale de Guinée. It was expected that Curaçao's highly profitable middleman position in the Spanish slave trade would thereby be terminated, even though that did not prove to be true. Amsterdam's merchants also believed that it was only a matter of time before France would control Spain's trade and colonies. They therefore closed their warehouses in Seville and Cádiz, which had traditionally supplied the Spanish fleets sailing back and forth to the Americas. In the end, this measure made little difference, as Spain's government suspended the fleet system for the duration of the war, afraid as it was of silver shipments falling into the hands of its enemies.[43] The consequences of this decision would be felt as far away as the East Indies, where the VOC (the Dutch East India Company) was left without regular shipments of Peruvian silver, which served as a means of payment throughout the Indian Ocean.

Whereas Dutch troops saw action in the Iberian Peninsula, the republic was spared the horrors of war. Targeted by the French, the Dutch colonies were not so fortunate. The first to be invaded was St. Maarten, the colony that had shared an island with the French since 1648. The arrival of six hundred French privateers led to a massive exodus.[44] The next Dutch colony to suffer personal and material damage was the plantation colony of Essequibo, as the French looted Amerindian villages and set plantations on fire. To prevent further damage, the Dutch commander capitulated and struck a deal with the invaders, to whom he was to pay 58,000 guilders. Since cash transactions of this magnitude did not occur in the eighteenth-century Caribbean, the Dutch paid the French largely in enslaved Africans, meat, and provisions. Four months later, other French privateers completed the colony's destruction by looting and burning the remaining plantations and carrying off numerous slaves and barrels of sugar.[45]

These actions proved to be merely the prelude to the havoc wreaked by Jacques Cassard in four other Dutch colonies during the same War of the Spanish Succession. An outsider in the French naval establishment, Cassard proved highly skilled in obtaining huge amounts of ransom after attacking the colonies.[46] His initial targets in the Caribbean were the English colonies of Montserrat and Antigua, but after France and England had buried the hatchet (October 1711), the Dutch remained as the sole French enemies in the New World. After a failed attempt to subdue Suriname, Cassard sojourned in Martinique, where he mounted a second attempt. This time, he landed 900 soldiers and 150 freebooters at the port of Paramaribo on October 9, 1712, forcing the Dutch authorities to surrender and pay a ransom of 622,800 guilders or 747,350 livres, to be paid in slaves, sugar, cash, silver, and letters of exchange.[47] Cassard also dispatched a squadron of 600 men to the Dutch colony of Berbice, located to the immediate west of Suriname. Following an impressive bombardment of the local fort, the Dutch surrendered and negotiated a ransom of 300,000 livres, to be paid in a letter of exchange, slaves, merchandise, provisions, and a sloop.[48] The colony's owners, the Van Pere family from Zeeland, refused to honor the letter of exchange, since in their estimation its value of 181,975 livres was worth more than that of the entire colony. After French diplomats in Utrecht had failed to reach an agreement, a consortium of Amsterdam merchants agreed to pay the letter of exchange and became the colony's new owners.[49]

Having returned to Martinique, Cassard set out again, first targeting the Dutch Leeward islands. On January 25, 1713, his ships appeared on the roadstead of St. Eustatius, only to find that the inhabitants had fled to St. Thomas and other nearby islands, bringing their possessions along. The Dutch governor told Cassard to do as he saw fit. The privateer squeezed 3,400 pesos out of the remaining residents, paid in a few dozen slaves and whatever cattle and provisions he could find.[50] At this juncture, Cassard received the information that Curaçao was only defended by 700 or 800 men, prompting him to steer to that island. Before approaching Curaçao, Cassard stopped at the coast of Venezuela to take in water. While there, the governor of Caracas provided him with pilots and maps of the island.[51] Although Curaçao's defenders had been forewarned about Cassard's fleet, their defense did not amount to much. Too late the government discovered a serious shortage of ammunition, guns, and men. After a relatively easy surrender, it took some time for the two sides to agree on the size of the ransom. The Dutch eventually managed to have the sum reduced from 300,000 to 115,000 pesos, payable mostly in merchandise, slaves, and cash.[52]

Most of the ransom costs were furnished by local residents, which led to loud complaints, dissent, and tensions with the colonial governments. The financial and economic setbacks of the invasions would reverberate for years to come, as they did in Essequibo, where the WIC bore two-thirds of the costs of the damages incurred. Not until the late 1720s did the population reach the same level as before the war.[53] In Suriname, not only did Cassard's invasion provide many slaves the opportunity to run away to the tropical rainforest, the ransom led to disputes between the Sociëteit van Suriname, which ruled the colony, and the planters, who were bound to pay ten percent of their property's value, but were reluctant to pay when the French had departed. Some planters even flirted with the idea of forming a government of their own.[54] By contrast, Cassard did not drive a wedge between the rulers of Curaçao and the island's residents, who consented to pay their share without complaint. The memory of the French invasion was still alive more than half a century later. In 1770, an anonymous settler complaining about taxes referred to Cassard's raid in a letter to the WIC, asking rhetorically, "What right do you have to this land, did you ransom it from the French in the year 13, didn't it come from our sweat and blood . . ."[55]

The damage Dutchmen inflicted on France during this war was relatively small and largely the work of Zeeland privateers. Their operations extended to the area north of Iceland, where French whalers were active, the Irish coast, the Mediterranean, the Venezuelan coast, and especially the coast from Brittany in France to Cape Finisterre in Galicia, Spain. In that zone, the Zeelanders seized many vessels carrying cod and ships bound for the West Indies or returning from there with sugar heading to Bordeaux, Nantes, or La Rochelle.[56] In the end, it is hard to assess whether Dutch privateering was a match for French corsairing, and therefore whether Dutch commerce was harder hit than that of France. While the total number of enemy prizes seized by the Dutch has been estimated at 1,800 with a net yield of 23.7 million guilders, it is not clear how many of these ships belonged to the French, although they must have made up the majority. The French corsairs captured no less than 4,543 prizes themselves, including many that had been fitted out in the Dutch Republic. At the end of the day, however, English shipping suffered more from the French than did the Dutch.[57]

The War of the Spanish Succession jeopardized Dutch economic interests in the Atlantic world. After all, Curaçao depended on the legal slave shipments to and a lively contraband trade with many Spanish colonies in the Antilles and on the Spanish Main. To fit out anti-Spanish privateers would therefore harm colonial Dutch interests. As the war broke out, the governor of Curaçao Nicolaas van Beeck tried to walk a fine line. While he issued letters of marque to privateers, Van Beeck tellingly advised captains of privateering vessels not to bother the residents of the Spanish Main and especially warned them against destroying plantations or cacao trees, since that coast was "the main [source] of this island's prosperity."[58] Instead, anti-French privateering made more sense, especially in light of the *asiento* granted by Philip V to the French. Besides, eliminating French shipping would induce Spanish settlers to embrace the Habsburg cause, whose champions supplied their necessities.[59]

The "Austrian" cause was also fomented by a move from the Habsburg emperor of Austria, Leopold I. Seeking to rally support for Charles in the

Americas, the emperor dispatched the German count Bartolomeo Capoce-lato to Venezuela. In 1701, Capocelato traveled from Vienna via Amsterdam to London and began his transatlantic voyage. But instead of heading directly for Venezuela, where he would have run the risk of arrest, he disembarked at Curaçao and installed his headquarters there. He found various men willing to assist him, including the French Capuchin priest Victor de Dôle and the merchant Phelipe Henriquez, a Jew who put some of his sloops at the count's disposal and let him use his wide network of commercial contacts on the Spanish Main. For the services he rendered, Henriquez was promised the governorship of Venezuela in the event Archduke Charles would win the war. Henriquez's presence in the Netherlands shortly after the war broke out suggests high-level deliberations on these matters. Although Capocelato eventually went ashore in Venezuela and built up a following among clergymen, officers, and government officials, his cause was doomed. He was arrested, escaped from prison, and returned to Europe without accomplishing his mission.[60]

Capocelato's mission seems a minor affair compared to the draft Dutch plan of December 1707 to seize all of Spanish America in the name of Archduke Charles. The plan, signed by A.H.—Anthonie Heinsius, the grand pensionary of Holland—provided for an Anglo-Dutch expedition with six to eight thousand soldiers from each of the two allies that would have blocked Bourbon access to the Peruvian mines that financed the enemy war effort.[61] The plan, which had been discussed in Britain's highest circles ever since the start of the war, was never implemented, probably, as Jonathan Israel has argued, because the leading Dutch politicians feared that Britain—having a superior navy—would secure most advantages from this scheme. They saw their suspicions confirmed later in the war. While the Bourbon side was closing in on victory, Britain struck a separate deal with France that provided for Philip V to remain on the Spanish throne and for the *asiento* to be switched from France to Britain. The only gain for the Dutch was that the French were not to enjoy commercial privileges in the Spanish Indies.[62] During the peace negotiations in Utrecht, the directors of the West India Company exerted pressure on the Dutch delegation to ensure that Britain did not end up with a monopoly contract for the slave trade. If they failed in achieving that, the Dutch should be granted the right to supply half of the Africans bound for Spanish America.[63] But the die had already been cast.

Dutch weakness at the negotiating table in Utrecht in 1712–13 was largely a reflection of growing British power. On the one hand, the Dutch army expanded during the war to over 100,000 men (its largest ever size in the early modern period), but on the other hand, the Dutch could not keep up with British subsidies to the Holy Roman Emperor and allied princes, nor with the British investment in the war effort in Spain. Once the war had ended, the Dutch lost more ground, as the size of the army was reduced to 40,000, whereas the other warring parties all tried to keep the numbers up. No longer was the Dutch army one of Europe's largest.[64] And yet overseas ambition was not abandoned. The Dutch remained a force to be reckoned with, not least because of the power they projected in the Indian Ocean *and* in the Atlantic, where their interimperial trade continued vigorously for much of the eighteenth century.

Peaceful Partnerships

In the four decades following the Treaty of Utrecht (1713) that ended the Spanish Succession War, the Dutch Atlantic world enjoyed an uninterrupted spell of peaceful relations, and hence trade, with its competitors. While Britain fought a brief and limited war with Spain (1727–29), relations with Spain never again occupied center stage in Dutch governmental and commercial circles. The geopolitical position of the Dutch Republic was mainly triangulated with the interests of Britain and France. That had been the case since the start of the first Anglo-Dutch War in 1652 and would not change until Napoleon's defeat in 1815.

At the same time, the interimperial Dutch slave trade had been severely damaged by the Treaty of Utrecht. In the aftermath of the war, it became clear that Curaçao would no longer be able to continue its traditional role in the *asiento* slave trade. British traders simply did not need the Dutch island.[65] Nonetheless, Curaçao remained a lively center of contraband trade, sparking frequent Spanish diplomatic complaints about the ongoing contraband trade by the colonial Dutch with Spain's American possessions.[66] With great frequency, Curaçaoan sloops and schooners sailed to the "coast of Caracas," where countless bays, coves, and inlets provided shelter for illicit exchanges with traders or planters. Preeminent among the products obtained were tobacco, hides, and especially cacao. While

Venezuela was the world's largest producer of the crop until the early nineteenth century, Curaçao became one of the main cacao providers to Europe by virtue of this massive illicit trade with the Spanish Main. The costly and cumbersome Spanish trade system, combined with the evasion of customs duties by Curaçao's merchants, enabled the island to compete favorably with their Spanish colleagues. At times, the latter were forced to travel to Amsterdam to buy cacao from their own colonies.[67]

The Spanish answer to rampant smuggling in Venezuela was the establishment of the Real Compañía Guipuzcoana, whose task it was to redirect the flow of the colony's products to Spain and put a stop to illegal trade. The company's vessels were remarkably successful in seizing both locally-owned Dutch vessels and ocean-going Dutch ships, prompting the introduction of an annual convoy service from the republic to the West Indies in 1737. Convoying was irregular, however, and depended both on the needs of mercantile firms and the finances of the Amsterdam admiralty. The navy ships accompanying ocean-going Dutch merchantmen were not designed to confront the Guipuzcoana inside Caribbean waters, where the company was successful for many years.[68] In order to eradicate Curaçaoan smuggling, the Spanish company also targeted Curaçao's trading partners on the Spanish Main. One of them, an outlaw nicknamed Andresote, had gathered followers among both the indigenous population and runaway slaves. He had regularly traveled to Curaçao and interacted with the island's vessels to conduct trade.[69] After the Guipuzcoana defeated him and his group, he returned to Curaçao, where he was later reported to have become, once again, the leader of a band of outlaws.[70]

The Guipuzcoana failed to root out Dutch smuggling, however, and the Curaçaoans continued to obtain much-coveted Spanish American silver. One senior Spanish official noted that most of the silver pesos Venezuela received in payment for the cacao it sent to New Spain ended up on Curaçao, where they were exchanged for all kinds of European produce.[71] If Curaçaoans dominated Venezuela's foreign trade, Jamaican traders were the most prominent foreigners on the adjacent littoral of New Granada, to the west of Venezuela. The division into two spheres of activity was conditioned by the prevailing winds, which made it hard for Curaçaoan vessels to do business in the southwestern corner of the Caribbean. Transportation costs were therefore twenty percent higher than those of vessels from Jamaica.[72] Nonetheless, Curaçaoan merchants were also a fixture in the port of Rio Hacha, where they shipped firearms, gunpowder, and linen in exchange for pearls, precious metals, cacao, dyewood, hides, and mules. As early as the 1690s, the Dutch kept public shops there, and by 1734, the Crown considered closing the port off because of rampant smuggling.[73] In Rio Hacha, the Bay of Honda, and in smaller ports of their own, the native Guajiro were major trading partners of the Dutch colonists.[74]

In a letter to merchants in the Dutch Republic, a Dutch trader by the name of Daniel Apelius described the commercial scene in Curaçao during the commercial boom of the 1740s. Two-thirds of the departing vessels, he wrote, left for the Venezuelan coast, where they transacted business with a profit margin of 70 percent, according to his perhaps overly optimistic calculations. One-third of the vessels sailed to Cartagena, Portobelo, Havana, and Trujillo (Honduras), where they obtained gold and silver and reportedly even made an 80 percent profit.[75] "Havana" usually referred to the island of Cuba and not its capital city, where surveillance made foreign trade very hazardous. Curaçao's smugglers preferred to deal with the inhabitants of Cuba's southern districts, which were neglected by Spanish merchants and where hides and tobacco were abundantly available. Hides were also sought after by Curaçaoans anchoring at ports in Santo Domingo, the Spanish part of Hispaniola. Half of all the hides officially leaving the colony in the first half of the eighteenth century were bought by traders from the Dutch island.[76]

Curaçao's traders were not the only ones procuring Spanish American tobacco. Occasionally, Barinas tobacco was also smuggled by Spanish subjects or Dutchmen to Essequibo by way of Spanish Guyana.[77] Settlers of Essequibo also imported enslaved Amerindians, whom they obtained not for reexport but for use in the Dutch plantation colonies. In Suriname, the number of Amerindian slaves declined from 500 to just over 100 in the years 1671–84 and dipped even lower thereafter, but planters in Essequibo continued to rely longer on slaves from the interior.[78] While the importation of enslaved Africans was expensive, Amerindian slaves were relatively cheap. One Spanish official asserted that the Dutch could afford ten or twelve Amerindian slaves for the price of one African.[79] The practice of native slavery in Essequibo endured despite an ordinance of 1686 which only allowed for those who were already enslaved among the Amerindians themselves to be used as slaves.[80] The WIC itself also put native slaves to work, although these formed a small minority—no more than 49 of all 656 slaves in 1727.[81] Most of the natives who ended up as slaves in the Dutch colony were supplied by the Carib allies of the Dutch. The sale of natives, among whom children predominated, was linked to the Dutch introduction of firearms that must have enabled Caribs to hunt down potential slaves or other enemies.[82] The Dutch connection was indispensable to the Caribs, whose livelihood, the Dutch director general of Essequibo wrote in 1746, was after all derived from the slave trade.[83] This trade went on until the States General, having succeeded the WIC as the ruler of Essequibo and Demerara, enacted a law in 1793 that forbade the purchase of Amerindian slaves entirely.[84]

Slave trading also continued, of course, on the African coast, where the West India Company captured scores of Brazilian ships involved in illicit trade. The seventy-six ships seized between 1685 and 1729, some of which were captured far from the Gold Coast, added to the WIC's commercial inventory and provided the company with the sweetened tobacco that was coveted by the local African population, as well as cowry shells—an important means of payment in the slave trade—firearms, gunpowder, and gold dust.[85] Legal Brazilian commerce was, however, the rule, and for every seized ship, one or two dozen vessels traded with an official permit from Elmina. Measured by ships, this trade showed a clear decline in the eighteenth century, from an annual average of twenty-eight in the 1720s to fifteen to sixteen in the 1740s and fourteen from 1759 to 1772.[86] While the WIC continued to collect the ten percent customs duty, its role in the slave trade diminished after 1734, when Dutch free traders were legally allowed to engage in commerce all along the African coast. They bypassed the company to engage in direct business with the Brazilians and thereby secure Bahian tobacco, which accounted for ninety percent of all tobacco sold on the Mina coast. In exchange, the Brazilians filled their holds with enslaved Africans first bought by the Dutch, 3,602 of whom were imported between 1715 and 1731, and with cowry shells and textiles, especially in the subsequent period.[87]

The single most important commercial feature of the era from 1715 to 1755 was the growth of exchange with British colonies in North America and the Caribbean.[88] Of the 4,478 ships that historian Johannes Postma has counted as anchoring at Paramaribo from 1667 through 1795, an astonishing 4,000—or nearly 90 percent—hailed from North America. The vast majority of the 30,120 horses that landed at Paramaribo in the period of 1683–1794 originated in New England. They came off ships from Rhode Island and Massachusetts, and also from Connecticut, whose port of New London specialized in the horse trade.[89] A specific type of horse seems to have been bred for export to Suriname, as author William Douglass wrote in a 1755 book about British North America, "In New-England there is a breed of small mean horses called Jades or Surinamers, these run and feed in the waste lands at little or no charge, and are shipt [*sic*] off to Surinam for the use of their mills, &c. in the sugar plantations."[90] More than one in three horses did not survive the voyage, many of them perishing on the deck in storms. This helps explain why almost seventy percent of ships carrying horses landed fewer than three at Paramaribo, although an alternative explanation may have been the desire to sell foodstuffs and other commodities and keep horse sales to a minimum. In the latter case, British merchants observed the existing rules by introducing a token horse that enabled the conduct of other business. These horses were less in demand after 1750, when many sugar plantations relocated to the coastal lowlands, and tidal energy was used to power the sugar mills.[91]

The drive of the New England merchants to expand their commercial ties with Suriname was part of a broader initiative that encompassed the French Caribbean as well. Filling their holds with fish, flour, bread, butter, and building materials, scores of vessels cleared their home ports to do business in Martinique, Guadeloupe, Sainte-Domingue, and Suriname, where the captains sought to vend their wares in exchange for sugar, rum, and molasses. In 1731, the governor of British Antigua attributed Suriname's prosperity to these exchanges: "By this trade from Boston and Rhode Island, the French are not only vastly benefitted and improved, but the Dutch also at Surinam. This trade enabled them to make their first settlements there, and from a small beginning they have been able many years since to employ annually 40 or 50 sail of shiping [*sic*] in the trade to that place, and to make upwards of 40,000 of their hogsheads of sugar; whereas without this trade neither the French or the Hollanders would ever have made sugar to any advantage, much less to rival and exceed the Brittish [*sic*] Islands, and by a restraint of it they must soon decline and in time quite decay."[92] Conversely, the link with Suriname and the West Indies was also of great significance to Rhode Island, accounting for most of that colony's trade.[93]

Suriname's share of the New England trade remained larger than that of the French islands until at least the year 1730, when the Dutch colony accounted for twenty-four vessels entering Boston against a combined fifteen from Saint-Domingue and Guadeloupe.[94] The growth of sugar production in the French colonies explains the subsequent increase of New England's trade with the French colonies. What these islands and the Dutch colony had in common was the surplus production of rum and molasses, for which there was no substantial market in the respective mother countries. Molasses in particular could be used to purchase a variety of goods from North American merchants. As a consequence, Boston imported more than one hundred thousand gallons of rum annually from the Dutch by 1715.[95] The Molasses Act of 1733, designed by Britain's Parliament to outlaw precisely such transactions in order to secure a monopoly on the sales of British West Indian sugar and molasses on the North American mainland, was circumvented on a gigantic scale, and often with the help of officials. Just as North American customs officers allowed false entry,[96] the governor of Suriname helped captains of vessels returning to New England or the Middle Colonies evade the payment of customs duties by signing the false statements of the skippers, who listed Madeira as their destination. During "stopovers" on the way to their actual North American destination, the ships could pass the patrolling naval vessels and unload their molasses without paying taxes because they were supposedly in transit.[97]

Curaçao's ties with North America went back further than those enjoyed by Suriname. Since at least around 1680, a regular trade had been conducted between the Dutch colony and New York City, then still home to an ethnic Dutch majority, whose firms were conspicuously active in trade with Curaçao. Migration between both places must have consolidated the links.[98] One North American official asserted in 1700 that New York merchants had gotten estates by means of trade with Curaçao (and also Madagascar).[99] Bilateral trade increased to such a degree that by 1730 a ship departed for Curaçao from the New York harbor every other week. Numerous New Yorkers supplied regular but small cargoes to such vessels.[100] In addition to New York, Philadelphia and Rhode Island were the main trading partners of Curaçao. By contrast, the British West Indies did not feature prominently in the island's records of arrivals and clearances.

Connections between Jewish merchants resident in New York and Willemstad were a boost for mutual commercial ties. Nathan Simson organized twenty-three expeditions to the island between 1715 and 1722, making him the leading Curaçao merchant in New York in his day. As such, he was succeeded by Daniel Gomez, a man with no fewer than thirty-four business contacts on the island, all Sephardic Jews. In the period of 1739–72, he dispatched 133 ships to Curaçao. This commerce, which breached the English Navigation Acts, remained hidden from view until English officials discovered its scope in the late seventeenth century, following the creation in 1696 of vice-admiralty courts in mainland English America. Nonetheless, Curaçao's imports from New York almost doubled from just over five hundred tons (1715–25) to nearly one thousand (1763–64), while New York imports from Curaçao increased more slowly, to nearly for hundred tons in the mid-1750s.[101]

Both sides benefited from this trade, the New Yorkers obtaining highly-valued Venezuelan cacao, Peruvian silver, and Central American dyewood, and the Curaçaoans importing flour, bread, and other provisions. At times, the New York connection was literally a lifeline for the settlers of Curaçao. One of them wrote in 1747, "If they did not bring us flour, butter, and other foodstuffs, half the inhabitants of the island would be on the brink of starvation."[102] Not all provisions were imported for local consumption, and some of the foodstuffs that were reexported during war years must have ended up on the tables of Britain's enemies.[103]

Although some sloops sailed directly from New York with a cargo of flour—a voyage that usually took three weeks[104]—most expeditions were more circuitous. One preferred itinerary of New York's vessels was revealed when a Spanish privateer captured a British schooner in 1751. This vessel had first departed from New York for the Irish ports of Neury and Cork, exchanging its linen for butter and salted beef. With that cargo the captain steered the ship to Curaçao, from which it left for New York with consignments of cash and dyewood from twenty-seven Curaçaoan firms for their New York correspondents.[105]

Like Curaçao, St. Eustatius was frequented by ships from the British colonies in mainland America—the so-called Thirteen Colonies. Provisions formed the main import item from North America, cheese and fish coming from New England and bread and flour from New York and Philadelphia. Building materials were another North American staple, including planks, shingles, hoops, staves, bricks, turpentine, and tar.[106] Sheep and poultry were also in demand on St. Eustatius, a single ship from Virginia introducing nine hundred sheep in 1744.[107] In fact, what happened to St. Eustatius—as well as to St. Maarten—around 1750 had happened to the British West Indies in the four decades bracketing the turn of the eighteenth century. In those years, these islands had become strongly connected to the North American colonies, which henceforth became a regular source of provisions and building materials.[108]

St. Eustatius's main commercial contacts, however, were still the British and French Leewards. The Dutch free-trade entrepôt enabled the French and British to conduct bilateral trade, which was impossible on their own islands. The governor of the British island of St. Kitts observed that "[t]he pretence of the Dutch buying of the English and then selling to the French is a mere fallacy. The produce of all St. Eustatius is not above 500 or 600 of our hogsheads of sugar a year. . . . The English and French vessels meet there and deal together as principals, or they have their agents, Steward and Sagran, for the purpose. The Dutch have no concern but to receive the company's duties."[109] That was, of course, an exaggeration. Despite the increasing significance of foreign traders, the role of locals who identified as Dutch in trade on St. Eustatius remained important. They were the ones shipping 11,000 enslaved Africans to foreigners in the 1720s.[110] Still, British ships also supplied slaves to the island. Various Dutch merchants active in the Atlantic world lodged complaints with the West India Company in 1753 about these slavers introducing captives without paying customs duties.[111] St. Maarten, meanwhile, did not receive slave ships, although small vessels introduced Africans in addition to other commodities on a regular basis, probably both for local use and reexport.[112]

St. Eustatius benefited from its proximity to the French islands of Guadeloupe and Martinique. Commerce with Saint-Domingue, which would soon be the most profitable colony in the Atlantic world, remained marginal. Sales records for four of the human cargoes that arrived from Africa in 1726–27 reveal that 47.6 percent of the captives were sold to the French islands, though none to Saint-Domingue. The French Caribbean was thus the main customer for bonded workers in these years, edging out the Dutch Caribbean (43.8 percent).[113] Another indication of the significance of French Caribbean trade is the number of vessels arriving in

1733 from Guadeloupe (fifty-five) and Martinique (twenty-three)—one had sailed from Grenada, but again none from Saint-Domingue. Sugar, rum, and molasses came off the bottoms from Guadeloupe, while coffee was a staple from Martinique.[114] Brisk business with the French colonies was conducted in times of war, frustrating merchants in France. After France had declared war on Britain in January 1744, forty merchants from St. Eustatius began a massive trade with Martinique and Guadeloupe in particular, sending 262 vessels to the French islands in 1745 and 290 the next year.[115] These close connections infuriated Britain's minister-plenipotentiary at The Hague, who wrote to the States General that his king had "repeatedly received intelligence that the Governor of the Island of St. Eustatius, as a result of an odious affinity for the enemies of His Majesty, constantly furnishes the inhabitants of the French islands, not only with all manner of victuals, but also with arms and warlike stores and with everything that their armateurs [shipowners] require for their constructions."[116]

St. Eustatius was attractive because of the (imported) foodstuffs that were always available there and often lacking in the French colonies, even during peaceful years. For example, on three occasions during 1749–51, traders from Guadeloupe received permission from their authorities to purchase provisions in the Dutch island.[117] In value and volume, St. Eustatius's trade with the British Leeward Islands probably rivaled that with the French colonies. And similar to the French trade, the supply of slaves to British customers was an important ingredient of St. Eustatius's commercial success, especially in the 1720s, when the governor of St. Kitts estimated that more than a thousand slaves from St. Eustatius were sold to his island over a three-year period. The brisk trade in humans subsided in the early 1730s due to the large increase in the British slave trade to the Caribbean, which significantly reduced St. Eustatius's role in human trafficking.[118] St. Kitts continued to be a destination for slaves, but also a source of African labor shipped in from British islands and reexported to French colonies. In a twelve-month period between 1743 and 1744, 350 slaves came off a ship directly from Africa, while 579 slaves arrived from predominantly British Caribbean islands: 344 from St. Kitts, 159 from Antigua, 31 from Anguilla, 17 from Barbados, 22 from Saba, 4 from St. Maarten, and 2 from Guadeloupe.[119] The significance of the Dutch island as purveyor of bonded Africans further declined after 1766, when the

TABLE 2. Vessels arriving in St. Eustatius, 1733–85

	1733	1744	1762	1768	1776	1785	Average
British WI	20.4	44.1	32.0	27.6	39.3	23.3	31.1
Dutch WI	3.6	33.7	42.4	11.0	26.7	43.5	26.8
French WI	56.9	13.1	9.1	31.9	16.4	15.0	23.7
BNA/USA	17.5	3.3	0.9	16.8	3.3	6.2	8.0
Danish WI	0.0	5.0	7.8	4.9	11.4	10.7	5.9
Spanish WI	0.7	0.9	7.8	7.8	2.9	1.2	3.6

Sources: Adapted from Goslinga, *Dutch in Caribbean and Guianas*, 204–5; Knappert, *Geschiedenis*, 219; and Menkman, "Sint Eustatius' gouden tijd," 394–95.
Notes: The figures represent arriving vessels. The category "Dutch West Indies" includes Berbice, Demerara, Essequibo, and Suriname, and "BNA" stands for British North America.

British turned their recently acquired island of Dominica into an entrepôt in an attempt to rival St. Eustatius.[120] Yet since St. Eustatius, as we have seen, was not exclusively dependent on the sale of slaves, it continued to attract merchants from the British West Indies, who were often looking for cheap European manufactures, East Indian goods, and rum (see table 2). For their part, merchants based in St. Eustatius courted colleagues from Bermuda, who were the main suppliers of new vessels. In the 1720s, fifteen to twenty vessels were bought from Bermudians, a trade that continued in the following decades. Traders and sailors from Bermuda often remained on St. Eustatius, eventually comprising the largest group of British Americans on the island, who formed their own "Bermuda Quarter" in Oranjestad.[121]

The British islands were by far the chief commercial partners of the Dutch colony of St. Maarten, making up three-quarters of all foreign arrivals in 1735–36. St. Maarten shared its British West Indian contacts with St. Eustatius, both Dutch colonies conducting a lively trade with St. Kitts, Anguilla, and Antigua, in which the initiative lay with the British merchants.[122] The trade of St. Maarten and St. Eustatius with Britain's mainland colonies, still modest in the 1730s,[123] developed rapidly in the middle years of the century. In those years, Thomas Allen moved from Boston to St. Eustatius, where he maintained correspondence with individuals in Savannah, Philadelphia, New York, Newport, New London, Boston, Salem, and Newburyport. As the owner of several vessels, he was instrumental in selling goods from these places not only in the Dutch islands, but also in the Danish, British, and French Caribbean.[124] Merchants from Salem and other ports north of Boston also integrated St. Maarten into British commercial networks, at least until the end of the Seven Years' War. Among many examples, three will suffice. One vessel, the *Love* (in use from 1751 to 1757) linked Barbados and St. Maarten with Salem; another, the *Neptune* (1757–61) regularly sailed to both Gibraltar and St. Maarten; while a third, the *Speedwell* (1751–55) conducted a triangular trade with Madeira and the Dutch colony.[125] On average, thirty-four vessels from Salem touched at St. Maarten annually in the years 1751–64, undoubtedly importing salt and some locally-produced sugar and selling provisions. Likewise, St. Eustatius was involved in British networks that included Madeira or Irish ports such as Cork and Waterford, where salted beef was taken on board.

War on Trade and Wartime Trade

After four decades of relatively peaceful trade, the Dutch Atlantic could no longer escape the effects of international warfare in the period 1756–1784. Wars were a mixed blessing for Dutch merchants based in St. Eustatius and Curaçao. On the one hand, they offered new commercial opportunities, but on the other hand, they drove up freight and insurance costs. Wars also led to the capture of numerous vessels, damaging interimperial Dutch trade, especially that with the French Caribbean islands, which was the main area of commercial growth for the Dutch Atlantic in the third quarter of the eighteenth century. That Dutch transatlantic commerce was only now targeted by the British can be explained by the rivalry between Britain and France. Neither considered it in its own interest to shed the Dutch as a potential ally during the first stages of what historians have labeled the Second Hundred Years War (1688–1815). If, however, Britain had opted for *rapprochement* to France, the Dutch Republic would have been in jeopardy. Such a policy change was actually conceivable during the last years of the Spanish Succession War, when the leading British politician Henry St. John, Viscount Bolingbroke, and the inspector-general of imports and exports Charles Davenant presented themselves as strong supporters of ending the ban on French trade and stimulating the British economy by initiating free trade with France. They condemned the British policy to contain France by fortifying the Austrian Netherlands (today's Belgium), claiming that safeguarding the Dutch Republic had enabled the Dutch to continue their dominance of world trade.[126] These men ultimately failed in their ambition to have a commercial treaty signed between France and Britain.

As tensions between Britain and France and their allies flared up again in the 1720s and 1730s, one factor preventing Britain from adopting an aggressive course that might have resulted in war was the uncertainty about the Dutch stance. If the Dutch Republic were to remain neutral, they would have stood to benefit from British trade losses in the ensuing war. Any Dutch gains would have been at Britain's expense, or so the reasoning went. Anxious to preserve their commercial interests, the States General steadfastly refused to be cajoled into new joint ventures with Britain. They neither accepted the invitation to take part in a fleet to protect Portugal from a Spanish attack in 1735, nor did they yield to the pressure to help Britain during the War of Jenkins' Ear with Spain (1739–48), although the Dutch suffered equally from Spanish coastguard vessels.[127] The French, for their part, did all they could to prevent the Dutch from siding with the British by reassuring the Dutch about their fear that France might invade the southern Netherlands.[128]

The neutral stance the Dutch cultivated on the international stage was abandoned in 1741 during the War of the Austrian Succession (1740–48), which largely coincided with the War of Jenkins' Ear (1739–48). The main Dutch role was to protect the Austrian Netherlands from French incursions, but when push came to shove, the Dutch did little to resist the French. What is more, the French sent an army into the republic in 1747 that conquered parts of States Flanders in an attempt to force the Dutch to withdraw their support for Britain and Austria. The unintended consequence was a tremendous amount of turmoil in the Dutch Republic, where many inhabitants opposed the regents, which in turn enabled the restoration of the stadholderate. Willem IV, who was already stadholder of the provinces of Friesland, Groningen, Gelre, and Drenthe, now also embarked on a short-lived career as stadholder of Holland, Zeeland, Utrecht, and Overijssel.[129] After his untimely death, he was succeeded by his son, Willem V.

It was during his rule that the Seven Years' War (1756–63) broke out—the first war of global dimensions, with fighting in the Americas, Europe, and Asia. At the war's inception, the Dutch reverted to a policy of neutrality. Participating on the British side in this war that pitted France and Britain against each other would have made them vulnerable on land to the mighty French army. Conversely, a French alliance would have made them vulnerable on the seas, where British privateers could be expected to wreak havoc on Dutch global trade. Neutrality, the States General argued, guaranteed that neither of the two belligerents made a move that would drive the Dutch into their enemy's arms.[130] Nonetheless, Dutch interests did suffer during this war. By the summer of 1758, Britain ceased to respect Dutch neutrality in light of the manifold commercial services the neutral countries provided to France, especially in its Caribbean trade.[131] And since the Dutch outstripped other neutral shippers by a vast margin, their vessels were seized in large numbers, causing a loss to shipowners and investors of almost 22 million guilders.[132] Those were the losses reported at the time, though it seems that in reality, some of these ships— it is unclear how many—were eventually released, usually because their initial condemnation as prizes in North American ports was overturned by the High Court of Admiralty in London.[133] In general, trade remained lucrative enough for it to continue in spite of the numerous captures.[134]

These captures reflected a new emphasis of British geopolitics. Whereas Britain had previously relied on a network of European alliances that, inter alia, protected the Dutch Republic and Hanover from a French or Prussian attack, her new priorities lay overseas.[135] British trade with the Americas was constantly on the rise, while trade with Europe was rapidly diminishing. The growing importance of the Thirteen Colonies as a market for British manufactures and the perceived threat of French expansion in North America made for a reorientation of overseas policy.[136] As Britain relinquished the old European alliance policy, the Dutch Republic and its commercial activities were left exposed. British ministers were no longer held back if they wished to punish perceived Dutch wrongdoing. Violations of the restrictive Navigation Acts by the colonial Dutch, for example, had long been an annoyance to Whitehall. They raised even more concern after the Seven Years' War commenced. Mercantile firms from the Dutch Republic massively used St. Eustatius as an intermediary in their trade to the French colonies, which were largely cut off from supplies from France. Dutch metropolitan control of the trade with the French colonies was such in these years that Dutch traders offered French colonial sugar and indigo to the merchants of France.[137] Britain's naval response to St. Eustatius's trade with the French West Indies was resolute, its ships in 1758 blocking the passage to St. Eustatius of forty neutral ships from Europe, most of which had undoubtedly been fitted out in the Dutch Republic. Another blockade took place during British operations against Martinique and Guadeloupe in 1759. Privateers from the British islands of Montserrat and Antigua also targeted St. Eustatius's locally-owned vessels, capturing them time and again. By 1761, 238 vessels from St. Eustatius had been seized, causing damages worth over three million guilders. It is unclear how many were restored to their legitimate owners.[138]

Curaçao suffered less at the hands of British privateering, although the loss of its ships and cargoes amounted to 300,000 guilders in 1758 alone.[139] Although the island had traditionally been part of the Spanish American orbit, French colonial relations with Curaçao were intensified in the mid-eighteenth century. While no more than twenty French colonial vessels arrived in Willemstad during a twelve-month period in 1751–52, 102 vessels cast their anchor in 1785–86. Some came from Martinique, offering cacao, others from Grenada, but most now hailed from Saint-Domingue, where Curaçaoan merchants had developed close contacts with traders in the ports of Cap Français and Léoganne and in the southern part of the colony. In exchange for Curaçaoan supplies of textiles, copious amounts of sugar and indigo were imported.[140] By 1785–86, the number of vessels arriving from Saint-Domingue (fifty-four) was even higher than the number of United States bottoms (forty-four).[141]

To depict the trade of the colonial Dutch with the colonial French as merely bilateral does no justice to the full picture. The Dutch also presented themselves as intermediaries between foreign empires. The best example is Curaçao's function as a transit point in the mule trade from the Spanish Main to the French colonies, a business that developed into the main branch of Curaçao's commerce.[142] Mules, also used as a mode of transport and as pack animals but predominantly used as draft animals on Caribbean sugar plantations, were in high demand in the rapidly developing French colonies. Since mules could be bartered for slaves, who were always in short supply, Venezuelan traders were soon invested in this commerce.[143] For their part, French merchants often relied on the Curaçaoan merchants with their time-honored contacts on the Spanish Main.[144] The production of mules in the Venezuelan Llanos kept increasing throughout the century. The governor of Coro (Venezuela) complained in 1723 that Curaçao was a way station in his area's annual export of 1,500 mules to the Caribbean islands.[145] When the colony's first intendant arrived in 1783, he noted that each year 8,000 mules were exported illegally, especially to the French Antilles.[146]

Aruba and Bonaire were sites of these mule sales, as were the uninhabited Aves and Las Roques archipelagoes. These trading places were all close to Coro, one outlet of the mule trade, and comfortably far from surveilling Spanish officials.[147] Much further to the east in Venezuela, in the deserted bay of Las Esmeraldas close to Araya, the Curaçaoans also bought mules for use in sugar mills, and both mules and sugar were then taken on to Bonaire and Aruba. There, Frenchmen from Martinique bought the animals and brought them to their island.[148] Curaçao itself was no regular station in the trade of mainland mules to the French colonies, although some cases have been documented of local traders illegally introducing these animals in one of the island's outer bays.[149] Governor Jean Rodier provided the main incentive to transport the mules directly to the French Antilles by exempting the sloops active in this trade from paying import duties, as long as they sailed on after taking in water and provisions on Curaçao.[150] For most of the century, the Venezuelan mule trade to the French Caribbean was not allowed by the Spanish Crown, until a royal decree *(real cédula)* of August 26, 1777, legalized the exchange of provisions and mules, as long as these were paid in slaves, silver, or letters of exchange.[151] Though Curaçao may have been explicitly excluded from the legal form of this trade, the island could not be sidelined, whether as conveyor of mules or provider of vessels for mule shipments.[152]

Meanwhile, Curaçao's bilateral trade with the Spanish Main continued to prosper. In the mid-1780s, Venezuela still accounted for over eighty percent of the island's shipping traffic.[153] By then, the Real Compañía Guipuzcoana had been liquidated, to the relief of the many Curaçaoans involved in trade. The company had been a scourge of the island's shipping industry, seizing no fewer than 400 vessels in the period 1759–74 alone.[154] These captures constituted a war on trade during peacetime. A century earlier, such losses might have been a reason for the Dutch Republic to go to war, but this was never the subject of discussion in political circles. Likewise, there was no metropolitan Dutch response to growing Spanish encroachment on Dutch Guiana. While Spanish missionary activity on the

Essequibo frontier expanded, Dutch commercial ties to Spanish Guyana were increasingly interrupted by Spanish attacks. This was enabled in part by Spain's pacification of the Amerindian Caribs, who ceased to operate as important allies of the Dutch, resulting in a decline in Dutch military strength.[155] One Spanish assault on the recently-established Dutch trading post at the Cuyuni River in 1758 killed two Dutchmen and took several others prisoner. In 1760, the Spanish raided Dutch settlements on the Barima and Moruca Rivers and in 1769 laid waste to the Moruca post and once again that at Cuyuni.[156] Dutch communications with the interior were now completely disabled by local Spanish authorities, who were following instructions from their metropolitan overlords to occupy all of eastern Guiana. The turmoil wrought by the French Revolution would, however, hamstring that project.[157]

Further east, Suriname did not suffer as much from the various international wars as did the Caribbean islands. Only in the 1690s and during the War of the Spanish Succession had attacks by foreign privateers damaged the slave trade.[158] The British American connection was consolidated after the Seven Years' War. A wide variety of items arrived on New England ships. One sloop left from Providence, Rhode Island, in 1766 with the following items: 100 hogsheads of tobacco, 122 boxes spermaceti candles, 1,975 staves, 433 hoops, 4,000 bricks, 1,700 feet heading, 8 horses with awning, 3,500 bunches onions, 35 wood axes, 62 shaken hogsheads, 9 2/3 barrels beef, 5 2/3 barrels pork, 7 cwt. ship bread, 3 firkins butter, 30 oars, 12 barrels flour, 25 barrels tar, 8 barrels oil, 3 pigs, and 50 kegs oysters.[159] In this period, tobacco cultivated in Rhode Island also featured prominently in that colony's shipments to Suriname.[160] Some entrepreneurs specialized in the Suriname trade, such as furniture maker Benjamin Peabody of Newport.[161] The New England imports were at times so massive that there was not enough molasses to be paid in exchange. Instead, Dutch traders on the receiving end of this trade issued bills of exchange that could be cashed in the Dutch Republic. This arrangement was, however, far from ideal for the New Englanders, many of whom did not trade directly with the Netherlands and preferred other currencies over the guilder.[162]

A reexport trade of enslaved Africans from Suriname to British or other foreign colonies never took off. Even the reexport of human cargoes to one of the Dutch entrepôts was exceedingly rare. A shipmaster who once intended to buy Africans in Suriname from arriving slavers and sell them in St. Eustatius was denied permission, on the grounds that such an arrangement was "unusual."[163] This is easily explicable: for most of the eighteenth century, planters in Suriname were complaining that not enough enslaved Africans were imported. Occasionally, individual captives did end up in British colonies. Quaco, a slave accused of poisoning a fellow slave in Boston in 1761, was one example. He had been brought in from Suriname, as had another slave who was a witness in this case.[164] Conversely, North American slaves were sometimes carried to Suriname, such as the nineteen Africans Nova Scotia's governor sent in 1784 to his cousin, who owned an estate in Suriname.[165]

The relations forged by Essequibo and Demerara with British North America were equally complementary to those maintained by Suriname, prompting the United States envoy in The Hague, John Adams, to observe in 1783 that "the Colonies, upon the Continent, of Surinam, Berbice, Demerary and Essequebo . . . cannot Subsist without our Horses, Lumber, and Provisions, nor without the sale to us of their Melasses."[166] Lumber, however, did not enter but leave Essequibo and Demerara, especially on ships bound for Barbados, Suriname's old trading partner, where the demand for timber had never subsided. These shipments were not as valuable as those involving rum and molasses, for the sale of which the WIC collected high export duties: twelve guilders for every hogshead of molasses and thirty per hogshead of rum.[167]

What British merchants did provide was plantation hoes and provisions. British manufacturers developed a special hoe for use on sugar plantations in Demerara, which must have been introduced in large numbers each year.[168] Provisions were equally critical to western Guiana. Short of these foodstuffs, Essequibo would have starved on more than one occasion. Neither in the seventeenth century nor the eighteenth did the West India Company and the other Dutch firms active in Atlantic commerce succeed in furnishing enough provisions on a regular basis to Dutch America. Foreign imports were therefore a necessity to feed European settlers as well as African slaves, who, Essequibo's director general Laurens Storm van 's Gravensande warned, otherwise worked less hard when hungry and were more likely to revolt.[169] British traders also increasingly introduced enslaved Africans themselves, filling a void left by Dutch slavers who were not eager to extend long-term credit to the planters. Owners of slave ships therefore opted to sell slaves in Suriname, which only made local slave demand in Essequibo more pressing.[170]

Although foreign slave imports were officially prohibited, the WIC Chamber of Amsterdam realized as early as 1754 that the colonies would receive few slaves if trade by non-Dutch ships remained illegal.[171] Nonetheless, the ban on slaves imported through foreign channels remained in place, despite a petition sent by Essequibo's planters to the States General in 1769, in which they suggested paying a tax for every slave thus purchased. The WIC Chamber of Zeeland, which wished to monopolize trade with both Essequibo and Demerara, at the expense of Amsterdam, rebuked Storm van 's Gravensande for lending his support to this petition and for conniving with a foreign slaver to sell slaves worth 150,000 guilders.[172] Enslaved workers indeed regularly arrived by way of the British Caribbean, with British merchants smuggling them in on the same vessels that carried immigrant British planters who had the right to introduce their own slaves. Like their Dutch colleagues, British slavers may not have been happy about the planters' inability to pay in cash, but the determination of the planters to ignore the rules and pay their suppliers in produce (not only rum and molasses, but coffee and cotton) guaranteed the future presence of British slave ships.[173] British captives also found their way to Demerara during that colony's growth spurt after mid-century, surpassing Dutch supplies, which were more than twice as expensive and only constituted ten percent of what the planters needed.[174]

The British impact on the smaller Guiana colonies went far beyond these commercial links.[175] From the early 1740s onwards, British subjects settled in first Essequibo and later Demerara and Berbice, encouraged by the Dutch commander Hermanus Gelskerke and by Storm van 's Gravensande. The West India Company board responded enthusiastically to these initiatives, hoping they would enable the colonies to prosper. They agreed to the plan to offer British settlers free land and ten years' exemption from taxes.[176] The immigrants were also attracted by the fertility of the soil, which contrasted sharply with the depleted soil of Barbados and Antigua, from which many of them arrived. Other advantages included the absence of hurricanes and severe droughts, the abundant crops, and the availability of cheap water transport for produce as well as, increasingly, tidal energy for the sugar mills.[177] To the many planters arriving from Tobago after Britain had ceded that island to France in 1783, British rule in the Dutch Guianas (however temporary) must have been attractive as well.[178]

Once some British planters had achieved success, others followed in their wake, establishing plantations on the coast, up the rivers, and soon in Demerara and Berbice as well.[179] In 1781, Edward Thompson, a Royal Navy officer, reported that numerous immigrants "whose fortunes had been shipwrecked elsewhere, and no place was ever formed by Nature to replace them so readily and shortly," were arriving daily from the British Caribbean.[180] British investments and entrepreneurship rapidly transformed the colonies to dynamic and quickly-expanding producers of cash crops. Demerara emerged as the foremost of the three colonies. Although the first plantation was not set up until 1746, no fewer than 130 plantations were counted in 1769. Planters with other nationalities added to the dynamism, including Frenchmen, Germans, and Swiss.[181]

In the end, no colony illustrates the ultimate decline of the Dutch position in the Caribbean and hence the Atlantic at large better than St. Eustatius. Like the Dutch Guiana colonies, St. Eustatius offered massive quantities of rum and molasses to North American traders in the decades after the Seven Years' War, and substantial amounts of sugar as well—almost five million pounds in 1770 alone. Most sugar and molasses entering New York City, for example, had been purchased in St. Eustatius. Sugar and its by-products usually originated in the French islands, which gave rise to a thriving Anglo-French trade on the roads of the Dutch island. The North American demand for molasses was virtually insatiable. Massachusetts alone possessed fifty-one rum-producing distilleries, Rhode Island at least thirty, and New York twelve.[182] Moreover, resident Englishmen distilled French rum.[183] British merchants did not only arrive from North America. Their Caribbean colleagues were also attracted by "Statian" rum, which was priced 40 percent cheaper in 1770 in the Dutch islands than in Barbados and Jamaica. The vessels arriving from these and other British islands in 1762 and 1776 accounted for half of all bottoms hailing from non-Dutch ports.[184]

St. Eustatius's trade thrived from the 1750s through the 1770s. On the eve of the Seven Years' War, land was reclaimed from the sea to build new warehouses. Commerce only grew during the war, and by the early 1760s, more than two thousand vessels cast anchor at Oranjestad each year—a dramatic increase since 1733, when only 146 ships arrived annually.[185]

Figure 1. View of the Island of St. Eustatius, engraving by Carel Frederik Bendorp, 1756. Courtesy of Amsterdam Museum.

The early 1770s saw a similar number of vessels arrive, a number that increased to more than three thousand by the end of that decade. No longer was St. Eustatius simply an entrepôt where merchants traded across imperial boundaries. After the start of the American Revolutionary War in 1775, the island became a conduit in the consignment of war material to the Continental Congress and its partisans in their independence war, in particular by Dutch firms such as De Neufville and Van Staphorst. In exchange for arms and ammunition, Chesapeake tobacco and South Carolina indigo entered the hundreds of warehouses on St. Eustatius's beach.

Dutch collaboration with the North American rebels led to the capture of fifty-four Dutch ships sailing between the Dutch Republic and St. Eustatius in 1777 and helped provoke Britain's declaration of war against the Dutch in late 1780. Shortly after the Fourth Anglo-Dutch War commenced, a combined British naval and army force aimed to end St. Eustatius's prosperity with one blow. Led by Admiral George Rodney, the invaders arrested two thousand Americans, seized two hundred ships, stole bullion, and emptied all the warehouses. The next three months saw systematic British plunder. "In several instances," eyewitness Lambert Blair wrote, "where it was supposed Money was secreted by the people, Soldiers & Negroes were employed to dig up the Earth in their Yards & Gardens; the Floors of Houses were taken up & in one instance a Tomb in the Church Yard was broke open in order to look for Moneys which was supposed to be hid therein."[186] Total damages added up to more than seven million pound sterling.[187]

At Rodney's orders, St. Maarten and Saba were also occupied, but he abandoned his plan to conquer Curaçao, since it would leave a garrison in St. Eustatius that was judged too small to withstand a French attack. Rodney's fleet then made for the Guianas, where he ordered four British privateers to force the surrender of Demerara and Essequibo. This was accomplished after the invaders had captured all the ships at anchor and pillaged several plantations. Soon, Berbice also fell to a British force.[188] Suriname was spared a British invasion, although its planters did lose outgoing cargoes on ships seized by British privateers.[189] The Dutch Leeward Islands and the western Guiana colonies soon returned to Dutch rule, not by means of an expedition sent from the Dutch Republic, but through the intervention of three French squadrons that overpowered the British occupiers. Nor were the French willing to hand over the colonies to the

Dutch until they were obliged to do so by virtue of the Treaty of Paris that ended the American Revolutionary War.[190]

In the meantime, Britain had brought the war to the shores of Africa. Soon after the outbreak of the war, an army had been assembled in England, largely made up of men freed from military prisons. Their task was to conquer Elmina and other Dutch strongholds on the Gold Coast. The troops arrived at Cape Coast Castle, the British headquarters in West Africa, in February 1782. After bribing a number of African chiefs, the invaders were able to subdue one Dutch fort after another, but Elmina did not fall, due to the defense of local African troops faithful to the Dutch. The Dutch alone would have been no match for the British force and their own allies.[191] Thus, at long last, the decline of Dutch political and military power was catching up with Dutch Atlantic pursuits. Britain's raids of Dutch America in 1781 and its challenge to the Dutch presence in West Africa, like the unanswered British privateering success of 1758, revealed how vulnerable the overseas Dutch had become.

From an early stage, the European residents of Dutch America and Elmina were closely intertwined with foreign traders and colonies. In Suriname, this foreign connection stemmed from the English colonization that had preceded the Dutch era. Suriname and British North America were well-matched. North American foodstuffs and horses were exchanged for Surinamese rum and molasses, for which there was no market in the Dutch Republic. In due course, the colonies in western Guiana, which had initially gravitated to Spanish Guiana, also entered the commercial orbit of British North America. At the same time, international trade was the *raison d'être* of Curaçao and St. Eustatius, which developed into popular entrepôts for vessels from across the circum-Caribbean as well as North America's eastern seaboard. Their commerce continued in spite of British, French, and Spanish mercantilist policies, even when hundreds of locally-owned vessels were captured by British privateers and Spanish coastguard vessels. What distinguished both entrepôts was their function as liaisons between foreign empires. If St. Eustatius derived its significance in part from its role as a rendezvous between French and British subjects, Curaçao increasingly emerged as a bridge between the Spanish Main and the French Caribbean. As quintessential intermediaries, these Dutch Caribbean islands with their multiethnic populations thus contributed to the commercial integration of the New World.

2

INSTITUTIONS, FINANCE, TRADE

If interimperial connections formed one anchor for the Dutch colonies and trading stations, ties to the metropole were the other. For governance, investment, and the shipment and sale of Atlantic goods the overseas Dutch depended on the Dutch Republic. The West India Company provided the umbrella for most activities in the Dutch Atlantic world, although Suriname and Berbice were ruled by separate entities in which the WIC was only a partner. This chapter outlines the institutional framework of the Dutch Atlantic as embodied by these companies. Investments in the Atlantic world came both from these companies directly and from a variety of sources that represented the Dutch version of Britain's West India interest. Unlike the Catholic Church in the French, Portuguese, and Spanish colonies, the Reformed Church cannot qualify as an institution of the Dutch Atlantic. Such a designation would not be warranted, given the minor role it played everywhere, with the exception of Elmina. Nor can we compare the West India Company's commerce to that of the Dutch East India Company. The company only continued to be prominent in Atlantic trade until the 1730s, when it had to give up its last remaining monopolies. Henceforward its commercial role declined, even as Dutch import trade from the Americas blossomed, with cash crops arriving in ever-growing quantities from Dutch plantation colonies (Suriname and increasingly the lesser Guianas) and from the Dutch entrepôts in the Caribbean.

Institutions

The demise of the old West India Company (1621–74) was a long and protracted process. Although its financial condition had been worrisome for many years, politicians and shareholders did not begin to discuss serious reforms until the late 1660s, when the expiration of the company's charter was approaching. Because no consensus was reached, the charter was not extended. Instead, the States General kept the company alive by prolonging the charter seven times within three years and thereby allowing the WIC to die a natural death. But how was the legacy to be handled? Not eager to assume responsibility for the Atlantic colonies, the States General agreed to a plan from the States of Holland to dissolve the old company and replace it with a new WIC. Shareholders could convert their shares into new ones for 15 percent of the nominal value and bondholders could substitute their bonds for 30 percent of the nominal value. The directors' power was circumscribed, their number in each chamber was reduced, and the central board was cut from nineteen to ten.[1] Shareholders and depositors therefore paid the highest price for the formation of the new Company, losing 85 percent and 70 percent of their capital, respectively. These groups of investors, which were dominated by merchants and sugar refiners, remained of crucial importance for the new, leaner, and meaner WIC—they provided most of the capital for the new company. Conspicuous among the shareholders of the second WIC were also provincial states, individual towns, and public institutions such as the Middelburg Loan Office.[2]

Shareholders from Zeeland were certainly firm supporters of the new WIC, but as a portion of the overall investment, their contribution to the second WIC was modest, starting off at one-fifth and declining to one-sixth by 1710. The Chamber of Amsterdam owned two-thirds of the capital stock, while the combined share of the other three chambers—those of Maas (in particular the towns of Delft, Dordrecht, and Rotterdam),

Noorderkwartier (Hoorn and Enkhuizen), and Stad en Lande (the town and rural parts of Groningen)—was around 5 percent. Like its predecessor, the WIC was a financial fiasco and therefore a nightmare for investors and its board alike. The price of WIC shares was fairly stable during the new company's first decades, varying between 70 and 90 percent, but declined steeply to 30 percent in the 1730s and finally reached 14 percent in 1789. The trade in WIC shares, understandably, slowed down from 88 shares being sold in the early eighteenth century to 20 in 1791.[3] The WIC did not even pay dividend in most years. Around 1730 it still did every other year, but the subsequent intervals were five or more years. If a payment took place at all, dividends were usually only around 3 percent. Nor were such payments a sign of Company prosperity. Instead, they were mainly intended to halt the falling share prices. Poor as it was, the financial performance of the WIC did not deviate substantially from that of the VOC, whose shares were not very profitable either after the 1650s and reached often miniscule rates in the years after 1730.[4]

Company policy was determined by the ten-man board, which after 1684 met no more than once a year instead of twice. Their main agenda items were the fitting out of ships, the annual financial survey, and a discussion of the letters received from and dispatched to Africa and the Americas.[5] The main difference with the first WIC was that war and privateering no longer appeared on the agenda. Trade and government dominated instead. The area covered by the charter had not changed, comprising Africa south of the Tropic of Cancer (but excluding the Cape Colony), the Americas, and the islands in the Atlantic and Pacific Oceans—the latter never an issue of much importance in practice. The company monopolized trade to Africa and Essequibo, and allowed private merchants to engage in commerce everywhere else, as long as so-called recognition money was paid to the company.[6]

The WIC monopoly of trade with Africa was not challenged within the republic until the end of the War of the Spanish Succession in 1713–14. Since Britain ended up with the *asiento* at the Peace of Utrecht, the company was bound to lose ground in the slave trade to Spanish America. As expected, the WIC's overall commerce also fared badly in the postwar years, due to French and British competition in West Africa but also the seemingly ubiquitous Dutch interlopers, smugglers. In the first postwar decade, a debt was incurred of four million guilders. The suggestion of the

Chamber of Zeeland's major shareholders in 1714 to end the company monopoly on African trade and to allow private merchants to enter the slave trade received no support from the WIC board, but another proposal in 1728 of a group of Vlissingen merchants to open up all Atlantic trade met with a different response. A long debate ensued between politicians and company directors about discontinuing the company monopolies, resulting in a victory for the free traders. The States General extended the WIC charter in 1730, but the company only maintained the monopoly on the supply of slaves to Suriname, Essequibo, and Berbice, and kept a zone of sixty nautical miles along the Gold Coast where it enjoyed exclusive trading rights. Four years later, following new negotiations, that zone was also given up.[7] Finally, in 1738, after sustained losses, the company abandoned its active participation in the Atlantic slave trade. It had, in Pieter Emmer's words, become a "body without a soul."[8]

While the WIC directly ruled the Dutch Caribbean islands and the possessions on the Gold Coast, this was not the case with the Dutch Guianas. The States of Zeeland had fitted out the squadron that conquered Suriname in 1667 and had thereby become owners of the former English colony. Although the States tried to keep the WIC at arm's length, they eventually agreed to talk to the Chamber of Amsterdam, which represented the Amsterdam merchants who wanted the company to purchase the colony. In spite of the resistance of the major shareholders, who feared that ruling the colony would be costly, an agreement was signed in 1682. The company would rule Suriname, but the trade would be open to all Dutchmen with the exception of the slave trade. This plan was abandoned when it transpired that the WIC could not pay the stipulated sum of 260,000 guilders for this purchase, and a new plan was put forward: the company would share ownership with the city of Amsterdam and the wealthy Cornelis van Aerssen van Sommelsdijck. The three proprietors agreed to share gains and losses evenly in what was now dubbed the Societeit van Suriname.[9] Van Aerssen van Sommelsdijck himself became Suriname's governor, but his tenure was cut short in 1688, when he was killed by mutinous soldiers in the colony's capital Paramaribo. His family was to exit from the *societeit* in due course.

Similar to Suriname, Berbice was ruled by a societeit on behalf of the West India Company. Berbice had started its life in the Dutch colonial world in 1627 as a patroonship of the Zeeland merchant Abraham van Pere.[10] By virtue of being the patroon, Van Pere received the colony in fief from the WIC and was guaranteed the right of inheritance. He could distribute the colony's lands and levy certain taxes. In 1678, the WIC confirmed that Abraham van Pere (Jr., son of the original patroon) and his heirs possessed the colony "in immortal fief."[11] The French invasion and ransom of 1712 left Berbice in administrative disarray after the Van Pere family asserted that they had not authorized the colony's commanders to pay for a ransom that exceeded the colony's value. A consortium of Amsterdam merchants ultimately paid a negotiated sum to the French, thus becoming the colony's new owners. Both the merchants and the WIC struggled, however, to ship the number of slaves deemed necessary to the colony, leading the merchants in 1720 to set up a joint-stock company called the Sociëteit van Berbice, which (by an arrangement made twelve years later) paid an annual sum of a mere six hundred guilders to the WIC.[12] Essequibo and Demerara, meanwhile, did come directly under the control of the WIC, and more specifically, under the control of the Chamber of Zeeland. The WIC's control of these colonies became a matter of dispute between Zeelanders and Hollanders in the 1780s.

Dutch colonial governance in the Atlantic world was thus remarkably heterogeneous, due in part to lack of centralization in the heavily federalized republic. At home, the second WIC was a slimmed-down version of its failed predecessor. The number of men on the company's payroll in the republic was no more than fifty. They no longer included workers involved in shipbuilding or maintaining wharfs and warehouses. The WIC rented or bought ships and employed only administrators, bookkeepers, and those fitting out and loading ships. In addition to domestic personnel, the Company provided employment for at least five hundred seamen who maintained maritime connections in the Atlantic as well as the many hundreds of soldiers and administrative personnel that populated the forts and factories in Dutch possession.[13]

Apart from the fifty permanent domestic staff members, around fifty directors worked part time for the Company. They were distributed among the five chambers in a peculiar way: the relatively insignificant Stad en Lande and Noorderkwartier chambers employed more than did the influential Chamber of Amsterdam. Directors of chambers, almost invariably merchants, were selected from the company's principal shareholders. Their main task was to manage the company's activities in their area, appointing personnel, purchasing trade goods, fitting out ships, and auctioning off imported goods. This was no time-consuming task, at least not in the smaller chambers. Directors in Groningen, for example, did not need to meet more than one afternoon every two weeks. In Amsterdam, by contrast, meetings were held twice a week. Remuneration was modest, although officially amounting to ten percent of the dividend paid by the company. But as dividends were seldom paid, the directors were left without remuneration for their work. It has been estimated that they did not earn more than two guilders per day for their WIC activities—but, of course, they had other sources of income, too, and may well have made money in other branches of the Dutch Atlantic economy facilitated by the WIC.[14] That was certainly true for the governors and commanders serving in Guiana, the Caribbean, or West Africa. Having often secured their appointment through relatives or friends in senior company positions, they sought to enhance their salaries by overstepping their boundaries and engaging in all kinds of remunerative trade deals.

Finance

Although the WIC directors decided to discontinue transatlantic slaving voyages in the 1730s, they did not dismantle the company's African commercial apparatus. Despite the assertions of historians that the company's participation in the slave trade ended when its ships stopped carrying Africans to the Americas, the WIC's role in the slave trade endured, deriving from its purchase of slaves from African merchants and their sale to Brazilian merchants and private Dutch traders. Until the outbreak of the Fourth Anglo-Dutch War in 1780, this commerce—first reported in 1704—involved the sale of some 1,500 slaves each year.[15] Apart from some profit, this brokerage earned the WIC twenty guilders for each slave sold, and safeguarded the company trade in African products.[16] To maintain its physical infrastructure and afford transaction costs, such as the weekly gifts of brandy, tobacco, and pipes to African chiefs, the company levied a variety of taxes.[17]

Taxes were also numerous in the American colonies, ranging in the Guianas from poll taxes to land and production taxes, an import tax on horses, carriages, and poultry, an export tax on produce, an excise tax, a stamp tax, an income tax, and auction taxes.[18] Theoretically, these taxes were used to help fund a variety of tasks, most importantly administration, justice, infrastructure, and defense against internal and external enemies. In reality, the services rendered by the company in exchange for this wide array of fiscal obligations imposed on colonial subjects were so puny that in 1785, Demerara and Essequibo's "planters and residents" accused the company of stifling colonial economic development. They reminded the States General that the WIC had been founded for the sake of conducting trade. It was therefore unfit to direct agricultural colonies.[19] The accusation was not entirely fair. The settlers of these rapidly developing colonies had no reason to complain about most taxes, since they were rarely if at all collected.[20] What irked them, however, were the company's attempts to ban or tax the trade with British and North American ships. The company directors, of course, realized that interimperial trade provided the colonies with essential commercial contacts that the WIC itself could not offer. On the other hand, the company had to make money, which made it necessary to forbid the import of slaves carried ashore by non-Dutch vessels or the shipment of sugar to places outside the Dutch Republic. Only Dutch ships were allowed to perform these tasks. Besides, foreign ships that did conduct legal trade in the colonies were obviously expected to pay duties, but the company discovered that the income derived from these duties amounted to very little in proportion to the actual foreign trade that was carried on.

The WIC Chamber of Zeeland complained to Essequibo's governor in 1748 that British ships arriving in that colony paid little in the way of slaving duties and no import or export tax. The governor responded by arguing that even introducing minor customs duties would alienate the colonial residents, who expected British shipping to decline as a result.[21] The issue resurfaced in 1773, when the company board again prohibited foreign slave imports, stressed that foreign ships could only take in molasses, rum, and wood, and banned the import of any European manufactures from foreign vessels. Essequibo's ruling Council of Policy pleaded in vain to have the latter ban lifted, arguing that the colony was insufficiently supplied with manufactures by arriving Dutch ships. Evasion of the trade laws was, of course, rampant. The rules were often flaunted quite openly in both Demerara and Essequibo, where British slave supplies were more frequent, more reliable, and cheaper than those of Dutch companies.[22]

Such evidence could be given for all of the company's colonies. Their foreign trade ran counter to the WIC's goal of levying taxes in order to

Figure 2. The *West-Indisch Huis*, 17th c., once the seat of the West India Company in Amsterdam. Reproduced from Coomans-Eustatia & Coomans, *Breekbare Banden*.

execute its tasks. In the new company's first decades, those taxes did not yet loom large, since the main source of income were the indemnities received from Portugal, which amounted to 4,241,623 guilders in the period 1675–1728, more than the sale of stocks (3,772,500), colonial customs duties (2,875,074), captured ships (1,544,380), or subsidies from the provinces (1,103,544).[23] The Portuguese payments, agreed upon at a peace treaty in 1661 and revised eight years later, were in compensation for the Dutch loss of Brazil to Portugal in 1654.[24]

But even in the years while these payments still arrived, they could not solve the company's endemic cash shortage, which formed a major obstacle to its ability to cover running costs and outfit ships. At times, directors had to draw on their own capital and lend money to their chamber or issue bonds, raising interest charges. Only in the early 1720s was liquidity no problem, since the company capitalized on the speculation craze that had taken hold of Europe. The directors seized the moment by issuing new stocks, which were soon traded for 250 percent of their nominal value and yielded the amount of 3,765,000 guilders.[25] However, this bonanza masked the structural problems facing the WIC after 1713. The poor figures for direct trade between the republic and the colonies brought about a further erosion of the company monopolies, as we have seen, and made the directors refrain from making new investments in ships, which contributed to a series of very costly shipping disasters.[26]

Atlantic interests in the Dutch Republic, meanwhile, were voiced not merely by the WIC and the Suriname and Berbice sociëteiten, but increasingly also by lobbyists who acted on behalf of merchants trading with Suriname or planters residing in the republic. A pressure group "interested in trade and navigation with Suriname" surfaced in 1713, urging the Sociëteit van Suriname to sign an agreement with the WIC about African slaves to be supplied to the colony. Absentee planters also vociferated, pressing the sociëteit in 1718 to refrain from introducing new taxes in the colony, and making themselves heard during negotiations in 1730 about the ways in which colonial fortifications were to be financed. Absenteeism had become so widespread that Suriname's governor Jan Jacob Mauritius observed in 1743, "The rightful and wealthy owners of the colony largely live in the fatherland."[27] These planters made common cause in a joint request with Dutch merchants and shipowners in 1747 by insisting on the need for the States General to dispatch two men-of-war to Suriname in the event that France launched an attack.[28]

Suriname was not the only colony to bring about a "West Indian interest." In that same year of 1747, merchants involved in importing "French" sugar (i.e., sugar grown in the French Caribbean) through St. Eustatius and Curaçao also pulled together. The invasion by the French army of Dutch territory in the closing stages of the War of the Austrian Succession induced the States General to ban the import of French sugar. More than one hundred Amsterdam merchants, making up virtually the entire merchant elite, a few dozen merchants from Rotterdam, and insurers from both ports signed petitions to exempt the sugar that entered the republic by way of the Dutch islands. The States General responded with a compromise, allowing ships en route from the Caribbean free admission to Dutch ports.[29] The States General were also amenable to grant merchant requests for convoying ships by the admiralty of Amsterdam to and from the Caribbean in view of the persistent threat of pirates and privateers. In practice, financial obstacles usually prevented the implantation of this policy, but during the Fourth Anglo-Dutch War the government again allowed convoys to escort ships to Suriname. Once again, the States General responded to the lobby of men interested in trade with the colonies.[30] Convoying was never the norm, however. Many a vessel became the prey of foreign privateers, prompting shipowners and merchants to petition the government. In the 1740s and 1750s, their lobby to have confiscated ships and cargoes returned from other countries was often successful.[31]

Lobbying was also an instrument used by colonial planters and merchants, whose aim was often to maintain or facilitate interimperial trade. Local interest groups in Essequibo and Demerara successfully petitioned the States General to open up the colony's slave trade to foreign nationals, while St. Eustatius's merchants submitted a petition to facilitate foreign trade in general. In 1786, the WIC had unilaterally decided to impose an import duty of 8 percent on most articles from Europe and North America. On various Caribbean islands, free ports had been established in previous years with customs duties that were much lower than those that now applied on St. Eustatius, compromising the traders' competitiveness. Adding insult to injury, the company directors had also stipulated that the trade between colony and metropole be confined to ships fitted out by the WIC. After Amsterdam's merchants sided with their colleagues from St. Eustatius, the States of Holland declared themselves against the new duties, and the States General reversed the measure.[32]

The WIC directorate undoubtedly enacted the tariff hike in order to cover St. Eustatius's recurring expenses. Throughout the Dutch Atlantic, whether for the WIC or for the sociëteiten, the costs for military protection and governance far exceeded the taxes levied. On the eve of the Fourth Anglo-Dutch War, the WIC's debt reached three million guilders and it rose further to four million during the war. Nevertheless, the States General agreed to extend the company charter by another thirty years in 1761. One issue that dogged the company was the financial nightmare in which Suriname's planters had ended up precisely when the WIC's share in the Sociëteit van Suriname had grown considerably. After the Van Sommelsdijck family sold its share in the sociëteit to the city of Amsterdam, Amsterdam traded its newly acquired share to the company in 1773, which thereby became interested in the sociëteit for fifty percent. The timing was unfortunate, since this acquisition proved anything but a solid investment.

Starting in 1751, residents of the Dutch Republic who were eager to place their capital but limited by the small number of investment opportunities sank their money into Dutch plantations in Guiana and in particular Suriname. Enormous amounts of credit were extended against mortgages on overrated plantations unrealistically promising very high yields. As a result, the slave trade reached unprecedented levels, which made it possible for planters to double their output and the value of their exports. The system had serious flaws, however. The most serious one was that the amount of credit made available for plantation loans was linked to the appraised—as it turned out, highly inflated—value of the plantations, not a combination of production capacity and market prices for the plantation crops.[33] In the 1770s, when the planters jointly owed their creditors—mainly Amsterdam commercial houses—some eighty million guilders, the artificial prosperity they had enjoyed came to an end. During years of disappointing income from crop sales, many plantations were running at a loss, which could lead to bankruptcy, since these planters were unable to pay the interest on their loans. When their plantations were sold, it transpired that the value of the plantations was far too small to pay off the mortgage debt. Creditors in the republic now disposed of their shares in the mortgage funds. Many planters, both those in the colonies and those resident in the metropole, lost control of their plantations as administrators appointed by the trading houses began to run the plantations, not prioritizing the owners' economic interests. These administrators were obliged to consign plantation products at often relatively low prices to their creditors, the Amsterdam mercantile firms, and procure manufactures and other products at high prices from these firms.[34]

Similar to Suriname and the lesser Guianas, the Danish Caribbean ended up with massive debts in Amsterdam in these years. When the Danish Crown assumed direct control of its three Caribbean possessions in 1754, following the demise of the Danish West India Company, it collected the loans that were outstanding to that firm. Unable to pay, planters turned to creditors, who were not available in Denmark but were abundant in the Dutch Republic. Although not as large as the Suriname credits, the total amount of loans extended by Dutch creditors to Danish planters was huge, coming to over 13 million guilders. Since two-thirds of that amount was furnished by the Amsterdam firm Abraham ter Borch & Sons, ships with cash crops sailed to Amsterdam instead of Denmark, hurting the sugar refiners in Denmark. A royal ordinance therefore stipulated in 1772 that raw sugar would have to be shipped first to Denmark and remain there for four weeks prior to reexportation.[35] Tottering on the brink of bankruptcy, ter Borch & Sons suspended payments, rendering bills of exchange drawn on the company's name worthless. For three years, the governor of St. Croix put an embargo on all goods and claims ter Borch had in the Danish islands. Nevertheless, the indebtedness of the Danish planters to Dutch investors kept growing, finally leading the Danish Crown to buy the "Dutch loans" in 1786.[36]

In the Dutch Atlantic, Suriname was not the only colony to give the WIC directors a financial headache in this period. The ensemble of other colonies was also generating losses. Whereas St. Eustatius (with 102,000 guilders) and Curaçao (with 31,000) both had a surplus in the years 1779–89 (a period for which we have accurate data), Essequibo-Demerara (123,000) and "Guinea" (93,000) registered deficits in these same years.[37] Ever since the WIC's foundation, merchants had used its institutional cover to see after their own interests. Now the point was reached where that cover became a burden, since the company's overall health was rapidly deteriorating. It could no longer repay the interest on what it owed, dividends were no longer paid for lack of profit, the five chambers with their huge overhead costs recorded an overall loss of 92,000 guilders, and protest movements sprang up in the colonies to challenge the numerous taxes collected there. The States General could have intervened and pronounce the company dead, but they allowed the company to survive until the charter expired.[38] The financial morass was not the only reason to take the WIC off life support. If finances had been the government's main priority, the VOC should have been dealt with first, since its debt was many times larger. The difference was that resistance to dissolution of the WIC was much weaker, in part because of the low value of WIC shares.[39]

The directors' fortunes waned with those of the WIC. Once a lucrative office, the post of company director had become so unappealing that the Chamber Stad en Lande (Groningen), formally ruled by twelve directors, only had three left when the year 1791 began, the other vacancies not having been filled. Two of the remaining directors were 86 and 79 years old, while the third died in 1791.[40] The WIC dissolved that year, its shares taken over by the States General for 30 percent of their nominal value. The States General also assumed the government of the colonies and trading posts in Africa and the Americas. To that end, a special committee was set up that allowed overseas WIC officials to stay put.[41] From 1795 on, the committee's jurisdiction extended to Berbice and Suriname, whose respective sociëteiten were dissolved. The rationale that was listed reflected the deliberate break with the past that had occurred: three different types of government in Dutch America would only lead to rising expenses and be detrimental to the colonies. In the Netherlands, the ancien régime metropolis had been reinvented as the Batavian Republic (1795–1801), which was created after the stadholder fled to Britain. Leaning heavily on French support, this new Dutch state was now directly responsible for Dutch Atlantic policy.[42]

Meanwhile, Dutch investments in the Americas continued unabated. Coinciding with the American Revolutionary War, the Fourth Anglo-Dutch War saw both the decline of Dutch holdings in Britain's government debt and the start of Dutch loans to the young American republic. By 1803, Dutch investors held 22 percent of U.S. domestic debt. Dutchmen also invested massively in long-term United States portfolios. By 1804, such investments amounted to nearly 40 million guilders. Dutch capital also flowed to banks, canal projects, and land speculation in the United States.[43] In addition, a massive scheme to develop land in western New York and Pennsylvania was set up by six Amsterdam banking houses. Dutch capital was thus finding new outlets beyond the Dutch Atlantic colonies, particularly in the United States. By contrast, Dutch investments in the newly independent countries in Latin America were modest at best.[44] In the last section of this chapter, we will return to the question of the profitability of the Dutch Atlantic for its investors.

Trade

If the VOC was an organization that relied on monopolies, the WIC relinquished most of these during the first decades of its existence. The second WIC could therefore never aspire to the status of commercial giant, but instead had to share the Atlantic world with the two sociëteiten and many Dutch merchant houses. Most of the latter were financed by short-term investments in a specific venture rather than a company.[45] Some of these firms had an Atlantic focus, while others were marginally interested in the Atlantic. The trade house de Neufville, based in Amsterdam, which specialized in linen sales to England and the Dutch Republic, sold no more than 1 percent of the value of its goods in the Americas (St. Eustatius) in 1760.[46] At the same time, the loss of a single ocean-going ship could reverberate in the world of Dutch commerce because of the investments of numerous firms. Such was the case with the *Curaçaose Visser*, which was captured by British privateers on its return voyage to the Caribbean in 1758. As many as 119 merchants and trade houses were interested in the cargo, valued at half a million guilders.[47]

In the following, we will distinguish between seven types of transatlantic trades in the Dutch Republic's interaction with the Dutch Guianas, the Dutch Caribbean islands, and Spanish, French, and British America; in its commodity trade with Africa; and in the transatlantic slave trade.

Trade with the Dutch Guianas

Among the products shipped back from the Dutch plantation colonies, sugar was the leading crop from Suriname both in weight and value. Suriname's sugar production doubled in the decade from 1696 to 1706, its output increasing so rapidly that in 1710 there were not enough ships available to carry the sugar to the Dutch Republic.[48] In addition to numerous other metropolitan firms, largely based in Amsterdam (table 3), the West India Company participated in shipments of colonial produce to the Dutch Republic, albeit only on slave ships that had carried disembarked Africans.[49]

Sugar was the leading crop shipped from Suriname until the 1750s, when it was surpassed in market value by coffee, which had been grown there since 1723. Coffee would retain its lead until the end of the century. Cotton, cacao, and tobacco were the other staples shipped from Suriname (table 4).[50] Throughout the century, Suriname's exports to the Dutch Republic were more voluminous and valuable than those of Berbice, Demerara, and Essequibo combined. In these other Guianas, the same crops, except tobacco, were cultivated as in Suriname. In Berbice,

TABLE 3. Shipping between the Dutch Republic and Suriname

Years	Amsterdam	Rotterdam	Zeeland	Unknown	Totals
1683–1700	146	13	61	42	262
1701–25	491	4	20	6	521
1726–50	744	8	62	101	915
1751–75	1,236	104	165	48	1,553
1776–94	825	36	17	71	949
Totals	3,442	165	325	268	4,200

Sources: Johannes Postma, *Dutch Shipping and Trade with Surinam, 1683–1795*, DANS, https://doi.org/10.17026/dans-zeh-h82t. Table prepared by Gerhard de Kok.

TABLE 4. Exports from Suriname to the Dutch Republic (in average pounds per year)

Years	Sugar	Coffee	Cotton	Cacao	Tobacco
1683–1700	99,842,829	0	0	0	4,753
1701–25	349,291,173	52,772	36,072	78,751	1,215
1726–50	451,397,850	52,820,762	17,938	3,767,929	25,724
1751–75	410,198,736	261,898,820	1,880,882	6,383,555	20,540
1776–94	289,411,450	209,478,740	12,289,266	10,564,427	810,510
Totals	1,600,142,038	524,251094	14,224,158	20,794,662	862,742

Sources: Postma, *Dutch Shipping*. Table prepared by Gerhard de Kok.

cacao was the most valuable crop cultivated in the 1750s and 1760s, but it was eclipsed by coffee in the 1770s (table 5). The coffee boom continued in the period 1780–95.[51] In Demerara and Essequibo, sugar also dominated production and trade before being dethroned by coffee in the 1770s (table 6).[52]

The rise in shipping from the Dutch Republic in the third quarter of the eighteenth century (table 3) was remarkable. Seventy-one non-slaving ships arrived in the colony from the metropole in 1769 compared to forty-two in 1740.[53] The shipping boom was caused by the aforementioned credit bonanza and the accompanying increase in the slave trade to Suriname as well as the consequent growth in colonial output. The arrival of large quantities of plantation crops, however, did not translate into high profits. Historians Jan de Vries and Ad van der

TABLE 5. Exports from Berbice to the Dutch Republic (average annual value in guilders)

Years	Cacao	Sugar	Coffee	Cotton	Totals
1753–60	215,493 (44.6%)	152,115 (31.5%)	39,360 (8.1%)	76,498 (15.8%)	483,406
1761–70	148,603 (44.4%)	68,022 (20.3%)	38,641 (11.5%)	79,488 (23.7%)	334,754
1771–79	54,338 (9.8%)	89,172 (16.1%)	261,888 (47.3%)	148,364 (26.8%)	553,762
Average percentage	32.9	22.6	22.3	22.1	

Notes: Calculated on the basis of Kramer, "Plantation Development," 394–95. We have used the prices for the same crops from Suriname as listed by Posthumus (*Inquiry,* 1:126, 186, 197–98, 285–86).

TABLE 6. Exports from Essequibo/Demerara to the Dutch Republic (average annual value in guilders)

Years	Sugar	Coffee	Cotton	Totals
1745–50	262,145 (100%)	39 (0%)	0 (0%)	262,184
1751–60	132,933 (98.7%)	736 (0.5%)	1,076 (0.8%)	134,745
1761–70	438,916 (76.9%)	109,149 (19.1%)	22,368 (3.9%)	570,533
1771–80	716,786 (37.1%)	898,687 (46.5%)	319,046 (16.5%)	1,934,519
1781–85	520,203 (25.5%)	1,103,310 (54.2%)	412,781 (20.3%)	2,036,294
Average percentage	67.6	24.1	8.3	

Notes: Calculated on the basis of Bolingbroke, *Voyage,* appendix 1, 397. Van der Oest's calculations ("Forgotten Colonies," 350–51) contain serious discrepancies between tables 12.6 and 12.7, which invalidate their use. Bolingbroke lists hogsheads, tierces, and bags, which we have converted into pounds, using several conversion keys. A hogshead of sugar was taken as the equivalent of 800 pounds, a tierce of coffee as the equivalent of 350 pounds, a bag of coffee was converted to 120 pounds, and a bale of cotton to 300 pounds. For prices, we have followed Posthumus, *Inquiry.*

Woude have shown that the annual revenue from the sale of these crops in the republic—12 million guilders—in the prosperous years 1765–74 was canceled out by a variety of expenditures. The banking firms in the republic used 3.7 million for the reimbursement of transporters, insurers, and commission agents. The firms also paid the letters of exchange issued in the colonies for the purchase of African slaves and North

American provisions, which amounted to another 1.8 million guilders. Planters paid 2.2 million for products imported from the republic and spent another 1.3 million on taxes and plantation management. Finally, the interest on plantation loans ran to 3.0 million.[54] This sobering calculation reveals the limits of profitability, at least for this period, corroborated by studies of the long-term development, which equally suggest that after the mid-eighteenth century, rewards tended no longer to correspond to the investors' high expectations.

Trade with the Dutch Caribbean Islands

Although cash crop production was minimal in the Dutch West Indies, these islands obtained large quantities of tropical produce thanks to their interimperial trade. Cacao, hailing mainly from nearby Venezuela, was the chief cash crop shipped to the Dutch Republic from Curaçao, accounting for more than half (55 percent) of the market value of all products arriving from there in 1701–55 (table 7). Other prominent items included bullion and specie, tobacco, sugar, logwood, and indigo, all originating outside the island. Among St. Eustatius's reexports to the Dutch Republic, sugar—largely from the French islands—predominated (71.8 percent), far outstripping coffee (14.8 percent) and tobacco (6.3 percent).[55]

Bilateral trade with the Dutch islands gradually increased over the course of the eighteenth century. In the first half of the century, an average of fourteen or fifteen ships left Dutch ports annually for Curaçao—with Amsterdam far ahead of other cities—whereas war years in later decades saw an intensification of shipping. The years 1761 (sixty-two

TABLE 7. Product trade, Curaçao-Dutch Republic, 1701–55 (in guilders)

Years	Value of cacao	Overall value	Percentage
1701–10	691,540	1,012,753	68.3
1711–20	562,269	1,210,000	46.5
1721–30	759,768	1,227,131	61.9
1731–40	507,020	1,113,606	45.4
1741–50	1,244,513	2,487,306	50.0
1751–55	624,763	1,025,072	60.9

Source: Klooster, "Curaçao and the Caribbean Transit Trade," 203–18, table 8.4 (216).

TABLE 8. St. Eustatius's exports to the Dutch Republic, 1738–90 (average pounds per year)

Decade	Sugar	Coffee	Tobacco	Cacao	Cotton	Indigo
1731–40	2,876,347	182,937	4,600	6,829	119,699	11,312
1741–50	5,170,166	273,005	9,843	17,054	95,374	3,523
1751–60	7,462,645	4,381,367	50,666	137,408	112,027	44
1761–70	8,713,711	2,223,512	179,846	235,045	57,497	6,140
1771–80	11,871,983	3,006,252	2,924,119	188,095	98,575	150,612
1781–90	4,309,408	280,967	406,440	98,698	14,021	881

Source: Derived from Klooster, *Illicit Riches*, 226–27.
Notes: Averages are given, because annual data are available only for the 1740s and 1760s. The figures for two decades may be somewhat untrustworthy: those for the 1730s are only based on the years 1738–40 and those for the 1750s on 1751 and 1760.

ships) and 1783 (eighty) stood out.[56] The number of ships sailing from the republic to St. Eustatius was comparable, also averaging fourteen to fifteen per year in the period 1738–51 before reaching higher numbers during later wars; many of the ships sailing in later years were, however, captured by British privateers.[57] By the 1780s, after the sack of St. Eustatius, the volume of trade with that island declined to the level of the 1740s.

Direct Trade with Spanish, French, and British America

Some firms in the Netherlands opted to deal directly with foreign ports in the Caribbean and North America alongside bilateral trade with the entrepôts of St. Eustatius and Curaçao. The itineraries of the ships fitted out for expeditions to Spanish America usually included Margarita or Trinidad, Cumaná, Portobelo, Santo Domingo, and southeastern Cuba, but they steered clear of the coast of Caracas, where it was virtually impossible to compete with their "compatriots" from Curaçao.[58] Dutch metropolitan ships, in search of indigo, cacao, and sarsaparilla (a vine believed to have medicinal properties), also anchored in Spanish Honduras and visited nearby British logwood camps.[59] The most active company dealing directly with Spanish America was the Middelburgse Commercie Compagnie (MCC) in the years 1721–44. The Zeelanders imported mostly bullion and specie, followed by cacao, hides, tobacco, indigo, and sugar.

The annual value of their direct trade with Spanish America in terms of the value of the products imported was around 350,000 guilders.[60]

Direct trade between the Dutch Republic and the French colonies, almost negligible in peacetime, occurred twice during the wars of the mid-eighteenth century. In 1744 and the years immediately following, French firms licensed merchants from the Dutch Republic to maintain transatlantic commercial connections with the colonies.[61] This scenario repeated itself in the first years of the Seven Year's War. The few Dutch merchants who tried to do without a French passport risked confiscation, not only from British privateers but also from colonial French officials.[62] Usually, however, companies based in the Dutch Republic avoided the risks involved in direct shipping to the French colonies by using the two Dutch entrepôts in the Caribbean.

Much more important than direct trade with Spanish or French America was that with the British colonies. Before the Anglo-French warfare of the 1790s, ships fitted out in the Dutch Republic were frequent visitors to North America's eastern seaboard, usually doing business in breach of the Navigation Acts. Ships from the Dutch Republic did not suddenly bypass Barbados and the English Leeward Islands, where so much trade had been conducted in the mid-seventeenth century. Jamaica's governor noted in 1682 that the Dutch offered European goods thirty percent cheaper than their English colleagues and paid more for American goods.[63] Commerce with the English Caribbean paled, however, in comparison to that with North America. In the last decades of the seventeenth century, some fifty traders from New York included the Dutch Republic in their trading networks, using legal and illegal methods to transfer their goods to Amsterdam. Increasingly, Amsterdam was used to complement New Yorkers' trade with England, not as their main destination.[64] New York merchants eager to do business in Amsterdam in the early eighteenth century often procured safe conduct passes to that port at Scotland's Orkney Islands or somewhere in southern Europe. Once fully loaded, ships returning from Amsterdam would engage in trade at a spit of land south of the city called Sandy Hook, the site of much commerce that could not bear the light of day. References to exchanges at this site can be found from the late seventeenth century to the end of the colonial period. Some Dutch vessels also anchored in ports in Connecticut or sailed as far as Philadelphia to trade with the New Yorkers.[65] The significance of this trade was underlined when New York's authorities began to crack down on smuggled Dutch goods at the start of the Seven Years' War. The city's mercantile community was alarmed, since "vast Numbers of Vessels [are] expected with Prodigious quantities of Holland Goods."[66]

On their part, Amsterdam mercantile firms, all of them generous with credit and some maintaining agents and factors in New York, eagerly imported fur, lumber, dyewood, tobacco, wine, and fish from their North American colleagues and sold textiles, guns, gunpowder, and tea for prices lower than those asked by their British colleagues.[67] Tea reexported from Amsterdam featured prominently among the items filling the holds of ships destined for North America due to the high tax levied on English tea. The market for tea in the Thirteen Colonies expanded rapidly as commoners joined the elite in consuming the drink on a daily basis.[68] A boycott of all British goods also benefited the sale of "Dutch" tea, the trade in which—although illegal—did not abate after the Tea Act promulgated by British Parliament in 1773 made British East India Company tea cheaper than the smuggled Dutch variety.[69] Acquired taste may have trumped the price, but what also carried weight was the smugglers' argument that by enabling the British East India Company to market its tea directly in North America, Parliament set a dangerous precedent for monopolies supported by the government.[70] The battlelines drawn, the smugglers helped stage the Boston Tea Party, a landmark event in the growing alienation between Parliament and the North American colonies.

Rotterdam had traditionally maintained close commercial ties with both Britain and British America. For example, in 1722–24 thirty-seven British ships arrived directly from the British colonies, including thirteen from the West Indian islands, nine from Virginia, and nine from South Carolina. Three decades later, shipments to Rotterdam from South Carolina had increased to an average of fourteen per year. In this way, more than two million pounds of rice, Carolina's staple product, ended up in the republic annually.[71] Unlike rice, tobacco from the Chesapeake usually arrived on board British ships that first touched at English ports before proceeding to Rotterdam.[72] Rotterdam was also deeply involved in the shipment of German migrants to British North America, especially those bound for Philadelphia, a business dominated by two Rotterdam firms and one from Amsterdam. They derived their income not only from this "trade in strangers." The limited competition also allowed them to make significant profits in procuring cargoes and performing other services in outfitting and loading the migrant ships.[73] Besides, these firms used the cover of passenger trade to smuggle in tea.[74]

Dutch metropolitan trade with New England has been traced back to the 1670s, remaining robust in every subsequent decade. At times, Dutch shipping was so voluminous that warehouses were well supplied with cargoes originating in the Dutch Republic—in 1715, Boston merchant Thomas Moffat remarked that Massachusetts was filled "with Dutch ware."[75] In the mid-eighteenth century, the merchant house of Thomas and Adrian Hope of Amsterdam acted as agent for Thomas Hancock of Boston in a triangular trade over the West Indies. Hancock's ships left Boston for the Caribbean, where his main agent, Martin Godet at St. Eustatius, would guide the captains to the best markets for their fish, ideally in the French islands. Logwood, indigo, lignum vitae, and bills of exchange were received in return. Contravening the Navigation Acts, these ships then sailed for Amsterdam, where the Hope brothers provided cargoes of paper, tea, and other items. Completing the triangle, the ships would return to New England. This trade went smoothly until war broke out between France and Britain in 1744. In the next four years, the ships sailed from Amsterdam to St. Eustatius, from which sloops owned by Godet or Hancock carried the European manufactures to Boston.[76] Numerous other Boston merchants also traded directly or indirectly with the Dutch Republic. In 1742, the recently-arrived English-born lawyer William Bollan wrote to the Board of Trade that New England was supplied from Holland with "Reels of Yarn or spun Hemp, paper, Gunpowder, Iron and Goods of various sorts used for Men's and Women's Clothing."[77] His father-in-law, Massachusetts governor William Shirley, reported a year later that Dutch ships engaged in contraband trade were more numerous than legitimate traders from Britain, underselling their rivals in broadcloth through their New England agents. It had come to the point, he added, that New England's dependence on Britain was in jeopardy.[78]

When that dependence ended decades later, Dutch metropolitan merchants failed to reap special benefits. After the revolutionary war had gotten underway, sailing to North America became almost impossible due to a blockade by the Royal Navy.[79] Dutch merchants, like their French counterparts, hoped that North American animosity towards the British would lead to a dislike for British goods and open the door even further to Dutch commodities. But habit and taste proved hard to change, and the Dutch insistence on short-term credit or payment in cash did not win them new friends.[80] Nonetheless, trade with North America prospered in the years 1793–1807, when each year an average of 107 merchant-men reached Amsterdam alone with cargoes much richer than before. Almost all of these ships were U.S.-owned and -based, making use of the state of war between France and Britain to sail as neutral freighters across the Atlantic and carrying among other things French Caribbean sugar.[81] Those cargoes were a sign of the changing times: while sugar from the French islands had previously arrived on Dutch carriers, it was now supplied to Dutch ports by ships from the United States, whose commercial hegemony in the Caribbean ended the role of St. Eustatius and Curaçao as regional entrepôts.

Commodity Trade with Africa

Despite its decline, oceangoing trade with North America was much more important than that with Africa by the late eighteenth century. West Africa had been the leading Atlantic destination for merchants in the Dutch Republic in the early seventeenth century. In the period 1674–1740, the WIC fitted out five ships annually for the commodity trade in Africa alone (not counting the slave trade), but by the 1730s no more than one annual venture was organized.[82] Other firms began to operate on the African market, such as the Zeeland-based MCC and Coopstad en Rochussen from Rotterdam.[83] The Africa trade contin-ued until the Fourth Anglo-Dutch War, when British privateers blocked the passage to the Gold Coast. After the war, no real recovery set in. The number of Dutch ships paying duties on the Gold Coast in 1780–91 was less than four per year, and no more than two on average dur-ing the last three years.[84]

   In the import commodity trade from Africa, gold had always been the most coveted item and remained in high demand throughout the eigh-teenth century. Gold dust continued to arrive in considerable quantities in Dutch ports despite the steep decline in imports from the Gold Coast, because that drop was compensated by gold dust introduced by Brazilian merchants in exchange for slaves. Gold accounted for 86.6 percent of the value of WIC shipments from Africa to the Dutch Republic in the first quarter of the eighteenth century and for half of those of the MCC. Both companies were supposed to sell the gold after embarkation in a Dutch port to the master of the Dutch Mint or the VOC, which did not always happen. After gold, ivory was the main product imported from Africa. The base material for the manufacture of fans, snuffboxes, and utensils, ivory accounted for twelve percent of the value of the WIC's African imports.[85] The combined annual value of the gold and ivory imports was around 300,000 guilders in the period 1701–30.[86] After 1730, little information is available. The trade in ivory seems to have declined significantly, and the gold trade also diminished, while the shipment of enslaved Africans increased and became the mainstay of the Dutch trade with West Africa.[87]

Among the export items in the trade with West Africa, textiles were paramount. In the first quarter of the eighteenth century, they made up half of the value of the cargoes sent there by the WIC (table 9). They accounted for 36 percent of the value of the cargoes shipped by illicit Dutch traders, who acted in breach of the WIC monopoly. Serge woolens were produced in Leiden and Haarlem, but most textiles were cotton cloth that had been shipped to the Dutch Republic by the VOC. Firearms and gunpowder, which formed the next category in Dutch exports to West Africa, were Dutch-made, as was some of the brandy. Specifically included for the slave trade were cowrie shells, which originated in the Maldives in the Indian Ocean. They were exchanged on the West African coast for

TABLE 9. WIC Exports to West Africa, 1700–1723 (in guilders)

Years	Textiles	Military stores	Cowrie shells	Alcoholic drinks	Other
1700–1704	466,390	84,250	114,860	33,030	181,080
1705–9	479,730	134,750	97,280	44,260	247,050
1710–14	574,220	91,990	128,830	21,680	243,790
1715–19	281,240	110,530	93,430	47,280	138,750
1720–23	728,720	218,300	157,010	78,690	398,400
Totals	2,660,300	639,820	591,410	224,940	1,142,070
Percentage	50.6	12.2	11.2	4.3	21.7

Source: Based on Den Heijer, "West African Trade," 153 (table 6.2).

slaves. The MCC, which fitted out 28 ships for the African trade and 23 for the triangular trade in 1730–55, sailed with the same commodities to exchange for African products and slaves.[88]

The Transatlantic Slave Trade

The Gold Coast may have provided most goods bought by the Dutch in Atlantic Africa, but it was outstripped in slave sales by the Bight of Benin, an area that included today's Togo, Benin, and western Nigeria, designated by the Dutch as "Slave Coast," where half of all Dutch slaves originated in the last quarter of the seventeenth century and two-fifths of the WIC slaves in the period 1700–38. Illegal Dutch slavers in the latter period preferred the Loango-Angola coast.[89] In the free trade years after 1740, the main procurement area was one that had previously hardly attracted Dutch ships: the Windward Coast (the area from northern Liberia to eastern Côte d'Ivoire) was responsible for forty percent of all slaves shipped by the Dutch. The choice of this coast by Dutch firms compensated for the decreased Dutch presence in the Bights of Benin and Biafra, where they had to compete not only with the British, but also with Portuguese and French merchants.[90]

Several ports in Holland, led by Amsterdam and by the province of Zeeland with a share of over 45 percent, were involved in the African slave trade from the late sixteenth up to the early nineteenth century. The invaluable Trans-Atlantic Slave Trade database, building on the pioneering work of Johannes Postma, lists the embarkation of some 554,000 enslaved Africans shipped in Dutch vessels, 475,000 of whom arrived alive in the Americas, hence a mortality rate of 14 percent. Recent research has produced some upwards revisions, putting the overall estimate around 600,000 embarked Africans. With a mortality rate recalculated on the basis of additional data at 13 percent, this would mean that approximately 525,000 captives were landed alive from Dutch ships.[91]

The Dutch share of the total transatlantic trade, now usually estimated to have amounted to 12.5 million people, was therefore roughly five percent. While this proportion was not particularly significant in comparative perspective, the Dutch share was higher in the period 1626–1800, in which virtually all (98.9 percent) of their slaves were transported. Instead of one in twenty, the Dutch carried one of every fifteen slaves

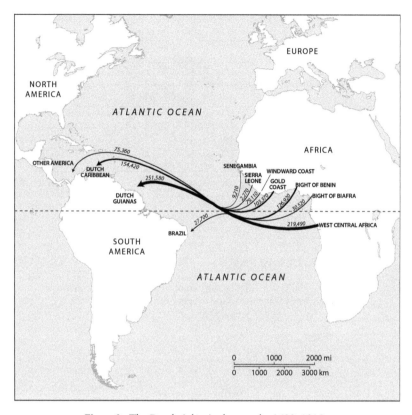

Figure 3. The Dutch Atlantic slave trade, 1600–1815.

to the Americas during those years. The Dutch share was even higher in the critical early period of the Caribbean plantation revolution, at over twenty percent in the mid-seventeenth century (fig. 4). The Dutch share in the overall slave trade thus clearly peaked early, in the decades after 1640, when merchants in the republic shipped bonded Africans to the French Caribbean and directly or indirectly benefitted from the Spanish *asiento*. This period ended when the *asiento* was transferred to Great Britain at the Peace of Utrecht (1713). The subsequent annual volume of the Dutch slave trade fluctuated with an upwards trend from 1720 to 1780, but the Dutch share in the overall Atlantic slave trade dwindled (fig. 4). The third quarter of the eighteenth century topped all other periods in terms of the number of slave ships fitted out and the number of Africans transported to American destinations (fig. 4 and table 10).

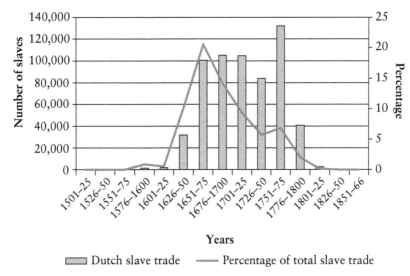

Figure 4. The Dutch Atlantic slave trade, 1500–1866. Trans-Atlantic Slave Trade Database (slavevoyages.org); Paesie, "Zeeuwen." Graph prepared by Gerhard de Kok.

TABLE 10. Dutch slave ships per twenty-five-year period

Years	WIC	Interloper	Private	Totals
1576–1600			4	4
1601–25			5	5
1626–50	116	1		117
1651–75	50	218		268
1676–1700	173	65		238
1701–25	125	140		265
1726–50	73	7	132	212
1751–75	2		436	438
1776–1800	5		141	146
1801–25			12	12
1826–29			2	2
Totals	544	431	732	1,707

Sources: Trans-Atlantic Slave Trade Database (slavevoyages.org), accessed on June 7, 2016; Paesie, *Lorrendrayen op Africa*, 357–69. Table prepared by Gerhard de Kok.

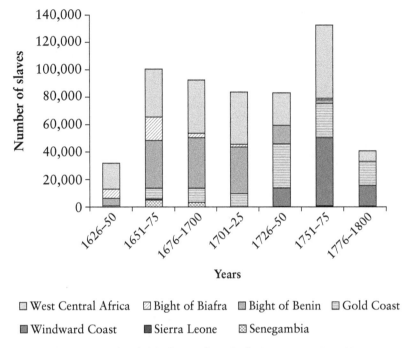

Figure 5. Dutch Atlantic slave trade: embarkation zones, 1626–1800.
Trans-Atlantic Slave Trade Database (slavevoyages.org); Paesie,
"Zeeuwen." Graph prepared by Gerhard de Kok.

While we know that male adults were dominant in the overall Atlantic
slave trade, there are only very loose estimates of the gender and age distribution. According to the Trans-Atlantic Slave Trade database, 58 percent
of all 12.5 million Africans embarked were men against 42 percent women,
while roughly one-quarter of all captives were children. There is no reason
to assume that these proportions do not correspond to the Dutch slave trade.

The embarkation zones varied considerable over time (fig. 5), due
mainly to developments on the supply side—no matter how much, for
example, observers complained that Africans from west central Africa
were less adaptable to plantation settings than captives from more north-
erly regions, in the end slavers along the West African coast bought wherever they could at prices they deemed reasonable, and so did planters and
merchants on the other side of the Atlantic.

TABLE 11. Embarkation zones of the Dutch transatlantic slave trade by decade

	Senegambia	Sierra Leone	Windward Coast	Gold Coast	Bight of Benin	Bight of Biafra	West Central Africa
1591–1600						83	1,282
1601–10							878
1611–20							951
1621–30							326
1631–40					1,988	1,630	2,834
1641–50				755	3,452	5,139	15,605
1651–60	846	752		1,437	10,059	9,561	3,328
1661–70	2,314			2,597	18,731	6,231	18,719
1671–80	4,655			8,309	11,123	1,969	17,897
1681–90	612			3,956	17,730	2,513	15,671
1691–1700				1,905	13,672		11,786
1701–10			142	4,166	17,754	514	13,013
1711–20				1,411	13,014		8,010
1721–30				12,990	6,728	10	12,065
1731–40	352		420	16,877	9,347		2,461
1741–50			12,898	6,191	638		17,880
1751–60		315	14,816	12,334	1,469		12,110
1761–70	426		23,168	8,224	864	83	27,032
1771–80		334	21,771	6,649	344	891	17,723
1781–90			3,867	10,395			2,513
1791–1800		180	948	4,877			1,770
1801–10			399	272			934
1811–20		211	523				
1821–30		484	150			53	
Totals	9,205	2,276	79,102	103,375	126,913	28,677	204,788

Source: Trans-Atlantic Slave Trade Database (slavevoyages.org), accessed on June 7, 2016.

Overall, west central Africa (the region of Kongo-Angola) was the dominant supplier to Dutch slavers, accounting for over one-third of all embarked captives (fig. 5 and table 11). The Bight of Benin supplied 21 percent, followed by the Gold Coast with 17 percent. The Windward Coast became a supplier at a late stage, accounting for 13 percent of the total but almost 40 percent in the booming third quarter of the eighteenth century. The other supplying regions were of lesser significance, while the departure zone of roughly five percent of all slave voyages could not be established. One striking feature of this distribution is that less than one-fifth of all Africans embarked on Dutch slavers departed from the Gold Coast, and that hence the share of Elmina, the one major Dutch fortress on the entire West African coast, was modest. This only underlines the fact that most of the slave trade was not conducted via Dutch-owned fortresses but rather by ships cruising along the coast and buying wherever they could.[92] Finally, all of the Dutch Atlantic slave trade was a West African affair, with neither the Cape Colony nor Eastern Africa providing captives for the Americas.

Overall, the share of the WIC was almost one third, mainly in 1626–1750; the share of interlopers a quarter, mainly between 1651 and 1725, and that of licensed private companies, mainly after 1726, 43 percent (table 10). The average number of slaves carried by the Dutch in the last quarter of the seventeenth century was 3,538. In the first three decades of the eighteenth century, illicit Dutch slavers even accounted for one-third of all Africans embarked by Dutch ships. The annual average imported from Africa during the free-trade era (1740–1803) declined to around 3,000 per year for a total of 194,773 slaves carried by Dutch frigates and yachts. The peak period during this era was 1756–73, when annual averages hovered around the 5,000 mark.[93]

The Dutch Atlantic slave trade is exceptional because of its dual character. On the one hand, there was the standard trade geared towards providing the Dutch plantation colonies with the necessary labor force. This trade was initiated in Dutch Brazil and was then established for the Guianas. On the other hand, there was considerable transshipment of enslaved Africans. The overwhelming majority of Africans disembarked in Curaçao and St. Eustatius were destined for reexport to the surrounding Spanish and French colonies. Hence over one-third of Africans shipped in Dutch vessels ended up in non-Dutch colonies, a higher proportion than for any other slave trading nation except the Danish and Swedish, both minor traders.[94] British reexports of enslaved Africans to foreign colonies may have been numerous, but they accounted for under 10 percent of the overall British slave trade.[95] The significance of non-Dutch destinations in the Dutch transatlantic slave trade is even more remarkable when we divide the slaving era into twenty-five year periods. In each of the quarter-centuries from 1675 through 1725, most slaves shipped by the

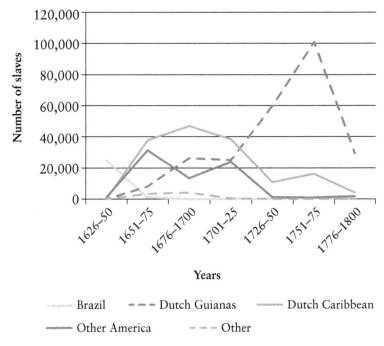

Figure 6. Dutch Atlantic slave trade: disembarkation zones, 1626–1800.
Trans-Atlantic Slave Trade Database; Paesie, "Zeeuwen."
Graph prepared by Gerhard de Kok.

Dutch were intended for foreign customers. It was only in the following three quarter-centuries, from 1726 through 1800, that Dutch plantation colonies dominated, claiming 85 percent of the slaves carried on Dutch bottoms (table 12).

During the long period in which the WIC controlled the slave trade, Curaçao was the main destination of slavers, receiving 43.7 percent during the years 1675–1739, followed closely by Suriname with 40.0 percent (fig. 6). St. Eustatius was a distant third with 7.7 percent, receiving as many slaves as the three remaining recipients combined: Essequibo (3.1 percent), Spanish America (2.9 percent), and Berbice (1.8 percent).[96] Precise information is lacking for the destinations of the Dutch interloper trade in 1700–1730, but it is beyond doubt that St. Eustatius and Danish St. Thomas were the preferred landing places.[97] The contrast with the free trade slave ships is conspicuous: during their crossings in the period

TABLE 12. Disembarkation zones of the Dutch transatlantic slave trade, 1576–1825

	Dutch plantation colonies	Dutch insular Caribbean	Foreign colonies	Other	Total	Percentage of Dutch plantation colonies
1576–1600			1,282	83	1,365	0
1601–25			1,829		1,829	0
1626–50	30,308		1,421		31,729	95.5
1651–75	12,468	45,000	38,342	4,716	100,526	12.4
1676–1700	30,140	49,988	4,096	1,623	85,847	35.1
1701–25	28,876	34,072	10,868		73,816	39.1
1726–50	70,335	12,255	505		83,095	84.6
1751–75	113,618	17,616	1,096		132,330	85.9
1776–1800	34,555	4,374	1,844		40,773	84.7
1801–25	1,971		482	216	2,669	73.8

Source: Trans-Atlantic Slave Trade Database (slavevoyages.org), accessed on June 7, 2016.
Note: The category "Other" includes Africa and Europe.

1730–1803, Suriname was by far the principle destination, accounting for 69.1 percent of all slaves shipped to known destinations. Demerara and Essequibo followed with 9.9 percent, and next were Curaçao (4.6 percent), St. Eustatius (4.1 percent), and Berbice (3.5 percent).[98]

On the western side of the Atlantic, the Dutch colonies received not a uniform "African" community but, rather, an ethnically diverse group of captives. The ethnic makeup of the first-generation African population varied per colony, depending on the chronology. A constant influx of enslaved Africans implied permanent reinforcement of ethnic diversity, while an absence of such and/or a growing numerical significance of locally born "Creole" slaves implied creolization; hence, the gradual emergence of more homogeneous, localized Afro-Caribbean communities in the various Dutch Caribbean colonies. The pace of creolization differed considerably within the Dutch Atlantic. The population of African origin in Curaçao, where the slave trade had become peripheral by 1730, was far more creolized by the late eighteenth century than its counterpart in Suriname and, a fortiori, the lesser Guianas.

The gross proceeds from slave sales, defined as the value of these sales before deducting the expenses of the slave trade, varied from year to year

TABLE 13. Average annual gross proceeds of Dutch slave sales, 1701–1800 (in guilders)

Years	Proceeds
1701–10	773,225
1711–20	482,608
1721–30	722,554
1731–40	616,086
1741–50	816,471
1751–60	969,863
1761–70	1,836,467
1771–80	1,654,836
1781–90	816,578
1791–1800	378,473

Notes: Calculated on the basis of Postma, *Dutch in Atlantic Slave Trade*, 264 (table 11.2), 265 (table 11.3), and 406 (appendix 24); and the Trans-Atlantic Slave Trade Database (slavevoyages.org), accessed on June 8, 2016. For Curaçao, we have used the average between contract and auction prices in the years 1701–40; for St. Eustatius, the average between high and low in the 1720s; and for Suriname, the average between upper and lower prices in 1701–40. For sales to other parts of the Caribbean, we have assumed the price level of Curaçao. For 1741–50, we used the average slave prices listed by Postma for 1740–49 and followed the same rule for the 1750s, 1760s, and 1770s. We used the average slave prices for 1780–95 for both 1781–90 and 1791–1800.

and decade to decade, spiking in the 1760s and 1770s, when abundant credit enabled massive slave purchases (table 12). Gross proceeds, of course, are no measure of the slave trade's overall profitability. Our most reliable figures pertain to the MCC. The net profit this company registered in its slave trade was 3.6 percent in the years 1740–55, rising dramatically to 17.6 percent in the years 1756–60.[99] Such margins were considerably higher than the profits recorded by the same company in its non-slave commerce with the Spanish Caribbean.[100] Historians Karwan Fatah-Black and Matthias van Rossum have recently argued that historians of the Dutch slave trade should focus on the trade's gross margins, defined as the difference between the price paid for enslaved Africans in Africa and the sum received for those landed in the Caribbean or the Guianas. On this basis, they calculate the total gross margin for seventeenth and eighteenth centuries at between 63 and 79 million guilders, an annual average in 1675–1800 of 0.4–0.5 million guilders.[101] These outcomes are all larger than previously assumed, though even 0.5 million is not a significant share of Dutch national income, which amounted to 265–79 million guilders in 1742. While there is serious debate about the methodology and hence the outcome of these calculations, it is likely that the economic impact of the African slave trade on the local economies of the Zealand port cities of Middelburg and Vlissingen was significant.[102]

Contributions to the Dutch Economy

If the contribution of the slave trade to the Dutch economy was limited, what about the benefits of the Atlantic commodity trade? Several imported crops, including sugar and tobacco, engendered industrial activity. Sugar refining was one of the major Dutch manufacturing industries in the eighteenth century. The buildings housing the refineries (or "sugar bakeries") may have been the only early modern Dutch constructions that rivaled the nineteenth-century factories in size. Refining first enjoyed a boom in the mid-seventeenth century before declining in the latter part of the century. The industry rebounded after the War of the Spanish Succession, and by 1751, 145 refineries were counted across the republic, 90 of which were operating in Amsterdam, 30 in Rotterdam, and 14 in Dordrecht.[103] Dutch sugar refiners stayed ahead of their French rivals due to sugar imports from and through Dutch colonies and through France; due to their access to affordable English coal, for which the French had to pay high customs duties; and due to their proximity to the northern European markets.[104] Government protection was another factor in the industry's competitiveness in the later eighteenth century. When refineries sprang up in mid-century in the southern Netherlands, Denmark, Norway, Sweden, Russia, Alsace, and Lorraine, reducing the clientele, Dutch authorities lent their support by reducing the tax burden, offering premiums, and prohibiting sugar refining in St. Eustatius. Sugar production could therefore grow, although the sugar business still lost ground internationally.[105]

In contrast with the sugar refiners, Dutch sugar traders did not receive protection from the States General. Sugar from the Dutch Guianas therefore had to compete in an open market with sugar produced in foreign— especially Caribbean—colonies under advantageous fiscal regimes (table 14). While global price levels consequently applied in Amsterdam

TABLE 14. Dutch Atlantic import of sugar in pounds, 1750–90

Year	Suriname	Berbice	Ess/Dem	Curacao	St. Eustatius	France	Other	Totals
1750	24,646,800	526,384	1,839,912	100,000	2,663,526	30,000,000		59,776,622
1765	16,837,600	195,056	2,676,202		5,005,729	20,000,000		44,714,587
1775	18,632,024	681,615	3,918,518	400,000	4,802,400	34,400,000		62,834,557
1780	14,185,488	350,000	3,439,641	400,000	30,433,600	256,000		49,064,729
1786	14,716,512	350,000	4,295,145		2,766,900	38,730,340		60,858,897
1790	20,429,640	350,000	4,403,072		7,524,100	23,716,989	1,926,435	58,350,236

Sources: Suriname: Postma, *Dutch Shipping.* Berbice: 1750: Kramer, "Plantation Development," 54–55. We used the 1753 figure for 1750. 1765–75: Kramer, "Plantation Development," 54–55. 1780, 1786, 1790: De Hullu, "Memorie," 394. Essequibo/Demerara: 1750–80: Bolingbroke, *Voyage,* 397; 1786: Bolingbroke, *Voyage,* using the figures for 1785. 1790: NAN, WIC 1136, cargo lists of 1790. Curacao: 1750, 1775, and 1780: Van der Voort, "Westindische Plantages," 260–61. St. Eustatius: 1750: Klooster, *Illicit Riches,* 226–27, appendix 5; 1775, 1780: Van der Voort, "Iets dat tot voordeel," 333, appendix L. We converted hogsheads into pounds using Van der Voort, "Westindische Plantages," 260; 1790: Klooster, *Illicit Riches,* 226–27, appendix 5. France: Van der Voort, "Westindische Plantages," 260–61. Other: Van der Voort, "Westindische Plantages," 260–61. Table prepared by Gerhard de Kok.

to sugar from the Dutch Guianas, French and British planters enjoyed much higher price levels in their protected home markets. This seriously affected the profitability of the Dutch Atlantic plantation economy. The Dutch home market was especially attractive to foreign sugar producers and merchants. Barbados was an important source of sugar sold in Amsterdam and Middelburg, shipped on Dutch ships directly from Barbados until Dutch refiners began to buy English sugar in London in the late seventeenth century.[106] In addition, Brazilian white sugar, which arrived by way of Portugal, had a stock-exchange listing in Amsterdam for most years from 1671 through 1710 and after 1750.[107] Likewise, the abovementioned "French" sugar was imported directly from St. Eustatius and Curaçao in much larger quantities—accounting for close to two-thirds of all arriving sugar—on board French ships from France. Vast amounts of reexported Saint-Domingue and Martinique sugar arrived, especially from Bordeaux, since the War of the Spanish Succession. Initially, French exports to the Dutch Republic outshadowed those to what the French called "the North"—Germany, Denmark, Sweden, and Russia—but by the second quarter of the century, the roles were reversed both for raw and white sugar.[108] Sugar from the French Antilles continued to dominate the Dutch market through the end of the century. By then, sugar from the British Caribbean was shipped in very small quantities, while the growing role of the Hansa towns of Hamburg and Bremen was illustrated by their reexports to Amsterdam of New World sugar.[109]

Like sugar, many other New World crops arrived by way of foreign European ports. Foreign crops quoted in Amsterdam included coffee from Saint-Domingue (1760–1859), tobacco from Barinas (since 1674), and tobacco leaves from both Virginia and Havana tobacco (since 1731).[110] Hides from both Brazil and Buenos Aires, some of which were supplied on the Gold Coast by Brazilian traders in exchange for slaves, were also available almost uninterruptedly since 1671. Equally, indigo from Guatemala, cochineal from Mexico, and wood from Pernambuco, none of which were regularly carried by ocean-going Dutch ships, were listed from the seventeenth through the nineteenth centuries.[111]

Tobacco from Virginia and Maryland was used massively in Amsterdam's tobacco workshops, where it was blended with domestic Dutch tobacco—grown in the eastern parts of the Dutch Republic—and equally cheap German leaf.[112] At its height in the late seventeenth and early eighteenth centuries, three thousand people worked in the Amsterdam industry, but their number declined drastically in the decades after 1720 due to the price drop in Chesapeake tobacco. An increasing share of reexported tobacco was henceforth left unprocessed.[113] At the same time, the manufacture of snuff tobacco became an important industry in its own right. While in the Zaan region (north of Amsterdam), Cuban tobacco was mixed with Dutch and other leaves to produce imitation Cuban snuff for the Spanish market, Virginia leaves—intended for the German inland market—predominated in the Rotterdam industry. In that town, like in Amsterdam at an earlier stage, no fewer than three thousand men found employment in the production of regular and snuff tobacco in the second half of the eighteenth century, before foreign competition began to affect these industries.[114]

Although Amsterdam was Europe's leading cacao market from the last quarter of the seventeenth century through the last quarter of the eighteenth, no large-scale cacao industry sprang up in the Dutch Republic. Most cacao was reexported raw to the Mediterranean, France, Spain, and Germany.[115] Only in Zeeland was a modest number of chocolate mills established, starting probably in 1705. Most cacao processed there came from Suriname, supplemented by supplies from the other Guiana colonies and varieties imported by the WIC and the MCC.[116]

The impact of Atlantic trade extended beyond the processing industries. The companies involved in Atlantic trade also employed thousands of people in the Dutch Republic. An average of forty to fifty men were employed in the eighteenth century by the MCC, most of them working in occupations related to shipbuilding, including sawyers, dock workers, and carpenters. Shipbuilding in turn created jobs for side industries such as sawmills, roperies, canvas weavers, and forges.[117] Around 1770, the outfitting of the company's slave ships (e.g., repairs and providing victuals and medicines) was largely in the hands of local suppliers, and trade goods such as gunpowder and spirits were also produced locally. Asian textiles and guns, however, had to be obtained elsewhere. According to a recent estimate, the share of Middelburg's income attributable to the slave trade was 11 percent; for nearby Vlissingen, it was 35 percent.[118]

The economy of Amsterdam also benefited from the city's intimate connection to Atlantic shipping. Fitting out ships in Amsterdam for Suriname, the anonymous author of a memorandum from around 1740 argued, provided a livelihood for shipwrights, sailmakers, mastmakers, timber merchants, anchor makers, gunsmiths, carpenters, masons, painters, compass makers, boat builders, coppersmiths, powder millers, tar merchants, paint merchants, grocers, brickmakers, oil and candle sellers, butter and cheese buyers, stockfish buyers, pea, beans and barley buyers, ship-biscuit bakers, brewers, wine-merchants, butchers, dockworkers, boatsmen, and pilots. In addition, exported textiles were partly manufactured in Leiden or bleached in Haarlem, while imported sugar created work for potters and coopers.[119]

Manufactures produced in these towns not only made their way to Suriname and—as we have seen above—West Africa, but also to Curaçao, intended for the Spanish American market. An alternative route to Spanish American customers was through Cádiz, the port in southwestern Spain from which Spanish fleets departed to New Spain and Panama. On the far side of the Atlantic, the European manufactures carried by these fleets were exchanged for precious metals and local products. A list of products sent from the Dutch Republic to Cádiz in 1684 reveals that many industrial companies were involved in shipping goods intended for Spanish American markets. Leiden supplied woolen fabrics, as did Haarlem, which also sent silks and white or colored striped linens. Amsterdam's consignments were numerous, including silk quiltings and satins, lamps, plush, cloth, hats, staves, and bleached wax.[120] By the early eighteenth century, the average value of the cargoes sent by Amsterdam companies to Cádiz intended for shipment aboard the Indies-bound fleets was 5,000–20,000 guilders.[121] At times, ships arriving from the Dutch Republic were allowed to become part of a Spanish fleet or sail outside the fleet system. For these purposes, some of the vessels were sold to Dutch or Flemish merchants residing in Cádiz.[122] Textiles intended for the Spanish colonies also filled the warehouses of Curaçao, including vast amounts of coarse linen that was either manufactured or bleached in Haarlem.[123] What is really conspicuous, then, about the import of New World products is that they overwhelmingly originated in non-Dutch colonies. This dramatically underscores the entangled and empire-crossing character of the Dutch Atlantic. Most tobacco imported into the republic came from the Chesapeake, followed by Spanish America. Cacao was predominantly a Venezuelan crop, while indigo arrived indirectly from Guatemala, Saint-Domingue, and South Carolina. Even sugar, cultivated on such a large scale in Suriname and to a lesser extent in the other Guianas, arrived largely (for 61.1 percent in 1750–90) from other parts of the Americas, mostly the French Caribbean (table 15). The only exception to this rule was coffee. The lion's share of this crop (on average 70.4 percent in 1750–90) was harvested in the Dutch Guianas (table 16).[124]

TABLE 15. Relative share of Dutch Guianas in Dutch sugar import, 1750–90 (in pounds)

Year	Dutch Guianas	Total	Share
1750	27,013,096	59,776,622	45.2%
1765	19,708,858	44,714,587	44.1%
1775	23,232,157	62,834,557	37.0%
1780	17,975,129	49,064,729	36.6%
1786	19,361,657	60,858,897	31.8%
1790	26,182,712	58,350,236	44.9%

Source: Based on table 2.11 in this chapter.
Note: We have not included the very small amounts of sugar produced in St. Eustatius and St. Maarten, for which data are missing anyway.

TABLE 16. Dutch import of coffee, 1750–90 (in lbs)

Year	Suriname	Berbice	Ess/Dem	Curaçao	Statia	France	Totals
1750	3,593,423	69,976	120	99,370	148,638	1,500,000	5,411,527
1775	20,331,934	707,871	1,276,800	500,000	2,330,030	9,692,000	34,838,635
1780	11,363,077	1,572,785	5,305,710	500,000	10,075,920	612,000	29,429,492
1786	12,527,630	2,250,000	1,639,960		289,500	5,122,762	21,829,852
1790	14,815,275	2,250,000	4,233,770		288,070	4,142,596	25,729,711

Sources: Suriname: Postma, *Dutch Shipping*. Berbice: 1750 (figure for 1753): Kramer, "Plantation Development," 54–55; 1775: Kramer, "Plantation Development"; 1780: Kramer, "Plantation Development". (figure for 1779); 1790: De Hullu, "Memorie," 394. Essequibo/Demerara: 1750–80: Bolingbroke, *Voyage*, 397; 1786: Bolingbroke, *Voyage*, using the figure for 1785; 1790: NAN, WIC 1136, cargo lists 1790. Curacao: 1750: NAN, NWIC 566–98, 1146–61; 1775, 1780: Van der Voort, "Westindische Plantages," 260–61, and Klooster, *Illicit Riches*, 193n49. St. Eustatius: 1750: Klooster, *Illicit Riches*, 226–27, appendix 5; 1775, 1780: Van der Oudermeulen, "Iets dat tot voordeel," 333, appendix L. Conversion of bales and tierces into pounds is derived from Van der Voort, "Westindische Plantages," 260; 1790: Klooster, *Illicit Riches*, 226–27, appendix 5. France: Van der Voort, "Westindische Plantages," 260–61. Table prepared by Gerhard de Kok.

Finally, what was the sales value of the products imported from around the Atlantic basin, and what does this tell us about the relative contribution of the Dutch plantation colonies, the Dutch entrepôts, and the trading posts in Africa? The interimperial connections are once again shown to have loomed large. The value of foreign reexports that reached the Dutch Republic by way of St. Eustatius and Curaçao accounted for 57.1 percent of the value of all products coming from Dutch America in 1701–40 and

47.3 percent in 1751–80 (table 16). Suriname was the foremost supplier of cash crops produced in Dutch colonies; not until the latter part of the eighteenth century did the other Guiana colonies export sizable amounts of crops.

The unmediated Dutch commercial engagement with the Atlantic world also includes the direct trade with Spanish, French, and British America, but hard data are largely missing here. The abovementioned annual figure of 350,000 guilders for the MCC's trade in Spanish America alone (1721–44) indicates that these trades were far from negligible. In these years, they surpassed the value of Dutch trade with Africa, which never claimed more than 6.5 percent (only in the 1710s) of Dutch Atlantic trade.

Overall, the import trade of the Dutch Republic with the Atlantic grew from 4.7 to 21.1 million guilders from the 1700s through the 1770s (i.e., by a factor of 4.5). Atlantic Dutch trade thus caught up with Dutch trade with Asia, which had been much larger all along, but only increased from 18.2 to 20 million guilders in the period 1720–70.[125] At the same time, the Atlantic share of Dutch international trade never approached that of foreign European empires—French imports from the Americas, for example, were worth 7.7 times more than French imports from Asia by 1772.[126] Nor did the eighteenth-century Atlantic trade of the Dutch come close in volume or value to that of their rivals. Those same French imports in 1772 from the Americas totaled the equivalent of 72.7 million guilders,

TABLE 17. Direct Atlantic imports of the Dutch Republic, 1701–80 (annual averages in millions of guilders)

Years	Suriname	Ess/ Dem	Berbice	Curaçao	St. Eustatius	Gold Coast	Totals
1701–10	1.8			1.5	1.1	0.3	4.7
1711–20	1.5			1.8	1.0	0.3	4.6
1721–30	2.2			1.8	1.0	0.3	5.3
1731–40	2.7			1.7	1.0		5.4
1741–50	4.2	0.3		3.4	1.3		9.2
1751–60	4.9	0.1	0.5	1.9	3.5		10.9
1761–70	7.8	0.6	0.3	2.8	4.2		15.7
1771–80	8.8	1.9	0.6	2.8	7.0		21.1

Sources: Suriname, Curaçao, and St. Eustatius: Klooster, "Overview of Dutch Trade," 379 (table 13.1). Essequibo and Demerara: table 6 in this chapter. Berbice: table 5 in this chapter. Gold Coast: Den Heijer, *Goud, ivoor en slaven*, 129 (table 5.8) and 136 (table 5.9).

while the annual sales value of British imports from the Americas came to more than 94 million guilders in 1772–73.[127] The Dutch figure of 21.1 million (1771–80) is modest by comparison. The republic's Atlantic trade had grown remarkably in the eighteenth century, but the Atlantic trade of its rivals had grown far more, and had given these empires a far stronger Atlantic profile than that of the Dutch Republic.

The trade between the Dutch Republic and the Atlantic world was largely the work of a multiplicity of small firms, rather than just the WIC. Commerce with Africa and the transatlantic slave trade initially remained West India Company monopolies, but the WIC's poor performance finally enabled the introduction of free trade in all commercial branches. After giving up its last monopolies, the WIC's commerce was confined to the sale of slaves to Brazilian merchants on the Gold Coast. In the other theaters of the Dutch Atlantic, the company's role was reduced to governance, either solely or in a consortium as in Berbice and Suriname.

As the importation of Suriname's plantation crops increased steadily in the eighteenth century, coffee joined sugar as a leading product, surpassing sugar in value by the 1750s. The same process occurred for Berbice, Demerara, and Essequibo, the three lesser Guianas, which would never match Suriname's value in terms of crop sales. In mid-century, the Dutch Guiana colonies offered Dutch investors attractive opportunities, which led to the transfer of tremendous amounts of credit. An artificial boom followed, failing to produce high profits and ending in a credit crisis that would thwart the further plantation growth of Suriname.

In addition to the Dutch cash crop colonies, a second linchpin of the Dutch Atlantic was formed by the two Caribbean entrepôts, which represented half of the sales value of New World plantation crops. If we add direct trade between Dutch metropolitan firms and foreign American colonies to the picture, the Dutch plantation colonies become even less important in comparison. In this way, the Dutch stood out in the Atlantic world. The two linchpins survived until the turbulent decades of the Fourth Anglo-Dutch War and the French revolutionary wars. That era saw the British conquest of the lesser Dutch Guianas and the permanent decline of the Dutch Caribbean entrepôts. The economic significance of the Dutch trading stations in West Africa had dwindled long before.

The lively trade of the Dutch in many parts of the Atlantic may have led to much hustle and bustle in maritime ports, but beyond a few examples, such as the MCC, there is no evidence of much profitability. If Atlantic trade contributed significantly to the economies of Spain, Portugal, Britain, and France, it had a less significant impact on that of the Dutch Republic. In spite of the many ships with Dutch flags plying the ocean, Dutch economic development never hinged on the Atlantic world.

3

WEST AFRICA

Conquered in 1637, Elmina was the one important permanent Dutch foothold in West Africa, crowning several smaller fortresses on the Gold Coast, which grew in number from ten in 1700 to fourteen in 1725.[1] It was a crucial link in the Dutch gold and ivory trades, and even if the Gold Coast never dominated the Dutch slave trade, the forts on the Gold Coast were indispensable to the functioning of the commerce in enslaved Africans. The nature of Dutch "society" in this area was distinct from that in Guiana or the Caribbean islands. Housing only sojourners, not settlers, the forts were home almost exclusively to male Europeans. Their high mortality rate—and eagerness to return to Europe—helped shape a community in perpetual flux, as its individual members were constantly replaced by newcomers. Although their world inside the forts was officially separate from the African world next door, this boundary was permeable in practice. Most men developed intimate relations with indigenous women, which led to a growing population of mixed off-spring, some of whom rose to high positions. Other free and enslaved

Africans also came to play an increasingly important role in the forts. The Dutch could not have maintained their commercial position without native brokers. Likewise, the close ties with neighboring African polities cultivated by the Dutch leadership proved valuable in times of war.

Commerce

As noted in the previous chapter, Dutch trade along the African coast was limited neither to the areas under Dutch control, nor to the exchange of European commodities for captives alone—items such as ivory and gold were also much sought after, at least until the 1730s. Nonetheless, the slave trade did become the dominant rationale for the Dutch presence in West Africa. Paradoxically, Dutch deployment of enslaved Africans in the forts for their own operations was very limited. The economic pursuits of the Dutch were largely limited to commerce, which they conducted on the coast with African rulers and traders.

The coastal strip occupied by the Dutch did not leave much room for agricultural activities of any kind. Besides, European planters would have faced a deadly disease environment. Producing foodstuffs was deemed virtually impossible, because as one Dutch surgeon explained, nothing grew on the arid, saline soil along the coast, and the rough woods and large plains were always full of salty moistures. One director general lamented that "to subsist on what grows here in this dry and forlorn land, without shipments from the fatherland, is . . . closely akin to famine."[2] That was an exaggeration. On the coast and in the interior, Africans were of course engaged in agriculture and produced rice, millet, yams, and potatoes. In addition, a variety of fruits grew wild. The Dutch also discovered that the soil did indeed lend itself to the cultivation of cash crops. For more than a decade, starting in 1697, cotton was produced, while a simultaneous attempt was made to raise an indigo crop, in both cases with the aid of residents of Curaçao—a black slave with cotton expertise and a white indigo planter.[3] Initiatives to start sugar cultivation failed due both to the lack of local Dutch expertise and the unsuitability of the soil.[4] Nor was the experiment with indigo and cotton successful in the long run. In the 1710s, the authorities concluded that the slaves who were employed in this production should be sent to the American colonies, where their labor was more in demand.[5]

If these attempts were incidental, more structural was the company's interest in Dutch gold production. Although the Africans jealously guarded the secret locations of their mines, the Dutch did make several attempts to mine gold themselves in the seventeenth and eighteenth centuries. It is unclear, however, if any prospectors were ever sent from Europe for this purpose.[6] One example of a WIC initiative to start gold production is the letter by the West India Company board to the council of Elmina in 1731 to express their desire that the Dutch Gold Coast be transformed into "a second Brazil"—a reference, in this case, to the economic boom experienced by Brazil since the start of gold mining there in the 1690s. In response, the council pointed out that gold was not mined along the coast, but rather several days' travel into the hostile and unpacified interior. The effective power of the Dutch, they added, was limited to their forts, and capturing lands was futile because of their numbers, which were so much smaller than the European population of Brazil.[7] In practice, indeed, no gold mines under Dutch supervision were ever established.

There was no alternative, then, to obtaining gold through trade. And trade with the interior was conspicuously different from elsewhere in the Atlantic world, starting with the logistics. Shifting power configurations in the African political arena, where Europeans could bring little influence to bear, constantly affected market conditions. Likewise, there were no trade routes here on which horses, mules, and carts could transport cargoes. Everything had to be carried on human backs and heads.[8] That was true for gold as well as ivory. Combined, these products represented 96.9 percent of the value of all commodities that the Dutch legally exported from the Gold Coast in the period 1675–1731.

Dutch gold shipments from this coast began to decline in the late seventeenth century, a trend that continued in the eighteenth. This downturn was, however, compensated for by increasing gold exports from other parts of West Africa. Falling gold supplies from the interior of the Gold Coast—as well as rising slave supplies—were due to the numerous wars between African polities, which were partly caused by the European competition on the coast. The WIC's rivals included not only the English—whose numbers rose substantially after the Royal African Company's slave trade monopoly was abolished in 1698—but also Dutch interlopers, Portuguese, Frenchmen, and Danes.[9] Various locations in the interior yielded gold, but its trade before 1701 had been a virtual monopoly of the Denkyira, who made all other states in the region tributary. After the Denkyira had been defeated by the Asante, the Dutch cultivated a commercial partnership with the new regional superpower, although that could not buck the trend of falling gold imports.[10] In fact, the expansion of the Asante kingdom led to a prolonged dislocation of the gold trade.

Like other Europeans, the Dutch paid for the products they bought with goods shipped in from Europe. A variety of textiles predominated, and alcoholic drinks, guns, gunpowder, and tobacco were also standard items among the Dutch cargoes. Cloth, in particular, was very popular—in 1725 alone, the WIC sold 31,000 pieces to its African trading partners. The company had to respond quickly to changing fashions, take local variations into account, and diversify its supplies in order to stay ahead of its rivals. Despite all diligence and hard work, however, the WIC could not avoid losing ground amidst ruinous competition. Especially the ascent of England, whose commercial power grew commensurately with the increase from five to eleven of the Royal African Company's West African forts in the years 1672–1713, was at the expense of the WIC's once impressive commerce.[11]

The rivalry with Britain led to occasional hostilities, starting with the inconclusive Komenda Wars (1687–1702). By means of violence and diplomacy, the Dutch at Elmina sought to secure a monopoly of gold purchases and bar other Europeans from the coast. Enraged at African traders at the town of Komenda, which was ruled by the inland state of Eguafo, for ignoring the agreements made about a Dutch monopoly, the Dutch allied with several inland states against Eguafo and its allies, including Britain.[12] In the years that followed, relations between Dutchmen and Englishmen remained tense, though warfare was avoided. A small spark was enough to set off warfare, however, in 1750, when a seemingly trifling dispute morphed into an attack on the British at Fort Dixcove by men from the Ahanta nation, supported by the Dutch at the nearby fort at Butri. The Ahanta then blocked access to Fort Dixcove for eight months, until an arriving British man-of-war forced the Dutch to come to the negotiating table. The conflict eventually ended when the Ahanta ceased their blockade after the British side made diplomatic concessions.[13]

A decade earlier, the Dutch had waged a war with their African neighbors at Elmina. The war was almost exclusively organized by Martinus François de Bordes, the Dutch director governor at Elmina Castle, who had no qualms about seeking military assistance from the Fante, traditional Dutch

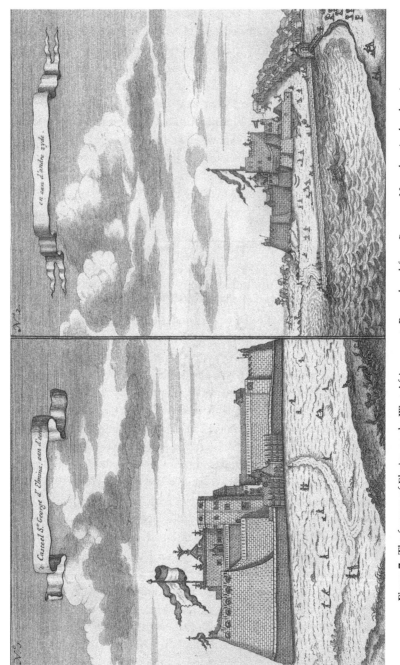

Figure 7. The fortress of Elmina on the West African coast. Reproduced from Bosman, *Nauwkeurige beschryving.*

enemies, to fight the Elminans. De Bordes's death (from natural causes) in March 1740 quickly led to the silencing of arms, but not before more than four hundred Africans had perished in the course of the war.[14] In the early 1760s, the Dutch became involved in another African war, this time also initiated by a single powerful individual. Amanahyia (or Amnichia), the de facto ruler of Appolonia, obtained much wealth through trade and robbery, which he used to build a power base west of Ahanta. A man of great ambition, he responded to perceived Dutch backing for a rival nation with which he was at war to attack the Dutch fort at Axim in March 1762, destroying the native settlements around the fort, killing many of their inhabitants, and almost making it to the gates.[15] Aided by several allied African nations, the WIC countered in January and March–April 1763 with expeditions against Amanahyia and his allies, but failed to achieve their objectives. In fact, they worsened the Dutch position, since Amanahyia, having received ammunition from Fort Dixcove, invited the English to build a fort in Appolonia. The English eagerly accepted the invitation, although the new fort would not be finished until 1771.[16]

Virtually every generation of Dutch officials thus faced a war with a neighboring African state, with or without the involvement of the British. As a rule, however, the WIC tried to avoid warfare, instead pursuing its goals by signing treaties and entering into alliances with African polities. Ultimately, the company was dependent on the goodwill of native leaders, calculating politicians who used the rivalry among European nations to their own advantage.

The WIC's rivals were not only to be found among foreign Europeans or Dutch interlopers. By engaging in illegal trade, the company's own employees also prevented the WIC from maximizing its profits. As long as the company had a monopoly of trade, commercial connections should have been a transparent affair, with the director dealing with African nobility and intermediaries in Elmina and the interior, and all trade with the republic and the colonies in the Americas being a company affair. In practice, however, WIC officials and increasingly, as we will see, also Eurafrican elite families tended to engage in illegal private trade. Although, because of their secretive character, these activities did not lead to the establishment of identifiable long-term commercial networks, they did undercut the company's profits considerably.

Until the end of the first quarter of the eighteenth century, the appropriately named Slave Coast accounted for most Dutch purchases of enslaved

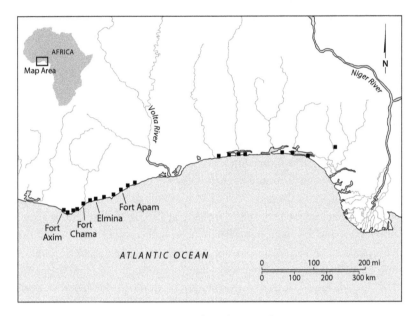

Figure 8. Map of Dutch West Africa.

Africans, even though the Dutch only had lodges there and no forts. The rise of Dahomey as a regional trading power starting in 1725 spelled doom for the Dutch on the Slave Coast. Hendrick Hertogh, the WIC's factor at Ouidah, seems to have helped the ruler of that state to resist Dahomey's expansion. After the king of Dahomey had demanded in vain that Hertogh be removed from the Slave Coast, the factor was murdered, probably by the king's agents. More important, Dahomey subsequently shunned the Dutch as a trading partner. The resulting decline in Dutch imports from the Slave Coast was compensated for by the increase in the slave trade in Elmina, where slaves originating in the interior were supplemented by those obtained at the outer forts as well as some bought on the Ivory Coast and the Bight of Biafra. The Gold Coast never dominated the slave trade, however, either before the WIC lost its monopoly in the 1730s—after which it confined itself to supplying slaves to the Portuguese—or after the start of free trade. Johannes Postma has calculated that during the free trade era (1730–1803), Dutch slavers had, on average, loaded nearly 70 percent of their human cargo before the ship reached

Elmina; most slaves had already been purchased on the Windward Coast (today's Ivory Coast and Liberia). By contrast with ships fitted out for the African commodity trade, the vast majority of which sailed straight from the Dutch Republic to Elmina only, Elmina was usually a slave ship's final stop and served therefore exclusively to complete the consignment.[17]

Demography and Lifestyle

Until 1760, the WIC employed on average 250 Europeans in each of its fifteen Dutch locations on the Gold Coast; after that year, the number of Europeans dropped until it totaled just a few dozen by the late eighteenth century, Eurafricans and Africans taking their place in the service of the company. Elmina employed over one-third of all Europeans, between seventy and one hundred in the years up until 1760. The WIC workforce in Elmina included some 300 enslaved Africans. Even so, the combined WIC personnel was only a fraction of the entire population of the town of Elmina with its 12,000 to 16,000 inhabitants— a population whose growth must have been related to some extent to the trading opportunities offered by the Dutch.[18] Military personnel, usually numbering well over one hundred at least until 1760, made up the largest contingent of resident Europeans.[19] In addition to their mercantile activities on behalf of the company, Europeans also occupied a variety of administrative and artisanal positions. In the late seventeenth century, the most competent soldiers could still be appointed as clerks, a career avenue that was later closed off.[20] The initial productivity of clerks—who were mainly tasked with copying documents—was negligible, since many of them were either sick or listless and tired, and once they were seasoned, it often turned out that they lacked basic reading and writing skills.[21]

West Africa was not a prized destination for potential WIC officials and soldiers, first because of health conditions. European mortality on the entire Western African coast was high, in the order of 20 percent per annum and probably much higher for new arrivals during their first year.[22] In some years, more than fifty European soldiers died as well as twenty to twenty-five sailors.[23] Nor were the other Europeans immune to the epidemic diseases that regularly depleted the white population.

Residents complained bitterly about living conditions, and if their concerns had been widely known, they would have kept potential sojourners from coming to Elmina. The only escape route for soldiers was desertion, which was relatively easy given the proximity of England's Cape Coast Castle. When Elmina's fiscal and chief merchants arrived at the English headquarters in 1700 to request permission to capture a Zeeland interloper anchored at Cape Coast, they were stopped by a Dutch soldier who had recently run away from Mouree. An agreement between Cape Coast and Elmina, which provided for the return of deserters to their fort of origin, failed to halt the flow of runaways.[24] What lured many a soldier to the English stations was the—probably justified—expectation of improved conditions. Whereas English soldiers received a wage and an allowance, new Dutch recruits were burdened by expenditures on transport and outfit as well as payments to the home front. Like employees of the Dutch East India Company, those in the pay of the WIC sometimes stipulated that a part of their wages would go to their wife or relatives. As a consequence, they could not start earning money for themselves until some years into their contract, allowing them to buy new clothes for the first time only then.[25]

Soldiers were not the only arrivals with debts. More than a few men who signed up as administrative personnel with the WIC in Elmina left debts behind in the republic. Among them was the former bailiff of the town of Zierikzee, who had lost his job because of misconduct. He got a fresh start in Elmina as the fiscal, in which capacity his main task was—ironically—to investigate misbehaving company officials, who often resorted to illegal trade. Another case of voluntary exile from the republic was that of a beer brewer from Groningen, who left for the Gold Coast after incurring debts. He served as the director general's steward and the commander of Fort Coenraadsburg.[26] In spite of such examples, there were plenty of men whose motivation was more entrepreneurial, hoping to strike it rich. In a letter to her son, the mother of one clerk hinted at this impetus when she mentioned the desire that he would return home as a rich man in a few years' time.[27]

The scattered data on Europeans—nearly all of them transients, with only a few surviving and continuing to live in Dutch West Africa for an extended period—reveal that a mix of Dutch, German, and Scandinavian migrants was common throughout the Dutch Atlantic. Virtually all of them were males, due to the company ban on bringing wives along. The rare minister who came with his wife from the republic sent her back, since "no married woman could possibly live a fulfilled life here."[28] Females, as a rule, may have been conspicuously absent among the WIC personnel, but one day a fight broke out among soldiers in the Elmina garrison that exposed one of them as a woman. After she confessed that she had disguised herself because she felt the urge to travel, the director saw to it that the woman was dressed in female garb and placed in a separate lodging house. There she fell in love with a soldier who would soon become her husband.[29]

Because of the high mortality rates, upward mobility in the local WIC hierarchy was one of the few incentives to enlist in Elmina. Only the position of director—sometimes called "director general" or "governor"—remained a prerogative of Protestant Dutch officials. For all other ranks, requirements were gradually eased. It was hard to find suitable candidates who wished to work in what director Pieter Nuyts called these "dreadful and heathenish regions." Thus, the Amsterdam Chamber of the WIC was flabbergasted that a man of some prestige, Abraham Houtman, was willing to serve as director of Elmina in 1722. Bad financial and personal luck explained his willingness—and his administration was no success story, as Houtman died within a year, but not before having perpetrated serious fraud against the company.[30]

Senior company employees such as Houtman were often eminently able to use their position for their own benefit. That was the case with Pieter Woortman (1700–1780), who after an initial stint in WIC service on the Gold Coast in the 1720s spent the next decade in the Netherlands, only to return to Africa in 1741. He worked his way up from bottler and captain of a company vessel to commander of Fort Lijdzaamheid at Apam, governor of Fort Crevecoeur at Accra, and finally director general in Elmina. Maintaining close relations with the local population and relying on his African wife's family ties, Woortman spun a trading web, which he and two of his sons extended in due course to the wider Atlantic. As a result, they became active participants in the Dutch slave trade in a network that included Amsterdam, Rotterdam, and Middelburg.[31]

Another man who cashed in on his company service was Nicolaas Mattheus van der Noot de Gieter (1715–55). Having joined the WIC in 1732 as an assistant on the Gold Coast, he was named junior official (*ondercommies*) at Fort Oranje at Sekondi, where he was later appointed commander. By 1742, he was the commander of Fort St. Anthony at Axim.[32] The authorities at the Dutch trading stations blocked all private trade in these years. Shipmasters of arriving Dutch merchantmen complained that they were allowed to initiate commercial contact with Africans, but as soon as the Dutch trade goods were brought ashore in canoes, sloops, or other vessels, they were confiscated by the commanders in the Dutch service. The same happened when goods were exchanged on land. Various shipowners and merchants in the Dutch Republic therefore joined forces and petitioned the States General to prohibit company employees from trading on the African coast—a ban that would echo a company regulation established in 1734.[33] In their testimonies, one captain after another accused Van der Noot de Gieter of the most outrageous self-serving behavior. He was said to employ a Dutch soldier and a number of local Africans to patrol the beach and prevent any trade between Dutch ships and the indigenous population. Moreover, the commander owned a ship that was used exclusively to trade for his account. The WIC refused to proceed against the alleged culprit, clinging to a decision it had made in 1740 to allow employees to engage privately in the slave trade, as long as they paid a duty of twenty guilders per slave—a poll tax imposed on each slave trader.[34] How lucrative his time at Axim was emerged after Van der Noot de Gieter returned to the Dutch Republic and married in 1746. In their mutual will, he and his wife declared that they possessed over 100,000 guilders.

Company personnel who survived the seasoning period did not necessarily lead a healthy lifestyle. Alcoholism was rampant—many a company employee allegedly drank through the night, which at times led to reprimands by superiors, but never to dismissal. One Dutch official in Elmina wrote that he did not know one person "in this melancholy land" who did not take a morning drink.[35] In the 1780s, one group of young clerks broke with the traditional combination of heavy drinking and playing dice, which frequently degenerated into fistfights or knife wielding, by performing plays, starting with one on the death of William of Orange. The theater may have been operative for a decade or two, but was eventually abandoned.[36] Aside from this initiative, high culture was largely absent from the forts, making the director general Jan Pieter Theodoor

Huydecoper, with his immense library and his love for the transverse flute, an object of ridicule.[37]

Spiritual life was also in short supply in Elmina, where the Reformed Church had a religious monopoly, but where the church's two sacraments—baptism and the Lord's Supper—were seldom administered. Nor were Reformed services well attended, except by soldiers, who were obliged to go to church. Even men who were church members in the Dutch Republic did not go to church. Informed that most company employees on the Gold Coast "led an unseemly, godless, and debauched life," the WIC board even feared that God would inflict his wrath on the area under Dutch control. In contrast to some Reformed ministers, Dutch Elmina's councilors were not particularly concerned about the adherence of most personnel to Lutheranism or even Catholicism. In 1744, they accommodated resident and visiting Brazilians, who were active in a decades-old trade that saw the Dutch exchange slaves for sweetened tobacco, as they allowed them to build a small church in Elmina, where Catholic priests henceforth led religious services for their compatriots.[38]

Free and Enslaved Africans

Trade tied Elmina to the wider Atlantic world, impacting Africans in two ways. It both enabled local Africans to have access to a variety of European products and increased the ranks of enslaved men, women, and children to be shipped across the Atlantic. The commercial routes to the American colonies that were used for their transport were occasionally also employed for another end: the exile by the Dutch ruling council at Elmina of undesirable Africans. For example, the brother of the king of Eguafo—who had been a Dutch broker—was exiled to Suriname for helping Komenda in its war with the Dutch. Six years later, the WIC accused the brother of the king of Komenda of preventing his servants from fighting for the Dutch and exiled him to the same colony. He was repatriated after a few years. Three decades later the WIC exiled another prominent Elmina man by the name of Tekki to Suriname after he had fallen from grace with his peers ruling the city-state. Eleven years and several appeals to the WIC later he returned to the Gold Coast and was accepted again in Elmina.[39]

The only free Africans to sail on Dutch slavers were a few sailors and the so-called *bombas*. These men were employed as paid overseers of the captives on board the ships bound for the Caribbean. As such, they served as intermediaries between their fellow Africans and their Dutch employers. After disembarking the slaves, they rejoined the otherwise European crew for their home leg, and spent time in the republic before returning to Elmina.[40] And yet even these men were never far removed from slavery. Jan Jansen, the son of an Elmina slave woman and a native of the town, had regularly served as bomba on board slave ships when the authorities accused him of knavery and threatened to send him to the colonies as a slave. A Fante man intervened and arranged for his manumission, but Jansen ran away from him. Elmina's fiscal subsequently took him as a slave to the republic and sold him to a merchant on Curaçao.[41] Another man, named "Jan de Bomba," surprised the Dutch after his ship's arrival on Curaçao. It turned out—or, at least, so the bomba asserted—that among the human cargo that had sailed from Africa was his own wife. He now requested to buy her freedom, which he was allowed to do. Husband and wife then presumably returned to their home, making them probably the only married African couple that ever completed the triangular voyage.[42]

The Dutch relied much more on Africans for their trade in West Africa than they did on bombas for the Middle Passage. African middlemen were, in fact, crucial for commercial purposes. Free Africans were also essential to the food supply of resident Europeans. While Elmina was partly provisioned by the republic, grains, animals, palm oil, and other locally procured foodstuffs enabled the Europeans to survive. And while enslaved Africans were employed in the company's gardens, the WIC's employees bought much of their food from the local free suppliers.[43] Elmina thus developed into a unique type of city-state, in which the Dutch fort was fully dependent on the African city.[44]

Elmina's function the trade in enslaved Africans had an impact on the wider demographic development of Western Africa, but the Dutch residents could not travel beyond the immediate surroundings of the forts. Only the main fortress and its immediate environment formed a place of significant cultural contact that featured a measure of creolization. The influence of Dutch culture may therefore have been larger here than in other parts of the Dutch Atlantic. Demographics explain why this was the case. Apart from a few exceptions, the WIC only sent single men to serve at Elmina Castle, and mortality among new arrivals was high. This meant, first, that a constant supply of new arrivals from Europe was necessary to fill the ranks, and second, that local Europeans turned to local females for sexual and sometimes also affectionate relations. The situation was not unique for the Dutch trading stations. It was no different in the British castles on the Gold Coast.[45] European men often dwelled in the city among Africans, ate the same diet of fish, maize, cassava, and yams, and drank palm wine—reputedly in large quantities. A growing share of Elmina's population, both in the castle and in its immediate surroundings, was *tapoeyer* (those of mixed Eurafrican birth or descent), and this segment was consistently exposed to European influences.[46] The WIC had no ambition whatsoever to spread Dutch culture beyond the fortress, but within it, the policy was to retain the exclusive use of the Dutch language and exclusive administration of the Dutch Reformed religion. Senior positions in the administration continued to be reserved for Dutch or, if need be, other European immigrants. Nonetheless, some tapoeyer children, having been recognized by their European fathers, became members of the small and secluded colonial world of Elmina, unlike their African mothers.[47] In the course of the eighteenth century tapoeyers attained prominent positions in Elmina society, and as a consequence were socialized into a local variant of Dutch culture which included both the language and dominant religion of the Dutch Republic.

Enslaved Africans faced a fundamentally different type of creolization. The entire stretch of misery starting with their capture in the interior and continuing through the overland marches and the internment in open air camps or fortresses and finally into the ships preparing for the Middle Passage, implied an instantaneous and violent process of creolization, as "Africans"—a post hoc denominator of no immediate significance at the time—of various ethnicities were forced to start understanding one another even before setting sight on the Europeans and the ships that took them aboard. Scholarly work in this field has seldom explicitly included the Dutch Atlantic, but we assume that the overall pattern was similar, in the sense that those enslaved Africans that were shipped by Dutch slavers and eventually arrived in Dutch colonies went through the same agonizing processes of early creolization. This included a sense of humiliation and loss that has often been described as "dehumanization," an awareness of being surrounded by an overwhelming variety of both African and

European strangers, and perhaps the first acquisition of a pidgin language. At the same time, individual captives may have found comfort in retaining or creating bonds with fellow victims.

No evidence has survived of possibly recurrent resistance by Africans earmarked for sale in the Americas when they were still under Dutch control in Africa, although we do know that aboard Dutch slave ships sailing across the Atlantic there were cases not only of individual protest—including attempts at escape or suicide—but also of conspiracies and revolts. Johannes Postma found some twenty-five cases of collective uprisings, usually only involving a minority of the slaves aboard. He suggests that there must have been many more. Ultimately none of these revolts were successful, but they did cause merchants to urge captains and their crews to refrain from any behavior that might provoke uprisings.[48]

One of the most horrendous stories in the history of the Atlantic slave trade was directly connected to the fear of revolt aboard slave ships. In 1738, the Dutch slave ship *Leusden*, which had departed from Elmina six weeks before, was stranded in the Marowijne River just off the coast of Suriname. As the ship was slowly capsizing, the captain concluded that she would soon sink. The crew rescued itself and sixteen slaves, but not before having closed and nailed all escape gates for the enslaved Africans on the decks below, 664 of whom drowned in the slowly sinking ship. The reason the captain later advanced for this cold-blooded mass murder was the fear of a deadly slave revolt if the crew would have allowed the captives to climb up to the deck. Incidentally, the sixteen enslaved Africans who helped the crew to escape were not rewarded, but sold shortly afterwards in a public auction. The captain was acquitted.[49]

In Elmina and the outforts, the WIC itself used only a limited number of local company slaves to support the procedures—some three hundred slaves were employed in Elmina, as compared to up to one hundred company officials. The slaves' duties included carpentry, masonry, forgery, rowing canoes, and loading and unloading ships. To avoid close ties with free Africans on the Gold Coast, company slaves were to be distinguished from trade slaves and hence introduced from the Slave Coast and the Niger Delta. Although uprooted and enslaved, they did not face the ruthless labor regime of New World plantation societies and were more likely to be manumitted. On the other hand, their food allowances were set at only one-third of that of the European soldiers, which helps explain why company slaves rose in revolt at least twice in the 1780s.[50] In due course, the company slaves came to live in a separate ward in the town of Elmina and form a social world of their own that straddled the divide between freedom and slavery. The slaves who were imported were all males, and just like the free company men, most of them ended up in sexual and affectionate relationships with free native African women.[51]

Common Ground

The Dutch never nurtured any illusion or ambition for genuine colonialism on the Gold Coast, where the expansion since 1700 of the Asante and Dahomey kingdoms translated into a concentration of military power of which the Dutch could not dream. The WIC wisely remained neutral when possible,[52] realizing, as one director general wrote, that the company's soldiers would be unable to defend Elmina Castle against a foreign European enemy or an African foe without the assistance of the local population.[53] This was shown in 1782, when a British force, reinforced by Fante allies, invaded, only to be rebuffed by the Elmina natives on behalf of their Dutch partners. Conversely, Dutch soldiers helped protect the residents of Elmina during a large-scale attack by the Fante in 1740.[54]

That the Dutch were able to maintain their presence in Elmina for so long is therefore not explained by their military strength, which was never on a par with their African neighbors. Dutch trader Willem Bosman had worried in his *Nauwkeurige beschryving* (1703) about the effects of the great quantities of guns sold by the Dutch to Africans: "In this way we give them a knife to cut our own throat."[55] But such concerns were hardly ever necessary and shared interest in trade and hence stability explains why such fears seldom became reality. The WIC wanted trade, and so did local leaders. This was the logic of Elmina and the lesser outposts.

The emergence of native brokers who were appointed by the WIC and lived in the vicinity of the Dutch forts was therefore in the interest of both Europeans and Africans.[56] Operating as intermediaries between the WIC and African traders, they were an elite among the constantly arriving Africans eager to profit from the commercial opportunities. Because these Africans came from different regions and represented various ethnicities, historian Harvey Feinberg has rightfully characterized Elmina as "multi-ethnic." Even so, Akan speakers were dominant in Elmina throughout the period under discussion. Their regional connections, however, were weak. The local leadership had no strong military tradition and did not entertain close relations with other Akan-speaking communities along the Gold and Slave Coasts.[57]

All of this meant that for most of the period after the Dutch conquest of the Portuguese fort, Elminian society was characterized by a pragmatic coexistence and sense of mutual benefit between the local African leaders and the WIC officials. Their collaboration was formalized in regulations drawn up at Elmina Castle that were binding for both parties. The WIC director general was even invited at times by Elmina's king (*ohen*) and his entourage to act as mediator in judicial cases among the African population, always remaining within the limits of local customary law.[58] Mutual medical aid formed another point of contact, albeit only in case of emergency. After the king of Akwamu could not be cured by his own physicians, the treatment by a Dutch barber surgeon seems to have led to his recovery. Conversely, when the number of these surgeons in the Dutch forts was reduced to only two, sick company personnel relied on native female doctors.[59] Collaboration also extended to military matters. The African residents of villages near the Dutch forts swore an oath of allegiance to protect the Dutch. In return, they were protected against both African adversaries and sexual indiscretions of Dutchmen, while their chiefs received regular gifts—especially brandy, pipes, and tobacco—in a system of reciprocity that developed overtime. Initially distributed only on special occasions, such as the New Year, Akan celebrations, or the arrival of a new director, Dutch gifts had become a weekly phenomenon by the early nineteenth century.[60] These gifts came on top of the tribute paid by the Dutch to the Asante government since the mid-eighteenth century.[61]

In all, then, there was an entente of mutual interest between the leadership of Elmina and the WIC, and only in rare case was this equilibrium broken. It took the erratic behavior of two directors general to disturb the harmony. In 1739, as we have seen, the director general De Bordes sparked a bloody armed struggle, and in 1808 a possibly nerve-wrecked interim director, Johannes Petrus Hoogenboom, also provoked local anger. He was butchered by a local mob, the fact that his genitals were cut off suggesting that part of the scorn he provoked may have had to do with sexual transgressions.[62]

If trade and defense provided an interface between the WIC officials and the town of Elmina, religion did not. Nowhere in West Africa was missionizing a priority on the Dutch agenda. Dutch clergy did target children of mixed descent, but otherwise refrained from spreading the gospel among their African neighbors. Attempts to introduce Christian learning through a school were unsuccessful. The school that one minister set up for tapoeyer and black children in the mid-eighteenth century attracted about twenty children, but folded within a decade.[63] Religious rapprochement would have contradicted the WIC policy for its employees to keep their distance from the Africans. Company men were forbidden to spend the night outside the Dutch forts and African women were barred from spending them inside those forts. The appearance of Dutch superiority was paramount. When one misbehaving company official was chased by a superior from the lodge where he was stationed to Elmina Castle, nobody took pity on him. He was thus forced to beg for food outside the fort until a female Eurafrican innkeeper provided him with food and drinks without charge. At that point, the WIC fiscal intervened and employed him as one of his own assistants, arguing that the man would otherwise bring shame to the company.[64] Another official may have expressed the opinion of many of his fellow Dutchmen when he openly doubted the possibility of truly converting adult Africans, barring miracles. The only method that he thought might work was to send young children to a special colony or inside a walled city, where Christians would educate them in religion.[65]

What came closest to this plan was the practice of socializing Eurafrican and African boys—more so apparently than girls—into Dutch culture by sending them to the republic. The remarkable story of Jacobus Capitein springs to mind: born in 1717 from two African parents, he was apparently either never a slave or was manumitted at a young age. He was taken to the republic at the age of eleven by his repatriating master, educated at the Leiden Latin School, and enrolled as a theology student at Leiden University. Capitein propagated in a famous 1742 *dissertatio* the notion that slavery was not incompatible with the Christian fate—a good

Figure 9. Jacobus Capitein, portrayed by Pieter Tanjé as
a protestant clergyman, 1742. Courtesy of Rijksmuseum, Amsterdam.

return to his investors, a cynic might say. Capitein went back to Elmina
that same year as a minister with the explicit task to spread the Reformed
religion among the local population. His efforts were futile and his life
ended in despair only a few years after his return.[66]

While Capitein's story is well known, there are similar lesser-known stories. According to Ghanaian oral tradition, Anton Wilhelm Amo, born near Axim on the Gold Coast as the son of a chieftain, was sent in 1706 by his African mother to her sister living, remarkably, in Amsterdam, for his education. He simultaneously functioned as a pawn to guarantee his nation's trade agreement with the company. Although not enslaved, the WIC seems to have sent the young man nonetheless as a gift to the prince of Brunswick-Wolfenbüttel, where Amo was baptized and employed as a lackey at court. He became conversant in Hebrew, Greek, Latin, French, German, and Dutch, and took up studies at the University of Halle, culminating in his public disputation on the legal position of Africans in Europe. He defended his dissertation in philosophy at the University of Wittenberg. At some point after 1747, Amo returned to his native soil, where he found his father and brother still alive. He lived as a hermit, practicing soothsaying, moved to the Dutch fort of Chama, and died at an unknown date.[67]

Recent research—not just in archival repositories, but also in museum collections—has uncovered many more cases of blacks in the Dutch Republic employed as servants, but also performing as painters' models.[68] Around one hundred young African or tapoeyer boys were sent to the republic in the eighteenth century, apparently to be immersed in Dutch culture and hence to fortify the links between the metropolis and Elmina. There are even several known instances of African (and also Caribbean) servants employed in the service of the quasi-royal stadholder family.[69] Usually, African boys sent to the metropolis were placed under the custody of a business partner or relative, where some at least learned the linguistic and commercial skills to pursue a career in Atlantic trading with Elmina as their base. These boys were commonly the offspring of African women and WIC employees, and some of them made a career in Elmina or other Dutch forts as if they were privileged whites.

That was the case with Nicolaas van Bakergem (1735–86). A native of Elmina, he departed to the Netherlands at the age of nine, presumably to receive a proper Dutch education, and returned to West Africa in WIC service. He represented the company three times on the Guinea coast, serving in a variety of capacities, such as governor of Fort Crêvecoeur in Accra and commander of Fort Lijdzaamheid in Apam. He did well for himself as a merchant in slaves and ivory, as shipowner, as West Africa factor for the Rotterdam firm Coopstad & Rochussen, and as coowner and finally sole owner of a plantation in Suriname.[70] Another example is that of Jacob Rühle (1751–1828), also born in Elmina. The son of German-born WIC servant Anthony Rühle and the African woman Jaba Botri, he climbed the ranks, rising to the posts of warehouse manager and *equipagemeester* (master of works), supervising personnel and managing stock. He gathered wealth in the slave trade, became a member of the ruling council in Elmina, and was the main financier of the local Dutch administration around 1790.[71] The rise of these tapoeyer families, as well as others, such as Nieser, Bartels, Van der Pluije, Vroom, and Huydecoper, indicates that people of mixed ancestry made it to the upper layers of colonial Elmina, more so than in the rest of the Dutch Atlantic world.[72]

Unsurprisingly, most company servants lacked the means to send their Eurafrican sons to Europe, if they nurtured such an ambition at all. Whether they took their parental responsibilities seriously or not, their departure or death must have left many Eurafrican children out in the cold. To prevent that, a relief fund was established in the 1720s to which the fathers were supposed to contribute.[73] Initially, Eurafrican men made a living mainly as farmers and fishermen.[74] Later on, as in many New World societies, military demand and demographic realities enabled them to play an increasingly important role in the colonial defense forces.[75] Around the mid-eighteenth century, tapoeyer soldiers began to outnumber whites in Elmina's garrison. While Europeans, if they survived at all, tended to return to the metropolis, tapoeyers served their entire career in the garrison, from which they derived status in local Akan society.[76] Their role in the Dutch armed forces was such that when the WIC banned further recruitment of Eurafricans in 1774, many posts remained unoccupied. The company was thus forced to reverse its decision.[77]

The Eurafricans' soldiering lives did not differ much from those of their white colleagues. It is true that remuneration for the whites was higher, officially because having been born in Africa, Eurafricans were supposedly used to smaller portions of food.[78] Yet both groups were required to attend church services in the fortress church and they must have socialized together. Perhaps these martial Eurafricans were behind the formation of a separate "mulatto" ward in the town of Elmina in the early 1780s.

Feinberg has speculated that this initiative was the result of their desire to distinguish themselves from the larger Elmina community and underline their European identity.[79]

Tapoeyer women had no employment opportunities of any kind in the Dutch forts, but frequently served as concubines of European men. These relationships were recognized in Akan customary law, which also determined that the status of children born of such "marriages" depended on the mother. Children inherited her legal condition, whether she was free or enslaved.[80] White fathers cherished these common-law liaisons, which kept them from baptizing their daughters, because Christian morality and a common-law marriage were considered incompatible.[81]

Although Europeans stationed on the Gold Coast may have been exempt from enslavement, their lives were not enviable. Disease-ridden and prone to alcoholism, most of them were eager to return to the republic at the earliest occasion. Only the lucky ones survived to see their native soil again. When their ship departed from Elmina, they left behind a world that mixed European practices with African culture, one in which European men and African women mingled and where their offspring sometimes advanced to positions traditionally reserved for whites. In these ways, Dutch West Africa resembled the urban sites of the societies that took shape in the Dutch Caribbean and Dutch Guiana.

The conquest of Fort Elmina from the Portuguese in 1637 set the tone for the Dutch position in West Africa for the rest of the seventeenth century. Even as other European powers established footholds, the Dutch remained the strongest power. That allowed trade in slaves, gold, and ivory to flourish, at least until the turn of the century, when a series of developments began to undermine the Dutch position. The abolition by England's Parliament of the Royal African Company's monopoly on African trade (1698) led to more English competition for the Dutch. In addition, the Komenda Wars and the ascendancy of Asante created an almost permanent state of war between African polities, which disrupted trade and led to a decline in gold supplies. The loss of gold was partly compensated for by the simultaneous increase in the slave trade on the Gold Coast as a consequence of the rise of Dahomey, which reduced Dutch slave imports from the Slave Coast. However, the Gold Coast would never be the main source of Dutch slaves.

Elmina and the neighboring Dutch forts were no more than trade stations. They never functioned as a colony that welcomed immigration. Few European women ever set foot in the Dutch castle, which led resident European males to forge emotional and sexual ties with local African women, especially from the adjacent town of Elmina. Economically, Dutch Elmina also depended on Africans, since virtually nothing was produced in the area under Dutch jurisdiction. Attempts to grow cotton and indigo failed, while gold production always took place in the interior. The Dutch also increasingly employed Africans—especially Eurafricans—inside the forts, where Eurafrican soldiers outnumbered Europeans after 1760. This reliance on Africans coincided with the withering of Dutch political and economic clout as well as waning respect for the Dutch from nearby African authorities. The British conquest of several forts during the Fourth Anglo-Dutch War only confirmed that the Dutch were no longer the powerhouse they had once been.

4

The Guianas

In spite of their eccentric location, the Guianas are generally considered part and parcel of the Caribbean, as they share with that region a history of colonization, the introduction of enslaved Africans, and slave-operated plantations. In a sense, they might even be thought of as islands during the colonial era, as these societies were mainly concentrated in a narrow coastal strip oriented towards overseas places, while the extensive tropical rain forest was relatively peripheral, even if it was home to inhabitants potentially hostile to the colonial state. Occasionally, contemporary sources indeed refer to the Guiana colonies as islands.

Early European exploits along this stretch of the Atlantic coast had been inspired by expectations of profitable trade with the Amerindian population, and some Europeans nurtured high hopes of finding El Dorado, a mythical place that British explorers such as Sir Walter Raleigh projected somewhere in the deep interior of the Guianas.[1] None of this materialized. Parts of the Guianas were developed as plantation colonies, just like the Caribbean isles. Expectations ran high, as the abundance of the natural environment was mistaken to be unlimited and easy to reap. In 1659, Otto Keye advocated the colonization of the "delicious" Guianas "to the comfort of so many miserable people" back home. In his 1718 description of Suriname, J. Herlein extolled its natural riches as well as its opportunities for profitable plantation agriculture. The colony, he insisted, "possesses her talent of blessings in abundance, excessively graceful, attractive and full of relish, to the extent one feels as if one were in Paradise."[2]

Economic Structure

In reality, the Dutch started to develop parts of the Guianas mainly because they had not succeeded in conquering, defending, and exploiting Caribbean islands suitable for profitable plantation agriculture. And while the colonists would be remarkably innovative in the ways they adopted the plantation model to the specific conditions of the Guianas, these colonial economies remained fragile and growth would increasingly depend on credits extended from the republic. France did not bother to develop its part of the Guianas at all, as its plantation colonies in the Caribbean Sea offered better opportunities. British competitors had no need for more colonies beyond the Caribbean proper until the second part of the eighteenth century. By then, the soil depletion of the old sugar colonies stimulated the migration of capital and people to the long-neglected lesser Dutch Guianas of Berbice, Essequibo, and its annex of Demerara. The de facto British takeover of these colonies was consolidated by episodes of formal British occupation in the 1780s and 1790s and, eventually, their permanent cession to the United Kingdom after the Napoleonic wars.

Throughout this period, the Dutch Guianas were embedded in a multidirectional commercial network, with Africa providing the crucial enslaved workers and with bilateral exchanges of people, commodities, and capital with the Dutch Republic, but also with an increasingly vital nexus including British North America and the British West Indies. The migratory links were crucial for the development of these colonies towards one end of the spectrum of New World slave colonies, characterized by an extremely uneven racial composition. Africans and Creole slaves made up some 95 percent of the populations of the Dutch Guianas, not counting the Amerindians and Maroons in the interior rainforest. The European population formed a small minority only, strongly differentiated along national and ethnic lines. This singular demographic composition contributed to the emergence of a society characterized both by endemic violence and remarkably bifurcated processes of creolization—one process on the plantations and in the interior, mainly among the African majority, another urban and involving Europeans and Africans alike.

The first European explorations along the "Wild Coast" of the Guianas had been driven by both geopolitical and economic ambitions. The natural habitat of the Wild Coast was far more hostile than that of the Caribbean islands, but the mighty rivers and tropical rain forests did hold the promise of exotic treasures, particularly the precious metals associated with El Dorado. Mineral exploitation, however, would not become a serious industry in the Guianas until the twentieth century. As for trade opportunities with the indigenous population, these were taken up at the start of Dutch colonization and have continued ever since, but they would form a decreasing and soon futile portion of the colonial economy simply because the number of Amerindians was too low and the products they had on offer were of little commercial significance.

By contrast, plantation agriculture, including timber production, was a highly promising endeavor—and the choice for this developmental model involved the large-scale importation of enslaved Africans, exactly as the British and French were doing in their newly-acquired Caribbean islands. There were some significant differences though. While initial British and Dutch experiments with sugar production in various parts of the Guianas were promising, they also highlighted problems associated with the particular geography of the Wild Coast. For one, the most fertile soil along the various rivers was difficult to cultivate because of problems with water management. Moreover, the location of the Guianas was quite disconnected from the insular Caribbean. And finally, the vast savannahs and tropical rainforests in the interior were both the existing habitat of Amerindians and increasingly a safe haven for runaway slaves. The presence of Maroons in the hinterland entailed major risks for the maintenance of social order in these slave societies and would time and again force Dutch colonial authorities to engage in costly military expeditions or peace settlements. None of these problems were as acute in the British and French Caribbean islands—which probably explains why the French never really bothered to turn Cayenne into a plantation economy, and why Great Britain only began to encroach on the lesser Dutch Guianas when the productivity of its oldest insular slave colonies started to decline.

The migration of the "plantation complex" from the Old World to the Americas, and later from Brazil to the Caribbean, as well as the subsequent development of the typical Caribbean plantation, may be read as the story of a series of innovations to which all European powers contributed and which was to tie them together in a vast network in which technical and management expertise was shared, voluntarily or not. The specific Dutch contribution to this history is threefold. First, it has long been thought that the Dutch in particular were responsible for bringing the plantation revolution to the Caribbean. Second, there was reputedly a distinct Dutch role in adding coffee to the major plantation crops of the Caribbean. And finally, the Dutch introduced a major innovation in plantation agriculture by adopting the metropolitan *polder* system—a system of water management defined by low-lying tracts of land enclosed by dikes, thus forming an artificial hydrological entity—to the Guianas.

As for the first claim, it was long taken for granted that after the Portuguese re-conquest of Pernambuco both the commercial networks and technological expertise acquired in Brazil migrated with the departing Dutch settlers and Portuguese Jews to the north, either directly to the Caribbean, particularly Barbados, or via the Dutch Republic. Thus, the story goes, while the practice of sugar production was stagnant in Spanish Hispaniola and Cuba, a powerful new impetus was given in the Lesser Antilles. The latest technology was imported by planters moving north from Brazil, while Dutch and Portuguese Jewish capital allowed for the necessary investment in land, capital goods, and enslaved Africans. This version of a crucial Dutch contribution to the development of the Caribbean has been subject to considerable nuance. John McCusker and Russell Menard in particular have emphasized the proactive role of British financers and planters on Barbados, in addition to the role of the Dutch. It is still commonly accepted that in the early phase of the development of the plantation Americas, Dutch (including Portuguese Jewish) actors helped spread the technologically and financially innovative sugar industry to the Caribbean, including the model of the slave plantation as both an agrarian and processing production unit. It should be underlined, however, that at this stage the Dutch had not contributed anything to the innovation of the

Figure 10. Sugar plantation in Suriname: enslaved Africans, sugar cane fields, water-powered sugar mill. Reproduced from Pistorius, *Korte en zakelijke beschryvinge*, 1763.

process of sugar production itself, but only, critically, to the transatlantic logistics and finance.[3]

As for the introduction of coffee as a major crop alongside sugar in the early 1710s, this innovation linked Java in the Dutch East Indies, via the botanical garden in Amsterdam, to Suriname. There is then a relation there, but apparently not a unique one. Dutch agents of the VOC had first smuggled coffee seeds from Yemen to Java in 1696. From Java, a specimen was sent to Amsterdam where botanists cultivated the plant in a purpose-built hothouse. A British botanist smuggled a specimen to London in 1714, while the Dutch donated another to the Royal Physic Garden in Paris. From these three specimens, Markman Ellis writes, coffee made it to the Caribbean—though in the 1760s there circulated another, perhaps more romantic story of two citizens smuggling coffee seeds from Suriname to Cayenne and hence Martinique.[4] Either way, this crop migration indeed has a Dutch dimension, and initially Suriname was the main coffee producer, but within a few decades the Dutch were no longer dominating coffee production in the Americas.

The one unique and lasting Dutch contribution to the technology of sugar production was developed in their own colonies on the Wild Coast of the Guianas.[5] New World plantations operated under a shared set of human resource management and agrarian and processing principles, always adapted to local conditions. While the transfer of agro-industrial inputs (crops and agricultural technologies) was initially unidirectional from the Old World to the New, the later phase was marked by a constant circulation of technical expertise in all fields within the Americas, as producers everywhere strove for optimization of their yields. Following Smith and Marx as well as abolitionist ideology, the institution of slavery has often been misinterpreted as anachronistic from an economic (in addition to an ethical) point of view. In fact, throughout its history, the Caribbean plantation achieved remarkable technological innovations by the standards of its time while stubbornly clinging to enslaved labor.

This was particularly true for the dominant institution of the sugar plantation, one of the world's first agro-industrial enterprises. The Dutch Guianas were no exception to this rule. Relevant technological innovations developed either in Europe or in competing Caribbean colonies were quickly implemented. Well into the nineteenth century, Suriname's estates even belonged to the technologically most advanced and hence most productive New World plantations. This applies to some extent to the agrarian part of production, but particularly to the subsequent processing technology. Surinamese planters' manuals testify to a vivid interest in issues such as finding the optimal match between type of soil and crop, crop selection, implementation of manure and fallow, and irrigation and drainage.

In the processing phase of the milled sugar cane, the Surinamese planters clearly participated in a wider international circulation of technological expertise. But the one truly unique dimension of the Guiana plantation was the adaptation, since the late seventeenth century, of the Dutch polder system to plantation agriculture. The best soils for agriculture were the lands adjacent to the Atlantic and the various rivers of the Amazon basin, but these lands were continuously swamped through the ebb and flow of the tides. The first sugar plantations, established during the short English rule of the colony, were therefore laid out on drier but less fertile grounds further inland. An adaption of the metropolitan institution of the polder proved to be the way forward. Plantations were laid out in quadrangles with the short side alongside the rivers, stretching a mile or more inwards. Enslaved Africans were put to the backbreaking work of building dikes to control the level of water within the plantation and delving an internal system of dikes and trenches to regulate water levels, allowing for both irrigation and drainage. This multifunctional system of canals and trenches also facilitated easy bulk transport in flat barges. On sugar plantations, an additional innovation was introduced. Sugar technicians learned to make use of the considerable tidal variation of the rivers as a source of hydraulic energy for the sugar mills, by taking in water as the tide was rising, and during ebb tide letting the water recede from the canals to the river through a water wheel powering the sugar mill.

The innovation of the polder system spread fast in the Dutch Guianas for all types of plantations, whether producing sugar, coffee, or cotton. The adoption of a water-powered sugar mill was costly, but crucial for a plantation's chances for survival. In the mid-eighteenth century, animal traction was still more prevalent than hydraulic energy, but by the 1770s water mills were dominant and would remain so until the adoption of the steam mill in the nineteenth century.[6] The productivity of the Surinamese polder plantations was rising and spectacular indeed, well above regional averages into the nineteenth century. In his 1774 classic, *Histoire philosophique et politique,* Abbé Raynal praised the Dutch for "having domesticated the ocean in the New World just as they did in the Old World." In the later eighteenth century, the prospects of this unique technological complex were promising enough to attract increasing numbers of planters from the overexploited British West Indies to Essequibo and Demerara, thus setting the stage for the eventual British takeover of these colonies.[7]

Only after 1800 would the Dutch planters lose their vanguard position in Caribbean plantation production. Apart from their use of polder technology, they had been keen followers rather than initiators of innovations in sugar and coffee production.[8] As was the case elsewhere, the introduction of the steam engine caused a substantial increase of the average scale, capital input, and productivity of the Surinamese plantation, but, as the nineteenth century progressed, the colony could not keep up with the new Caribbean frontiers, particularly Cuba and, ironically, British Guiana, once colonized by the Dutch. As for the polder technology, its reach would remain limited to Suriname and British Guiana.

Crop selection reflected the adaptability of the planters and investors, even if a keen eye for maximum profits could, and did, end up in unduly risky investments—the rise and fall of coffee would ultimately produce a story of windfall profits.[9] While sugar dominated exports from the Dutch Guianas in the first half of the eighteenth and again in the nineteenth century, in between coffee was dominant, at least in Suriname. Cotton and timber were export crops of far less importance. The average plantation size increased across the board in much of the eighteenth century. The slave population of the average coffee plantation in Suriname oscillated roughly between 70 and 125 in the second half of the century, and between 100 and 150 on sugar plantations. Plantation growth in the same period in Berbice and particularly Demerara and Essequibo is less documented, but export figures indicate that in the 1770s and 1780s, coffee dominated, as against sugar both before and after.[10] In all, the Dutch Guianas were never among the largest producers of sugar and coffee in the Caribbean. Suriname was somewhere in the league of the smaller British and French West Indies, whereas Berbice, Demerara, and Essequibo jointly became a major sugar producer only in the nineteenth century, after the British takeover.

Labor on the plantations of the Dutch Guianas was primarily provided by enslaved Africans and their descendants. Amerindian slaves, who were still found in modest numbers on plantations in the late seventeenth century, were a rarity in early eighteenth-century Suriname and soon after also became exceptional on plantations in the lesser Guianas. Slaves spent a considerable part of their time providing for themselves rather than producing export crops. No matter how much plantation owners and directors might have preferred to have their bonded labor produce nothing but highly-prized tropical staples, there was simply no alternative. Every plantation inventory discloses that a considerable portion of the plantation grounds was planted under surveillance with provisions including plantains, yams, and cassava. Moreover, slaves had their own little plots where they cultivated a range of subsistence crops, "on their Sundays" and other moments not devoted to plantation routines. Fishing and hunting provided additional proteins.[11]

This was not all. Time and again, official placards detailing regulations for plantation management and the treatment of slaves stipulated that good care should be taken that the plantation slaves have sufficient food, as food was considered to be "the soul of the plantation."[12] According to the regulations imposed on the planters, this should include the distribution, at least twice a year, of imported items such as dried fish (particularly cod, but also herring) and salt. In addition, minimal amounts of imported clothing and utensils (fish hooks, knifes, and the like) were to be distributed each year. In other words, the enslaved populations of even the most isolated plantations, days of rowing upstream in the interior, were connected as consumers to European fishermen, artisans, and textile workers (such as the producers of Osnabrück linen), as well as to producers of salt, possibly slaves toiling elsewhere in the Atlantic.

The model of the export-driven slave plantation was by definition a prime mover of the entire early modern Atlantic and has been addressed extensively in the historiography of plantation America. We need not discuss here in much detail either the organization of the typical Guiana plantation and the specifics of planters' management or slaves' suffering and agency. It is relevant nonetheless to point to a few key questions. First, the cost of the polder technology to the enslaved population was high, as the labor input was extremely demanding. In addition to all the requirements of agrarian work in any plantation, there was the backbreaking work of delving and maintaining the infrastructure of dikes, canals, and trenches, work that even in contemporary Maroon oral traditions is mentioned as a reason for their forebears to escape the plantations. Moreover, the use of tidal energy to propel the sugar mill meant that most of the milling needed to be done when tidal difference was highest. In these days, demands on the enslaved were even higher than otherwise. Calculations of demographic performance of the various types of plantations disclose that, indeed, the toll exerted on slaves working on sugar estates was higher than on plantations producing coffee, cotton or timber.[13]

The combination of harsh ecological circumstances (climate, disease environment) and the heaviness of the labor demand on the polder plantations in turn made for a highly unfavorable demographic performance, with population loss in Suriname staggeringly high at around five percent per year during much of the eighteenth century.[14] Not only expanding a plantation's work force, but even keeping it at the same level therefore required a steady influx of enslaved Africans. This implied that demographic creolization proceeded at a low rate—which in turn aggravated the negative demographic growth, as first-generation immigrants experienced far higher mortality than Creoles (whether slave or free, and of whatever color) born in the Americas.

Plantation production in the Dutch Guianas was concentrated in Suriname, while the share of the lesser colonies only started to increase spectacularly in the last decades of the eighteenth century. Sugar dominated the value of exports from Suriname prior to 1750 and after the Napoleonic wars; in between, coffee exports were most important. Cotton export started in the 1760s but was never of much significance, while timber production was mainly for domestic use. With the crucial exception of subsistence production, all other production and exports were negligible.

Trade relations were far more complex than a simple bilateral colonial exchange. The Dutch Republic furnished capital for investment mainly in the plantation sector, as well as capital goods and a wide range of commodities for consumption either in Paramaribo or on the plantation. In exchange, the Dutch Guianas exported plantation produce to the Netherlands, mainly through Amsterdam but also through Rotterdam and Vlissingen. Trade with West Africa was mainly the one-directional commerce of enslaved Africans, procured all along the West African coast rather than primarily through Elmina. Indispensable in this commercial network was the cross-imperial trade with the British colonies—primarily British North America, but also the West Indies. Without these exchanges,

Suriname would not have expanded, and the lesser Guianas would not even have been developed in the first place. As it was, these cross-imperial networks not only made the initially mercantilist intentions of the WIC and the Berbice and Suriname Sociëteiten obsolete, but also added to the international character of Paramaribo.

Population Development

The populations in the Dutch Atlantic were predominantly African, and well into the nineteenth century population growth depended on massive imports from West Africa. When shipments into Curaçao—which mainly occurred for reexports anyway—dwindled after 1730, most of this trade was directed to Suriname. Ironically, the explosive growth of the lesser Guianas in the late eighteenth century was fuelled by imports of enslaved Africans managed by British traders with little or no formal link to the Dutch authorities.

Suriname's colonial population—excluding Amerindians and Maroons—increased from some 3,800 in 1684 via 40,000 in 1752 to 63,000 in 1774, later dropping to 53,000 in 1795 and 50,000 in 1813, mainly due to the African slave trade. As discussed in chapter 3, the embarkation zones of the Dutch trade in Western Africa were diverse and changed continuously, fuelling the ethnic diversity of the African and Creole slave community in the Guianas. Throughout the eighteenth century, the share of the enslaved population was well above 90 percent. The share of mixed-race Surinamers in the free population must have increased steadily, but in contrast to the insular Dutch Caribbean, we do not have specific figures to illustrate this in much detail.

While much the same can be said for the ethnic composition of the lesser Guianas, the major contrast is the late development of these colonies. The colonial population—again, excluding Amerindians and Maroons—of Berbice was some 4,000 around 1760 and 4,500 by 1780, but exploded to perhaps over 40,000 in the mid-1790s. Essequibo had fewer than 500 inhabitants, mainly enslaved Africans, prior to 1715 and some 2,700 by 1735. In the late 1760s, the colony, with its offshoot Demerara, counted just 10,000 souls, as against 24,000 in 1782 and 30,000 by 1796. Around the time of the British takeover in 1815, the number of slaves alone was put at 77,000—by then in absolute numbers well above Suriname, and surely also far more African in character than the slowly creolizing slave community of the older Dutch colony.[15]

As usual, the information stored in archival sources tells us far more about the European minority in these colonies. A first census in 1684 counted 652 whites in Suriname, 163 of these Jews. The free population was set at 2,000 around 1750, some 2,700 in the mid-1770s, nearly 5,000 in 1795, and over 6,000 in 1813. The numbers in the lesser Guianas were much smaller—probably not even 200 in the 1730s, some 500 in the 1760s, over 3,000 by the late 1790s, and surely more thereafter. Over time the share of free non-whites grew, and by 1811 free blacks and people of color outnumbered whites in Paramaribo in a ratio of three to two.[16]

This rise of the free non-white population was one of many unintended consequences of colonization. Against the odds—the combination of a heavily male European minority and the asymmetric power relations inherent to any slave society—colonial legislation persisted in forbidding "carnal conversation" between whites and blacks well into the eighteenth century. In contrast to Curaçao, placards in Suriname forbade interracial intercourse up to 1759, accepting its inevitability only in 1784, provided this would not cause disorders on the plantations. This caveat was important. Governor Mauricius had earlier attributed much of the "disorder among the slaves" to white "debaucheries" with the female slaves.

It stands to reason that the European segment was less stable in the Guianas than in Curaçao, with its longstanding Protestant and Portuguese Jewish communities totalling over 3,500 in the late eighteenth century. In this period of over 150 years, Suriname in particular must have attracted larger numbers of new European arrivals than Curaçao, as the expanding economy offered plenty of job opportunities. A particularly nasty disease environment, however, adversely affected first-generation European settlers.[17] In addition, and with the exception of the Jewish settlers, there was far more permanent return migration to Europe from the Guianas than from the insular Dutch Caribbean—Governor Mauricius complained in 1742 of the *animus revertendi* of the white population, eager to make money quickly and return to safer European shores. Possibilities to actually make a fortune in a short time diminished considerably in the later eighteenth century, so it is likely that both European immigration and remigration subsided.[18]

Around 1600, the earliest European colonists of the Guianas were mainly English, Dutch (mainly from Zeeland), and French—not counting the Spanish further to the West—and they settled all over the Guianas. By the 1670s this had changed. The colonies—or rather their coastal strips—had been divided between the French in Cayenne and the Dutch in the rest. Prior to the 1667 conquest by Zeeland, parts of the region around the Suriname River had been colonized by English planters from Barbados, as well as some Jewish planters who had dispersed across the Caribbean after the collapse of Dutch Brazil. The transition to Dutch rule entailed the departure of virtually all the English and an unknown number of the Jewish planters, even if Zeeland attempted to force the latter to remain with the argument that they were not British subjects but, rather, belonged to a separate nation.[19] Meanwhile new Jewish arrivals had settled, some via Amsterdam and others by way of a few short-lived Guiana colonies under Dutch rule.[20] The subsequent period witnessed more direct Jewish immigration from Amsterdam, initially only from the Portuguese community, but soon also of generally poorer Ashkenazim. Suriname would thus become the only colony in the early modern Americas with a considerable Ashkenazi community, and the only plantation colony where Jews had a considerable share in the planter class. While the Jewish population in Suriname increased from 232 in 1684 to 1,330 in 1791, its share in the European population decreased from 35 to 27 percent.[21]

The Christian European community was highly diverse. The largest contingent of immigrants originated in the republic, but these included recent immigrants exiled for religious reasons from France (Huguenots, Labadists). The colony received increasing numbers of German and Scandinavian settlers and, to a lesser extent, settlers from elsewhere, including the British Isles. Over time, exogamy and creolization mitigated the initial importance of national origins in the Christian population, leaving the Christian-Jewish divide as well as class distinctions as the two main defining lines within the white group.

Paramaribo, the colony's only port city, developed slowly. Initially most planters lived on their plantations, while the Jewish planters lived upstream from the Suriname River, where they founded their own village of Jodensavanne in the 1680s. As trade expanded and as absentee ownership increased, however, the capital expanded to nearly 12,000 inhabitants in the late eighteenth century, at the bottom of the top-20 port cities of Atlantic America, occupying more or less the same rank as Willem-stad.[22] The number of whites living on the hundreds of plantations in the interior was very limited, on average hardly ever more than two oversee-ing a slave community of anywhere between 75 and 150.

These Europeans were increasingly responsible for managing the plan-tations of absentee owners. Initially resident owners acted both as planters and merchants, but over time absenteeism grew. In the mid-eighteenth century, only a quarter of all plantations were in the hands of absentee owners, but this had risen to two-thirds in the 1790s. Trade patterns were increasingly dictated by metropolitan merchant houses, whose control over plantation loans entitled them to the consignment of provisions for the plantations and return cargoes of tropical produce.[23] Hence we see the emergence of a local class of merchants (*administrateurs*), overseeing all affairs of the plantations entrusted to overseers (*directeuren*) on behalf of both the absentee owners and the creditors in the metropolis.

As the eighteenth century progressed, not planters but rather their rep-resentatives came to form the elite of Suriname society. Some of these merchants were elites from the start, such as the director of the Sociëteit van Suriname, Mauricius, who alongside his official duties had a lucrative side job administering ten plantations. Others attained this status by their own efforts. The Protestant planter elite dominated the colonial councils from which Jews were excluded.[24] Their names reflect the amalgam that the gentile community had become: Dutch family names such as Van den Bergh, Blom, Gootenaar, De Graaff, and Steenbergen appear alongside French ones such as Rocheteau, Planteau, Saffin, and Taunay, or German ones such as Becker, Wolff, and Stockel.[25] The number of German settlers was especially large. A German sailor who regularly visited Suriname even made the exaggerated claim that it would be more appropriate to call Suri-name a German colony, since 99 percent of the white settlers had come from all parts of Germany to both Paramaribo and the plantations.[26]

While the spoils of the system surely benefited these Paramaribo-based merchants, decision-making was the exclusive preserve of their overseas superiors based in the republic. After the 1770s credit crisis, the metropol-itan merchant houses in Amsterdam and also in cities such as Rotterdam called the shots over and above the absentee owners of often hopelessly indebted plantations.[27] Planters and merchants alike were functioning in commercial networks that tied them both to the Dutch Republic, Africa, and the Americas. Differences between Christians and Jews were not of major relevance in this respect. Surely the Jewish community entertained intensive trade relations in the Americas. The prominent Jewish planter and merchant Samuel Nassi, son of David Nassi, a refugee from Dutch Brazil who may be considered one of the founding fathers of Suriname, was instrumental in the opening up of the trade network linking Suriname to British North America in the early eighteenth century.[28] The colonial authorities' reluctant permission to engage in this trade reflects not only their pragmatism but, equally, the necessity of dealing with Jewish merchants on a par with gentiles.

In contrast to the Curaçaoan *kleine vaart* in the Caribbean region, the ships sailing the inter-American routes were overwhelmingly North American, not owned by Surinamers. This trade therefore involved a steady stream of (British) American ships unloading and loading their cargo in the Suriname River off Paramaribo, but also the constant presence of North American merchants and above all sailors in Paramaribo, adding to what must have been a polyglot urban environment.[29]

There was a modest two-way migratory circuit between the Dutch Republic and Suriname. The annual average of passengers from the Netherlands to Suriname steadily increased from some 115 around 1730 to nearly 200 in the 1770s, while figures for the flow in the other direction were 60 and 135, respectively. Most travelers were whites, but non-whites—mainly slaves—accounted for some 15 percent of the sailings to the republic and ten percent on the way back.[30] The higher average of outward sailings from the republic reflects both mortality and permanent settlement in the colony. The larger proportion of non-whites on the outward voyage from Suriname can also be explained. Returning planters often brought some slaves with them, presumably both for household services and exotic display. Some of these servants did not return, because of death, because they were allowed to remain, or because they engineered their own stay—there was ambivalent legislation in the republic about the status of West Indian slaves once they landed in the republic, where slavery was not allowed.[31]

Individual travel between Suriname and destinations in the Caribbean or North America was much less frequent. This underlines the fact that, in spite of the diversity of trade relations, demographically the metropolis was still the prime spoke connecting the nodal point of Suriname to the outside world—with the obvious exception of the one-directional link to West Africa. Interestingly, the average of continental outward sailings from Suriname was consistently higher than the arrivals. This suggests that, given a choice, many passengers preferred to settle elsewhere, probably particularly in North America.[32]

With most metropolitan interest directed to Suriname, the neighboring plantation colonies of Berbice and Essequibo/Demerara developed slowly, the former primarily with input from Amsterdam, the latter from Zeeland. As discussed above, demographic growth was slow until the spectacular growth in the last decades of the eighteenth century. As in Suriname, the European segment of the population was always well below 10 percent, reflecting the colony's structure as a plantation economy. Prior to the boom period, this segment had consisted of the usual mix of transients and settlers from the Dutch Republic, German lands, and the Nordic countries. One remarkable contrast to Suriname was the near-absence of Jewish settlers. Much to the indignation of Jews in Amsterdam and Suriname, the lesser Dutch Guianas remained officially closed for Jewish immigrants. This regulation was not completely enforced—an 1818 list of plantation owners mentions a few Portuguese Jewish planters with roots in Amsterdam—but their number was certainly small in comparison to Suriname.[33]

The other difference between the lesser Guianas and Suriname was the steady increase in the proportion of British citizens in the European population after 1760, predominantly originating in Barbados. The growth of this community was the direct result of the policy of the Essequibo director Laurens Storm van 's Gravesande, who invited planters and investors from the "depleted" British West Indies to continue their plantation business in the fertile grounds of the Guianas.[34] In their wake, merchants and ship captains from British America followed. Storm's policy of "development by invitation," combined with British metropolitan support, ended up loosening the ties with the Dutch Republic and caused a gradual insertion of these colonies in the anglophone Atlantic. At the time of the British occupation in 1795, British subjects were a sizeable minority among the Europeans. By the time of the definitive transition to British rule twenty years later, they formed the majority.[35]

As in Suriname, the proportion of the free non-white population in the lesser Dutch Guianas was low, between 5 and 10 percent in the

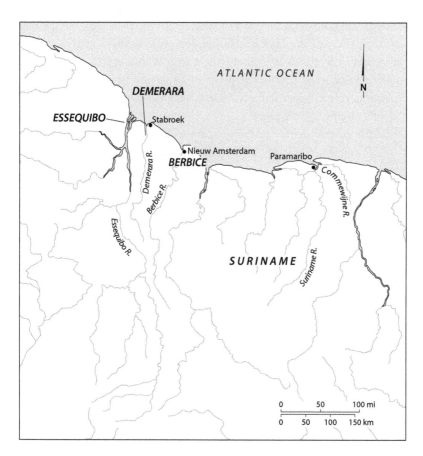

Figure 11. Map of the Dutch Guianas.

1780s and 1790s. There are no indications of significant participation of this group in trade networks. Curaçao remains the one Dutch Atlantic exception to the rule that maritime trade was a white privilege.

Regimes of Slavery

Scholarly work on slavery in the Americas has resulted in an increasing appreciation of the great variety in time and space of the conditions under which the enslaved were made to work and live, and of the considerable differences in opportunities and constraints for the enslaved to shape their own lives. From the Dutch Atlantic perspective, these approaches tie in with a very old debate about the nature of slavery in Curaçao versus Suriname—the traditional point of departure being that slavery in Suriname was of a particularly "harsh" character, as against a relatively "mild" variant in Curaçao.

Much of this debate is unfortunate as the use of concepts such as "mild" might erroneously suggest that there were benevolent types of slavery. All slavery involves a policy of dehumanization and exploitation, and by definition there cannot be anything "mild" about it. But that being said, some comparative conclusions may be suggested, relevant not only to Curaçao and Suriname, but also for the understanding of regimes of slavery in the entire Dutch Atlantic.

As for the drive to engage in the Atlantic slave trade and to exploit enslaved Africans in the Americas, there is nothing exceptional about the Dutch dimension in this central feature of early Atlantic history. The basic understanding was that the expected economic benefits of the system sufficed as a motive to participate in the system—opposition was weak and did not have any impact in Dutch politics or society. The eventual abolition of the slave trade was imposed by the British during the Napoleonic Wars, and slave emancipation would not occur until 1863—and even then followed by an apprenticeship period up to 1873 in Suriname. The Dutch participation in the slave trade peaked early, making up 5 percent of the slave trade overall and almost 6 percent in the period up to 1800.[36] The low and declining share of the Dutch reflected their loss of geopolitical and commercial clout, not concerns of a humanitarian or economic nature. The late-eighteenth-century British and North American deviance from the European-Atlantic consensus that slave-trading and slavery were acceptable was not taken up by the metropolitan Dutch at all.[37]

Regimes of slavery within the Dutch Atlantic varied considerably. Local conditions were decisive and there was no encompassing metropolitan legislation trying to impose some sort of generalized "Dutch" regime of slavery. Local political and juridical councils were decisive for the establishment of regulations regarding the treatment of slaves, as well for the observance of these regulations. Such councils were presided over by a metropolitan governor, but otherwise dominated by local slave owners, with obvious implications for the priorities set. Regulations for "moderate" treatment and against the deployment of "excessive" violence were frequently proclaimed, departing from the maxim that a "not too harsh nor too soft" handling of the slaves resulted in optimal productivity and minimal resistance.[38] The fact that such legislation and control over its observation was not a metropolitan affair must have helped to keep slavery in the overseas colonies at the margins of public awareness in the Dutch Republic. The occasional metropolitan minister protesting the excesses of slavery or well-trained lawyer trying to see to impartial juridical procedures to deal with both slaves and free non-whites invariably found out that the governing local elites did not welcome such niceties.[39]

The quality of life of slaves in the Dutch Atlantic depended more on specific local conditions than on legislation. Again, "quality of life" is a difficult concept—one may well argue that under slavery quality of life was by definition poor or horrible. Even so, there were considerable differences. Such variants seem to have been related most of all to ecological conditions and hence the type of labor imposed. The best indicator is demographic development, though it is impossible to differentiate between natural conditions and particularly disease environment on the one hand, and the labor regime imposed on the other. Having said that, the few detailed demographic studies available do indicate that the demographic toll paid by the slaves on Guiana plantations was much higher than in the Antilles. This was in part the result of earlier creolization on the islands, which caused further improvement of demographic performance, as survival rates were much better for Creole slaves—and whites for that matter—than for first-generation immigrants.[40] That the type of labor demanded of slaves mattered as well seems evident, also from comparative work in other parts of the Americas. For Suriname, this has been substantiated in case studies indicating that, overall, slaves working on coffee plantations in Suriname had better demographic prospects than slaves on sugar plantations, where labor demand was even higher.[41]

Demographic performance is obviously a very crude proxy for "quality of life," and moreover in itself a puzzling one. Food consumption, for example, could be considered a high-impact factor for demographic performance. Most sources would indicate that slaves in the Guianas had better access to food and a more diverse diet than their peers on the Dutch islands. There are indeed more references to hunger and even famines, mainly because of droughts, in reports on Curaçao. Yet the overall demographic development on Curaçao was not as bad as in the Guianas. It seems likely that the horrific demographic toll exerted by the Guiana plantation regime added to slave resistance, as in the Berbice revolt of 1763 and the remarkably high levels of marronage in Suriname.

Harsh discipline and punishment were part and parcel of slave regimes throughout the Atlantic, and this was not any different in the Dutch Atlantic, nor was there much variance from one colony to the other. There is clear evidence of slave resistance in all Dutch colonies, and revolts as well as marronage were punished in horrible ways wherever. Surely there was no "mildness" in retributions meted out to ringleaders of slave revolts or maroon groups anywhere. Anything in this sphere of repression and punishment heavily affected the quality of life for all slaves, as the specter of arbitrarily deployed violence must have been an everyday concern for all. This constant awareness of danger, rather than its direct demographic consequence, must have been the key impact of colonial violence in the Dutch Atlantic world—whether on board the slave vessels on the Middle Passage, on the plantations, or in urban settings.

Another important dimension of slavery regimes is the opportunity of exiting the system by legal means, hence through manumission. The frequency was low in the Guianas, in contrast to Curaçao. In the Guianas, the numerical imbalance between black and white remained enormous, and the number of mixed relations and children born out of such relations was low—and their manumission was anything but evident. Gender divisions within the rural slave population were not unlike those seen anywhere in plantation America. The majority of men and women worked as field slaves. A male elite was employed for skilled trades, while privileged female labor was mainly in the services. Such privileges within the framework of slavery could be maintained for generations.[42] The numbers of free non-whites remained negligible on plantations. Anecdotal evidence suggests that urban domestic service was the domain of both enslaved and manumitted women, with hardly any competition from whites.

Obviously, there were also illegal ways to escape from slavery. With the exception of the Haitian Revolution, slave revolts never ended up freeing an entire slave population, even if they did provide individuals opportunities to turn their backs on their slave masters. Both in the Guianas and in Curaçao, marronage did provide a significant avenue for escape. Suriname provided the best and most widely used opportunities in this respect and

stands out as exceptional because the major route out of slavery was marronage rather than manumission.

Last but certainly not least, cultural autonomy is a significant dimension in assessing the features of a particular slave regime. Again, there
were major contrasts within the Dutch Atlantic. Demographics were far
more important than colonial policies, which were hardly relevant for
cultural issues in the first place. The larger the European proportion and
the more intense the contact between white and black, free and slave, the
more one would expect cultural exchange to be two-directional, but also
the space for cultural autonomy for the enslaved population to be limited.
In this sense, it is only logical that the slaves' cultural autonomy was far
greater in the Guianas than in urban Curaçao or St. Eustatius.

The extreme demographic and ethnic imbalance of the Guiana populations meant that the cultural development of the slave majority—not to
mention that of the various emerging Maroon communities—took shape
in a world to which whites had little access. The resulting cultural autonomy produced highly idiosyncratic Afro-Caribbean cultures, more so than
in the Antilles, where the economic and hence demographic and ethnic
development took a significantly different turn.

By the late eighteenth century the international reputation of slavery
in Suriname had become remarkably bad even by comparative standards.
Much of this reputation owed to visitors' devastating criticism based
on first-hand observations of gruesome mutilations and punishments of
slaves and Maroons. John Gabriel Stedman's famous 1796 *Narrative, of
a Five Years' Expedition, against the Revolted Negroes of Surinam* is the
best known indictment, but there were others as well. The case of Stedman's *Narrative*, and the quick succession of subsequent translations of
his travelogue, also indicate how both news and reputations circulated
quickly throughout the Atlantic world. Framing news for specific political
or personal motives ("spinning") was part of that process. This may have
been of an individual nature, such as Voltaire in his *Candide* denounc-
ing slavery in Suriname rather than in, say, St. Domingue, partly or perhaps mainly out of frustration with his Dutch publisher. It may also have
been of a more political nature. Thus it served British entrepreneurs quite
well to denounce Suriname slavery as extremely oppressive and cruel at
the very moment when the British themselves were taking over the lesser
Dutch Guianas to convert these into a new frontier of plantations and

The Execution of Breaking on the Rack.

Figure 12. Gruesome images of slavery in Suriname: "The Execution of Breaking on the Rack." Engraving by William Blake, reproduced from Stedman, *Narrative*, 1796.

hence slavery—arguably of a "milder" nature than the exceptionally cruel Dutch variant.[43] But at the end of the day, the bad reputation of slavery in the Dutch Guianas was probably well deserved—not necessarily worse than in Caribbean colonies such as Jamaica, St. Domingue, or Cuba, but surely not better at all.

Amerindian and Slave Revolts

In contrast to their counterparts in the Antilles, European settlers in the Guianas had to reckon with the resistance of indigenous peoples. Though their numbers were modest and their share in the total population soon dwindled as more and more enslaved Africans arrived, their pacification was crucial for the establishment and consolidation of a viable plantation colony. Early settlers sought to deal with Amerindians of various ethnicities, of which Caribs and Arowaks were the most important. There was some commercial exchange, but its importance diminished quickly, and ultimately the Europeans just wanted the indigenous people not to interfere in their project of setting up a plantation colony. In the first phase of plantation development, planters and colonial authorities alike did recruit Amerindians as allies in their efforts to curb marronage. To avoid conflicts, it was decided early on in Suriname that Amerindians were not to be enslaved for plantation labor, and by the early eighteenth century Amerindian slaves were a rarity on plantations. Colonial policy towards the indigenous communities was based on a divide and rule strategy that generally functioned quite well. Only once, in the early history of Suriname, did Amerindian resistance jeopardize the survival of the colony. The "Indian Wars" of the late 1670s proved to be the decisive moment in their pacification.[44] Thereafter, there were no more significant confrontations with the various Amerindian communities, who were increasingly outnumbered by the ever-growing population of the plantation colony and remained largely at the margins of this new colonial world, sporadic commercial transactions notwithstanding.

In the lesser Guianas, Amerindians remained a force to be reckoned with. There was constant bickering and manipulation back and forth. The nomadic Amerindian communities did not heed the nebulous colonial borders drawn over the interior of the Guianas, easily "trespassing" from Portuguese to French, Dutch, English, and Spanish territory and back. The Amerindian presence in the lesser Dutch Guianas was probably more significant than in Suriname with its expanding plantation zone and Maroon communities. As the development of the plantation economy finally accelerated, colonial authorities and planters in Berbice, Demerara, and Essequibo needed to coopt the Amerindians—in particular "my good friends the Caribs," as Essequibo's governor Laurens Storm van 's Gravesande wrote in 1772. Colonial archives indicate that this was quite successfully achieved by a mixture of commercial trade-offs, presents, and divide-and-rule strategies. Amerindian support became crucial for colonial control in the suppression of African slave revolts and in preventing the emergence of Maroon communities as had already been the case in Suriname.[45] Nor did their leverage diminish over time. The occupation of Demerara and Essequibo during the Fourth Anglo-Dutch War by first British and then French forces only strengthened the native negotiating position when the Dutch tried to reestablish their authority.[46]

As the well-worn cliché has it, wherever there is slavery, there is also slave resistance, and this resistance ranged from cultural expressions to outright armed struggle. Dutch Atlantic history forms no exception to this rule. In the remainder of this section, we gloss over the many forms of everyday resistance ranging from malingering to all sorts of mild sabotage, and instead address the major slave revolts as well as marronage.

In addition to many smaller, localized slave revolts in the Dutch Atlantic, we know of three major slave revolts in the early modern history of the Dutch Atlantic, one in Curaçao (1795) and two in the Guianas. The 1763 slave revolt in Berbice took place during a period when the lesser Dutch Guianas were only beginning to expand along the model of Suriname. At the time of the revolt, the colony had no more than 350 Europeans and 3,800 slaves, probably the majority of these African-born. In February 1763, a group of slaves led by African-born men (judging by their names—Cuffy, Cosala, Accabre, Atta, Akara, and Goussari) revolted. The revolt quickly expanded to the entire plantation sector. In successive assaults and revolts on individual plantations, some forty whites were killed. The colony nearly collapsed, but ultimately, after over a year of guerrilla warfare, order was reestablished in July 1764. This had been possible because of the dispatch of soldiers from the Dutch Republic, Suriname, St. Eustatius, and even Barbados, but equally because Amerindians sided with the colonial troops. The revolt and its bloody suppression—including the execution of 140 rebels—cost a large number of mainly African lives. In 1765, the total number of slaves was estimated at only 2,500, hence 1,300 less than three years before. This dramatic decrease reflected both marronage and the human cost of warfare.[47]

During the entire period of guerrilla warfare, there was also a process of negotiations going on, and fragments of the rebels' messages have survived in copies of letters dictated by the insurgents' principal negotiator, Coffy, or Coffala. He was quoted as saying, "That the Christians were rude to them; and that they no longer wanted to endure Christians or Whites in their Country and that they wanted to rule Berbice." He also stated that "planters and directors are the cause of this war as they have severely mistreated the people and have treated them to floggings and whippings beyond tolerable limits." Another letter recorded Coffy and his companion Accara explaining the revolt in similar terms, putting the blame on "Masters that have not given the Slaves what they deserved." Not much later, Coffy wrote again, offering peace, but adding that if no peace would be signed, "they will fight until no Christian is left in Berbice." Proposing to split the colony in two, he emphasized that the people in his part of the colony would never be slaves again, while the governor could continue to have a plantation colony with enslaved Africans at his side. Post hoc interrogations of both leaders and followers of the revolt and of Amerindians help us to understand the complexity of the entire revolt. On the one hand, we see that the rebels managed to coopt Europeans deserting from the colonial army to their ranks. On the other hand, there were cases of reenslavement of slaves unwilling to join the rebels' war. They were simply forced to continue their slave labor, this time producing sugar, molasses, and alcoholic "kill-devil" for black masters.[48]

The Berbice revolt was the first major slave revolt in the lesser Guianas and probably the first ever in the Americas that nearly brought down European colonial rule and slavery—decades before the Haitian Revolution. Perhaps the timing of the revolt indicates an awareness of developments in Suriname. In 1760, just a few years before the start of the Berbice revolt, the colonial authorities in the adjacent colony had signed a peace agreement acknowledging the sovereignty of the Ndyuka Maroons, followed by a similar treaty with the Saamaka Maroons in 1762. This episode had started with the 1757–60 Tempati revolt, a crucial episode in the successive Maroon Wars in Suriname.

Marronage was an early feature of the colony's history, and soon became far more of a threat than slave revolts. As the plantation zone in Suriname expanded and plantations were laid out ever further from Paramaribo, a major concern of the few whites on the plantations was to protect their fragile status. Force alone did not suffice; plantation management required a more subtle approach that included finding a balance that would keep the enslaved from open resistance. In the process, as time progressed, the slave communities acquired more bargaining power—though resistance never subsided altogether. Short-term marronage was frequent and often condoned or only lightly punished as long as the escaped slaves returned by themselves within a few days. Permanent marronage was an altogether different issue, not only because this implied a serious loss of capital and planters thought of it as a bad example, but also because escaped slaves often returned to their former plantations to take revenge on the white managers, to spark a revolt, or to convince or force other slaves—particularly females, as the escapees were predominantly males— to join them in the interior. In this sense slave revolts and Maroon raids were two sides of the same coin.[49]

Marronage in Suriname started most likely already in the early English period, but accelerated after the assault of the French corsair Jacques Cassard in 1712. Hundreds of slaves took refuge in the interior and did not return once Cassard had left. In the subsequent decades, Maroon communities deep in the interior expanded through natural growth and the regular influx of new runaways. Four different communities were established, the Saamaka, the Ndyuka, the Aluku or Boni, and the Kwinti, by 1750 totaling some 3,000 Maroons as against roughly 38,000 slaves and only 2,000 free inhabitants, non-whites included. The growth of the Maroon population worried the colonial authorities enormously, and there was talk about pacification through peace treaties modeled after the 1738 Jamaican example—another clear indication of the interconnectedness of the Atlantic beyond the domain of trade.

While hardliners in Suriname had long prevailed, those in favor of peace treaties gained the upper hand after the revolt in the Tempati region in 1757. For three years, revolting slaves disrupted the plantation regime in this part of the colony, and eventually these "Tempati Negroes" joined forces with the Ndyuka Maroons. This combination was deemed very risky and convinced many who had previously opposed a treaty that there was no longer an alternative. Negotiations were initiated, and resulted in a peace treaty in 1760. This document basically acknowledged the autonomy of the Ndyuka as long as they remained in the interior. Two years later, virtually the same treaty was signed with the Saamaka and in 1767 also with the Matawai, an offshoot from the Saamaka. All peace treaties included the stipulation that the "pacified Maroons" would no longer harass the plantation economy and would return new runaways to the authorities—a particularly painful demand on the Maroons that was often sidestepped in the years and decades to come.

This left only the Kwinti and Aluku/Boni as potential enemies, and indeed in the 1770s the so-called Boni Wars erupted, later immortalized by the Dutch-Scottish soldier John Gabriel Stedman in his *Narrative*. His account, published two decades later, not only provides glimpses of the harshness of slavery and of the cold opportunism and sadistic whims of individual slave owners, but equally of the riches and the surprising diversity of Paramaribo society in its heyday. Stedman, moreover, describes in much detail the guerrilla war between Maroons and the often hopelessly ineffective colonial troops disoriented in the intimidating and deadly tropical rainforest. The *Narrative* also underlines the crucial importance of free black soldiers on the side of the colonial troops.[50]

Peace was signed in the 1770s, but war flared up again in the 1790s and the last round of Maroon wars would only be concluded in 1793, when the Aluku's chief Boni was killed by a leader of the Ndyuka and the Aluku moved to French Guiana. By then the Kwinti were also pacified. The various Maroon communities would expand in the interior in the decades to come, and *petit marronage* would remain a feature of slavery in Suriname—but the "pacified" Maroons no longer posed a threat to the colony's survival. Neither did slave revolts. Slave society survived into 1863 and was only abolished at this late stage by metropolitan legislation.

Although the plantation system in Demerara and Essequibo also produced runaways, no lasting maroon settlements seem to have been founded in these colonies. It was relatively easy for slaves in Essequibo to reach the Orinoco and from there make their way to Spanish towns. After 1750, they could count on sanctuary upon arrival. The large distance to the Orinoco made the voyage (by way of the ocean or the forests) from

Demerara much more hazardous, which may explain why absconding slaves there opted to become maroons. Regular Amerindian scouting parties, however, prevented their hideouts from becoming permanent.[51]

Slave Cultures

Just like interracial relations, the transfer and mixing of cultures was a phenomenon despised and feared by the Europeans, but equally impossible to curtail. A great variety of cultures went into the making of the various, deeply contrasting cultures of the Dutch Atlantic—particularly European inputs from different parts of the continent and an equally wide array of African influences. Amerindian contributions to creolization were less critical.

In contrast to the Iberian powers, and to a lesser extent France, the Dutch—like the British in their Caribbean colonies—had no interest whatsoever in Christianizing their captives, whether prior to their departure from Africa or after their arrival in the colonies. This had significant long-term consequences. Only a small minority of the enslaved Africans arriving in the Dutch Caribbean and Guianas colonies—specifically those baptized in Portuguese ports in Congo or Angola—had been exposed to Christianity prior to the middle passage. In Curaçao, the enslaved population was also confronted with Christianity through Catholic missionaries arriving from the Spanish Main. Not so in the Guianas, where the enslaved populations reconstructed a religious universe without significant Christian input. In Suriname, Christian missionaries were only allowed to propagate the gospel on the plantations beginning in the 1820s. In Berbice, Demerara, and Essequibo, Christianization was only started under British rule. As a consequence, for over two centuries the overwhelming majority of the enslaved population of the Guianas developed and practiced an Afro-American religion combining polytheistic and animistic features with scant Christian—or Jewish, for that matter—elements.

To European outsiders this religion represented nothing but primitive superstition, an additional justification to keep their slaves under the whip. Such denigrations may have been of little relevance to the practitioners of this creed, later summarized as *winti* in Suriname. The slaves' religion reflected their continuous confrontation with a tropical world dominated by the logic of the polder plantation—cults such as that of the *watramama* assumed particular importance. Deep in the interiors of Suriname, Maroon communities continued to develop their religions, which even there represented innovations rather than simply retentions of African religions. Reports from often desperate missionaries and studies of contemporary Afro-Surinamese religion alike indicate how the nominal conversion to Christianity in the last decades of slavery did not erase Afro-Surinamese religion, but rather caused the emergence of a religious continuum incorporating *winti* at one extreme, and "European" Christianity at another.[52]

For the enslaved rural populations and the Maroons, religious creolization mainly involved the adaptation of diverse West African traditions to new local circumstances. Conditions were different in the urban setting of Paramaribo. There was considerable room for religious diversity among the free population. This must have had some impact on the slaves working in and around European households as well, broadening the parameters of creolization to include a European dimension. The most conspicuous evidence of this is the emergence of a small Eurafrican Jewish community, children of Jewish men and African women who served in Jewish households. Religious influence is evident in wider Afro-Surinamese culture in conventions of impure food designated as *trefou* in Sranantongo, from the Hebrew word *tereefa* or the Yiddish *Treife*.[53] Conversely, Suriname's enslaved Africans helped shape the Jewish holiday of Purim, transforming it into an Afro-Caribbean festival, a local version of carnival.[54]

Language was a crucial domain of early creolization. While Dutch was the dominant and particularly the administrative language among the white settlers of Suriname, Portuguese (among the Sephardim), French, German, and English must have been spoken widely. But the colony's lingua franca, the indispensable vehicle for communication between the free minority and the massive slave majority, was Sranantongo, at the time known as "Negro-English," a Creole language with an African syntax and a predominantly English vocabulary. The first written evidence of Sranan is Aphra Behn's novel *Orinooko* (1688), which has a few words in the language, followed by more extensive passages in Herlein's *Beschryvinge van de volk-plantinge Zuriname* (1718). Subsequent sources reflect that the language was becoming entrenched. That this Dutch colony should have an English-, rather than Dutch-based Creole as its lingua franca speaks to its emergence and consolidation in the first years of colonization under English rule.[55]

Other languages were spoken as well in the Guianas, starting of course with the pre-European Amerindian languages. Individual Dutch traders learned at least bits of these languages in order to be able to trade with the indigenous populations, but in the end the latter had to acquire new languages if they wanted to communicate with the colonial world at all. Sranantongo rather than Dutch became this medium. By that time the Amerindian population had been forced to share its habitat in the tropical rain forest with several separate Maroon communities, each again developing its own Creole language. The differences between these Maroon Creoles again reflected the earliest histories of these communities. Saramaccan has a stronger Portuguese vocabulary, echoing the first generation's escape from plantations owned by Portuguese Jews and the emergence of the Creole "Dju-tongo" ("Jew-language"). The other Maroon languages are closer to Sranantongo, the dominant language at the plantations at the time the first generations escaped.[56]

If the emergence and dominance of all these various Creole languages indicate the crucial impact of speakers of African languages, it also raises the question of why Dutch was rather marginal, and why no Dutch Creole language emerged. The first question may be answered by reference to demographics, timing, and colonial policy. In the various Dutch colonies, the share of Dutch speakers was always small, even among the European segment; the dynamics of early settlement by non-Dutch speakers simply aborted the chances for Dutch-based Creole languages to emerge. As for colonial policy, the strictly businesslike WIC and other Dutch companies were not putting any cost or effort into spreading the Dutch language. At the same time, the use of Dutch as the only language of government—both in the meetings and minutes of the colonial councils and in placards and the like—as well as in the Dutch Reformed Church ensured that anyone with an ambition to become part of the colonial elite needed to have a proper command of Dutch anyway. On that level, Dutch was not marginal and would retain its position to the present.

As for the second question, three Dutch-based Creole languages actually *did* develop, all based on the Zeeland dialect of Dutch: "Negro-Dutch" in the Danish islands of St. Thomas and St. John, and two in the Guianas, "Berbice Dutch"—spoken *inter alia* by Coffy, leader of the

1763 slave revolt—and "Skepi" in Essequibo. The explanation for this phenomenon does not contradict the conclusion just advanced, as all of these languages reflected the early presence of settlers from Zeeland, prior to other Europeans. Remarkably, even these three Zeeland-based Creole languages were very dissimilar from one another.

Creolization was not limited to the realms of language and religion, but touched most facets of life, from agricultural practices and cuisine to the arts, from kinship arrangements to oral traditions, and so on. A more extensive discussion of this cultural history of the Dutch Atlantic falls beyond the scope of this book. Suffice it to state the obvious, that the roots of contemporary expressions of Dutch Atlantic culture such as the Antillean *tambú* and *tumba* music, the *ocho día* funeral practices, or Surinamese oral traditions such as *odos* and a wide array of ritual practices surrounding the cycle of life lay in the early modern period. The best evidence of a continuous process of cultural creolization may however be found among the Surinamese Maroons, whose oral traditions and artistic creativity demonstrate an unbroken linkage to their forebears' determination of making sense of, coping with, and ultimately also embellishing the grim new realities of life in the early modern Dutch Atlantic.[57]

Cultural creolization emerged from the interaction between generations of immigrants arriving in a new environment populated by indigenous populations as well as previous immigrants and their descendants. New arrivals—whether free or enslaved—were "seasoned" by earlier settlers to facilitate integration. Power asymmetries characterized the new setting, with race, legal status, gender, and increasingly also class as the most significant dimensions. But in addition to these factors, demographics played a crucial role, both in patterns of immigration and in the frequency of interethnic relations. These two dimensions were closely intertwined.

The demographic transition from a predominantly Old World to a New World population occurred only well into the nineteenth century in the Guianas, much later than in the insular Dutch Caribbean. Likewise, the share of white and mixed-race inhabitants was many times lower in the Guianas. These two factors combined explain why the creolized cultures of the Guianas were predominantly African-based, less mixed than in the Antilles where, to cite the most telling case, the Creole language Papiamentu became the native tongue of all inhabitants of the Leeward islands, irrespective of color.

We have exceedingly few first-hand accounts of how creolization actually came about. The "seasoning" of new arrivals was one crucial facet; education of locally born children was another. For Suriname we do have some descriptions as to how Creole slaves were allotted the task of socializing new arrivals from Africa. From the planter's perspective, the only thing that really mattered was that this socialization would secure optimal productivity, and this is what planters' manuals indeed conveyed. But a wide array of cultural and social matters was also transmitted from Creole slaves to newly arrived Africans. Much of this remained an enigma for the European population, a menacing one at that. Thus we see constant attempts at monitoring and curtailing music-making, singing, and dancing among the enslaved, as it was never clear whether such cultural expressions were simply entertainment or instead held deeper religious and social, possibly disruptive, meanings. While this *baljaren*—a neologism based on the Spanish *bailar*—was tolerated at specific occasions on individual plantations, there were always worries that the party could be dangerously subversive, and for that reason participation of slaves from other plantations was repeatedly forbidden.[58] "African" culture was a constant concern in the Guianas, where the world of the enslaved was far more isolated from the world inhabited by the European minority than in the Dutch Antilles. This contributed to the markedly bifurcated pattern of creolization in the Guianas among Africans and Creoles, with the latter embracing an urban variant with a more distinct European influence.

In the urban setting of Paramaribo, creolization involved more intensive transfers across race and class borders. A crucial figure in this process was the female servant, usually enslaved, who was entrusted the task of caring for the young white children. Through these nannies, European children learned the local Creole and many more things from the world of the slaves that would gradually become part of the entire social and cultural fabric of these societies.

The Free Population

The entire economy of the Guianas depended on the plantation sector, and the overwhelming majority of the colonial population lived on these plantations, all located along the rivers and only connected to one another and to urban settlements by boat. Most Europeans loathed and feared the fairly isolated life on these plantations, where in spite of official ordinances blacks outnumbered whites in ratios of fifty or even hundred to one. In Suriname, the alternative was Paramaribo. In the lesser Guianas, urban development was weak, with an early urban settlement in Essequibo (Fort Kyk-over-al), followed in 1764 by Nieuw Amsterdam in Berbice and Stabroek in Demerara in 1784. None of these places expanded beyond tiny administrative centers prior to 1800. Paramaribo in contrast continued to expand and became a multicultural city of some significance.

Governors and a few other senior officials were sent in from the Dutch Republic, while other officials were recruited locally from the European population (though not its Jewish segment). Most governors returned to the republic after their tenure ended. Who were the members of the colonial elites they encountered? In the Guianas, merchants or *administrateurs* and planters were on top of the social hierarchy. Dutch-Scottish soldier John Gabriel Stedman described the typical Suriname planter as a despotic and absolute "little king."[59] After the mid-eighteenth century, most plantation owners moved to the Dutch metropolis, leaving the supervision of their plantations to merchants, who emerged as the wealthiest and most powerful class in the colony. The *administrateur* would appoint a director to each plantation, usually a European immigrant but at times an impoverished planter or a planter's son.[60]

Bureaucratic and planter careers were not entirely separate tracks. More than a few planters had started out as officials in the service of the Sociëteit of Berbice or Suriname, afterwards becoming director for absentee owners or obtaining the wherewithal to buy a plantation, often by contracting an advantageous marriage. The most successful ones moved further up to become administrators.

The defense of the colony against internal and external threats required armed forces—the eternal complaint was that there were not enough military men around. Most of these were poor immigrants, many born in the Holy Roman Empire. As they were hired specifically for this service, and often did not linger if they survived at all, these soldiers were poorly integrated into urban life. There were recurrent tensions with resident civilians, and soldiers could be punished harshly. These poor whites also faced hardship of another kind, battling endemic tropical diseases. Because mortality was extremely high, the garrison was perpetually understaffed.

In times of military crisis, additional recruits had to be supplied from Europe, which usually took long as the interested parties disagreed over who was going to foot the bill. Apart from an artillery unit of 170 men, 900 soldiers were garrisoned in Paramaribo and the interior in the first quarter of the eighteenth century, a number that rose to 1,200 in 1772. The following year, another 1,200 soldiers disembarked to fight the Boni Maroons.[61] The garrisons in the lesser Guianas were much smaller and hopelessly inadequate. In 1785, Governor Lespinasse of Essequibo wrote that "our fortresses are useless & and even if they were of use, we don't have the men to defend them nor gunpowder to give them." Five years later, his successor, Von Meyerhelm, dryly confirmed that there was no gunpowder whatsoever.[62]

European soldiers who survived the transatlantic voyage, the seasoning period, and finally the years for which they were contracted could choose to remain in the colony, and a significant number of sailors did so. In the Guianas, such men could choose to work on a plantation as a *blankofficier* (assistant to the director). Many lasted only short periods in this position, but there are also examples of poor whites who worked their way up to become plantation directors.[63]

As in all American colonies, European artisans added to the social landscape. A German settler in Suriname listed the colony's various artisanal pursuits. They included apothecaries, gold- and silversmiths, clockmakers, wigmakers, barbers, painters, woodturners, cabinetmakers, book printers, book binders, glaziers, coach builders, boxmakers, saddlers, carpenters, butchers, masons, millers, coopers, shoemakers, tailors, and knife grinders.[64] As impressive as this list may appear, artisans were often in short supply, both in Suriname and elsewhere. By 1762, Paramaribo was home to only two tailors, two bakers, two butchers, two carpenters, one mason, and one smith, too few therefore for an expanding urban population.[65] Only by century's end had free people of color filled this niche in Paramaribo, much later than in Willemstad, where slaves and particularly free people of color were active in numerous artisanal pursuits as early as the 1710s.[66] The growth of this group accelerated after the economic crisis of the 1770s, which set off substantial white emigration out of Suriname. Free males of color then began to fill positions that had traditionally been occupied by the white population, and soon most blacksmiths, carpenters, tailors, and shoemakers were men of African birth or descent.[67] The labor market in the thriving port city of Paramaribo was increasingly variegated anyway, with foreign sailors, local poor whites, and free blacks performing all kinds of chores alongside slaves.[68]

While European immigrants were predominantly male, there was more of a gender balance among the white settler population. The public role of women from this small group is poorly represented in the archives, which reflects the entirely male-dominated domains of governance and defense and the almost equally gendered domain of trade and production. In these records, white women therefore figure mainly as spouses, daughters and possible marriage partners—not infrequently as very attractive partners, widows of wealthy planters. Oral traditions and travel accounts represent European women in more active and at the same time less innocent modalities, as in stories about cruel female slave owners cutting of the breasts of their husband's favorite female slave or drowning enslaved babies for making too much noise. Travel accounts such as Stedman's *Narrative* offer a wider range of testimonies of white women administrating their own plantations from their luxurious urban households in Paramaribo.

Imports of food supplemented local production, particularly for the urban population. The well-to-do made sure a wide range of often luxurious consumables were shipped in from the Dutch Republic and North America, but the lower echelons depended on imports as well. Soldiers and officials were utterly dependent on these supplies and therefore in dire straits whenever a ship was delayed or failed to arrive at all.[69] Surely there was white poverty, though this was held in check by denominational poor relief.[70] A French voyager noted that one did not see in Suriname the same crowds of poor people as in "our European cities."[71]

To some arriving settlers, the colony must have represented a frightening new world. The hardships experienced by migrants of the Labadist sect, which moved to Suriname in 1684, were typical. The dense forest, the swampy ground, their ignorance of local plants, the ubiquitous mosquitoes, ants, and snakes, the hostility of the Indians, and, finally, disease and death, made life short or miserable at best.[72] New settlers continued to risk their lives by settling in the Guianas. Epidemics of smallpox, yellow fever, and the like struck with frightening frequency.[73] As everywhere else in the Americas, and indeed the tropics per se, native-born whites and nonwhites alike fared much better than immigrants, but even in the long-standing Portuguese Jewish community epidemics continued to exert a heavy toll.[74]

The high levels of alcohol consumption were notorious. Sundays in Suriname, as an ordinance from the same year reveals, saw residents sailing with boats and ferries, while the liquor flowed abundantly and inebriation was the norm.[75] Impressive alcohol consumption was a fact of life. A plantation director once remarked that the local custom was to "measure life by the wineglass rather than the hourglass." European visitors invariably described lavish meals consumed with astonishing quantities of spirits.[76] Excessive drinking was a serious problem among artisans and officials employed by the Sociëteit van Berbice, and among overseers, estate managers, and bookkeepers in Demerara.[77] Not surprisingly, complaints about misbehavior of planters—sexual abuse, harsh punishment—were frequently connected to intemperate consumption of alcohol.[78]

Tobacco smoking was equally common, and less conducive to social problems. White men—as well as blacks of both sexes—all over the Dutch Atlantic could be seen after a day's work sitting in front of their house and smoking pipe tobacco.[79] In Stabroek around 1800, an English visitor wrote, "[I]t is a rarity . . . to meet a person in the streets at evening without his pipe or segar, and it is always considered a mark of attention, when two people meet smoaking, to discharge a mouthful of smoak at each other."[80]

Much of this smoking and drinking was done in a range of bar and taverns which might also serve as semi-brothels and which attracted an international set of predominantly male sailors and local whites and free blacks. For the higher echelons of the urban population, other more "refined amusements," as Stedman called them, included dancing, horseback riding, and card playing. Besides, he added, in Suriname "they have erected a small theater of late, where the genteelest inhabitants act tragedies and comedies for their amusement and that of their friends." This theater, the "Hollandsche Schouwburg," was opened in 1775 in the first period of cultural fervor in the colony. Concerts of European music were given both in private parties of the rich and in the governors' residence and, later, such theaters. In Paramaribo Christians and Jews alike, sometimes together, sometimes separately, developed a Europe-derived cultural life in the later eighteenth century.[81]

Throughout the Americas whiteness was a condition to become part of the local elite, and Suriname was no exception to this rule. But as the number of free people of (partly) African origins grew, they forged their own, gradually more noteworthy place in the economic and social life of Suriname. Commensurate with the preponderance of males in the white population, many whites sought free women of color as concubines, a phenomenon that became socially accepted as the *Surinaams huwelijk*, marriage Suriname-style. But there are also incidental cases such as that of the wealthy black plantation owner and merchant Elisabeth Samson, who in the 1760s chose her own white companion and, in defiance of the local elite, entered into a legal marriage with him.[82] Most free women of color were less well-off and worked as seamstresses or housekeepers, while free black women were employed as laundresses and market vendors.[83]

Status and regular pay must have attracted free blacks and people of color to join the military in Suriname, where they stood guard and went on patrol in Paramaribo and its surroundings. Although individual free blacks had served in the colonial militia throughout the century, not until 1775 did the government set up separate companies of "mulattoes and negroes."[84] Their role in the government's wars with Maroons was negligible, unlike that of the Corps of Black Rangers, established three years earlier and made up of slaves bought from planters lured with promises of manumission. Their contribution to the Dutch victory over the Boni Maroons was decisive.

Whereas religious life among the vast majority of the population was characterized by creolized forms of African religion, the European population held onto either the Christian or Jewish creed. Free non-whites hovered in between—some sort of integration in white-dominated urban society required an adoption of European standards. As European immigrants retained their home religion, most Dutch immigrants belonged to the Dutch Reformed Church, which retained its privileged position in the colonies as it did in the metropolis.

Immigrants from other parts of Europe brought their own variants of Protestantism. Huguenots from France were among the early immigrants in Suriname in the later seventeenth century and they were apparently welcomed. As elsewhere in the Dutch and even more so British colonies, these immigrants were supposed to support metropolitan geopolitics rather than to build an ethnic enclave. In the Dutch Guianas, too, Huguenots would ultimately blend in with the local white population rather than preserving their distinct French Protestant culture—business, shared interest, and intermarriage were the key.[85]

Many of the soldiers arriving in the Guianas were Lutherans hailing from Germany and Scandinavia. Their strand of Protestantism was initially banned throughout the Dutch Atlantic. Only in 1742 was the first Lutheran minister allowed to arrive in Suriname. The acceptance of his work inspired a plea from sixty Lutherans in Berbice for a congregation of their own. This was granted by the Sociëteit van Berbice in 1744. Decades later, the Lutheran Church was still nominally present, but in dire straits because of lack of preacher and means.[86]

The German Moravians, too, encountered considerable opposition. Maintaining close contacts with coreligionists both in Herrnhut, Germany, and in Bethlehem, Pennsylvania, Moravians settled in Suriname in 1735 and in Berbice five years later.[87] They saw it as their primary task to administer to blacks and Indians, not to whites. The Moravian settlement of Pilgerhut in Berbice started well, but an epidemic killed almost half of its members in 1760 and the settlement was destroyed by rebelling slaves three years later.[88] Suriname's Moravians were initially condemned by the Reformed Church council and scorned by Huguenot and Lutheran clergymen alike, who equated their communal living with "whoredom."[89] The Moravians took up missionizing in the interior Guianas, with little result; in Suriname, their real success would have to wait until the 1820s and beyond, when they were admitted to spread the gospel on the slave plantations.

Catholicism was condoned in the Dutch Republic, but it took a long time before the immigration of Catholics into the colonies was tolerated. Apart from their belief that Catholic settlers aided and abetted the enemy, the Protestant elites outside of Curaçao also adhered to the notion that the introduction of Catholicism among the black population could spark slave revolts. Only in 1785 did Suriname's governor and council honor a request from Amsterdam Catholics to tolerate their religion in the colonies, "considering that tolerance is gaining steady ground among civilized peoples." In spite of concerns among the Sociëteit van Suriname's directors, the governor and council also consented that free blacks and coloreds might adopt Catholicism. It stipulated, however, that no slaves were to adopt Catholicism, to prevent slaves from engaging in disturbances under cover of religious services.[90] Together with the Moravians, Catholic missionaries would be responsible for the Christianization of the enslaved populations of Suriname during the post-1815 amelioration. By then, colonial authorities and planters alike accepted and indeed stimulated Christianization, as part of a package deal entailing both pacification and socialization in a "proper" family and work ethic.[91]

The only non-Christian population group that enjoyed considerable religious freedom throughout Dutch America was a sizable one: the Jews. As mentioned above, Jews formed an important part of the European population of the Guianas, and indeed elsewhere in the Dutch colonies.[92] This reflected not only the relative tolerant climate for Jews in the Dutch Republic, where in Amsterdam alone the number of Portuguese Jews increased from 350 in 1610 to 2,230 in 1675 and some 2,800 by 1750, the number of Ashkenazim from 60 in 1630 to 1,830 in 1675 and perhaps as much as 20,000 in 1750; but also the immediate consequences of the loss of Dutch Brazil.[93] Well aware that the Portuguese authorities would reintroduce the prosecution of Jews, the entire community of many hundreds left the colony for either the Dutch Republic, Livorno, or the Dutch, English, and initially also the French Caribbean. French policies would soon disallow the creation of Jewish communities in the French Caribbean, although isolated New Christian[94] or even openly Jewish merchants might be tolerated half-heartedly because of their commercial value to the colonies. Jewish settlers were admitted on a wider scale in the English colonies, but the proportion of this segment in the overall European population remained low.[95]

Of all Jewish migrants leaving the Dutch Republic for the Americas, most opted for Suriname. This certainly applies to the second half of the eighteenth century, when migration was often imposed on poor Jews by their own community in the Dutch Republic. Of these so-called *despachados*, most were sent to Suriname, followed by Curaçao.[96] They added to a growing Jewish population soon making up one-third of the white populations both in Curaçao and Suriname. A similar presence in Essequibo, Demerara, and Berbice was thwarted time and again by the local councils. Notwithstanding support from the WIC, Jews as a group never obtained permission to settle here. As an argument, local officials invariably referred to the large-scale marronage in Suriname, which they ascribed to Jews' maltreatment of slaves.[97] Repeated requests from

Amsterdam Jews to admit Jews from Suriname as cultivators to Berbice were thwarted by the local authorities. In 1763, the latter seemed to give in, but the plan foundered when most of the thirteen prospective settlers turned out to be destitute. Only a few Jewish individuals received the right to settle in this colony.[98]

The contrast with Suriname is the more remarkable, since the rights they received there had first been codified in the privileges—"liberty of conscience" and respect for their religious practices, but no right to political representation—granted to Jewish settlers of Dutch Essequibo in 1657.[99] In Suriname, they created the world's largest Jewish agricultural community in the tropics, centered on the village of Jodensavanne.[100] The Jewish community consisted of both Portuguese Jews and Ashkenazim and stood out for its balanced sex ratio, in itself a result of creolization, and for its tendency to remain in the colony and not return to Europe within a few years.[101] Community leaders nurtured a vivid remembrance of their early history in the Dutch Atlantic and their escape from the Inquisition into the Dutch Atlantic world.[102]

The 1657 Dutch Essequibo privileges may have served as a blueprint for the privileges extended to the Jews of English and next Dutch Suriname, but these were not uncontested. Thus when the Jews, unlike the Protestants, failed to contribute to a new hospital in 1695, the Council of Policy threatened the leaders of the Jewish congregation that failure to comply would make the Jews lose their privileges. The parnassim instantly gave up the fight, took a collection, and wrote back that 25,905 pounds of sugar had been amassed.[103] Anti-Semitism was surely not absent, as the refusal to admit Jews to the recently built theater Hollandsche Schouwburg in 1775 demonstrates. Although Jews built their own theater in response, their community's regents lamented that the Jews preferred the affection of people around them to their privileges.[104]

Religious toleration among the free population in the Guianas did not do away with the fences between the various religious communities, but stimulated their members to interact with other groups. Examples of cases in which the gap between faiths was bridged abound, not just on an individual basis, but collectively. While the Lutherans and the Reformed had their own poor relief boards, the orphans and the poor of Catholic persuasion were placed with the boards of other religions for lack of one of their own. Moravian relations with Jews and Catholics were also known to be good, the leaders of the communities inviting each other to important events like a funeral or the inauguration of a church or synagogue. After initial tensions, Reformed laymen also warmed up to the Moravians, occasionally visiting their services.[105]

Throughout the Dutch colonial world, the Reformed Church could be expected to invest in the education of the Protestant youth, but realities were often different. The Sociëteit van Suriname prided itself in 1707 on the progress made with sixty to seventy boys and girls, aged nine to eleven, in reading, writing, mathematics, and Christian prayers.[106] In the long run however, the quality of education in Suriname left much to be desired. Former planters, soldiers whose term of service had expired, and foreigners who were barely able to speak Dutch were among those appointed as teachers in Paramaribo.[107] A first school for "mulattoes and negroes" was founded in 1760, but the number of students would remain low, as it did in all-white schools.[108] As late as 1791, David Nassy, born and raised in the colony as a faraway descendent of his seventeenth-century namesake mentioned above and himself surely a renowned intellectual, nevertheless maintained that the colony provided insufficient means to develop even mediocre qualities.[109] Things cannot possibly have been any better in the neighboring Guianas, where the first school on record was set up in Stabroek as late as 1800, under British rule.[110]

This observation might lead us then to the conclusion that the Dutch Guianas were not only crassly materialist and exploitative societies, but also stagnant colonies that were somehow inward-looking and contained within themselves. This was clearly not the case, economically or in a social and cultural sense. For the urban population and also for the whites on the plantations, the colonies' intensive commercial relations meant constant contacts with transient visitors from Europe, the West Indies, and North America, and as we will discuss later in this book, there was a surprisingly intense circulation of ideas alongside the constant flow of people and commodities. Much less documented, and mainly due to the constant new arrivals of "salt water negroes", new cohorts of enslaved Africans, the enslaved majority too continued to be connected with the wider Atlantic world.

Developed from the start as plantation colonies, the Dutch Guianas resembled the British and French sugar islands in many ways: the dependence on a constant supply of enslaved Africans, the brutal exploitive and racist system of slavery, the technological and managerial set-up of the plantation system, the export of the resulting tropical cash crops to the metropolis, the dependence on metropolitan credits, and the stark demographic imbalance between a tiny white minority and an overwhelmingly enslaved black majority.

But there were also considerable contrasts. Alongside and even above sugar, coffee was a major cash crop. Moreover, commercial relations were not restricted to a mercantilist framework, particularly because of trade relations with North America and post-1750 massive British investment in the lesser Guianas. The military defense of the colonies, not directly ruled by the Dutch state but rather by semi-public companies, was fragile. European migration was highly diverse, including significant contingents of Sephardic and Ashkenazi Jews alongside Germans, Scandinavians, and British.

Again in contrast to much of the insular Caribbean, there was an Amerindian population to be reckoned with. In the major Dutch colony of Suriname, this threat was neutralized early on, and the Amerindians were consequently relegated to the periphery of the colony. In the lesser Guianas, Amerindians continued to be significant in their own right, but also a party used by the colonial authorities to quell slave resistance. As elsewhere in the Americas, slavery implied slave resistance, and the Dutch Guianas witnessed a few major revolts, including the 1763 Berbice uprising. But the most conspicuous dimension of slave resistance was marronage and the early establishment of significant Maroon communities deep in the tropical rain forest of Suriname.

Slavery in the Dutch Guianas was brutal, but it also left some remarkable legacies, such as the Creole language of Sranantongo, its English vocabulary derived from the early English colonization of the colony. Creolization created a new cultural form out of various African cultures as well as inputs from the indigenous population and the various European segments of the population. Up to the early nineteenth century, such processes of creolization were exclusively African-based on the plantations where over ninety per cent of the colonial population was living, and included a diversity of European inputs in the urban environment of, particularly, Paramaribo with its multi-ethnic population.

5

THE INSULAR CARIBBEAN

Something remarkable transpired between the early Spanish disqualification of the Lesser Antilles, including those islands that would later become Dutch, as *"islas inútiles,"* and the 1770s, when Adam Smith, in his *Wealth of Nations*, admired the fact that the Dutch had made the "barren" islands of Curaçao and St. Eustatius into prosperous commercial hubs.[1] Surely it was not their scale—all Dutch islands were small even by Caribbean standards—nor their ecological habitat that had first attracted Dutch colonizers to any of these islands. Whereas the Guianas were depicted from the start as places of immense fertility and promise, the agrarian potential of the islands was rightly understood to be poor, at best suitable for subsistence farming. While no profitable agrarian export economy emerged, trade proved to be essential for the economies of Curaçao and St. Eustatius.

Commerce was not the first economic activity undertaken by the Dutch in St. Maarten, St. Eustatius, and Curaçao. Salt collecting was the rationale for the settlement of St. Maarten (1631), food production occupied the first non-military residents of Dutch Curaçao (1634), and tobacco cultivation lured the initial Dutch settlers of St. Eustatius (1636). Gradually, however, these islands came to revolve around trade. Agricultural pursuits were not completely sidelined, however. St. Eustatius was home to 76 plantations in 1775, St. Maarten boasted no fewer than 92 plantations by 1789, and Curaçao reportedly already had 111 plantations before 1700. The plantations, however, produced foodstuffs such as maize or raised cattle, and many ended up combining these two activities. Cash crop production failed on Curaçao, despite repeated attempts, but fared better in the other two colonies, especially St. Maarten, where 35 of the 92 plantations were sugar estates.[2]

Even in the best years, however, output was minor compared to the Dutch Guianas and foreign producers of sugar in the Caribbean. What did make the Dutch islands special, in particular Curaçao and St. Eustatius, was their function as regional entrepôts. Traders in Willemstad shipped the European manufactures they obtained from the Dutch Republic to the Spanish Main and other parts of the Spanish Caribbean, as well as to the French islands. Merchants in St. Eustatius—and on a much smaller scale those in St. Maarten—also made good use of their location by establishing commercial bridges to nearby British and French islands as well as to British North America. Apart from merchants involved in long-distance imports and exports, a large part of the free and enslaved population of these Dutch colonies were to some degree involved in trade. Commercial booms and busts therefore had a direct impact on local prosperity.

Demography and Mobility

Of the six Antillean islands, only Curaçao and, later, St. Eustatius had a substantial population—and their population densities were well above regional standards.[3] The only reliable census for Curaçao prior to 1800 dates from 1789. That year, the island had around 21,000 inhabitants, just over half of whom lived in Willemstad, which was the only genuine city in the insular Dutch Caribbean.[4] The proportion of slaves on Curacao was just over 60 percent, that of the Protestants 12, the Jews 5, and the free non-whites 18 percent. The prominent share of the European segment, compared to most other Caribbean islands, reflected the mercantile character of the island.[5]

The gentile European immigrants surviving and settling on the island gradually merged into the one segment categorized as "white Protestants." Marriage data relating to this group suggest that women formed a stable element in the Curaçaoan community. In the early eighteenth century, white brides tended to be natives of the island, whereas most bridegrooms were European-born. In the last two decades of the century, brides were still almost exclusively locally-born, but now Curaçaoan-born grooms outnumbered those from Europe by a 2:1 ratio.[6] The colonists' European origins were diverse. Of the 47 Protestant families settling on the island between 1634 and 1800 and still living there by 1950, 18 had Dutch origins, 12 German, and 5 French, with the remainder hailing from various countries.[7] While there were sharp class divisions within this group, exogamy and cultural creolization affected all whites and gradually diminished the importance of national origins within the white and Christian population. Protestants formed the great majority among the owners of agrarian mansions and farms, but Protestants and Jews alike participated heavily in all trades connecting the island to the wider Atlantic. Protestantism was also dominant among the soldiers stationed on the island, who were bracketed together with "the poor slaves" by one resident physician as "the most despised section of the colony's population."[8] There was a large amount of turnover among the soldiers because of their high mortality rate. 166 of the 700 soldiers arriving on Curaçao in the period 1702–44 died within a year, and 43 percent did not survive their contract period.[9] Many of them must have fallen victim to yellow fever or smallpox.[10]

Throughout the early modern period, the proportion of Jewish settlers was remarkably high in Curaçao, as in Suriname and, later, St. Eustatius. The Jewish community in Curaçao dates from 1650 and was largely Portuguese. Some of the earliest Jewish settlers came from the Guianas, other Caribbean islands, or Livorno, but the most important point of origin was the Portuguese-Jewish community in the republic, in particular Amsterdam.[11] The island's community expanded through both natural growth and continuous migration from the republic. On the other hand, in times of economic decline, Jews were among the emigrants in search of better opportunities in places such as Rhode Island (1693) and the free ports of St. Eustatius and St. Thomas.[12] The number of Jews seems to have increased to 1,500 by mid-century, half of the total white population.[13] Thereafter there was an absolute and relative decrease of the Jewish inhabitants as the census of 1789 counted 1,095 Jews, just under one-third of the total white population.

The role of Curaçao's Jews in retail trade was such that, according to one Christian inhabitant, no meat was sold on Saturdays.[14] But Jews were not only important in local retail trade. The Jewish mercantile community with its wide Atlantic network was crucial to the development of Curaçao both during the period of the *asiento* and during the subsequent ascent to the position of leading free trade center—by around 1790, Willemstad still ranked seventh among the port cities of the insular Caribbean, even if its heyday was over.[15] The Curaçaoan merchant community continued its intensive relations with trading partners, both Jewish and gentiles—legally within the Dutch and British Atlantic, and illicitly with French and Spanish partners. Jews had their own ships sailing in the *kleine vaart* in Caribbean waters, and to a lesser degree in the transatlantic *grote vaart*.

Not listed in the 1789 census—possibly because they were seen as transients—but certainly present on the island were some Catholic merchants who were instrumental in maintaining commercial links, particularly with the French Caribbean. Because of their religion, they had an ambiguous position in white Creole society, but otherwise they were apparently fully accepted in their commercial capacity. This again underlines the pragmatism prevalent in WIC circles in both the colony and the metropolis.

If the percentage of Curaçao's residents who were white was unusual by Caribbean standards, the relative size of its enslaved population was rather large for a New World society not based on cash crop production. The number of slaves has been estimated as hovering between 8,000 and 13,000 in the eighteenth century, and the only exact number available is that of 12,864 slaves in 1789, or 61.3 percent of the total population. In that same year, 321 enslaved Africans were counted on Bonaire and 78 on Aruba.[16] Africans arrived in large numbers on Curaçao during the heyday of the island's transit trade in slaves to the nearby Spanish colonies, which effectively ended by 1730. The subsequent population growth must have been due largely to natural increase.

Another conspicuous demographic feature of Curaçao was the early development of a considerable community of free people of African and

Figure 13. View of the island of Curaçao, 1800. Painting,
courtesy of Nationaal Archief, The Hague.

Eurafrican origins, which set the island apart from all other Dutch colonies. By the late eighteenth century, half of the island's free population was non-white. This community was indispensable to the emergence of the island as a commercial hub. While the majority may have worked in modest occupations ranging from shipmate to dock worker, there are numerous indications of free Curaçaoans of African or mixed descent, both men and women, owning ships or conducting extensive trade in the region.[17]

In sum, then, Curaçao's role as a commercial center in the region was the work of a heterogeneous population in which Dutch Protestants formed but one element. That both Protestant and Jewish merchants were involved in trade with the Dutch Republic has long been known, even if it remains to be seen whether there were really distinct gentile and Jewish trade networks. The fact that a much broader group participated in the regional trade indicates that "Dutch" agency in the wider Atlantic should be understood as a cross-cultural endeavor on all sides.

Unlike Curaçao, St. Eustatius experienced considerable demographic growth only a century after its colonization. While the total population stood at 785 in 1700 and 1,274 in 1715, it grew from 1,641 (1738) and 2,515 (1747) to 3,205 in 1779; an all-time high of 8,123 was reached in 1789.[18] Throughout this period, slaves made up between 60 and 75 percent of the population. In 1789, 63 percent of all residents of St. Eustatius were slaves, 29 percent whites, and 8 percent free non-whites. Some of the island's long-standing leading Protestant families in the later eighteenth century, such as the Heyliger, Doncker, de Graaff, and de Windt families, had Dutch origins and had been on the island for many generations. There was an early Jewish segment as well.[19] The growth spurt beginning in the 1730s was connected to developments in the British Atlantic. The proclamation of the Molasses Act in 1730 led to the settlement of agents acting for North American merchant firms in St. Eustatius, where they could minimize the effects of British mercantilism.[20] The island's white community also grew as some members of both Curaçao's and Suriname's Jewish communities moved there, intending to build the equivalent of Curaçao in the northern Caribbean, but their numbers remained modest.

In the late 1750s, of some 160 merchants, only 10 belonged to the long-established Dutch elite. The rest were more diverse, consisting of Dutch, French, and British migrants, either from the metropolis or from the colonies.[21] Over the next decades, the European merchant community was among the most cosmopolitan in the Americas, with Protestant Dutch settlers a minority group and English as the prevailing language. This vibrant community connected the island to the Dutch Republic and West Africa via the *grote vaart*, and even more intensely to British North America via trade and to surrounding islands, particularly the French Caribbean, via the *kleine vaart*. By the 1780s, the majority of recent immigrants were non-Dutch, with the greatest segments out of a very diverse community of European merchants being either British, British West Indian (particularly Bermudan), or from rebellious North America. Locally established merchants maintained intensive relations with a wide range of port cities. As a contemporary put it, the policy of "giving the greatest possible accommodation to all strangers, of whatever nation" had not only made St. Eustatius a "universal repository for the produce and manufactures of every quarter of the globe," but had also made its merchant community truly cosmopolitan, "as in great fair."[22]

The centrality of trade made for a different type of elite in the islands than in the Guianas. If planters and administrators were on top of the social hierarchy in the Guianas, merchants were held in the highest regard on Curaçao and St. Eustatius. On both islands, people from all walks of life were involved in commerce. Curaçao's governor Isaac Faesch wrote that a good part of the island's trade was conducted by less well-off people who bought a sloop on credit and could not afford to pay it off until the sloop's return. Investing all their fluid assets in a single voyage, such ship-owners were usually not men of substance, but rather part-time traders and sailors, who formed a significant part of Willemstad's population. These men supplemented their monthly wages by engaging in petty trade. They carried small amounts of merchandise on their Caribbean trading voyages, risking total loss in case of confiscation of these contraband commodities by foreign authorities.[23] An increasing number of those involved in Curacao's trade were people of African or mixed descent. In St. Eustatius, by contrast, where their share of the total free population was small (6.5 percent in 1790), there is no indication that non-whites acted as ship-owners and merchants.

Mobility in the Dutch Antilles was the highest among the enslaved Africans. Of course, the major factor in this mobility was their nearly immediate reexport upon arrival in the free ports of Curaçao and St. Eustatius to the surrounding Caribbean islands and the Spanish Main. After a brief stay on one of the two islands, these slaves were moved to other nations' colonies and, in a sense, disappeared from the Dutch Atlantic, mostly without leaving a trace. Much smaller numbers of Curaçaoan slaves left cultural traces in other parts of the region as they fled Curaçao's slave regime. Maritime marronage led to the formation of a free black community in the Coro region of the nearby Spanish mainland where Papiamentu was long spoken.[24] Likewise, both free and enslaved men from the island, some African and some Creole, some black and some of mixed origins, traveled as sailors on various Caribbean trade routes, and, inevitably, served as messengers as well. These sailors were instrumental in passing the news of the Haitian Revolution on to other colonies, their own included.[25]

Large numbers of slaves disappeared from Curaçao during the revolutionary decades. The island's total population shrank by one-third from some 21,000 in 1791 to 14,000 in 1816, and the number of slaves was halved from nearly 13,000 to just over 6,700.[26] Some of this decline reflected the migration of slave owners bringing their chattel to the northern Caribbean, particularly Danish St. Thomas. As late as 1830, a Dutch visitor to that island remarked that Papiamentu was widely spoken among the non-white population.[27]

Something of the same sort must have happened on St. Eustatius. Its development as a free trade port for the northern Atlantic had involved the immigration of merchants from Curaçao, who most likely took their personal slaves with them. The 1781 sack of St. Eustatius and its definitive decline by 1800 triggered two waves of emigration, with the adjacent competing free trade port of St. Thomas as the major destination. In the later eighteenth century, there were also free blacks born in Curaçao working as sailors out of St. Thomas. In 1803, out of 1,000 free people of color in the capital of Charlotte Amalie, 156 were born in Curaçao and another 62 hailed from St. Eustatius.[28] Settlers of Dutch islands also moved to the new Swedish colony of St. Barthélemy, which developed into an entrepôt of regional significance, albeit for a short period. Some merchants from St. Eustatius and St. Maarten first moved there in the mid-1780s, followed by so many sailors from the Dutch Caribbean that these dominated in the early nineteenth century.[29]

Evidence of migratory links between the Dutch colonies is mainly anecdotal. There was no metropolitan policy to connect the colonies through public servants, nor was it helpful that each colony had its own institutional arrangement. There are only isolated examples of colonial careers linking the various colonies, such as that of the Swiss-born Isaac Faesch, who first served the WIC in St. Eustatius (1736–40) before becoming the company's governor in Curaçao (1740–58). Antony Beaujon, born in a merchant family from St. Eustatius with strong relations with Curaçao and appointed director of Essequibo and Demerara in the late eighteenth century, was a rare example of personal and elite connections between the Dutch Antilles and the Guianas.[30] Nonetheless, some planters from St. Eustatius moved to Essequibo after the 1740s. There is also some evidence of planters, merchants, and public servants moving from Suriname either to Berbice, Essequibo, Curaçao, or St. Eustatius, or between the latter two.[31] Trade connections also involved travel from Dutch colonies to other parts of the Americas, which must have led to occasional resettlement. Curaçaoan settlers moved to Rhode Island in the late seventeenth

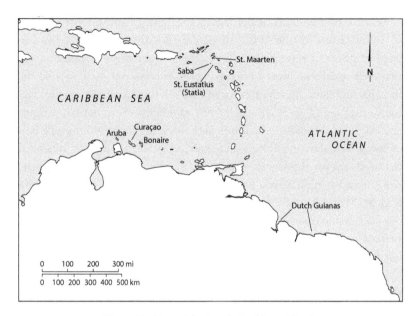

Figure 14. Map of the Dutch Caribbean islands.

century, while merchants from Curaçao and St. Eustatius settled in St. Thomas during the eighteenth century. Intensive trade connections with British North America must have involved some permanent migration. There is little indication of permanent European migration from Curaçao to the Spanish Main, if only because the presumably most mobile segment, that of the Jewish merchants, could only obtain permission to settle in Venezuela in 1819 because of their religion.

Slavery and Free Non-White Labor in the Antilles

In 1753, Spanish American privateers targeting smugglers captured the *Aurora*, a Curaçaoan vessel with a fairly typical crew. One of them was born in Amsterdam, another one in Swabia (Germany), yet another was an Amerindian from Aruba, and the others were all natives of Curaçao: eight adult whites, five adult blacks, and five black boys.[32] The historical record does not specify the status of the ten blacks, but it is very likely that they were enslaved, like many other Curaçaoan sailors.

Black slaves worked in the Dutch Caribbean from the earliest days of colonization by the WIC. In Aruba, Bonaire, and Saba, the proportion of the enslaved of the overall—in itself tiny—population was relatively small, at most between one-third and one half. Aruba and Bonaire remained poorly populated, mainly functioning as pastureland for Curaçao, and employing a modest number of local mestizo farmers and enslaved Africans—the latter also working the scorching salt pans of Bonaire. Labor in the salt pans was, likewise, one of the jobs allotted to slaves on the Dutch side of St. Martin, in addition to agrarian work on a few plantations producing sugar or crops for local consumption. St. Maarten's slaves outnumbered the white population throughout the documented period from 1736 onwards. In that year, 1,382 slaves worked for 599 whites. By 1790, three-quarters of the colony's 5,571 inhabitants were slaves, while the number of free people of color and blacks was not even 200. Much the same applies to St. Eustatius, where the share of slaves was some sixty percent for much of the eighteenth century, whereas the number of free non-whites remained small. In Curaçao, finally, as we saw, the intermediate group of free non-whites grew apace to near one-fifth of the insular population in 1789 and one-third in 1816, the proportion of slaves declining from 61 to 48 percent. The share of whites remained stable at roughly one-fifth, which would have been low for the Spanish Caribbean, but was high for a typical Caribbean plantation colony.[33]

Of course, none of these islands fit the mold of anything "typically" Caribbean, as long as we take the plantation colony as a model. In comparison to the French and English Caribbean, the societies that developed in the insular Dutch Caribbean evolved along a different trajectory in which slave labor still mattered, but was put to other uses and exploited in different ways and perhaps degrees. In both cases, the economy was divided into a commercial sector and an agrarian one. The former maritime branch was well known throughout the Atlantic and has cemented the idea of "the Dutch"—or at least these two Dutch islands—being indispensable lubricants in the wider Atlantic system. The agrarian branch of both economies has attracted much less attention, probably for being less spectacular and seemingly less important. And yet without local food production, the commercial growth of the port cities would not have been possible. Additionally, much of the slave labor in both islands was not deployed in urban, commercial settings, but rather in agriculture catering to the local population.

While older studies such as Cornelis Goslinga's *The Dutch in the Caribbean and in the Guianas* do refer to local agriculture and sugar plantations and hence slave employment on the Dutch Windward Islands, most recent scholarly work on St. Eustatius understandably focuses on the island's unique commercial function in the wider Atlantic.[34] As a consequence, the function of the local economy and the recruitment and exploitation of enslaved labor has not been richly researched for the island. The enslaved population must have been put to work both for agrarian purposes and around the warehouses. In all types of work relating to the loading and unloading of ships, they will have worked together with the sailors manning the boats, most of these free men of many shades of color.

The economic history of Curaçao is much better documented, and hence the contours of slave labor and the wider labor market, as well as the characteristics of the local regime of slavery, are better known. The obvious contrasts between the regimes of slavery in the two main Dutch Caribbean colonies, Curaçao and Suriname, were first discussed in a comparative framework by the Dutch anthropologist Harry Hoetink over half a century ago. Pointing to the supposedly "harsh" system of slavery in Suriname as against the alleged "mild" character of slavery in Curaçao, he rightly argued that metropolitan culture alone could not be seen as a decisive factor in the development of variants in Caribbean slavery. Neither did he find any hard evidence of causality between types of slavery and subsequent race relations.[35]

Many of the issues Hoetink raised have been taken up in later research. On the basis of thorough archival research, historians Wim Klooster and, more recently, Linda Rupert and Han Jordaan have filled in many blanks in our understanding of the development of Curaçaoan society and particularly the role of slaves and free men and women "of color" in this small yet cosmopolitan island.[36] These studies have unearthed a wealth of material on the participation of both slaves and free women and men of color in the urban and maritime branches of the economy. Much of this, in particular the autonomy exerted by many of these islanders, is remarkable by Caribbean standards. And yet we should not forget that over half of the island's slaves remained tied up in agrarian work, producing food that was indispensable for the growth and survival of the maritime sector that has attracted so much more attention. It is likely that there was a considerable distance between the two groups of slaves and even more so between agrarian slaves and the urban free non-white community—that conclusion can at least be drawn from the major slave revolt of 1795, which apparently attracted mainly agrarian slaves and was suppressed not only by white colonials, but also by the "colored" (mixed-race) militia.

According to the 1789 census, 55 percent of Curaçao's population lived in and around Willemstad and only 45 percent in the countryside. The enslaved population of nearly 13,000 made up 61 percent of the total population, but its distribution was clearly more rural, with 58 percent living in the countryside and 42 percent residing in the city.[37] Not much is known about this rural majority. They were working on a type of plantation uncommon in the Caribbean and sometimes likened to continental *haciendas*, producing food for local consumption only. A typical Curaçaoan *landhuis* or mansion, usually home to a white owner of Dutch Protestant origin, was small-sized, employing between a few dozen to a rare maximum of perhaps one hundred slaves who worked a limited surface of mostly arid land. The ecological conditions were far less favorable than in most of the Caribbean, allowing only for low-productive agriculture and some cattle-breeding. The most important crop grown was sorghum, the basic element in the diet of the slaves and poor free men and women. Among the cattle, goats predominated.[38]

Just over 100,000 enslaved Africans were brought to Curaçao between 1658 and 1800, the overwhelming majority (86 percent) arriving in the period between 1662 and 1730. Most of these captives were resold to buyers in the Spanish Main, while a small percentage went to the British and French islands. Of those that were retained on the island, the majority was put to work on the countryside to produce food both for the local population and for the enslaved Africans held in custody until they were shipped to other places. In 1696, the number of private plantations and gardens was calculated at 111. The West India Company only owned a limited number of slaves itself. In 1700, the company employed 558 slaves at plantations and another 165 in the city.[39]

The work of the agrarian slaves was atypical by Caribbean standards, and heavily marked by the recurring problems of drought. Even if the majority of local slaves were employed in agriculture, local production was not enough to feed the islands, making food imports from New York,

Philadelphia, and Rhode Island, as well as the Spanish Main and to a lesser degree the Dutch Republic, indispensable—which again underlines how much Curaçao was dependent on the broader Atlantic connections it also helped to foster.

Much of the historiography of plantation slavery in the Caribbean is based on correspondence between interested partners on various sides of the Atlantic, a high-intensity exchange of vital information regarding management, production, trade, cost, and benefits—management always including issues regarding the enslaved population. As Curaçaoan plantations were locally owned, financed, and managed, and as their produce was strictly locally sold without the need for merchants, very few archival materials are available that could lift the veil about plantation life on the island. The only major study deals with the nineteenth century, and focuses primarily on agriculture and finance rather than on slave labor and management or slave culture. Anthropological work on the immediate postslavery period has unearthed oral traditions going back to the time of slavery. From this work, we get at least glimpses of how life as an agrarian slave must have been—and indeed the struggle for survival, the challenge of securing enough food, is a recurring theme, alongside musings about master-enslaved relations.[40]

More is known about urban and maritime slavery, because most archives pertaining to Curaçao resulted from Willemstad's function as a hub in a network of Atlantic connections. Scholarly studies have revealed several features. First, we see enslaved Africans and their Curaçaoan descendants working in a wide range of occupations, often alongside free laborers of all shades. Next, historians have documented that these occupations implied frequent contacts with other parts of the Atlantic. Third, there is ample evidence of high manumission rates, and anecdotal evidence of social ascent of Curaçaoans of African origins. Finally, and more implicitly, studies on urban slavery in Willemstad raise the question of the extent to which rural and urban slaves were inhabiting the same colonial space.

As for the first characteristic, slaves were working in urban settings, in Willemstad's buzzing harbor, and on ships, and their labor was possibly put to several such uses at the same time. Most important among the jobs in the city was domestic service, predominantly reserved for women. Labor in and around the harbor was allotted mainly to men who were employed in the warehouses, in loading and unloading ships, in ship repairs, and so on. Maritime slave labor was again a male affair, with slaves serving as sailors—fishing for local consumption was most likely primarily an occupation for free people. In all of these occupations, enslaved laborers were working with free men and women, both white and non-white, often performing the same tasks. The lines between free and enslaved in this highly monetized urban economy were comparatively thin, at times even enabling slaves to pass for free when it suited them.[41]

Enslaved people based in the city could make money in several ways. Owners—both the WIC and private individuals—would hire their slaves out to third parties, allowing them to keep a modest proportion of the net benefit for themselves. Perhaps more important, slaves could engage in small entrepreneurial ventures on the side while working for their owners. Thus an enslaved sailor traveling between Curaçao and St. Domingue could engage in illicit petty trading, and a seamstress hired out to do her work could arrange to have some side jobs herself.[42]

Even if rural slaves were less isolated than slaves on Guiana plantations, they did spend most of their times on the farm, with limited contact with city people and probably even less with the international clientele of Willemstad. Urban slaves in contrast were constantly in contact with foreigners, if not professionally then at least casually, as all shared the same space in the city quarters. Enslaved sailors employed on Curaçaoan vessels had even more opportunities for international contacts, as their masters' commercial pursuits would bring them to a range of port cities in the Caribbean, the Spanish Main, and North America, where they must have had some contact with the local population.

Unlike most parts of colonial America, recorded manumission rates in Curaçao were high, as borne out by the large proportion of free non-whites in the total population—almost 18 percent in 1789. According to Jordaan's calculations, between 1722 and 1800, the number of recorded manumissions was 3,310. Almost half of the manumittees (48 percent) were children, 38 percent were women, and only 14 percent were men. The greater part of these manumissions (58 percent) were achieved through payment, as against 34 percent without a monetary transaction—a category including affectionate manumissions by owners—and 8 percent in other ways. In over 40 percent of all cases, slaves bought their own freedom or that of their kin without interference of a third party, indicating that they had secured the necessary money themselves. Overall, the majority of manumissions was financed by people of African origins, themselves free or enslaved, a clear indication that the urban and maritime economy provided this group with chances for capital accumulation.[43] It has long been thought, on the basis of anecdotal evidence, that in times of drought, when plantations did not even produce enough food to feed their own people, slave owners let their slaves temporarily fend for themselves or even resorted to manumissions out of calculated self-interest, leaving it to the freed men and women themselves to escape starvation. Recent research, however, suggests that this was not a major impetus for manumission.[44]

Slave Resistance

Manumission was far more prevalent in the Antilles, particularly in Curaçao, in contrast to the Guianas, where demographic and geographic factors enhanced the chances for collective revolt or escape. This does not imply that there was no marronage in Curaçao, where the phenomenon was known since the early days of black slavery. In the early eighteenth century, some slaves even sailed with oceangoing ships to the Dutch Republic, hoping to reach the shores of freedom, but nearly all of them seem to have been sent back to New World slavery.[45] Enslaved Curaçaoans also profited from the ransoming expedition of Jacques Cassard in 1713. On that occasion, a large number ran away to the French ships, where they found a place to hide.[46] More commonly, just like on the three Danish islands, marronage took the form of maritime escape. The best chance for Curaçao's runaway slaves was to canoe or sail to Tierra Firme, a risky but navigable forty miles away. Archives mention the presence of runaway Africans from Curaçao in Coro, present-day Venezuela, as early as the end of the seventeenth century. Over the decades, thousands of enslaved Curaçaoans must have used this escape route. Between 1759 and 1766 alone, 380 slaves were recorded as having escaped to the Spanish Main. In 1774, a year in which Curaçao faced a severe food crisis, another 140 slaves escaped. This migratory tradition drew the Coro region and Curaçao close to each other throughout the eighteenth century.[47]

Marronage may have functioned as a safety valve for the slave system, but outright revolts also occurred on Curaçao on at least four occasions: in 1716, 1750, 1774, and 1795. The first of these recorded rebellions saw eleven Africans who had arrived on the island only seven months before kill three whites on a WIC plantation. Facing opposition from fellow slaves, they failed to implement the plan to start a general revolt, and their attempt came to naught. Around one hundred Africans from Willemstad and its surrounding area, also predominantly recent arrivals, were involved in the next revolt in 1750. Their target was a government plantation and their victims were one white overseer and 59 enslaved blacks. The fear this uprising instilled among the whites was reflected in the harsh punishments—39 rebels were executed and 13 exiled. The outburst of 1774 was a mixture of rebellion and marronage. All 72 slaves belonging to one plantation rebelled and boarded a large canoe, heading for Coro. After they were discovered, most took to the woods, after which they were gradually apprehended. No executions followed these events.[48]

The revolt of 1795, by far the most important one, started on August 17 in apparent protest against an infringement on the usual daily routines, but soon turned into an attempt to launch an island-wide revolution inspired by the Haitian Revolution started just a few years before. Within two days some 2,000 of the island's 12,000 slaves were in revolt. The slaves won the first battles, but then the tide started to turn. Negotiations were started in late August, when one of the leaders, aptly named Toussaint, affirmed in French, "We are here to win or die," but they failed. In the end, the combined white, colored, and black militias prevailed and the leaders of the revolt were executed in what authorities called an "exemplary," extraordinarily cruel manner.

Contemporary accounts left dramatic testimonies of the revolt's foremost leader, Tula, who may have been born outside of Curaçao and most likely had spent time in the French Caribbean; he was also known as "Rigaud," an unambiguous reference to the revolutionary leader from Saint-Domingue he claimed to have met. He was reportedly well abreast of the French and Haitian revolutions. "We have been badly treated for too long," he was quoted as saying. "We do not want to do anybody harm, but we seek our freedom, the French [Caribbean] blacks have been given their freedom, Holland has been taken over by the French, hence we too must be free."[49] Drawing on Christian rhetoric, Tula argued that all people share the same parents, Adam and Eve, and hence are entitled to the same liberty.

The 1795 revolt was inspired by the news of the French and Haitian Revolutions, as well as the establishment of the French-leaning Batavian Republic in the Netherlands. News traveled fast, particularly to a maritime hub such as Curaçao and to the slave population intimately tied to the bustling port. Indeed the revolt seems a textbook example of Eugene D. Genovese's thesis that after the French and Haitian revolutions, slave revolts throughout the Americas were dominated by Creole slaves using the rhetoric of universal human rights and aiming at ending slavery per se—indeed, there was also a failed slave revolt in Dutch Demerara in 1795, equally inspired by the French and Haitian revolutions.[50] However, a straightforward picture of enslaved but revolutionary blacks against repressive *ancien régime* whites brushes aside the support of free blacks and coloreds and even slaves in the crushing of the slave revolt. The reality of this revolt, like so many others, was a more complicated one.

Free Blacks and Coloreds

Although early Dutch colonial legislation forbade "carnal conversation" between whites and blacks, in Curaçao, the prohibition for whites to engage in "lewd" or "non-Christian" ways with female blacks was not renewed after 1655.[51] Nor was it forbidden for whites and nonwhites to marry, as was confirmed in 1752 by a Curaçaoan committee appointed by governor and council.[52] The initial divide between enslaved blacks and free whites soon made way in all Dutch colonies for a tripartite demographic division, as the number of free nonwhites grew apace in the eighteenth century. By 1716, whites had become a minority in Willemstad, visited that year by Spanish official Marcos Betancourt y Castro en route to Caracas, where he would start his tenure as Caracas's new governor. His impression of the port was that very few "Hollanders" lived there, whereas the bulk of the population was made up of blacks and coloreds, numbering, according to his estimate, four to six thousand.[53] Those among them who were former slaves cannot have been more than a few hundred. This group, however, grew steadily, in spite of some apprehensive white families who aimed to maintain whiteness by only marrying fellow whites. Free nonwhites on Curaçao were more numerous than whites by 1789.[54] By contrast, the number of whites in St. Eustatius and St. Maarten still exceeded free nonwhites by wide margins in 1789 of 7:2 and 6:1, respectively.[55]

Commensurate with their growing demographic weight, free blacks and coloreds occupied an increasingly significant place in the economic life of the Dutch Caribbean, as they did in many other parts of the West Indies. And yet the lives of most of the recently freed persons and their offspring were precarious. Archives abound with concerns about the poverty of the free coloreds and corresponding issues of law and order such as vagabonding and theft. On Curaçao, a minority among the free people of color lived outside town, especially women who cultivated some crops or raised cattle on small plots of land.[56] Most free nonwhites, however, lived in Willemstad, where they scraped a living as artisans and sailors. By the 1780s, most captains of the island's ubiquitous sloops were mulattoes. Some free people of color suffered from deprivation, Governor Rodier asserted, especially in times of slack trade, which frequently forced them to seek employment off the island.[57]

There is some evidence, though, of both men and women who attained both considerable property and status, reflected among other things in their slave ownership. Anna Maria Koningh, granddaughter of an enslaved woman who worked on the WIC's Hato plantation, owned several houses. In her will, she stipulated that each of her nine children (fathered by her Jewish lover David Cohen Henriquez) was to receive one or more slaves. One son, Nicolaas Henricus, made a living as an insurer, shipowner, and merchant, and also worked for the island's courts as a translator from Portuguese and Spanish.[58] His contemporary Gaspar Antonio Quirigazo, a free black ship captain, made a good living off the contraband trade, engaging among other things in the sale of small groups of slaves. His wealth allowed him to buy and sell rural landholdings in the 1740s and 1750s.[59] Likewise, the trade with the coast of Caracas allowed free black ship captain, supercargo, and shipowner Antonio (or Anthonij) Beltran to buy a house in the Otrabanda neighborhood and to own slaves—ten in 1748 and seven in 1775. For three years, he also owned a plantation.[60] The porch of his house served as guardhouse for the free black militia, of which Beltran was the captain. In that capacity, he helped defeat the 1750 slave revolt.[61] As in other parts of the Americas, leadership of the black militia must have been synonymous with leadership in the overall black community.[62] Despite his prominent position, we know little about Antonio's life. In 1760, as the Seven Years' War raged, he seems to have been on board a sloop that was seized by a British privateer as it sailed from Martinique to Curaçao. All freeborn or freed black crewmembers were subsequently auctioned off as slaves on St. Kitts. Among them was "Anthonij Bertrand."[63] If this was indeed Antonio, he did make it back to Curaçao, where we find him manumitting slaves in 1765 and 1766.[64]

Beltran's military service was not exceptional. Freedmen on Curaçao had been assigned a military role since the early eighteenth century. Starting in the War of the Spanish Succession (1701–13), free black and colored men, as well as enslaved Africans, were enrolled in the island's militia companies, both to defend the island against foreign intruders and to maintain public order.[65] One of the militia's tasks was to hunt down runaway slaves, which would sometimes take the form of a two-week expedition, during which the militiamen were allowed to visit all plantations.[66] By the end of the eighteenth century, not only were free black and colored local sailors incorporated into the militia (dubbed "National Guard" in 1796), but a small number of light-skinned coloreds were given officer posts, in spite of indignation in white circles.[67] The issue of non-white citizenship and loyalty remained contested, both in private and among the island's all-white ruling council. Thus in 1789, several council members argued that in case of an attack by Spanish forces, free blacks and coloreds would side with the enemies, who were fellow Catholics and whose priests they held in high regard.[68]

Some outsiders ascribed an enviable status to free nonwhites in the Dutch Atlantic. They included Julien Raimond, a wealthy indigo planter from St. Domingue, one of whose grandparents was of African descent. During the French Revolution, he emerged as perhaps the principal advocate of racial reforms in the French Caribbean. In a published letter, he mentioned Curaçao as example of a colony where prejudices against skin color were virtually absent.[69] Raimond was clearly misinformed. Racist ordinances circumscribed the freedoms of Curaçao's free and enslaved blacks and coloreds. Playing loud music was forbidden, as was carrying a stick, or walking in the street after dark. Any white was allowed to punish nonwhite behavior considered impertinent with a cane. Besides, the legal testimony of black or colored witnesses lacked judicial force. Specific legislation discriminating against free nonwhites did not exist, with one important exception. After complaints from less affluent whites, legislation was introduced in 1749 prohibiting blacks and coloreds from keeping a shop in town, although they could continue their commercial dealings in their homes and take merchandise to town during the daytime.[70]

Poverty came and went among all ethnic groups on Curaçao, whose commercial sector was more vulnerable to economic downturns, and besides produced insufficient foodstuffs itself. Lack of provisions sometimes made Aruba's Amerindians relocate to the Coro region in Venezuela, only to return to the island when food was plentiful again. Even those among them who were in WIC service were poorly endowed, receiving no more than a little corn from Curacao, and at times animal bones instead of meat.[71] Food scarcity affected whites as well. In a sermon delivered in 1753, Rabbi Jeosuah Hisquiahu de Cordova deplored the plight of the poor who could not feed their children.[72] The poorest segment of white society on the Caribbean islands was made up of sailors, whose families in times of commercial slumps like the 1750s could lose their livelihood. On Curaçao, their best hope was to eat what was considered slave food: corn bread and okra.[73] Two decades later, middling whites responded to another economic downturn by selling their golden rings, silver forks, and spoons, as well as their best clothes, in order to buy corn and other provisions.[74]

Interruptions in overseas food imports could exacerbate the indigence of poor whites and nonwhites alike. Ports from British North America supplied many of the dietary needs of both the Dutch Guianas and the insular Caribbean, including flour, butter, bread, beef, and fish. The local meat supply never met the islands' need, especially in times when food for cattle was in short supply. Residents of Aruba and Bonaire refrained from slaughtering cattle in 1789 because the animals were all skin and bone anyway.[75] Shipments of provisions from North America were so important to Curaçao, that the outbreak of the American Revolution had serious consequences. Since the States General initially refused to recognize the young republic as a sovereign state, maritime ties with North America were temporarily severed, with immediate consequences. The governor reported in 1779 that the supply of meat and bread in the island's warehouses only sufficed for six more weeks.[76]

Creolization

After 1730, the demographic growth of Curaçao's African and ethnically mixed population depended on natural reproduction, not on slave imports. This in turn means, first, that the influx of African culture became minimal at a relatively early stage, and second, that interracial sexual relations early on caused the emergence of an ever-growing intermediate group. Moreover, European immigration seems to have been modest, while both the Protestant and the Jewish communities were well established at an early stage. Metropolitan Dutch cultural influence was therefore limited and did not block the emergence of a relatively stable Creole culture nurtured more by the island's regional connections than by its links to a faraway metropolis. These regional connections marked not only the European population, but also the urban and to a lesser extent rural population at large, whether slave or free, black or of mixed origins. The emergence of a Creole culture in Curaçao therefore was a process affecting the entire population at once.[77]

The most conspicuous form of Creole culture in all three Leeward islands off the continental coast was the Papiamentu language, which emerged in an as yet undefined moment in the early colonial era, possibly already in the seventeenth century and with significant pre–Middle Passage Afro-Portuguese impact.[78] As early as 1704, the Jesuit Alexius Schabel referred to the local "broken Spanish"; in 1732 another Catholic priest, Agustín Caicedo, wrote of a separate local language existing alongside Dutch, Spanish, and Portuguese; and fifteen years later, sailors on board a Curaçaoan vessel taken by a British privateer told a judge in Newport, Rhode Island, that people in Curaçao commonly spoke "Poppemento." The first written text in the language is a letter from 1775 exchanged between two Jewish lovers. By the end of that century, Papiamentu was clearly the island's first language—with Curaçao's governor Johannes de Veer referring to it as "the national language" in 1795—as it was, one assumes, on Aruba and Bonaire. By that time Guene, another local Creole language but of a more African nature and restricted to the rural enslaved population, was still used as a semisecret vehicle, but was on the way to vanishing.[79]

Papiamentu was not a Dutch-based Creole, but rather a language with an African syntax and a predominantly Iberian, and particularly

Portuguese, vocabulary, echoing the early recruitment of enslaved Africans in Portuguese Africa, the Portuguese spoken by the local Jewish population, and the intense commercial contacts with the Spanish Main. Whereas creolized variants of European languages throughout the Caribbean tended to wear the stain of lower class inferiority, Papiamentu gradually acquired a more prestigious position. By the late eighteenth century Papiamentu had become the lingua franca for all inhabitants irrespective of class, color, or legal status. Gerrit van Paddenburgh, a schoolteacher arriving in Curaçao in 1816 after the reestablishment of Dutch rule, deplored the dominance of Papiamentu even among the local white Creoles. While Van Paddenburgh disqualified Papiamentu as a "mixture of corrupted Spanish, Indian and Dutch . . . insupportable to the more delicate ear of the European," and many more Dutch visitors would repeat such denigrations, the language's emancipation would continue into the present.[80]

The Amerindian contribution to the process of creolization was of limited significance. This is not surprising given their early decimation on the islands. A late-eighteenth-century report estimated that only three or four "worn-out" Amerindians were living on Curaçao. Their number was higher, but still limited, on Aruba and Bonaire.[81] As Aruba, in particular, had relatively few inhabitants of African origins, its population was more mestizo in character. Indeed, the Papiamento—with an "o" rather than "u" at the end—spoken on the island to this very day has a slightly stronger Spanish American bent to it in pronunciation and orthography.

While the Spanish environment affected Curaçao, Bonaire, and Aruba linguistically, in the northern Caribbean islands the English language became dominant at an early stage under influence of the islands' anglophone environment and the many English settlers with temporary jobs. During the Anglo-French war in 1744, a French corsair mistook a ship from St. Maarten for an enemy English vessel. After all, the crew knew no Dutch, nor did the ship's owner and skipper, despite being born in the colony.[82] In the same colony, a newly arriving minister of the Reformed Church discovered in 1763 that none of the churchgoers understood his Dutch.[83] A contemporary Dutch observer wrote that the lifestyle of St. Eustatius's inhabitants was so perfectly English in morals, manners, clothing, and interior design that only a flag was lacking to make the island completely English.[84] When the last Reformed ministers left St. Eustatius and St. Maarten in 1792 following the abolition of the West India Company, the Dutch language also exited these islands.[85]

Ironically, the Dutch language did survive remarkably long on the nearby Danish islands of St. Croix, St. John, and St. Thomas. When the Danes colonized St. John in 1718, one historian has explained, "those same planters and their slaves settled the island, taking the Dutch Creole language along with them [from St. Eustatius]. When St. Croix was purchased in 1733 and settled in the following year, a similar scenario ensued . . ." Apart from regular Dutch, Dutch Creole developed in the first years of Danish colonization of St. Thomas, when most planters were Dutch and arriving Africans used some Dutch as well, resulting in the Dutch Creole language being used as the island's lingua franca. Creole Dutch spread from St. Thomas to the other two Danish islands.[86]

Religion

In the Dutch Republic, the Reformed Church was the "public church," the official spiritual organ of society, but not the only established church. Membership was not required by law. What is more, the Union of Utrecht (1579), the philosophical foundation of the new polity, recognized individual freedom of conscience—the freedom to worship, that is, in private homes. As the interpretation of religious affairs was left to each individual province, the extent of religious freedom for non-Calvinists depended on local conditions.[87] Buttressed by the West India Company—which appointed its ministers and made sure that its overseas servants were church members—the Reformed Church also took root as the public church in the Dutch Atlantic, albeit not without difficulties. One obstacle was the need to accommodate large sections of the white colonial populations who were not Calvinist. The borders of the "Reformed Atlantic," incidentally, did not coincide with those of the Dutch colonial realm. Ethnic Dutchmen in the Danish islands attended services at the Dutch Reformed Church. Ministers arrived from the Netherlands on St. Thomas until they could not make themselves understood anymore, which happened only in 1827.[88]

In most colonies ruled by the Dutch Republic (and even some foreign colonies), the Reformed Church was thus dominant in the leading circles.

Another common feature was the initial ban on Lutheranism, maintained well into the eighteenth century. Like in the Dutch Republic, Catholics were deprived of religious rights beyond the freedom of conscience, except in Curaçao, where they lived a full Catholic life. The interimperial context overrode the traditional Dutch animosity vis-à-vis Catholicism. Priests from the nearby Spanish Main arrived regularly to baptize and sermonize among the enslaved islanders. Catholicism thus became an important ingredient of Afro-Curaçaoan culture. On St. Eustatius, it was Methodism that began to spread around the time of the American Revolution; although the religion was banned from other Dutch colonies around the turn of the nineteenth century, it was allowed to flourish on St. Eustatius. Jews, meanwhile, were granted extensive privileges in Suriname, Curaçao, and St. Eustatius and established crucially important communities there, but surprisingly were not tolerated in Essequibo and Demerara. To every rule, there was an exception, and the metropolis did not enforce homogeneity.

Although religion enabled the white community to get together at least once a week, encouraging sociability, Reformed services were poorly attended in most colonies. St. Maarten's minister complained in 1763 that he had an audience of four or five people. The reason, he added, was that the church was half an hour's walk from the town of Philipsburg, and no Dutchman owned a horse.[89] Likewise, many white laypeople on Curaçao rarely went to church, not even for their own wedding, which was allowed to take place at home. The domestic setting obviated the need to invest in a new outfit.[90] At one point, a group of impoverished people sent a request to the Reformed Church council not to include bell-ringers, gravediggers, and undertaker's men in funerals of the poor to save them money. The request was denied.[91]

Connected to the indifference many showed towards the Reformed Church was the lack of schoolteachers. One minister on Curaçao complained in the mid-eighteenth century that the post of official schoolmaster (employed by the WIC) had been vacant for two years, while the interim teacher was not equal to his job.[92] As Willemstad expanded, private schools sprang up in outlying parts of town, but they were always short-lived.[93] The contrast with the Jewish community, where in the 1730s 180 boys between the ages of five and thirteen attended one of two schools five days a week, was conspicuous. No fewer than five Jewish teachers were on the island, whose instruction was supplemented by two rabbis.[94] The situation on the other islands did not differ much. On the tiny island of Saba, for example, the Reformed Church displayed almost no activity. Only between 1736 and 1739 was there a resident minister. Nor does there appear to have been any school. Small wonder, then, that in 1790 only four of the island's 730 whites could read and write.[95]

Where Dutch ministers were active, they preached not only to Dutch natives, but also to Germans, many of whom were soldiers and almost all of whom were Lutherans. In both St. Eustatius and Curaçao, Lutheran churches were prohibited until the second half of the eighteenth century. In 1700, a Lutheran resident of Curaçao did receive the last sacraments from a Lutheran clergyman, but one that arrived by ship from Danish St. Thomas to that end.[96] Lutheran ministers dwelling on the island were expelled in 1685 and again in 1704. In the mid-eighteenth century, Lutherans came close to getting their own congregation after fellow Lutherans in Amsterdam set up a fund in 1743 to pay for a minister and other expenses.[97] The authorities on Curaçao only relented a dozen years later, following requests from local Lutherans who stressed the increase of their coreligionists due to the growing navigation from the Danish Caribbean, the arrival of large numbers of Lutheran soldiers, and the birth of many children in their community.[98] The affluence of the Lutheran community, which had no poor in their midst, must have been a factor as well.[99] On St. Eustatius, Lutheranism appeared in the open in 1780, seventeen years after fifty-two Lutheran had requested a minister of their own. The minister sent by the Lutheran church in Amsterdam, however, served for only two years.[100]

Inhibiting the establishment of Lutheran churches was not only Calvinist pressure but also the fear of white disunity, which would make whites even more vulnerable to the non-white majority. White friction did indeed occur when the recognition of Lutheranism tempted some settlers to leave the Reformed church benches and attend the new services. A Lutheran minister in Curaçao proved to have speaking skills superior to those of his Reformed colleagues.[101] Adding insult to injury, Lutheran ministers on Curaçao occasionally baptized children of members of the Reformed congregation, even if this only happened for lack of a Reformed minister.

In such exceptional circumstances, the Reformed congregation preferred a priest at the baptismal font.[102] Animosity between the two Protestant churches only faded in the nineteenth century, when membership numbers dwindled away. In 1825, both merged to form a single Protestant congregation.[103]

On St. Eustatius, the Methodist Church began its successful mission in the 1780s. Buoyed by the visit of Thomas Coke, the first Methodist bishop, and the evangelical work of "Black Harry," a former slave who hailed from the United States, Methodism grew by leaps and bounds on St. Eustatius in spite of government persecution. By the time it was recognized and a chapel was built in 1804, many residents of St. Eustatius, both free and enslaved, had joined it.[104] No such Protestant missionary movements were allowed on Curaçao, whose free colored and black population adhered almost exclusively to the Roman Catholic belief and were not welcome in the Dutch Reformed church to begin with. Priests had sojourned on the island from 1680 onwards, as the *asiento* contracts or subcontracts stipulated that Curaçao could only be a transit port in the slave trade if the spiritual needs of Catholics were met. Ten priests were to see to the arriving Africans and two Capuchins were granted the right to wear their habits in public and use a chapel that opened onto the street. These Capuchins celebrated mass in the open air, took care of the sick, and celebrated marriages.[105] Although a total of fifty-five Catholic clergymen spent time on Curaçao in the last two decades of the seventeenth century—several of them unlicensed—it was not until the early years of the next century that priests settled on the island.[106] Apart from the Capuchins, they represented the Jesuit, Dominican, Augustinian, and Franciscan orders, each of which needed permission from the Dutch States General, the WIC in both Amsterdam and Curaçao, and the diocese of Caracas, which continued to claim spiritual jurisdiction over the island long after the Dutch takeover of 1634.[107] The priests' missionary work was quite fruitful, at least quantitatively. By the 1730s, the number of Catholics on the island had risen to seven thousand, the overwhelming part of the insular population both free and enslaved.[108]

Missionizing cannot solely account for the massive adherence of Africans and their descendants to Catholicism. Also relevant is that demographics precluded the autonomous emergence of a local Afro-Caribbean religion. In comparison to the Guianas, the ethnic composition of the population was less extremely polarized, with Europeans making up a substantial majority and the African-origin inhabitants, whether enslaved or free, having far more frequent and intensive contact with the white population. The room for autonomous cultural development was therefore limited, particularly in the urban setting of Willemstad.

There, the Reformed service on Sundays was invariably overshadowed by that of the Catholics, especially after the completion of the St. Anna Church in Otrabanda in 1768. Built largely with construction material illegally imported from the Spanish Main—in keeping, one might say, with Caracas's spiritual authority—the church accommodated no less than 3,000 people when a new Dominican priest arrived in 1774.[109] The bulk of them were nonwhite; in the mid-eighteenth century, no more than a few dozen European Catholics called the island home.[110] Earlier in the century, their number may have been larger. In his diary, the Bohemian-born Jesuit Alexius Schabel mentioned a seventy-seven-year-old native of Brabant who had lived on Curaçao for fifty years. Although married to a Protestant woman, the man had raised all his children as Catholics.[111] Schabel, who had arrived in 1704, related that Catholic Spaniards, Portuguese, Germans, Dutchmen, and others approached him to confess their sins. Many of the Dutch, Germans, and the native-born whites had not been in a confession booth for five or six years, at least not with a priest who understood their tongue. Although formally they had to belong to the Reformed Church, officials were well-represented among these white Catholics, including the commanders of both Aruba and Bonaire, if we are to believe Schabel. Bonaire's commander enabled him to baptize thirty Indians. Other examples were Curaçao's governor Jan Noach du Fay, a Swiss native converted by an Augustinian priest,[112] and the captain-lieutenant Herman Winkler, introduced to the Catholic faith along with many other Reformed men by an unnamed Jesuit priest. Following a complaint about the latter case by Curaçao's governor, the WIC decided to send the States General's ordinance against Jesuits and to have the priest removed from the island.[113]

Prior to 1785, when two Catholic priests disembarked in Suriname, Catholic services and all outward display of the Catholic religion were anathema anywhere in the Dutch Atlantic outside of Curaçao.[114] One prevalent notion was that Catholics were a potential fifth column, which echoed concerns in the Dutch Republic.[115] That same year saw tensions rise on Curaçao after a French priest arrived from Saint-Domingue.[116] And yet Catholicism continued to flourish on the island. How can we explain that? The Reformed Church had never seriously missionized among people of African descent, explaining Catholic conversion rates on Curaçao by reference to the alleged superficial nature of Catholic missions and the supposed inclination of blacks to Catholicism.[117] The rationale for this tolerant policy was the authorities' conviction that Catholic priests managed "to keep [the blacks] in check," an achievement that could not be expected from Protestant preachers, as Curaçao's Governor de Veer put it in 1795. He was convinced that the Catholic faith of slaves and free nonwhites was more in the island's interest than the Protestant creed, since the authority of Catholic priests was more despotic. Consequently, de Veer continued, no rebelliousness was in evidence among the nonwhites, whereas in Suriname, Essequibo, and Berbice, where slaves lacked any Christian instruction and were left to their pagan beliefs, revolts were bound to happen and slave-owners fancied they could treat their slaves as beasts. Ironically just half a year later Curaçao witnessed its largest slave revolt ever.[118]

The Protestant white elite of Curaçao tenaciously excluded the non-white population from their own churches, thus making sure that there were clear lines of religious distinction. The early nineteenth-century visitor G. B. Bosch, himself a Reformed minister, observed that skin color basically defined one's creed: "From half an hour's distance I could already notice from someone's appearance to which church he belonged." After a few years' service in the colony, he concluded that there were more than simply religious motives at stake. The rationale for reserving Protestantism for whites, Bosch wrote, was "a colonial policy of contempt for people of black and brown skin. The larger one made the distance between whites and [nonwhites], the more one denigrated the latter, the stronger and longer, one thought, would colonialism remain in place."[119]

The Jewish leaders followed the same line of thought. They belonged to the only non-Christian population group that enjoyed religious freedom in Dutch America—and beyond—throughout the long eighteenth century. Jews received religious privileges in the more important colonies of Suriname, Curaçao, and St. Eustatius, while St. Maarten was also briefly home to a Jewish congregation.[120] What provoked criticism and derision on the part of their Christian neighbors was the customary welcome given by Curaçao's Jews to new governors. Protestants alleged that the Jews had an ulterior motive, aiming to obtain new privileges. Governor Nicolaes van Liebergen was greeted in 1680 with the gift of a *lampet*, a wash basin with a water pot. Van Liebergen initially declined and then accepted the offer. The Jewish leaders vowed in a deposition that they had not sought to obtain the privilege to trade with the island's Indians, as some had contended.[121] In 1704, when Jacob Beck was inaugurated as the new governor, word had it that the Jewish leaders offered him a huge silver platter, covered with gold, and promised him an African slave as an alternative gift when he turned down the initial offer.[122] Such rumors were ultimately predicated upon anti-Semitism, which surfaced again in 1727. After conceiving a plan to build a hospital for wounded sailors, Governor du Fay called a meeting with Protestant and Jewish representatives, proposing to generate the costs for the new building from a one percent increase in import duties. The Jewish delegates immediately consented, eliciting the sneer from a notorious anti-Semite that the Jews would come up with a trick to avoid paying or would deduct the expenses from something else. An enormous uproar followed.[123]

Despite these incidents, members of different religious communities interacted with other groups on a daily basis. As in the Dutch Republic, their coexistence involved what historian Willem Frijhoff has called an "ecumenicism of everyday relations," partly spontaneous and partly based on enforced toleration.[124] In the insular Caribbean as elsewhere in the Dutch Atlantic, this ecumene was reinforced by race relations. The rule by a white minority over an enslaved black majority spawned a pragmatic solidarity among the Europeans that would otherwise have been much less pronounced. This solidarity translated into the habitual acceptance of everyday violence vis-à-vis slaves and the subordination of free nonwhites. Dutch America thus underwent the same transformation that historian Kirsten Block has observed for the Caribbean as a whole, where the foundation of European identities changed from religion to race.[125] The case of the Dutch islands shows that this transformation did not require a plantation setting.

By all standards, Curaçao and St. Eustatius were the chief Dutch colonies in the insular Caribbean, eclipsing the other ones both demographically and economically, although St. Maarten was not insignificant in either respect. The interimperial trade networks of which they were an integral part largely bypassed the sparsely-populated islands of Saba, Bonaire, and Aruba. Another distinguishing feature of the entrepôts of St. Eustatius and Curaçao was their slave majority. The slave trade marked the development of Curaçao ever since the 1660s, when it became a major transit port in the *asiento* slave trade. After its participation in the regional slave trade steeply declined after 1730, the island's black population reproduced naturally. Not all people of African birth or descent were tied to the mercantile economy, since most of them worked on plantations producing provisions for the home market. Without new cultural influences from Africa after 1730, black Curaçaoans embraced Catholicism, though certainly in a local variant with African influences. Their conversion was also testimony to the island's close relationship with the Spanish Main, from which many priests arrived to administer to the population. Similarly, the close ties to nearby British islands enabled Methodism to flourish on St. Eustatius.

Allowing Catholicism on Curaçao was a pragmatic decision by the Dutch authorities. Economically indispensable and demographically strong, Jews were also granted religious freedoms, but otherwise religious heterogeneity was anathema, in part because of the need for the white elite to remain united. The Reformed Church therefore enjoyed a privileged position, at least until the mid-eighteenth century, when its role declined all over the Dutch Caribbean. Church attendance was dwindling and Lutheran groups in Curaçao and St. Eustatius received the liberties they requested. The recurrent attempts by anti-Semitic Christians to have Jewish freedoms withdrawn also seem to have faded in the latter part of the century. Racial tensions, expressed in a number of slave revolts that rocked Curaçao, served to mitigate strife between whites, allowing for government-sanctioned religious openness. Both religious exclusivity and diversity were thus informed by the dominant white fear of black insurrections.

6

THE CIRCULATION OF KNOWLEDGE

In *Main Currents in Caribbean Thought,* Gordon K. Lewis characterized the intellectual debates in the early modern Caribbean colonies as
"crassly materialist and spiritually empty," and as expressions of "cultural philistinism." Likewise, in *Slavery and Human Progress,* David
Brion Davis observed that by the eighteenth century, slave societies
throughout the Americas "were acquiring the image of social and cultural
wastelands." A contemporary once sniffed that "[l]a canaille de l'Europe,
c'est l'aristocratie des Indes," meaning that the trash of Europe formed
the elites of the tropical colonies. Contemporary reports about European
settlements along the West African coast were even less flattering.[1]

Bearing in mind the small number of free citizens, the dearth of
local educational facilities, and the crassly exploitative character of
their societies, we may safely assume that such bleak characterizations
also apply to the Dutch Atlantic colonies—Elmina offered even fewer
intellectual opportunities than the capitals of the Dutch Caribbean.
Around 1790, the leading local intellectual of Suriname, David Isaac

Cohen de Nassy, affirmed that even this most developed Dutch Atlantic colony "lacked whatever one needs to train and develop a mediocre intellect."[2]

None of this is particularly surprising. Whereas the settler colonies of the Americas soon developed their own intellectual institutions and traditions, this was not the case in those parts of the Atlantic world exclusively developed in the context of plantation slavery—both on the African side and in plantation America. It will not come as a surprise that the accumulated knowledge mainly served the pragmatic needs of a colonial endeavor defined by economic interest. But as we will see, ideas, technology, and expertise circulated within a Dutch Atlantic world that transcended the narrow boundaries of the metropolis and its colonies and involved a quite extensive network across the wider Atlantic world.

Webs of Communication

News traveled throughout the Dutch Atlantic and beyond, and at times surprisingly fast. Merchants as well as representatives from governing and religious institutions on all sides of the ocean communicated with one another on a permanent, even if often interrupted basis. These reasonably efficient information networks were indispensable for the functioning of the colonial system. Through these same channels, correspondents in the colonies learned of major political developments in Europe and in the Dutch Republic—such as wars, financial crises, and regime changes—and informed their counterparts about the latest developments in the colonies. As transatlantic sailings could take months, there was always a considerable time lag in communication, so news about the Dutch Caribbean colonies would reach other nations' colonies in the Americas long before it landed in the republic. In the late eighteenth century, local Caribbean newspapers such as the *Bermuda Gazette,* the *St. Christopher Journal,* and the *Bulletin Officiel de Saint-Domingue* indeed provided casual commercial information and sometimes political news about the Dutch Caribbean. Thus, according to the *Antigua Gazette*, news about the surrender of Suriname to the British on August 22, 1799, already circulated in places such as St. Pierre, Martinique, long before it could have been known in Europe.[3]

Similarly, when a major slave revolt erupted in Berbice in 1763, a call went out for armed assistance not only to Suriname and St. Eustatius, but equally to Barbados. Dutch settlers agonizing about "the fatal, ruinous, and terrible case of Berbice" hoped for Dutch intervention and prayed "that God the Lord will protect us." But this might have taken many months, if only for the time of travel. Laurens Storm van 's Gravesande, governor of the adjacent twin colony of Essequibo and Demerara, decided he could not wait and through the local British community requested military help from both the British governor of Barbados, Charles Pinfold, and from Gedney Clarke, a merchant and planter from New England with business interests throughout North America and the West Indies. Clarke himself organized and financed the dispatch of ships carrying some 300 military men from Barbados to help quell the revolt and prevent it from spreading to Essequibo and Demerara. Storm would later write that this British support, "next to God," had secured the survival of the colony, while Clarke wrote to his son that without this help the colony "would have been lost."[4]

A constant flow of correspondence linked the various parts of the Dutch Atlantic internally as well as across imperial borders. The men—and occasionally women—reading and writing these letters were mainly educated whites, but within the insular Dutch Caribbean, white, free colored, and enslaved artisans and sailors alike facilitated the transfer of information from one colony to another. Through these intermediaries, the enslaved populations of the Dutch colonies learned about major events that occurred elsewhere. Thus, just as news brought in from France had helped inspire the Haitian Revolution, so news conveyed by sailors about the events in St. Domingue in turn sparked the major 1795 slave revolt in Curaçao. Recent research has uncovered an intricate web of messengers and information linking the French Caribbean revolt to conspiracies in Curaçao and the Spanish Main. The leaders of the Curaçaoan rebels were crystal-clear about their sources of inspiration. As mentioned in the previous chapter, its major leader, Tula, was also known as Rigaud—the name of the foremost "mulatto" military leader in revolutionary Saint-Domingue—and had most likely spent time in that French colony; another leader spoke French ("Nous sommes ici pour vaincre ou mourir") and went by the name of Toussaint. In explaining the revolt to a Catholic priest, Tula revealed that he knew not only of the Haitian Revolution, but also that the Dutch Batavian Republic was a vassal state of revolutionary France: "The French [Caribbean] blacks have been given their freedom, Holland has been taken over by the French, hence we too must be free."[5]

Every ship traveling in the Atlantic carried letters, printed materials, and particularly people conveying information from one port city to the next. While this information was mainly of a commercial or political nature, individuals also exchanged information of a more personal character. This has become particularly evident from the "Sailing Letters" project, based on many thousands of letters once stored aboard Dutch vessels taken as prizes by the British Navy.[6] This treasure trove demonstrates how poorly state and business archives represent the overall contents of the correspondence circulating across the seas. Many of these prize papers are letters written by or on behalf of modest sailors, housewives, and artisans addressing faraway family members or friends—and some sixty percent of this unique archival collection pertains to the Atlantic, and within that category, primarily the West Indies. Through these letters we get glimpses of the ordinary lives of the people inhabiting the Dutch Atlantic world— and again, we also see that the world of those setting out from the Dutch Republic to West Africa or the Caribbean was not necessarily limited to Dutch colonies.

Some of these letters also testify to the creolization of Europeans. Thus in Curaçao, 1783, a certain Anna Elisabeth Schermer-Charje wrote to her in-laws in the Dutch Republic in a mixture of Dutch and Papiamentu. Her little boy is quoted expressing his mother's and his own longing for his father temporarily residing in Holland: *"Mi mama ta warda boo, mie jora toer dieja pa mie papa"* ("My mother waits for you, I cry all the time for my father"). Likewise, a Dutch immigrant to Essequibo, Wernard van Vloten, wrote letters to his family back home in Dutch, but included some phrases in Skepi, such as: "En sok kum kloeke dagka van noom di sitte bi warme lantta en als um kom weeran bi Bikkelante, Hom sel brengk van die 4 blabba moye goeto" ("And when the great day arrives for uncle who lives in a warm country, and when he returns to the Netherlands, he will bring along nice things for those 4 kids").[7]

None of the Dutch Atlantic colonies was exclusively linked to the republic, and this circulation of ships, people, and all sorts of information cemented their entanglement with the wider Atlantic world. But in addition to multidirectional flows of communication, there were also more restricted circuits of information. The more systematic collection and dis-semination of knowledge about the Dutch colonies and their wider habi-tat was a predominantly unilateral process directed from the republic. We will explore this story of Europeans from various nationalities building up and aiming to disseminate a body of knowledge of faraway places. The remainder of this chapter focuses on the circulation of a variety of printed materials, consumable goods, and individuals, and their impact on the transfer of information within the Dutch Atlantic and, possibly, beyond. In this context we will formulate some tentative answers to the question of what type of information on the colonies reached which residents of the Dutch Republic, and what its impact may have been.

Language is key to communication, and a reminder of the means of communication within the Dutch Atlantic is appropriate. Dutch was probably the dominant language only in the tiny European community that inhabited the Elmina fortress. In Suriname, the language most widely spoken was Sranantongo, while early in the eighteenth century, the ver-nacular in the Southern Antilles had become Papiamentu, and (West Indian) English in the Northern Antilles. Most white settlers in Suriname must have been multilingual, speaking one or more European languages next to Sranan, and we are not even sure that Dutch was the language most widely spoken among them. On the islands, this was surely not the case, given the dominance of Papiamentu in the Southern Antilles and English in the Northern Antilles—but judging from the commercial net-works, Spanish, French, and English must have been spoken widely too. Thus, a researcher working in Dutch archives mainly with the Dutch-language documents resulting from the written communication between the metropolis and the various colonies is far afield from the linguistic realities of these colonies, as the fragments in Papiamentu and Skepi just cited so nicely illustrate.

Technology and Scholarship

It is neither possible nor particularly helpful to differentiate between curiosity-driven scholarly research and experimentation and the transfer of information aiming for practical results. The whole gamut was practiced, and added to early modern Dutch and hence European understanding of the natural habitat of the colonies, their pre-Columbian and new inhabitants, and ways of domesticating these exotic places.[8] The production of practical knowledge, both by scholars in academic settings and by practitioners in all types of trades, was crucial to European expansion.[9] Innovations in cartography, maritime technology, and the art of warfare preceded and accompanied Western colonialism, and in the Americas the plantation complex was characterized by a drive for optimization of production processes. While much of this technological progress was one-directional, European overseas exploits also stimulated the development of metropolitan science, and incorporated indigenous and African knowledge in a process that was, as Delbourgo and Dew write, "often the product of commercial contingency rather than of imperial design."[10]

From a scientific perspective, Dutch Atlantic history was nowhere more exciting than in Dutch Brazil (1630–54), where Governor Johan Maurits van Nassau-Siegen invested heavily in the arts and sciences, an exceptional approach in the entire reign of the VOC and WIC. Once more we need to emphasize that in view of the diverse backgrounds of the European population in the Dutch Atlantic, the usage of "Dutch" has a certain arbitrariness to it. Thus Johan Maurits himself was born and died in German territory. The contemporary Brazilian remembrance of this "humanist prince" emphasizes his patronage of painting, both ethnographic and naturalistic (Albert Eckhout and Frans Post), as well as his active support for the sciences. In Maurits's entourage were the German cartographer, mathematician, and astronomer Georg Markgraf and the medical doctor Willem Piso, a Dutchman educated in Leiden and Caen, France. The two studied the local flora and fauna and also engaged in medical, meteorological, and astronomic research, resulting in their massive joint publication *Historia Naturalis Brasiliae* (1648). The volumes written by Piso, *De Medicina Brasiliensi*, are still considered pioneering works on tropical medicine, while Markgraf's volumes have a similar standing in naturalist scholarship. The *Historia Naturalis Brasiliae* was concluded by a historical and ethnographic account written by WIC director Johannes de Laet. The scholarly and artistic fervor characteristic of the Brazilian adventure would not be replicated. Along with the optimism about the WIC and its prospects in the Americas, the drive to invest in scholarly exploits waned.

Henceforth, Dutch scholarly interest in the Atlantic colonies, if any, centered on Suriname, with its promising plantation sector and spectacular biodiversity. From the early sixteenth century, illusions of Eldorado and the existence of rich gold mines had inspired European explorers to venture into the interior of the Guianas. The fate of most of these expeditions was dismal, as gold was seldom mined and many explorers found instead a miserable death in the tropical forest. Systematic geological research on Suriname would only start in the late nineteenth century, long after the Humboldtian revolution had gathered momentum elsewhere in the Americas and beyond.

Cartography, too, had mainly an early promising start. Dutch map-making was far more extensive for the area covered by the VOC than for the Atlantic, and by the mid-seventeenth century, the WIC retreated from Atlantic map-making. By then, good maps of the Atlantic including the Antilles and the Wild Coast provided essential mapping for colonization and trade. Johannes van Keulen's *Zeefakkel*, produced in the early 1680s, was a navigation manual of the entire Atlantic available in Dutch, Italian, and Spanish versions, based on hundreds of detailed maps. Van Keulen's maps would remain internationally cutting-edge until the mid-eighteenth century, except for France and England, where state-sponsored alternatives displaced Dutch cartography earlier on.[11]

The development of the Guianas' plantation sector was accompanied by a series of fairly adequate maps of the coastal region. In contrast, serious reconnaissance of the interior of the Guianas started only in the later nineteenth century. There is little indication of local academic interest in physical geography, but practical expertise was developed. Thus planters' manuals discussed issues such as types of soil and seasonal climatic variations in great detail, as these directly influenced productivity in the plantation sector.

Publications on the Guianas would often include verbal and pictorial evocations of a majestic nature, presenting their intended European readership with stunning images of the tropics. Few of these works had scholarly merits or pretense. One major, and certainly the earliest, exception was Maria Sybilla Merian's work on the flora and fauna of Suriname. While her personal history as a talented and enterprising female researcher and artist in a male-dominated world has attracted much interest, her lasting contribution as one of the "Great Naturalists" clearly stands by itself. Merian concentrated on insects and butterflies, but she also drew flora and reptiles. Published in 1705, her *Metamorphosis insectorum*

Surinamensium was to become a source of inspiration for scholars as well as a first introduction of Surinamese nature to a wider European audience. Her work stimulated further European scholarship. Many of her drawings were collected by Hans Sloane and were subsequently included in the treasures of the British Museum. Carl Linnaeus would use the *Metamorphosis* extensively for his systematic classification of nature. The tenth edition of the Linnaean *Systema naturae* (1758) has over one hundred references to her work.[12] Linnaeus even sent his Swedish student Daniel Rolander to Suriname in 1754 to collect specimens of the local flora.[13]

Other than this, there is only scattered evidence of European scholars taking the study of Surinamese nature seriously in the early modern period. Attempts to found botanical gardens in Paramaribo failed, but some remarkable local contributions to European botanical and hence pharmaceutical research were recorded, even if medical doctor G. W. Schilling criticized his fellow European settlers for discarding the wealth of knowledge treasured by slaves and free coloreds. Indeed, in 1730, the enslaved African Quassie demonstrated the medical uses of a local type of bitter wood. Word spread quickly. Through Carel Gustaf Dahlberg, a Swedish planter residing in the colony, a specimen was sent to Sweden and would eventually be classified in the Linnaean system as *Quassia amara* L. (1761). Dahlberg's interest was probably strengthened by the work of Rolander, the tutor to his own children. A few years later, C. M. Blom published a scholarly treatise on this *kwasibita,* as the bitter wood was known in Sranantongo. In 1751 Quassie was manumitted and in 1776 he was even invited to travel to the Netherlands to visit with the stadtholder. The high distinction awarded to him by Willem V probably honored his role as a spy for the colonial regime against the Maroons no less than his herbal expertise.[14]

The Antilles attracted little naturalist attention. Floral data collected by the English botanist Leonard Plukenet were included in Linnaeus's *Species plantarum* (1753) and added to by Nicolaus Joseph Jacquin (1763). The latter was born and educated in the Netherlands but had moved via Paris to Vienna, whence Holy Roman Emperor Francis I sent him on a scientific expedition to the West Indies and Central America (1755–59). Jacquin also provided the first descriptions of the flora of the Windward Antilles. Upon their return both Plukenet and Jacquin became leading botanists in Europe.[15]

While contemporary authors were deeply impressed by the fauna of Suriname and presented spectacular descriptions and depictions, they offered no systematic analyses and at times some very confusing information. Specimens of Surinamese wildlife, particularly birds, did find their way into eighteenth-century European collections. George Edwards's 1743 *Natural History of Birds*, for example, included ten birds from Suriname. In the 1760s, Dahlberg apparently sent over some seven hundred zoological specimens to Linnaeus. The Dutch medical doctor Philippe Armand Fermin, who had a practice in Suriname and authored various books on both nature and society in Suriname, built up his own collection, parts of which also ended up in Hans Sloane's collections. Fermin also experimented—on slaves, that is—with electricity discharged by eels. In fact, fascination with this fish prevalent in the rivers of the Guianas stimulated the emergence in the mid-eighteenth century of a lively network of scholars between the Dutch Guianas, Leiden and Amsterdam exchanging information on animal electricity; this network in turn fed into wider European debates.[16]

New World plantations operated under a shared set of human resource management and agrarian and processing principles, always adapted to local conditions. Technological innovations were an integral part of this, and the Dutch Guianas were no exception to the rule. Relevant technological innovations developed either in Europe or in competing Caribbean colonies were quickly implemented. Planters' manuals from Suriname testify to a vivid interest in innovation, and particularly the adaptation of the metropolitan technology of water management helped create a sophisticated system of irrigation, drainage, transportation, and water-powered energy for the sugar mills. In addition, the introduction in the early 1710s of coffee linked Java via the republic to Suriname—and many other innovations were introduced from non-Dutch parts of the Atlantic.

Marked by high morbidity, high mortality, and low fertility, the demographic performance of the populations of the Dutch Atlantic was dismal. While the constant threat of deadly disease haunted the European minority, aboard the slave ships and in the Caribbean colonies overseers also worried about condition of their enslaved personnel, indispensable and costly capital to them. Over time, there was a slow but unmistakable improvement in the demographic performance of all segments of the Caribbean populations. The explanations for this progress probably lie

mainly in the creolization of the local population and the growing proportion of locally born slaves resulting in better resistance to endemic disease
and smaller impact of foreign epidemics. It is not clear at what point this
logic became clear to the local elites. Regardless, out of evident self-interest the local authorities and planters were always interested in implement-
ing specific measures that would increase natural reproduction. Planters'
wisdom as expressed in manuals and correspondence departed from the
maxim that "wise" rule combined discipline—enforced if necessary by the
whip and worse—with some balance between high work demands and
"reasonable" treatment. In other words, the planters and overseers were
encouraged to extract the maximum productivity out of their enslaved
workers, without crossing the limits of what these slaves could tolerate
physically and mentally.

Next to factors such as nutrition, housing, and room for cultural
expression, health issues were constantly discussed among Suriname's
local elites and in all planters' manuals. This interest was not matched by
significant medical research or valorization of European medical scholarship. The major breakthroughs in medical knowledge date from the later
nineteenth century and beyond. As late as 1800, European medical science did not have very much to offer either to its own populations or
to colonial subjects in the tropics, although some modest advances were
made in preventive and curative practices. There was something of an
institutional colonial tradition in medical care, ranging from government
hospitals, pharmacies, and quarantine establishments to lay provisions
on individual plantations, but even contemporaries complained bitterly
about their quality. It would take until the early twentieth century before
widespread deadly or devastating illnesses such as cholera, yellow fever,
and leprosy would be fully understood and became curable, but before
that time resident physicians and medical specialists serving the maritime
trade with the West Indies made valiant efforts to describe and categorize the
many illnesses they encountered.[17]

Again, practical knowledge circulated in numerous ways and included
the adoption by some colonial practitioners of African and Amerindian
medicine. The few relevant Western medical innovations that were made
in the eighteenth century spread rather quickly to the colonies. The most
telling example is the preventive treatment of smallpox. The technique
of inoculation (with human material), first introduced into Europe from

the Ottoman Empire, was implemented in the British West Indies in the 1770s and quickly spread to the Dutch colonies. The safer technique of vaccination with animal material was discovered shortly before 1800 and was quickly adopted in the British West Indies and subsequently in the Dutch West Indies.[18]

While, in sum, the development of tropical medical sciences by local laymen as well as by physicians and pharmacists trained in the metropolis was modest, there was a distinct circulation of relevant knowledge within the wider Atlantic adding up to some incremental growth in medical expertise. Such exchanges transcended colonial borders, as many of the students from the British West Indies who took a degree in medicine at Leiden University probably returned to the colonies after finishing their studies.[19]

Intellectual Wastelands?

In view of the poor local facilities, an educational sojourn in the metropolis was requisite for the children of the colonial elites. These were predominantly whites from the Caribbean, but we also know of dozens of young Africans sent to the metropolis for educational purposes, including the famous Jacobus Capitein whose tragic story we already recounted.[20] By the 1730s, well-to-do settlers in Suriname had developed the practice of sending their children to Holland at age seven or eight.[21] Over one hundred Dutch West Indians, mainly from Suriname, studied at Dutch universities in the eighteenth century. Law was the favorite discipline, followed by medicine.[22] The majority of university-trained professionals arriving in the colonies were recent immigrants from Europe, and they often had no intention of making their residence in the colonies permanent.

Virtually all known educated people and (aspiring) intellectuals were white and part of the colonial establishment. As a group they were divided along lines of birth (European or colonial), religion (Christian or Jewish), and class, but they shared a clearly-defined distance from the non-white and enslaved population. Some of these local intellectuals published works on Suriname. They were really individuals—there is little indication of a network connecting intellectuals in the Dutch Atlantic and beyond on a regular basis. Within the colonies, these men—female participation in intellectual debates was extremely rare—must have known one another. As there were hardly any educational institutions, they must have arranged to meet elsewhere.

The second half of the eighteenth century saw the founding of some organizations aiming at the advancement of intellectual debate. Masonry provided an important venue. A lodge was founded on St. Eustatius as early as 1747 at the initiative of British settlers, while the first lodge on Curaçao dates from 1757. Both were among the first in the Americas. In the next few years, several more Masonic lodges were established on Curaçao. Apparently, there was no separate Jewish lodge on the island.[23] The first lodge in Suriname opened in 1761. In the late 1770s, there were no fewer than six lodges with over two hundred members; by 1800 the colony still boasted four lodges. Some of the lodges had been exclusively Jewish, while others were of a mixed religious character. Anecdotal evidence suggests that the greater part of the male colonial elites, including high officials and even governors, participated in one or more Masonic lodges.[24]

Not surprisingly, there was nothing revolutionary about this Masonic movement; a nineteenth-century pamphlet would even comment that the lodge in Suriname counted "the most brutal slave executioners" among its leadership. True to the ideals of international Masonry, the lodges did debate ways to advance the development of the colonies. Following the metropolitan model, Masons were instrumental in establishing local departments of the Maatschappij tot Nut van 't Algemeen (Society for the Public Good). The department for Suriname was established in 1794, much earlier than its Curaçaoan counterpart (1817); it lasted until 1800 and was revived in 1816. There was no trace of this sort of intellectual activity in Elmina.[25]

In the 1740s, Suriname had a governor with literary ambitions, Jan Jacob Mauricius, but the intellectually most active episode in the Dutch Atlantic colonies would be set in that same colony in the later eighteenth century. The central figure was the Jewish Surinamese David Isaac Cohen de Nassy, quoted in the opening section of this chapter. Nassy was a descendant of his namesake discussed earlier, one of the founding fathers of Dutch Guiana. The younger Nassy was the leader of the five-member Association of Learned Jewish Men that served as a debating club and ended up publishing one of the most noteworthy studies in the colony's historiography, the *Essai historique*. The fact that the book was first published in French (1788) and only later in Dutch (1791) not only illustrates Nassy's polyglot competences, but also suggests that Nassy and his associates were trying to appeal to a wider audience than the Dutch world. As we will see, this was very much in line with Nassy's own subsequent career. The *Essai historique* was the fruit of a circle of men who defined themselves firmly as both Jews and creoles. Its message was first, that Jews were honorable and productive members of their societies, wherever those societies might be; and second, that the authors and their community had made this particular colony their home and had worked tirelessly over the generations for its progress.[26]

Another type of institution for intellectual advancement, extant again only in Suriname, had no other ambition than to provide a platform for optimizing plantation production. Several debating clubs dedicated to this pursuit were listed at one time or another. The one book actually published as a result of such deliberations discloses a truly utilitarian agenda—and testifies to the commonsense approach of its membership to plantation agriculture, ruling slaves, and medicine.[27] Mention may also be made of short-lived associations such as the Collegium Medicum and the naturalist Kollegie van Natuur-Onderzoekingen (College for Naturalist Research; both ca. 1780), the Suriname branch of the economics division of the Hollandsche Maatschappij der Wetenschappen (Holland Society for the Sciences), and journals dedicated to medical issues (*De Surinaamsche Artz*, 1786–88) or plantation culture (*De Surinaamse landman*, 1801–5).

These initiatives of the later eighteenth century testify to a growing awareness of scholarly advances in Europe as well as a utilitarian ambition to apply this knowledge to local questions. As one of the protagonists of the "Suriname Enlightenment" observed in 1786, his compatriots shared in a spirit in which "the distribution of knowledge appears to be a general desire."[28] This same exceptionally dynamic period in Suriname (even in comparison to Batavia in the East Indies) saw the founding of associations with literary and theatrical ambitions. These included De Surinaamsche lettervrinden (1786), the Letterkundige Uitspanningen (1785–87), and the Jewish literary association Docendo Docemur (1783), of which, again, the exceptional Nassy was a leading member.[29] Scattered evidence regarding membership suggests that a prosopography of the local elites would disclose high levels of overlap in the membership of the various institutions discussed above, in spite of the discrepancies between their official ambitions, intellectual orientations, and religious affiliation.

What literature was available to the educated class? As there were no public libraries, we should turn to inventories of private libraries. Perhaps surprisingly, some of the higher-up inhabitants of the Elmina castle did possess quite extensive and diverse book collections. Thus, WIC director Jan Pieter Huydecooper had a library with scholarly works of all sorts. Stationed in Elmina in 1760, he ordered additional legal texts such as the *Codex Justitianus* and a recent publication on Dutch Roman law—only to find out that, for present purposes, he might better study local legal practices in Elmina.[30]

For Curaçao, we have an inventory from the 1730s describing the library of Juan Pedro van Collen, a former governor. His collection included at least six biographies, predominantly of Dutch military and political leaders, and a few other historical tracts, as well as some works of philosophy (Erasmus, Descartes), and a good number of literary works dominated by Dutch authors but also featuring Milton's *Paradise Lost* and Montesquieu's *Persian Letters*. What is most striking about the inventory is the virtually complete absence of classical authors and theological treatises.[31] An entire century separates this inventory from the next one discovered so far, the library of the prominent Jewish islander Haim Abinun de Lima. In his multilingual library, travel accounts, literature, and political, geographical, historical, and reference works dominated. Not surprisingly, in contrast to Suriname, planters' manuals were lacking.[32]

English, of course, was dominant in the Northern Antilles, and we may safely assume that North American influence was paramount. For example, all works offered for sale in 1792 by Edward Luther Low, editor of the *Sint-Eustatia Press,* were in English. His catalogue of 36 titles in 159 volumes mainly comprised works in history, literature, and travel accounts. A later book offer by another printer (1812) included encyclopedias and the Académie française's *Dictionnaire.*[33]

Again, and typically, we have more indications for libraries in Suriname. A first public library was established in 1783. In the *Essai historique,* Nassy boasted with some exaggeration that the combined private libraries of the prominent residents of the colony—including the governor and other metropolitan officials, medical doctors, and several Christian and Jewish "laymen"—were second to none among the libraries throughout the Americas and could rival the large libraries in Europe. David Nassy's private library alone, likely built up over the generations, was an impressive multilingual collection of four to five hundred books, two-thirds of it nonfiction. With many volumes on physics, chemistry, and physiology, the hard sciences were well represented. So were the medical and pharmaceutical sciences, no doubt because Nassy practiced these trades.[34]

David Nassy was an intellectual of exceptional proportions in Surinamese history, and an extraordinary individual on other accounts as well. While he failed as a coffee planter, he was more successful as a mainly self-taught medical doctor, an expert in pharmaceutical knowledge, a dignitary in the Jewish community, a sworn multilingual interpreter, and a public intellectual standing tall among the Surinamese elite. His remarkable career testifies to his individual capacities and drive, and moreover gives remarkable insight in the possibilities for circulation of ideas in the Atlantic world. Born in the isolated outpost of Suriname in 1747, he would link up with intellectual currents of Europe, and later in life also ventured abroad. Partly for health and family reasons, Nassy moved to Philadelphia in 1792. It is significant indeed that Nassy chose not to travel to the republic, but rather to settle in North America, using a long-established and intensively traveled commercial route. By then, Philadelphia was a vital center linking European and North American scholarship.[35]

In his new habitat, Nassy published a study on yellow fever the next year and was elected a member of the American Philosophical Society in 1795. He practiced as medical doctor first in Philadelphia and later on the Danish West Indian island of St. Thomas, another colony with long-standing Dutch connections. Upon his return to Suriname in 1795, Nassy did not even try to gain permission to pursue this profession, alluding to "the envy and prejudice against the Jews." In vain he advocated for the establishment of higher education modeled after, no less, Harvard and Princeton. He died in Suriname in 1806.[36]

Nassy's story illustrates that Suriname was not closed off from intellectual currents in the wider Atlantic, but he remains an isolated figure and his legacy seems to have been rather ephemeral. The Dutch lawyer and public official François Lammens, who arrived in Paramaribo a decade after Nassy's death, observed that among the local elites the arts and sciences were "never" a subject of discussion and that local cultural and intellectual associations were short lived in this materialist society.[37]

In summary, the circulation of knowledge within the Dutch Atlantic and beyond responded mainly to a utilitarian agenda, even if there was some interest in "pure" inquiry, involving both Dutch scholars connecting to peers elsewhere in the Atlantic and European scholars such as Linnaeus interested in the natural resources of the Dutch colonies. This is not surprising. Although the Dutch companies for Asia and the Atlantic did collect relevant maps and to some extent also works of art from the Indies, they did not display much interest in research. Individual researchers, even those employed to other ends by the companies, mostly worked at their own initiative and with their own means. The Dutch colonial companies were no active sponsors, and in comparison to the major competitors, "the knowledge infrastructure in the Dutch seaborne empire long remained fairly underdeveloped," as Karel Davids writes. Even the stadtholder Willem IV's collections of tropical exotica—which included, apart from maps, mainly naturalia, many of these bequeathed by VOC officials, and in large part not acquired in Dutch colonies but rather in China and other faraway places—did not reflect anything like a concerted metropolitan effort to add a scholarly dimension to colonialism.[38]

This conclusion is neither surprising nor exceptional in a wider Caribbean perspective, although some nuance should be discerned. Clearly the continental American colonies, in particular in the north, were partaking more intensely in circuits of knowledge of all kinds. Within the Caribbean proper, the Spanish, French, and British Caribbean colonies all had larger populations and (consequently) more of an educational and scholarly tradition. The first university in the Americas was founded in 1538 in Santo Domingo; Cuba's first university came in 1728. With the onset of the Bourbon reforms in the 1760s, the Spanish Crown began to revive academia in Spanish America. The first institution for higher education in the British West Indies was established in 1743 (Codrington College, Barbados). Several local learned societies were established in the later eighteenth century all over the British West Indies, even if subsequent academic development in the anglophone Americas was concentrated in North America. In the 1780s, French Saint-Domingue boasted an academic infrastructure directly linked to the Royal French Academy of Sciences, then an international leader in scientific research—though even there, James McClellan writes, "utility and the promise of utility constituted the reasons why science and medicine became enlisted in the service of colonial development."[39]

This utilitarian agenda always implied the circulation of knowledge across imperial boundaries, as the permanent spread of technological innovation in the sugar industry illustrates. There was a keen interest in the technological advances made elsewhere, and much of this must have circulated by oral transmission of practical knowledge by specialists moving from one place to another. The transfer of more abstract knowledge required more sophisticated retrieval, as the greater part of scholarly publications was produced in the metropolitan centers and usually in the metropolitan language. Dutch metropolitan scholars and centers of expertise participated in this wider Atlantic web of knowledge, to which the Dutch Atlantic colonies were peripheral.[40]

Printing and Publishing

The later eighteenth century witnessed the beginnings of a publishing industry in the Dutch Atlantic world, once again with the exception of Elmina. Since the mid-1770s, a local newspaper was printed in Paramaribo, published under different arrangements and names, mainly as the *Surinaamsche Courant*. In the 1790s, the colony also had short-lived newspapers in French and German—not in English. Some books and pamphlets were locally published. The islands lagged behind. The short-lived English-language *St. Eustatius Gazette* (1790–94) was published by Edward Luther Low, an Englishman from St. Kitts who had started a printing press annex bookshop on the neighboring Dutch island but returned four your later to St. Kitts as the Statian economy descended in a downward slope. On Curaçao, no newspaper whatsoever was published until the founding of the *Curaçao Gazette* in 1812, during the British interregnum, by William Lee from Edinburgh. The paper was continued as the *Curaçaose Courant* in 1816.[41]

Publishing on Dutch Atlantic affairs was mainly a metropolitan affair, but not one of great significance, and certainly not in the period after the loss of Dutch Brazil and New Netherland. Benjamin Schmidt has argued that after the 1670s, Dutch authors and publishers were moving away from presenting specific images of various parts of the globe, in the process extolling the republic's exploits in faraway places, towards the construction of more generalized images of an exotic world, increasingly devoid of allusions to specific localities and metropolitan lordship and catering to the largest possible clientele. In Schmidt's analysis, in the half century up to the 1730s the Dutch Republic functioned as the foremost construction site of both an imagined exotic world and its antipode, the idea of a generalized European civilization. In the remainder of the century, Dutch publishing lost its edge to France and Great Britain, but would retain its position as one of the intellectual entrepôts of *ancien régime* Europe. Not coincidentally, this was also a period in which the republic was beginning to lose its leading technological position.[42]

Schmidt does not present a comprehensive analysis of publications specifically dealing with the Dutch colonial world, and indeed the most important and prestigious publications produced in the republic had a broader geographic and political reach. Famous works such as Arnoldus Montanus's much translated and copied work on the Americas, *De nieuwe en onbekende weereld: of Beschryving van America en't Zuid-land*, included passing references to the Dutch possessions. The same applies to works on global religions published in the republic such as Bernart Picart's *Cérémonies et coutumes religieuses de tous les peuples du monde* (1723–43). If we do focus on publications on the Dutch Atlantic colonies proper, we cannot but conclude that their number was conspicuously small—which reflects, we may presume, the low level of interest in these colonies among the educated classes.

As for nonfiction books, whether travelogues, treatises on faraway places, or planters' manuals, the harvest is meager and unevenly distributed. There was a significant pre-1680 Dutch tradition of publishing on sub-Saharan Africa, as witnessed in books such as Pieter de Marees's 1602 *Beschryvinge*, Dierick Ruiters's 1623 *Toortse der zee-vaert* and Olfert Dapper's 1668 *Naukeurige beschrijvinge*—many of these, according to the custom of this period, combining the authors' own observations with information drawn from previously published descriptions on West Africa.[43] In turn, perusing these works, but also drawing upon his own experiences as a servant to the WIC in Elmina (1688–1702), Willem Bosman published his acclaimed *Nauwkeurige beschryving* on the African Gold Coast in 1704—but while this book was soon translated into several other European languages, it would remain the only original Dutch book published on West Africa for the rest of the century, not counting some general works such as Isaak Tirion's multi-volume *Hedendaagsche historie, of tegenwoordige staat van alle volkeren*, published from the 1740s through the early 1760s. Some French-language titles added to the body of studies published in the Dutch Republic on sub-Saharan Africa, as well as summaries in compendia on the world beyond Europe, such as Pieter van der Aa's *Zee- en Landreysen* (1707). Van den Boogaart concluded that Dutch publishing on sub-Sahara Africa, even including the Cape Colony, was marginal in comparison to Dutch book production on Asia and the Americas—and this, we may add, is particularly evident for the eighteenth century.[44]

The short-lived Dutch colonization in Brazil did result in some important scholarly books—more so than was the case with New Netherland.[45] Particularly remarkable is the apparent lack of interest in the Dutch Antilles, islands that had been an integral part of the WIC's Atlantic domain since the 1630s. Johannes de Laet, a polyglot scholar, cofounder of the WIC and subsequently a leading official of the company, wrote about the Caribbean in his *Nieuwe Wereldt* (1625) and *Beschrijvinghe van West Indiën* (1630), and included some pages on the conquest of Curaçao in his *Historie ofte iaerlijck verhael* published in 1644. The French native Charles de Rochefort, who moved to the Dutch Republic and subsequently authored the well-known *Histoire naturelle et morale des isles Antilles de l'Amérique* (1658), also wrote an almost unknown book on Dutch Tobago (1665), where he seems to have lived; his 1658 *Histoire* offers only scant information on St. Eustatius, St. Maarten, and Saba, and none on the other Dutch Caribbean colonies.[46] Up to 1815, only one, short and tantalizingly superficial, history and general description of Curaçao appeared, written as late as 1779 by an author who had never visited the island (J. W. Hering, *Beschryving*). Hering's description of the island as "not a treasury of the richest products of nature" but rather "a warehouse" for international trade echoes Adam Smith's characterization of the surprising comparative advantages of this "barren island."[47]

Smith was referring to St. Eustatius, an island that inspired not one single book throughout this period. No matter what these islands' economic value to the metropolis may have been, Dutch interest was apparently small, and locals harbored little aspiration to introduce their island to readers in the republic. Only in 1789, in the dying days of the WIC, did the Dutch States General sent the Grovestins and Boeij commission to the West Indies in order to compile a report on the state of affairs on the Antilles, and on the lesser Guianas—and their reports were informative but reflected mainly an administrative interest.

The virtual absence of publications on the Dutch Antilles provides a stark contrast both to the significant number of books issued on the British, French, and Spanish Caribbean islands, and also to Dutch metropolitan interest in the Dutch Guianas, particularly Suriname. The colony was of greater economic promise and interest to the metropolis, and hence attracted more European visitors, some of these ending up as authors. Substantial parts of the books they wrote discussed topics related only indirectly or not at all to economic gain, presenting instead proto-ethnographies of the wondrous indigenous populations, as well as descriptions of exotic flora and fauna. This is not to say that the body of publications of the entire 1680–1815 period reflects an intensive metropolitan interest. The total number of books was in the order of twenty to thirty, most of these dealing with Suriname only, a few describing the Guianas combined, and only two on Berbice, Demerara, and Essequibo alone. The latter were written by British visitors (Edward Bancroft's 1769 *Essay on the Natural History of Guiana*, and Henry Bolingbroke's 1807 *Voyage to Demerary*)—no coincidence in view of the British interest in extending the frontiers of the British West Indies.

Of this modest body of writings, quite a few were written in languages other than Dutch and often by foreigners—demonstrating again the entangled nature of the early modern Atlantic. We should be prudent in attaching significance to this, as the republic's publishing industry remained multilingual throughout this period. Even so, it is striking how often books on Suriname aimed for a wider international audience. The most famous book on the colony, John Gabriel Stedman's 1796 *Narrative*, was published in English before it was translated and appeared in German (1797), French (1798), Dutch (1799–1800), and even Swedish (1800) and Italian (1818)—Stedman himself was of mixed Dutch-Scottish descent and spoke both Dutch and English.[48] As mentioned above, the 1788 *Essai historique* written by David Nassy and his consortium of "learned Jewish men" was published in Suriname in French and only subsequently translated into Dutch and published in Amsterdam (1791).

Nauwkeurige
BESCHRYVINGE
VAN
ZURINAME

TE LEEUWAARDEN, By MEINDERT JNJEMA.

Figure 15. Title page of an early book on Suriname, with an idyllic engraving of a presumably enslaved African family. Reproduced from Herlein, *Beschryvinge*, 1718.

The Dutch medical doctor Philippe Fermin first published two books in French (*Histoire naturelle*, 1765, and *Description générale*, 1769) before he issued a Dutch edition of the latter (*Nieuwe algemeene beschryving*, 1770), again followed by a French-language *Tableau* (1778). The Germans Johann Friedrich Ludwigs (*Neueste Nachrichten*, 1789), Johann Andreas Riemer (*Missions-Reise*, 1801), J. D. Kunitz (*Surinam*, 1805), and Christlieb Quandt (*Nachricht*, 1807) published their observations in their mother tongue, as did the Frenchman Pierre-Victor Malouet (*Collection*, 1802). The German Albert von Sack first published his account in English (*Narrative*, 1810) before it was published in German (*Beschreibung*, 1821) and Dutch (*Reize*, 1821).

Among the major works written in Dutch and published in the republic on the Guianas, mainly Suriname, we find a few general surveys, starting with A. van Berkel's *Amerikaansche voyagien* (1695) and J. D. Herlein's *Beschryvinge* (1718), next Thomas Pistorius's *Korte en zakelyke beschryvinge* (1763), J. J. Hartsinck's *Beschryving* and Fermin's *Nieuwe algemeene beschryving*, both from 1770, and Stedman's *Reize* (1799–1800). Otherwise, there are planters' manuals, particularly Anthony Blom and Floris Heshuysen's *Verhandeling*, Blom's 1787 *Verhandeling*, and the 1804 *Verzamelingen* published by a Suriname-based group of planters. Then there are a couple of polemic booklets by the renegade Protestant minister Joannes Kals (*Klagte* 1733, *Neerlands hooft- en wortel-sonde* 1756, and *Nuttige en noodige bekeeringe*, 1756) as well as the highly polemic and voluminous 1752 *Receuil van egte stukken*, which deals with intra-elite conflicts. And that is it. Even if Suriname was of more interest to a Dutch reading audience than the Antilles and Elmina, the number and certainly the character of the books published pales in comparison to the wealth of publications manufactured and marketed in the eighteenth-century republic on the exotic world writ large, and also in comparison to the number of works published on the domain of the VOC, an immense and highly developed Asian world that apparently interested and impressed the Dutch far more than the Americas or Africa.[49]

General introductions to the republic's history and present state included mainly superficial entries on the colonies.[50] Likewise, major encyclopedic works were not based on first-hand experience with overseas colonies, Dutch or other, but did include relevant information. Thus a metropolitan reading audience could learn of Suriname and to a much lesser extent the Dutch Antilles by browsing through the works of the Frenchmen Père Jean-Baptiste Labat in the 1720s and particularly Guillaume Raynal (*Histoire philosophique et politique*, 1774, and the 1781 *Suppléments*), and through the compendium written by the Dutch author Elie Luzac (*Hollands rijkdom*, 1780–83). Very often such works were published in the Dutch Republic.

The number of publications on the Dutch Caribbean colonies would increase considerably in the half century after 1815. Particularly from the 1840s onwards, a great deal was written on slavery—its justification or lack thereof, excesses, arguments in favor of and against its abolition, alternatives, and so on. Most of these books were written in Dutch, and predominantly by Dutchmen. While this may partly reflect the growing appreciation of the Dutch language in the new kingdom, it also indicates that the remaining Atlantic colonies were becoming more exclusively Dutch. In stark contrast to the Dutch East Indies, foreign interest in the Dutch Atlantic colonies had withered—and hence a new notion of the Dutch Caribbean and particularly of Suriname emerged in which its foundational transimperial connections were all but forgotten.

If we turn from books to pamphlets, we see not simply a low level, but even a decline of overall interest in the West Indies—not counting, that is, the many dozens of pamphlets that were published in the republic during the eighteenth century on Atlantic commercial and governance issues by the competing interested parties, particularly those in Zeeland and Amsterdam.[51] But beyond such pamphlets expressing hard-nosed interest in the economics and governance of the extant Dutch colonies, there is not much. We may take the National Library collection of pamphlets from the 1486–1853 period as a point of departure. Certainly this collection is not exhaustive, but still the broad pattern is telling. Of nearly 37,000 items, a mere twenty-four relate to the Dutch Atlantic in the period from 1680 to 1800. Thirteen of these deal with just one issue, the 1780–84 Anglo-Dutch War, especially the British ransacking of St. Eustatius, and the demise of Dutch power in Atlantic waters. The National Library's collection has many more relevant pamphlets published prior to 1680. Indeed, of the ninety-three items dealing with the Dutch West India Company, seventy-eight antedate 1680, hence relate to the ambitious first company. In the later pamphlets there is nothing to remind us of the "grand design" for

West Indian expansion once expressed by the protagonists of the Dutch West India Company.[52]

This is not to say that the educated classes could not access information on the Atlantic. By the mid-seventeenth century, the first newspapers were providing occasional reports about such faraway places as the Guianas, even if Asia was generally better covered than the Atlantic.[53] Newspapers were widely available in the Dutch Republic, and Amsterdam was a European clearinghouse for information, especially regarding trade and foreign affairs. The republic's major newspapers, all published in the province of Holland—the *Oprechte Haerlemse Courant,* the *Amsterdamsche Courant,* the *Leydse Courant* and the *'s Gravenhaegse Courant*—had a combined circulation of about 20,000 in the mid-eighteenth century. If the common estimate that each issue was read by some ten people is correct, their total readership must have been about 200,000, some 10 percent of the overall population of the country and perhaps as much as a third of the adult population, male and female.[54] Such newspapers featured sections grouped under geographic categories such as "Duitschland," "Vrankryk," and, indeed, "West-Indien." The latter was often the smallest section, but at least some information was regularly provided, often including references to the British, Spanish, and French Atlantic colonies as well.

Browsing through these newspapers one finds that major news in the West Indies was indeed covered, such as the 1763 slave rebellion in Berbice or the sacking of St. Eustatius in 1781. Occasionally less dramatic events were reported, such as a shipwreck, celebrations of the stadtholder's birthday, a hurricane, and so forth. It is hard to detect an editorial policy in this coverage; most likely the newspapers simply printed what happened to have been sent in. Newspapers reported more systematically on departures and arrivals of ships to and from the West Indies, including their cargo holds, and also of meetings of the WIC board. There were some advertisements, ranging from offers by the WIC of land for settlement to individual job propositions and sales of products from or books on the West Indies. In all, then, residents of the republic with a vested interest in the Atlantic must have gathered their information primarily from their business partners and reports of meetings of the institutional partners involved, while the general educated public could learn of the West Indies from the press in a less systematic way, and next to nothing about the Dutch presence in West Africa. Only those with friends and family overseas may have been better informed, as the prize papers disclose—but of course, the number of Dutch traveling to or living in the Atlantic colonies was low throughout this period.

Finally, a modest body of fiction emerged. Once more, the Antilles and Elmina were all but neglected. Novels, fictitious travel accounts, and a few theater works privileged the Guianas and focused on slavery and race—generally in a more critical way than nonfiction publications. The two most famous and probably relatively well-read works by far were written by non-Dutch authors. One is the 1688 novel *Oroonoko, Or the Royal Slave* (translated into French and German, not in Dutch) by the British author Aphra Behn, the other Voltaire's *Candide, ou l'optimisme* (1759, Dutch translation that same year). These works of fiction, together with Stedman's travelogue, did much to cement the image of Suriname as the nadir of brutalities inflicted on enslaved Africans. Indeed, few eyewitness accounts on the Atlantic and particularly on New World slavery were as much translated and as intensely circulated as Stedman's *Narrative*.[55]

As Bert Paasman has demonstrated, the total corpus of Dutch fiction on the West Indies and Atlantic slavery was negligible until the late eighteenth century. The two decades after 1790 witnessed more publishing, with a good dozen novels, poems, and plays, much of this inspired by British abolitionism and radical strands of the Dutch Patriot movement highly critical of the slave trade and slavery itself. As in Great Britain and North America, a considerable part of this work was written by women, such as Petronella Moens, Betje Wolff, Aagje Deken, and Elisabeth Maria Post.[56]

A Taste of the Tropical Atlantic in the Republic

In 1777, in the midst of the Surinamese financial crisis, a gentleman from Utrecht and his son, Jantje, visited Amsterdam for a few days. The purpose of this visit was business rather than leisure: the days were spent attending tedious deliberations with a notary about the financial problems of the West Indian plantations. Jantje was annoyed and suggested getting rid of the colony. His father understood his son's complaints. Thus he wrote down with evident despair: "Our Forefathers were rich and healthy, drank no Coffee nor Chocolate and never had losses on the Colonies. We instead drink Coffee, get ill and see our Capital and Interest diminish."[57]

The Dutch participation in the development of the Atlantic world indeed introduced new consumption patterns, first limited to the wealthy, but at quite an early stage filtering down to the lower classes. Tobacco was the first of the new tropical products to be widely consumed, probably as early as the mid-seventeenth century. Sugar, coffee, and (Asian) tea became ubiquitous in Dutch households and even orphanages in the course of the eighteenth century, sugar contributing a growing portion to a daily caloric intake that was increasing significantly anyway. Imported from the Spanish Main via Curaçao and later also directly from Suriname, cacao too was added to the Dutch diet, although more as a luxury item. The American potato became an increasingly important staple in Dutch households after the 1730s—but, of course, this had become a home-grown product. Evidence of the diversification and increase in Dutch consumption in the wake of European colonial expansion may be found in contemporary paintings and archives.[58]

Coffee houses, the first of which was established in Amsterdam in 1665, were becoming more numerous and less exclusive in the eighteenth century, and, at the same time, coffee became a household item.[59] English visitor James Boswell observed in 1764 great numbers of "wretches who have no other subsistence than potatoes, gin and the stuff which they call tea and coffee." Elie Luzac claimed that coffee, tea, and gin between them had destroyed "more than three-quarters of the breweries of Holland." These changes were not limited to the Dutch Republic. There is similar evidence from colonial powers such as France and Great Britain, but equally from places without direct colonial links. In Antwerp households, for example, equipment to prepare coffee became ubiquitous in the course of the eighteenth century. Coffee houses emerged all over Europe, and certainly not exclusively in cities with colonial connections.[60]

The number of Dutch tobacco-processing ateliers and sugar refineries had increased rapidly, particularly in Amsterdam, since the seventeenth century (see chapter 2).[61] The growing share of Atlantic commerce in overall Dutch trade brought business opportunities for the elites, innovation, and employment for the lower classes. So surely life in the republic was affected by Atlantic expansion. But did this mean that, beyond the leading public servants and business people, a substantial portion of the lower classes of the Dutch Republic were really aware of the overseas Atlantic?

We cannot assume that the processing or consumption of tropical produce automatically translated into awareness of the places where these were produced, and under what conditions. Absentee plantation owners, merchants, stock holders, or officials connected to the governing colonial institutions must have had some knowledge of all of this, but it is not evident that the same applied to ordinary consumers or even people working in retail business or related industries. Engravings of interiors of coffee houses do not reveal specific geographic markers, and, of course, unlike sugar, coffee came from many different places around the tropical world. In the republic, sugar was imported from Suriname but also from other Caribbean colonies, just like coffee. Tobacco processed in the republic did not come from Dutch colonies at all, but, rather from British North America and later also from the Dutch hinterland. The link, then, between tropical consumption goods and the Dutch Atlantic was not immediately evident.

Did the Dutch Atlantic somehow reverberate in Dutch cityscapes? Over the past decade, some interesting work has been done on architectural highlights in Dutch cities that somehow have a link to Dutch Atlantic history. Such research examines the Amsterdam offices of the West India Company, prestigious town houses of officials and businessmen with Atlantic interests, and the like.[62] While such memory sites do remind us of a long forgotten and perhaps intentionally silenced history of direct Dutch involvement in Atlantic expansion and, particularly, in the business of the slave trade and slavery, they cannot really be understood as strong indications that contemporary citizens or visitors to Dutch cities would have singled out the Atlantic connection of cosmopolitan cities such as Amsterdam and Rotterdam, and even less so cities in the country's interior. Perhaps this was more the case in the twin cities of Middelburg and Vlissingen in Zeeland, whose Atlantic profile was more evident. But generally, all Dutch seaports were linked into a European and a (quantitatively only secondary) global network of connections in which the share of the Atlantic remained modest by comparative standards.

Repatriates or temporary visitors from the Atlantic colonies were in and of themselves powerful reminders of Dutch overseas pursuits, the more conspicuous when these people brought with them enslaved servants of African origins. We have some figures on passenger traffic and some quite anecdotal evidence on the movement of people between Suriname and the republic—passenger travel and repatriation from the Antilles to the republic was less prevalent. While this data underlines that relations with Suriname were far more intense than with all other parts of the overseas Dutch Atlantic, one should be very careful in attributing too much importance even to the former. On the basis of eighteenth-century travel statistics, we may conclude that there was steady movement between Suriname and the republic, but equally that it is unlikely that at any given time a considerable number of "West Indians" were actually living in the metropolis.[63]

This probably explains why, in spite of much recent research, the anecdotal evidence on blacks in the republic has not really altered the picture of a peripheral presence. We have some exceptional cases such as Johannes Capitein from Elmina, Quassie from Suriname and an increasing number of lesser-known cases, but that is all. As for the presence of repatriating or sojourning Europeans, again, the evidence is mainly anecdotal and pertains mainly to repatriates from Suriname. We know of a few cases from the mid-eighteenth century such as that of the Suriname-born Dutch planters' scion Johan Alexander van Sandick, who, owing to his forbears' successful plantations, was reputed to be extremely rich, hence an attractive marriage partner for even the stadtholder's daughter. His repatriated father, Jan, had left him his planters' fortune in the same will of 1743 that manumitted his two enslaved servants Crispijn and Angelica, now residing in The Hague. But if we follow him and his family's history in the republic closely, we see little indication that their lives continued to gravitate towards their West Indian interests, but, rather, a diversification of their economic and social world away from this connection.[64]

The impact of Atlantic expansion on Dutch arts was minimal, with the exception of the early phase in Dutch Brazil, when Johan Maurits patronized not only the sciences but also commissioned paintings, resulting in the truly spectacular works of Frans Post and Albert Eckhout. Very few other professional painters worked in the Atlantic colonies, apart from Merian, though she would probably not have thought of herself that way. The one truly magnificent painting from Suriname, "Slave Dance," painted by Dirk Valkenburg, dates from 1709, after the painter's return to the republic—his few other paintings from Suriname are less spectacular as they portray mainly landscapes, not people. The modest number of other preserved paintings mainly portray the ports of Paramaribo and Curaçao, and St. Eustatius's roadstead. In addition, a fair number of engravings and drawings were made, mostly produced as illustrations for maps and the meager body of books published on the Dutch colonies. With the exception of the engravings made by William Blake based on drawings by John Gabriel Stedman, few of these captured either the Amerindian or the African populations of the colonies beyond stereotypes. This has led to the odd situation that we have more paintings by Rembrandt and other masters of the few dozen black servants living at one time in the republic than we do paintings of the hundreds of thousands of slaves that at one point were on board Dutch slave ships or who once lived in Dutch colonies.[65]

All of this is not to suggest that the Dutch Republic ceased to matter to the Atlantic colonies and vice versa, but, rather, that there were distinct asymmetries. To all but a fraction of the indigenous minorities and African-origins majorities of Dutch America, it must have been impossible and perhaps also irrelevant to imagine the republic that shaped their lives. The white settler population of Suriname, by contrast, continued to think of the metropolis not only as a crucial economic and political patron, but also as the place to send its children for education and perhaps one day to repatriate, and probably also as a model of civilization. The constant arrival of seaborne passengers as well as letters and newspapers from the republic helped to keep the settlers abreast of developments in the "motherland." But even in Suriname, there was far more information going around. Ships arriving from the British West Indies and North America carried information from other parts of the Atlantic, and ships departing in the opposite direction carried not just molasses, but also people and tidings of this Dutch colony to places outside of the Dutch realm. While bilateral links with the republic probably remained crucial for Suriname, this was no longer the case after mid-century for Berbice, Demerara, and Essequebo, where links to anglophone America were becoming dominant. As for the Dutch Caribbean islands, their prominent place in intraregional networks implied that connections to, and information on, the republic was not dominant among their many linkages to the outside world.

In a way, then, news about the Dutch colonies may have circulated as much, or more so, in non-Dutch colonies in the Western Atlantic as it did in the metropolis. Moreover, one should not overestimate the extent to which such news was distributed and digested within the republic. Surely many in the republic had some vested interest in the Atlantic, and indeed both the West India Company and the institutions governing the Guianas by definition represented an official West Indian interest with immediate access to the States General. The same goes for the business houses specializing in Atlantic commerce, absentee owners, and the like. At various times, representatives from these circles lobbied for their interests, demanding economic, military, or diplomatic support, thus testifying to a vivid interest in the overseas colonies. But there is little evidence that such lobbying reflected, or stimulated, awareness of the Dutch Atlantic colonies beyond these directly interested parties. This may help explain why, as we will discuss in the next chapter, the republic never produced a serious public debate about the legitimacy of the Atlantic slave trade.

Not only people and commodities circulated in the Atlantic, but so did knowledge and ideas—whether by formal correspondence, publications and research, or informally through travelers. Institutional and commercial parties—and also increasingly local gazettes and the like—spun webs of communication linking the various parts of the Dutch Atlantic to one another and beyond. Unsurprisingly, given the highly diverse character of the Dutch Atlantic, much of the resulting sources are not written in Dutch but rather in one of the many other European or Creole languages prevalent throughout the Dutch Atlantic.

Perhaps more so than one might expect given the crassly materialistic and exploitative character of the Atlantic world and of the Caribbean in particular, we did find considerable evidence of scholarly research and its practical uses, ranging from geography and the natural sciences through medicine and agrarian expertise to ethnography. Practical and scholarly expertise circulated widely throughout the Atlantic. In the Dutch Atlantic, this was more a question of individual initiative than of colonial policies. In spite of the absence of a truly intellectual ambience in Caribbean slave societies, we revealed remarkably enlightened efforts to establish scholarly, educational, and cultural practices beyond a merely utilitarian agenda. Meanwhile the Dutch Republic managed to remain a renowned center for publications on exotic places including the Dutch Atlantic colonies well into the eighteenth century, as well as a world market that absorbed and distributed ever more tropical products to its own citizens and any more on the European continent.

It remains a thorny question how exactly the Atlantic and particularly the Dutch colonies in Africa and the Americas reverberated in Dutch society. At this point, we can only arrive at very tentative answers. Surely the political and commercial elites most directly involved were well aware of the Dutch Atlantic world they had helped to build, and certainly literate Dutch citizens could have access to relevant printed materials and the like. By contrast, it is crystal clear that hardly any among the Dutch institutions and individuals involved had an interest in questioning the fundamental characteristics of the slave trade or slavery itself. As we will discuss in the next chapter, there was no such thing as a vibrant debate in the Dutch Republic about its legitimacy, in contrast to the United Kingdom and France at the time. One is tempted to think of this as indication of a more peripheral place of the Dutch Atlantic in the public mind, which in itself would run parallel to the comparatively lesser economic importance of the Atlantic to the Dutch Republic.

7

Contraction

"The Dutch are no longer the brokers or carriers for other nations," wrote the *English Review* of December 1786. "That trade, which was carried on solely through them, almost all kingdoms now carry on without their intervention. The forces of power thus continually drying too, no wonder that the decay becomes every day more visible."[1] This devastating observation stood in sharp contrast to Adam Smith's praise, just a decade earlier, of the ability and drive that had turned the "barren islands" of Curaçao and St. Eustatius into prosperous "free ports open to the ships of all nations" in a sea of suffocating mercantilism.[2]

The *English Review* was commenting on what would turn out to be only the beginning of the decline of the Dutch Atlantic. Over the next decades, the geopolitical weakness of the Dutch Republic would be exposed, resulting in its collapse at home and significant contraction of its colonial realm. After the Napoleonic Wars the Dutch state was reestablished as a kingdom, headed by a king with high ambitions for an overseas empire. But hopes for the Atlantic part of this realm were shattered early on, particularly hopes for a continuation of the commercial, empire-crossing services provided under the Dutch flag. As the Dutch were to find out, the end of the era of mercantilism meant that their services as brokers in the wider Atlantic were no longer needed. Surely they would find overseas alternatives, with spectacular riches, but these would be found in the Dutch East Indies.

This period of 1780–1815 constituted a transition. Both dates are marked by geopolitical events: the beginning of the Fourth Anglo-Dutch War and the end of the Napoleonic Wars. This was a period of enormous upheaval in the entire Atlantic, both because of a series of closely related political revolutions on both sides of the ocean and because of the British abolition of the slave trade, which would eventually mark the end of the triangular early modern Atlantic. All of this was of profound consequence to the Dutch Atlantic. What in the early 1780s might have seemed like a temporary crisis to some turned out to be the beginning of a long-term decline—not so much of the metropolitan Netherlands, nor of its possessions in the Indonesian archipelago, but certainly of the Dutch Atlantic. Against this backdrop we first discuss the entanglement of political developments in the various parts of the Dutch Atlantic and their relation to broader political developments in the Atlantic. We also explore the ways elites in both the Netherlands and the colonies dealt with the changing times. While the Dutch Atlantic somehow seemed out of touch with major political developments both in Western Europe (British abolitionism) and in the Americas (the Creole nationalism of North and Latin America), much of this was quite typical in a Caribbean context. Finally, we briefly look ahead at the nineteenth century by contrasting the atypically early implosion of the Dutch Atlantic to the explosive growth of the Dutch East Indies.[3]

The Collapse of the Dutch Republic

The *English Review* had other pertinent observations to make. The Dutch Republic's once celebrated, decentralized, and relatively open system of governance had come to a grinding halt. "Their complicated form of government, too, acts like a dead weight on a declining state. Incapable of exertion, except when set in motion by a general ardor for public good, it is ill suited to the circumstances of a corrupted and debilitated common-wealth, where a thousand jarring and incompatible claims throw every thing into confusion: and where nothing but the strong arm of power could still the agitated and contending elements, and bring this political chaos into order and form." In other words, unlike the neighboring monarchies, the Dutch Republic lacked a firm hand to guide it through this crisis. Instead, internal bickering and French intrusion only made matters worse. "The present situation of Holland naturally suggests these reflections. The unprosperous state of its affairs, which is always productive of bad humour, the spirit of faction, and some mutual causes of complaint, have revived ancient political animosities; all these, aided by the fostering hand of France, have excited a ferment which we sus-pect will not end favourably, either for the happiness or prosperity of the community."[4]

Fears that things "will not end favourably" were indeed omnipresent in the Dutch Republic at the time, and many were looking to France rather than to Great Britain for a way out. The economic crisis hit hard and would prove to be structural. Since the 1713 Peace of Utrecht, the Dutch had performed their role as middlemen in the Atlantic on a basis of neu-trality between the larger European rival states. The Fourth Anglo-Dutch war demonstrated that this rewarding role could only be performed as long as the competitors tolerated this. When the British decided that the republic's neutrality was no longer convenient, the Dutch found out that they lacked the military means to defend their interests. Unable to protect their own merchant fleet and colonies, their future lay in the hands of the British, and to a lesser extent the other Atlantic states.[5] During its golden age, the republic's leading role in international trade had been based on a combination of optimal cost-efficiency and a strong naval presence, if nec-essary, but throughout the eighteenth century these economic advantages had diminished, and Dutch naval strength had crumbled. By the 1780s, the Dutch Republic had no serious means to protect its colonies against British or French aggression in times of war. Moreover, the ransacking of St. Eustatius had taught the sobering lesson that the empire-crossing so typical of merchants operating from the Dutch Caribbean free ports had only been possible because, and as long as, stronger naval powers had found it expedient to tolerate this undermining of their mercantilist policies. This period of strategic lenience was drawing to a close in the

1780s—and after the Napoleonic Wars, the Dutch would be confronted with the end of mercantilism as such.

The Anglo-Dutch War had been a devastating confirmation that the Dutch were no match for the British, and the ensuing political humiliation and economic disaster had provoked a deep crisis and polarization among the Dutch elites. No doubt the correspondent of the *English Review* was referring to these antagonisms. Inspired by Enlightenment ideas, the Patriot movement emerged against the governing aristocratic elite and its leader stadtholder Willem V in 1781, one year into the war. The Patriots were inspired by the American Revolution—a nice rebound of the trans-atlantic circulation of ideals, bearing in mind the earlier Dutch inspiration for American nationalism. In the mid-1780s, they started organizing themselves in militias, and by 1787 there was a genuine Patriot coup. Pro-Orange Prussian intervention, however, prevented regime change and the Patriot leadership had to seek exile in France. Some of the leading Patriots would return in late 1794 as members of an armed force supporting revolutionary France's invasion army, thus contributing to the fall of the Dutch Republic and the exile of Willem V to England.

The proclamation of the Batavian Republic in January 1795 signaled both a victory for the Patriots and their absolute dependence on revolutionary France. The Patriot movement was internally divided, particularly on the issue of the continuation of a federal state versus the shift to a unitary state. Moderate factions differed from radical ones in their plans for reform and the implantation of revolutionary projects. But all Patriots were anti-British and pro-French. Their now defeated Orangist opponents were pro-British. The Batavian Republic lasted until 1806, at which point Napoleon Bonaparte decided to turn the country into a dependent "Kingdom of Holland" with his brother Louis Napoleon serving as its first king. In 1810, against his brother's wish, Napoleon annexed the Netherlands altogether. Three years later, the Anglo-Prussian defeat of France resulted in the establishment of a Kingdom of the Netherlands, with the last stadtholder's son appointed as King Willem I.

This long and at times revolutionary intermezzo had crucial consequences for the management of Dutch colonial affairs. First, the institutional framework was reorganized. The semi-state-owned VOC and WIC were dissolved and the direction of the colonies was entrusted to genuine state institutions, initially as part of the Batavian-French regime.[6] With the establishment of the Kingdom of the Netherlands, colonial affairs became a prerogative of King Willem I himself. Only with the liberal democratic reform of 1848 would the States General reclaim this authority.

British intervention resulted in first temporary and ultimately permanent contraction of the Dutch realm. During the Fourth Anglo-Dutch War, British privateers seized dozens of ships transporting tropical produce to the Dutch Republic. Moreover, due to the British government's order to seize all Dutch vessels it was virtually impossible after 1795 for Dutch ships to cross the ocean. Dutch colonial trade with the United States continued apace until the early 1790s, both from the Dutch Caribbean islands and the Guianas.[7] St. Eustatius and Curaçao could not be saved by new contacts in the United States. Within a few years, these entrepôts collapsed, as the permanent interruption of transatlantic trade made it impossible for the island's traders to conduct regional trade. What followed was an irreversible commercial exodus.[8]

Compared to the Dutch islands and Suriname, which had been experiencing a major debt crisis since the late 1770s, Berbice, Demerara, and Essequibo seemed to be full of promise, and British interest there was rapidly becoming more of a threat. In 1781, a group of British planters encouraged their King to add these colonies to his empire where they "would be equal to or rather exceed your Majesty's most flourishing settlements in the West Indies."[9]

The planters' letter was sent to King George III during the brief British occupation of these three colonies in 1781. The Fourth Anglo-Dutch War (1780–84) had entailed British and next French occupations of Dutch colonies, and had delivered a crystal-clear geopolitical message to the republic, with special relevance for the Atlantic. British military interventions would continue to narrow the orbit of the Dutch colonial domain. Upon taking up exile in England, stadtholder Willem V, in the so-called "Kew Letters," had instructed the overseas officers to admit the ships and troops that would be sent by the British king, "and to consider these as Troops and Ships of a nation that is in friendship and Alliance [with the purpose to] prevent that this Colony will be invaded by the French."[10] One assumes he did not anticipate that his protectors would not return all possessions after the wars. During the Napoleonic wars, the British indeed took possession of all Dutch colonies, albeit at different intervals. At the 1814–15 Peace of Vienna, the United Kingdom returned the Indonesian archipelago, Suriname, and the Antillean islands, but retained the Cape Colony and Sri Lanka as well as Berbice, Demerara, and Essequibo.

As for Africa, Elmina had remained Dutch throughout the Wars, but the Dutch slave trade was languishing anyway, dropping from a yearly average of 6,000 in the 1760s and 5,000 in the 1770s to a mere 2,000 in the first half of the 1780s and 1,400 in the next five years.[11] British political intervention sealed the fate of the Dutch slave trade, as the Dutch were simply forced to follow the 1807 British Abolition Act.

Dutch Patriots, Colonialism, and Abolitionism

While the Patriots, generally economic liberals, had been delighted with the dissolution of the semi-statal, monopolistic East and West Indias Companies, their movement had no colonial agenda of radical change. The Patriot intermezzo yielded a modest harvest of pamphlets addressing colonial affairs and sparked some debate in the new National Assembly about colonial policy, but all this was to be of limited importance. By the late eighteenth century, the Dutch Republic had ceased to be the intellectual powerhouse it had once been and the Dutch printing business was no longer export-oriented, so there was little Dutch contribution to international political or philosophical debates.[12] As elsewhere in Europe, enlightened Dutch politicians struggled with the contradiction between high ideals about the equality of men and the economic benefits of colonialism, and eventually concluded that the time was not yet right for ending either colonialism or slavery. As for colonialism as such, a 1796 Patriot state commission concluded bluntly that colonies served "exclusively" for the benefit of the metropolitan economy, and should therefore be "subservient to the Batavian people."[13] Neither would the National Assembly draw any radical conclusions regarding slavery, in spite of the strong opposition by Pieter Vreede, the leader of the radical Patriots.[14]

Antislavery thought had been conspicuously weak in the republic since the early days of colonization, and virtually absent in its colonies. Nonfiction works on the Dutch Atlantic—mainly on the Guianas—had offered elaborate descriptions of the exotic flora and fauna, the culture of the indigenous and enslaved populations, and the development of Paramaribo and the life styles of the European settlers. But ultimately most of this literature served to initiate its European readership in the ways money could be and was being made there, and how this related to metropolitan rule. This was not only discussed in planters' manuals detailing technology and human resource management, but equally in increasingly critical treatises on mercantilism as practiced by the WIC and the Society of Suriname. In this type of writings, mostly dating from the 1770s onwards, the institution of slavery was explicitly defended, and its presumed "excesses" routinely downplayed, condemned, or both.[15]

Slave resistance and particularly the problem of marronage was addressed in many of these books. Reflecting the planters' interest, the books argued that these problems should in no way be seen as an indictment of the system of slavery as such. But clearly an awareness of the violence involved did worry an increasing number of metropolitan authors. John Gabriel Stedman was not the instigator here—while he lived in Suriname in the 1770s, his famous *Narrative* was not published until the mid-1790s. Apparently, other worrisome tales of the slave trade and slavery in the Dutch colonies did circulate in the republic and unleashed some concern.

Surely there had been doubts at an early stage even within the West India Company—its Zeeland Camber had expressed "very little inclination to the slave trade" as late as 1677, and had favored at least the propagation of Christianity among "the Moors."[16] While many had agreed with the famous seventeenth-century Dutch scholar of law Hugo de Groot, or Grotius, that no individual was enslaved by nature, they likewise had followed his reasoning that under certain conditions slavery was acceptable. The WIC's founding father Willem Usselinx had been among those who conveniently relegated this issue to the domain of theologians and lawyers, implicitly condoning slavery in the process. Protestant ministers such as Godefridus Udemans and Johan Picardt had already provided convenient supportive arguments, including the familiar trope of the curse of Noah extended to his unrespecting son Cham. This type of reasoning, at times linked to the idea that exposure to Christianity would eventually open the way to spiritual freedom, had been supported by the Elmina-born, Dutch-educated minister Joannes Capitein in his 1742 *Dissertatio*.

In his 1704 description of the West African coast, Willem Bosman downplayed the disruptive effects of the slave trade and implied that those Africans transported to the Americas at least escaped the wrath of their African enslavers. Other interested parties in the African slave trade and slavery in the Americas had squarely reminded their readers that much money could be made this way, and, alternatively, that without it the Atlantic colonies would collapse. Thus the medical doctor D. H. Gallandat from Vlissingen had simply argued that whatever might be said in criticism of the trade, the advantages for all involved—"for the negro tribes and for the slaves, for the merchants in general, and for the settler colonies in particular"—were more substantial.[17]

Even as the *ancien régime* of the republic, including its colonial policies, was coming under attack, opponents to the semi-mercantilist West India Company did not align with the abolitionist thought that was making headway in Great Britain and North America and to a lesser extent in France. A multivolume, anti-mercantilist correspondence on the governance of Essequibo and Demerara published under the pseudonyms of Aristodemos and Sincerus (1785–88) as well as a treatise by A. Barrau (1790) continued to underline that there could not be economic development without slavery and hence the Atlantic slave trade.[18] Meanwhile, planters' manuals continued to rehearse the axiom of "righteous rule," meaning the need to strike a balance between excessively harsh and overly lenient treatment of the enslaved.[19]

Only gradually were Dutch readers also presented with more critical positions. In his 1774 *Histoire*, Abbé Raynal, deploring the loss of "public spirit" in the once extremely successful republic, also blamed its leadership for failing to mitigate the "tyranny" unleashed on Suriname's slaves, the "horrible cruelty" of the planters inevitably inviting slave revolts. He voiced similar criticism in his 1781 *Suppléments*. His entries on the Antilles were shorter, and had little to say about slavery.[20] In *Hollands rijkdom* (1780–83), Eli Luzac, a prolific lawyer and author from Leiden, deemed the complaints he had heard about the administration of justice in Suriname "unbelievable," but added that some of these might be warranted nonetheless. He was clearly addressing "the mean treatment" of slaves "of which one heard so frequently." Luzac apparently did not object to slavery, but he did condone the right of the enslaved, "as humans," to demand fair treatment. This approach was not abolitionist, and concurred with the stance taken in first-hand witness accounts in Suriname penned by Stedman, Johann Riemer, V. P. Malouet and many others, a non-radical acceptance of slavery with sensible moderation.[21]

Figure 16. Monument commemorating the 1795 slave revolt, unveiled in 1998 near Willemstad, Curaçao. Photograph by Gert Oostindie.

While none of the institutional players were giving abolition a serious thought, the number of treatises condemning the slave trade and slavery did rise, particularly in the 1790s. Various foreign anti-slavery tracts were published in Dutch translation, including the presumed autobiography of Olaudah Equiano. Prominent Dutch authors such as novelist Betje Wolff and Patriot Johan Derk van der Capellen wrote endorsements to some of these works.[22] Clearly, there were some local abolitionists active therefore, and the educated public had access to information on the debates both abroad and domestically, but this did not lead to widespread support for the abolitionist cause, nor to prolonged polemics on the question of whether the republic should continue condoning the trade and slavery itself.

There was one occasion that could have made a difference. In the 1797 meetings of the National Assembly, radical Patriot Pieter Vreede did condemn slavery as incompatible with the Rights of Man. Stressing the common humanity of Africans and Europeans, he fiercely argued that Dutch citizens "steal and buy humans with treachery and violence in Africa, to hurl them down in your American colonies to work forever on your plantations." His rhetorical argumentation against economic justifications for the trade was dismissive: "Is the accumulation of treasures everything, and virtue nothing!" But even Vreede, while urging for abolition of the slave trade as the Danes—much to their credit—had already done, thought an abrupt ending of West Indian slavery itself to be too risky—if only because of the unfortunate example of the slave revolt in French St. Domingue.[23]

In the ensuing debates considerations of national interest prevailed, and occasional allusions to the Haitian Revolution were used to illustrate that the enslaved Caribbean populations were not quite ready for freedom. The Assembly concluded that the idea of inalienable rights to freedom could not yet be extended to non-European colonial subjects, much less to slaves. The lack of radicalism is further illustrated by the fact that the 1798 constitution promulgated by the Batavian Republic even withheld full citizenship rights from Europeans in the colonies. Surely the earliest revolutionary debates in metropolitan France had reflected more radical thought.[24]

The rest is history: the British abolition of the slave trade imposed on the occupied Dutch colonies in 1807, the late rise of a moderate, elite abolitionist movement in the 1840s, and the final emancipation in 1863. While the educated Dutch public had access to the relevant international debates, apparently this information was not widely circulated and discussed, much less taken up in a significant abolitionist movement. The abolition of the slave trade was followed by another absence of debate in the first four decades of the nineteenth century. Why the Dutch failed to develop genuine abolitionist fervor has puzzled many scholars. The answers are mainly sought in the domain of political stagnation writ large and the absence of significant dissenting minorities within the Protestant Church that dominated the Dutch state. We may add that the Atlantic was never as central to the mindset of the Dutch educated class as it was in the other European colonial domains, in spite of the commercial links.[25]

The Patriots' lasting impact on colonial affairs was therefore confined to the fields of governance and economics. Enlightened thinkers had long criticized mercantilism with its supposedly stifling monopolies. It was quite logical that the Dutch Patriots were consistently critical of the VOC and WIC. In the debates leading to the constitution, the Patriot representatives agreed that neither of the companies—by then bankrupted anyway—should be revived. Henceforth, all colonies were to be simply possessions of the state.[26]

Patriots and Orangists in the Caribbean Colonies

The metropolitan conflicts between Patriots and Orangists had repercussions in the Caribbean colonies as they had elsewhere in the Dutch colonial world. Such conflicts arose after 1795, hence not before the establishment of the Batavian Republic, the stadtholder's Kew Letters, and the intermittent British occupations of Dutch territory. Just like colonial elites elsewhere in the Americas, the Patriots were keen to bend colonialism to their interest and to maintain slavery, the pivotal institution of their colonial societies. Thus, when Jan Bom, a Patriot official to Demerara and Essequibo, applauded the Batavian Republic as a "free" state no longer "in the chains of the Aristocratic and Orange slavery," this did not imply that he opposed black slavery. Instead he insisted that he and his fellow Patriots in the colony had demonstrated exemplary zeal in suppressing a "devastating Revolt of the Negro slaves" in 1795.[27]

More plausible, then, is the assumption that political strife within the Dutch Atlantic colonies was driven at best partly by ideological divides, and more by local idiosyncrasies and interests in which many protagonists demonstrated considerable opportunism. Thus Albert Kikkert, a Dutch-born member of the Curaçao elite, actively participated in the repression of the 1795 slave revolt, later became a vociferous member of the Patriot—and, hence, anti-stadtholder and anti-British—faction in local politics, was consequently expelled after the 1800 British takeover, but somehow managed to return to the island in 1816 as the first governor appointed by King Willem I. In his installation speech, he spoke of "the iron yoke of the French invaders," qualified Napoleon as "the worst of tyrants," and his monarch as "a caring father." This type of "weather-vane" conduct was quite characteristic in the context of the successive regime changes in the Netherlands, and ensured a high degree of continuity between the "French" period and the new monarchy.[28]

A summary of events in the various colonies during these revolutionary times may illustrate the limited impact of internal political bickering in all colonies except for Curaçao. With the symbolic support of the Kew Letters as a convenient justification, the British invaded all but one of the Dutch colonies, but not exactly at the same time. Berbice, Demerara, and Essequibo were the first to be taken over by the British, from 1796 to 1802 and then again in 1803, this time indefinitely. Suriname was British from 1799 to 1802 and again from 1804 to 1816; Curaçao, including Aruba and Bonaire, from 1800 to 1803 and again from 1807 to 1816; the Northern Antilles from 1801 to 1802 and from 1810 to 1816. Only Elmina remained nominally Dutch throughout this period—an indication of its insignificance, but nonetheless remarkable in view of its potential role in the Atlantic slave trade, made clandestine for the Dutch, too, after the British abolition in 1807.

There is an intriguing pattern here. In the Atlantic, the colonies that would eventually not be returned—Berbice, Demerara, and Essequibo— were the first to be occupied. Exactly the same transpired in the domain of the VOC, where the British occupied all Dutch settlements except for Deshima. Thus the British took over governance of the Indonesian archipelago late and only for a short period (1811 to 1816), while they intervened earlier in the colonies that they would eventually retain—the Cape Colony (1795 to 1803 and again from 1806), Sri Lanka (ever since 1796), and Malacca (1795 to 1818 and again since 1825). In a sense, then, the entire period of regime changes and warfare in Europe provided Great Britain with convenient arguments to expand its empire. It is not surprising that both British West Indian interest in the metropolis and local British planters and merchants in Berbice, Demerara, and Essequibo had applauded the takeover of the colonies in 1780 and again 1796, and thought of the Peace of Amiens (1802) as an annoying obstacle in their design to retain these promising plantation frontiers permanently.[29]

On the eve of the establishment of the Patriot Batavian Republic, the white elite of Suriname arguably identified more with the metropolis than did their peers either in the lesser Guianas, with their robust British West Indian community and connections, or Curaçao and St. Eustatius, with their traditionally stronger regional rather than transatlantic orientations. We may also assume that after the French and particularly the Haitian Revolutions, they worried about the establishment of a possibly revolutionary Batavian Republic. News that the civil commissioners in Saint-Domingue had abolished slavery was received in December 1793 with deep concern, as the slaves in Suriname might be inspired to rebel. Slave unrest remained limited, though. In March 1795 Governor Friderici still organized the usual celebrations for the stadtholder's birthday. But shortly after, the Kew Letters arrived and the governor and his Colonial Council had to make up their minds about what course of action to follow. Surprisingly, Friderici and his predominantly Orangist council decided to ward off a "protective" British takeover in spite of the stadtholder's instructions. The British reacted by establishing a maritime blockade, before attacking anyway in August 1799. The conditions of capitulation included a clause on a possible permanent transition to British sovereignty.[30] With a short intermezzo following the Peace of Amiens, Suriname would remain British until 1816. The British intervention did have one unexpected and, among the planter class, most unwelcome outcome, which was the abolition of the slave trade, a measure confirmed in the 1814 treaties.

How do we account for the initial resistance among the Suriname elite to surrender to the British? Surely there was no interest in revolutionary ideas, hence no sympathy for France—even though the Batavian Republic was recognized, the Colonial Council forbade public debates on "French" issues such as the Rights of Men. This ban must have been inspired by fears of a spilling over of revolutionary ideas from St. Domingue or, more close by, the colony of Cayenne.[31] And no one anticipated that the British intervention would end with the imposition of the end of the slave trade. Perhaps, therefore, the initial refusal to follow the stadtholder's instructions and invite the British in may be understood as a reflection of the emergence over the preceding century of a white Creole community out of an assemblage of European migrants of quite diverse backgrounds. This new Creole settler community defined itself both as part of the Dutch colonial realm and as a legitimate defender of local economic and political rights and therefore wary of any permanent change of imperial affiliation that might adversely affect their local interests.

This confident attitude is illustrated by the *Essai historique* (1788) discussed in the previous chapter. Throughout their book, David Nassy and his fellow "learned Jewish men" emphasize both their gratitude for having been allowed to live as Portuguese Jews in Suriname since its earliest days, and the crucial Jewish contributions to the colony's development. A deep loyalty pervades the book, starting with the opening dedication thanking the directors of the Sociëteit van Suriname for the opportunity to live "under the laws of the Republic of the United Dutch Provinces, and under your protection." But this did not keep Nassy from requesting that the directors lower taxes and allow free trade. This is a refrain uttered throughout the colony's history by gentile settlers as well—no matter how divided among themselves they may have been on scores of issues, including religious divides and bigotry, as contemporary judge Adriaan Lammens wrote.[32]

The British took over Suriname in spite of the local elite. For the local business community this would have the adverse long-term consequence of the end of the slave trade, but some positive short-term effects. The British intermezzo meant that no ships could be sent to French-controlled Holland and no debts paid off. Instead there was unrestricted trade with North America and within the British Atlantic. Suriname, therefore, partook in the advantages of the British market and the West Indies lobby in the metropolis, resulting in an accumulation of local wealth. But even then, this did not translate in a widespread longing to remain within the British fold. Only the planters of Nickerie, the most Western part of the colony and hence adjacent to Berbice, urged in vain for inclusion in what was to become the new colony of British Guiana. But these planters were mainly British nationals to begin with.[33]

The contrast with Berbice and particularly Demerara and Essequibo is stark. In the second half of the eighteenth century, British interest and presence in these colonies had been rapidly growing, and they had already been briefly occupied in 1780 during the Fourth Anglo-Dutch War. This episode lasted only a few months, but the letter of British resident planters cited above may have alerted the Crown to this new frontier. The supplicants advised their king not to return these "little-known" colonies to the Dutch, as they provided great opportunities.[34] The colonies were returned nonetheless, but the informal British takeover continued and was even applauded. Thus a 1790 report commissioned by the States General argued that further immigration of "planters from Barbados, Grenada and other isles, leaving their depleted lands" would make the colonies flourish to the benefit of the Dutch metropolis. At the same time, the report complained of massive illegal slave imports by and for British nationals. The criticism, obviously, was not about the trade as such, but about its illegal character.[35]

Shortly after the establishment of the Batavian Republic, and in accordance with the Kew Letters, a British fleet sailed up to the Guianas to assume protective custody against France. This offer was initially refused, against the judgement of the Orangist governor Willem August van Sirtema van Grovestins, who secretly left Demerara, tellingly on a British ship. His successor Antony Beaujon would turn over the colony a year later to the British anyway, to the applause of British Atlantic investors.[36] A delegation of local residents had already requested that the government in Barbados intervene, and when the British fleet came, as a contemporary wrote, "a great number of speculators" ready to invest their capital in this new frontier emerged, hence it was "more like a country resumed, than ceded, to England." Around 1800, two-thirds of the white population of Demerara was estimated to be British, while the rest was a cosmopolitan mix including, in addition to the Dutch, many other European nationalities.[37]

The position of the British settlers should not surprise us, but what of the loyalties of the local Dutch population in Berbice, Demerara, and Essequibo? It appears that there was more internal friction than in Suriname, which may have reflected a concern among the Dutch settlers that this was not primarily a struggle over political ideas, but rather hardnosed competition over the possession of valuable territory. Thus the above-quoted former local official and fierce Patriot Jan Bom blamed not only the "vile" British for the 1796 takeover, but equally the "egoism" of "corrupt" local Dutch, including the "perfidious" governors Van Grovestins and Beaujon. In vain had the Patriots attempted to protect the colony from Britain's "vile and cowardly means of treachery and bribery." Bom bitterly concluded that the Orangists had joined in "the triumph of the English settlers." He was convinced that the British would not return the colony, which they had hoped to add to their empire ever since the early 1780s.[38]

Calculating Dutch settlers may also have shifted their allegiances out of pure opportunism. There was always the concern that local conflicts could spark slave rebellions following "the terrible example of the French islands."[39] A transfer of sovereignty may also have rescued indebted planters from paying their dues, as a cynical commentator had remarked years before in the Patriot newsletter *De Post van den Neder-Rhijn,* in reference to the quick surrender of Demerara to the British in 1781.[40]

Upon their return to the islands in 1803, the British initially dealt cautiously with Dutch sensitivities, allowing the pro-British Dutch governors Antony Beaujon and Abraham van Imbyze van Batenburg to serve as lieutenant-governors under the new British governor.[41] Born in St. Eustatius, Beaujon came from a family of merchants who settled in both Curaçao and St. Eustatius, and was a rare example of family interconnectedness within the Dutch West Indies. A Patriot settler accused him of having no loyalty, "no heart for Patria [the Fatherland]," of being "a Foreigner, intruding in the Colony without the least interest in the public cause."[42] Perhaps we may indeed qualify Beaujon's maneuvering as sheer opportunism, but then again, in 1800 "national" loyalties were less defined and stable than they would be a century later. Meanwhile the British resolve was clear. A Dutch visitor observed that by 1810, the Dutch settlers had only second-class status. In 1834, there were still a number of Dutch owners among those compensated for the ending of slavery. But in 1840, the colony's European population was mainly English, "very few of the former Dutch settlers having remained in the colony."[43]

For St. Eustatius, there is little indication of Patriot versus Orangist strife. Both St. Eustatius and the adjacent Dutch colonies of St. Maarten and Saba were at the mercy of the British and French. This had first become clear in 1781 with Rodney's sacking of St. Eustatius and the subsequent three years of French occupation. In 1793, at the outbreak of the war between the French and the British, Dutch settlers had claimed the French part of St. Martin, but two years later, the French took over all of the three Dutch Windward Antilles. The British, in turn, ousted the French in 1801, returned the islands to the Dutch after the Peace of Amiens, and resumed control in 1810 for another three years. In 1816, the three islands' combined populations had been reduced to half the size of 1790, and over the next century and a half, this figure would remain that low.[44] Rather than worrying about political positions, the more enterprising settlers simply realized that the Dutch state had little to offer and left, taking their slaves with them to nearby locations such as the Danish islands.

While Curaçao witnessed a similarly drastic reduction of its population, this island did experience significant political turmoil in the first five years of the revolutionary period. Patriot versus Orangist strife, combined with successive outside interventions, led to potentially revolutionary regime change in the period from 1795 to 1800, after which a combined

British-American intervention secured the isolation of Curaçao from the Batavian Republic and revolutionary France. Thereafter, internal factionalism ceased to matter as no French-leaning Patriotism was tolerated anymore.

The history of the six revolutionary years is quite complicated.[45] Clearly there was some local sympathy on the island for the French Revolution, to the point that the government banned the singing of French revolutionary songs in 1789. By 1793 the governor also issued a ban on public criticism of the House of Orange. News of the establishment of the Batavian Republic intensified local strife in 1795, pitting Patriots and Orangists against one another. But then, in August, the island experienced its largest slave revolt ever, clearly inspired by the French and Haitians Revolutions. The ranks were immediately closed and the revolt was violently suppressed by a coalition including not only the white population, but also the (separate) militias made up of black and "colored" freemen.

In the summer of 1796, the Batavian Republic sent an envoy to ensure the island's loyalty. Pressed to choose, the Orangist governor De Veer refused to take the oath of loyalty to the republic and was consequently replaced by Beaujon. To Patriot dismay, the latter turned out to be Orange-leaning as well. This caused renewed factional strife between local Patriots and Orangists and ended in a coup d'état in which Lauffer took Beaujon's position, in December 1796. His appointment was made public in a declaration opening with the French revolutionary slogan "Freedom, Equality, Fraternity."[46] Yet Lauffer was no radical either. He had been one of the leading figures in a moderate Patriot movement demanding economic reform benefitting the local merchant class, but he nurtured no far-reaching ideas. Once in power as a "Batavian," and hence officially a pro-French governor, his policy was to repress the more radical Patriots and to keep the revolutionary French troops out of the island. In the next years, he attempted to steer a middle course in the long-standing Anglo-French belligerence as well as the "Quasi-War" fought between his assertive French allies and the United States. His only real interest in this was the defense of Curaçao's commercial interests—more radical ideas, particularly about slavery, were not relevant either to the local elites or to the three competing nations.

All of this climaxed when in 1800 predominantly black French troops from Guadeloupe landed on the island to preempt a possible British attack.

Conspiracies involving local French revolutionary agents had preluded this dramatic episode—though it seems likely that their "revolutionary" fervor had more to do with French geopolitical interests than with ideals about slave liberation and links to revolutionary Haiti.[47] In this decisive conjuncture Lauffer, who portrayed himself as a man inspired by the French Enlightenment *philosophes*, took no risk and requested American and British protection against revolutionary France. This explains why the British allowed him to continue as civilian governor after they had ousted the French and annexed the island.

Creole Triumphalism?

If the Dutch Atlantic elites were conservative, they certainly were not unique in this. Throughout the Atlantic and certainly in the Caribbean, we see a similar conservatism. Surely, if we are to understand "Creole Triumphalism," a concept applied by Bernard Bailyn to Latin America as well as to British America, as the pulsating circulation of revolutionary, anticolonial ideas leading to regime change, there is nothing in Dutch Atlantic history that comes close.[48] Nowhere did local white elites strive towards independence, and choices made in the Patriot versus Orange, pro-French versus pro-British dilemma were dictated by personal or local merchant and planter interests. Pragmatism or sheer opportunism prevailed. Within the margins dictated by the metropolis, everyday politics were made by Dutch and other European settlers in the colonies, and they embodied no revolutionary fervor at all in this Age of Revolutions. No striving for independence, no lasting urge for political reform, let alone social change. At the end of the Napoleonic Wars, the local elites in the restored colonies— if they had not left for better shores outside of the Dutch realm— simply accepted the new realities, welcomed the governors now appointed by a real king, had to accept the abolition of the slave trade imposed by the British, and had no qualms about slavery and extant socio-racial hierarchies.

But all of this is quite typical after all, in the Atlantic and particularly the Caribbean context. The drive towards independence was virtually absent in the Caribbean—the Haitian state emerged as an unanticipated and initially unsought outcome of a very complex social struggle, and this outcome in turn discouraged Creole political nationalism elsewhere. And even if the Latin American *emancipación* eventually sealed the fate of slavery on the continent, there had been no initial drive for social revolution or antislavery. Throughout the Caribbean, local elites clung to slavery as the foundation of their economy and way of life.[49]

Of course, the majority in the Dutch Atlantic was not made up of Europeans, let alone European elites, but rather enslaved Africans and their offspring, whether slave or free. As we discussed earlier, there were attempts to follow up on one of the most spectacular episodes in the Age of Revolutions, the Haitian Revolution. As elsewhere in the wider Caribbean, news of this revolution did reach the enslaved populations of the Dutch colonies. The massive 1795 slave revolt of Curaçao—involving 2,000 of the island's 12,000 slaves—was among the largest contemporary revolts in the wider Atlantic and was evidently inspired by the French and Haitian revolutions. Thus, the revolt's leader, Tula, emphasized the equality of all men as they all originated from Adam and Eva.[50] The 1800 French invasion of the island found support among the local enslaved population, but the invasion failed and again, there were no rewards for the slaves.[51]

It is likely that the news of the Haitian Revolution reached the enslaved populations of the Guianas as well. A merchant in Rotterdam, writing about this "terrifying news," shared with his agent in Paramaribo his hopes that the necessary vigilance would quell any "spirit of rebellion among the negroes" in Suriname. It is not clear whether more than the routine type of repression was needed in these years. As we have seen, the Dutch Guianas had a long tradition of slave revolts and particularly marronage, and the last "Boni" Maroon War (1789–93) had just been concluded. In the period that followed, only a few minor slave revolts were recorded, and these came to naught.[52]

By contrast, this period did have repercussions for the free non-white populations. First, this is a matter of figures. The proportion of the "free coloreds" in the total population of both Curaçao and Suriname increased, while the overall population contracted.[53] The growth of this group opened avenues for upward social mobility for some of its members, particularly in the economic sphere, even if the color line would remain divisive well into the nineteenth century and beyond. There is no doubt that revolutionary news spread quickly to the entire population precisely because of the mobility of the free blacks and "coloreds" in the wider region. But there was no concerted effort among the non-white population, whether free or enslaved, for regime change and the end of slavery. On the contrary, non-white militias were instrumental in suppressing both the 1750 and 1795 slave revolts and in the turbulent years 1796–1800.[54]

Ironically, the tiny island of Curaçao did contribute in indirect ways to the independence of "Gran" Colombia. This, again, is a story of interimperial connections. Two men from Curaçao, Pedro Manuel Brión and Pedro Luís Piar, worked closely with Simón Bolívar, contributing both their military skills and, in the case of Brión, significant financial resources accumulated in interimperial trade. This enabled the multilingual Brión to buy a man-of-war in Great Britain in 1815, lifting several *independistas* from Cartagena to Haiti the next year and there help Bolívar to be elected as commander for what would turn out to be a failed invasion, followed by a successful one a year later. Throughout the episode of the independence wars, Curaçao served as a haven for political exiles, including Bolívar himself in 1812. This was a function Curaçao would retain throughout the nineteenth and early twentieth centuries vis-à-vis the notoriously unstable republic of Venezuela.[55]

For the modest Dutch Atlantic realm itself, though, and apart from the loss of the "lesser" Guianas and the descent into insignificance of Curaçao and St. Eustatius, the crucial change in this period was the abolition of the slave trade, imposed by the British who emerged dominant from this entire period. There has been much discussion about the role the Haitian Revolution and slave resistance more generally have played in the trajectory leading up to the abolition of the trade and next of slavery itself. Whatever the conclusions one may draw from this debate, there is no indication that events in the Dutch Atlantic sped up this process. Nowhere within the Dutch Atlantic did local elites vie for an end to the slave trade or slavery itself. The one major revolt, in Curaçao, had no impact on debates on colonialism or slavery in the Netherlands, where abolitionism was absent or at best weak.

Indirectly, abolition did have a crucial bearing on the social and cultural development of the Dutch colonies and their majorities of African descent. The end of the slave trade meant not only that the process of demographic and hence cultural creolization accelerated, but likewise that the bargaining power of the enslaved population increased. In Suriname, this would stimulate state-controlled amelioration policies on the basis of the British model, as well the admission of Christian missionaries to the plantations, where slave owners, unlike their counterparts in the Antilles, had long thought of Christianization as casting pearls before swines and potentially disruptive for the slavery regime.[56] As the demographic link to Africa was definitely severed, oral traditions maintained spiritual links across the Atlantic, but culture-building became even more a locally and regionally rooted process than it had been before.[57]

Intraimperial Transitions

Without falling into the trap of overestimating the modernity of the early Atlantic world per se and construing what historian Pieter Emmer referred to as the "myth of early globalization," we may characterize the early modern history of the Atlantic as a watershed, the beginnings of a long-term process towards integration, starting in, but not limited to, the economic sphere.[58] Between 1600 and 1800, the Dutch were actively involved in this process. They were not primarily conspicuous in the field of plantation production, but they certainly were in commerce and finance, which also stimulated demographic and cultural border-crossings. Dutch economic policies were a mixture of mercantilist and free trade principles and practices, inspired more by pragmatism than by principles. Dutch free trade ports lubricated the predominantly mercantile Atlantic economy, and were therefore tolerated by their more powerful competitors. In the later eighteenth century, Dutch decline set in first because of failing credit arrangements, and hence a crisis in the plantation colonies, and next due to a lack of naval power to protect Dutch commercial networks—by then it was all too obvious that the Dutch had been at the mercy of the French and, particularly, the British fiscal-military states for many years.[59] Franco-British rivalry had long allowed the Dutch Republic to survive, as the two rival nations both sought to court the Dutch as an ally. By the late eighteenth century, such an alliance was no longer worth pursuing.

In the preceding two centuries, the Dutch Atlantic had been characterized by remarkable institutional heterogeneity, free and often unregulated flows of capital, strong cross-imperial commercial and demographic linkages, and hence high proportions of non-Dutch settlers among its white populations, adding to its ethnic and cultural diversity. Much in this period suggests a remarkably modern and flexible capitalist spirit, and as such the Dutch Atlantic passes the test of being a champion of early-modern "soft" globalization as suggested by economic historian Jan de Vries.[60] But in the end, neither the Dutch Republic nor its colonies—and much less the enslaved populations laboring in these same colonies—seem to have benefitted particularly from this precocious globalization.

For the Dutch Atlantic, the period roughly running from the outbreak of the Fourth Anglo-Dutch War to the end of the Napoleonic Wars saw over three decades of economic and political contraction, without lasting regime change and with only subtle long-range cultural change, sparked by the externally imposed abolition of the slave trade. The wider significance of the Dutch Atlantic to the early modern wider Atlantic came to an end in the Age of Revolutions, as did its economic significance for the metropolis itself.

The republic, in scale and military and naval power no match for the major Atlantic players, had used its neutrality to build a niche as a broker greasing the prevalent system of mercantilism. The years from 1780 to 1815 taught the Dutch the lesson that a weak state's neutrality lasts only as long as larger states condone it. After 1815, in the emerging post-mercantile Atlantic, there was no longer a need for trade zones such as Curaçao or St. Eustatius at all, no need for illicit connections at the margins of mercantilism, and the very issue of neutrality thus became insignificant. After the loss of the lesser Guianas, the Dutch were left with only Suriname as a potential asset, but this colony had declining comparative advantages in a quickly globalizing market for plantation produce. Surely Dutch interest in the Atlantic did not wane altogether, but judging by investments and since the 1840s also Dutch migrants—totaling some 175,000 up to 1914, and another 130,000 up to 1960—the focus shifted decisively from the Dutch Caribbean to the United States.

The Dutch role as an Atlantic broker operating from a range of regional hubs was already undermined in the previous period. Merchant ships outfitted in the North American colonies were increasingly active in the trade with the Caribbean, to the extent that as early as 1713 a merchant commenting on American trade to the French islands remarked that the Americans were taking over a role hitherto played by the Dutch.[61] That observation may have been premature, but indeed North American shipping was on the ascent and had even become crucial to the Dutch Guianas in the same period. After the American Revolution the new nation's commercial expansion in the Caribbean accelerated. Throughout the eighteenth century, British and British West Indian investments, shipping, and migrations had an increasing impact as well, culminating in the takeover of what was to become British Guiana.

To what changes did the major Dutch actors aspire in this context of decreasing significance in the Atlantic, whether in the metropolis or in the colonies? The imperfect monopolies of the West Indian companies were challenged and broken, eventually giving way to direct state control of colonial affairs. The colonial elites had no interest in anything more radical, surely not independence and not even a concerted effort to ensure political representation. Much less was there an abolitionist drive, on either side of the Atlantic. Colonials in the Dutch orbit were hardly inspired by the American, French, or Spanish American revolutions and positively abhorred the far more radical Haitian Revolution.

The changes, then, that really mattered—abolition, geographical contraction, loss of broker function—were all externally imposed and grudgingly taken for granted in the Netherlands and among the local elites in the colonies. Slavery remained the key institution in the Dutch Atlantic until 1863 and all considerations of those in charge derived from their concern about a social order constantly tested by the enslaved. The enslaved population had not been a direct party in the changes taking place between 1780 and 1815, but the Dutch colonies were at least entering the final phase of slavery, a period without slave imports from Africa and hence a period of intense creolization. The intermediate group of free men and women of (partly) African origins increased considerably, and at least in Curaçao developed into a presence to be reckoned with. But ultimately the gradual and unfinished emancipation of the non-white majorities under the Kingdom of the Netherlands would be accomplished in the context of progressive marginalization of the Dutch Atlantic colonies.

We should not assume that contemporaries were already anticipating this decline of the Dutch Atlantic. In spite of their painful awareness of Dutch decline, policy makers voiced optimism during the Age of Revolutions, or at least the conviction that the Caribbean colonies could play a vital role in helping the Netherlands regain the status of a serious world player. Thus in 1795, parliamentarians from the "revolutionary" Batavian

Republic were of the opinion that their new state could only survive with the support of its colonies, "in particular those in America."[62] After the Peace of Amiens, the Dutch quickly dispatched a large fleet to the Caribbean to restore their sovereignty, investing serious money in the expectation of future rewards. Even when Britain again "temporarily" took over almost all Dutch colonies during the Napoleonic Wars, these were expected to be recovered. In an 1806 report written at the request of the recently appointed king Louis Napoleon, the Dutch Department of Colonies argued that the Atlantic properties, including Berbice, Demerara, and Essequibo, were "among the most prominent colonies worldwide." A second memorandum expressed the conviction that these colonies, and the African slave trade, were "indispensable" for Dutch recovery as "a merchant state."[63]

Upon the restart of the country as the Kingdom of the Netherlands in 1813, King Willem I, too, hoped to make the colonies work for the benefit of the metropolis. In 1820, he still nurtured high hopes for his American possessions, in spite of the loss of much of the Guianas, for which incidentally Amsterdam merchants blamed him.[64] By 1825, government reports qualified Suriname as "a highly important colony," and "almost the only still flowering branch of trade and shipping for Amsterdam."[65]

This was the last optimism regarding the Caribbean. In the next decades, it would dawn upon government circles and entrepreneurs alike that the Dutch East Indies were becoming the only part of the colonial world that really mattered. Prompted by Willem I, the state assumed control of the East Indies' economy, with evident success for the national treasury. Income from the East Indies, mainly derived from the semi-feudal Javanese "Cultivation System," averaged 32 percent of state income in the 1830s, 53 percent in the 1840s and 45 percent in the 1850s.[66] In 1830, the Netherlands imported roughly the same quantity of cane sugar from Suriname and Java; in 1850 Java produced five times as much and in 1860 fourteen times.[67]

As the process of globalization intensified in the long nineteenth century, the Dutch interest in the Atlantic colonies waned, while the Dutch East Indies provided a new economic and geopolitical frontier. Contraction was the outcome of the Age of Revolutions for the Dutch Atlantic, while the following century, in spite of large-scale post-slavery recruitment of indentured labor from British India and Java, witnessed the demise of the Dutch Atlantic altogether. As the process of globalization progressed, its centers of gravity moved. By the 1870s, Dutch parliamentarians were happy with the transfer of Elmina to the British and, seeing neither economic nor geopolitical interest in the Caribbean colonies, started to think aloud about selling them off. Gradually the awareness that the Dutch Atlantic had ever mattered to the republic began to fade, just as it was forgotten that it had played a significant role in the emergence of the early modern Atlantic.

Paradoxically, in spite of all this contraction, the Caribbean is prominently present in the contemporary Netherlands, more than ever before. This is because of postcolonial migrations and the choice of the Antilles not to follow the example of Indonesia and Suriname and instead to remain non-sovereign parts of the Kingdom of the Netherlands. This historical irony no one could have foreseen one or two centuries ago.

The contraction of the Dutch Atlantic was in the first place a consequence of long-term geopolitical changes in Europe and particularly the rise of Great Britain to unprecedented hegemony, continuing even after the loss of the North American colonies. The Dutch Atlantic had never mattered as much to its metropolis as was the case for the Atlantic empires of the Dutch rivals, but even so, its economic importance had been on the rise throughout much of the eighteenth century. The major problem was of a geopolitical nature. As long as the stronger states tolerated the Dutch as intermediaries in a highly mercantilist world, the Dutch Atlantic could thrive. But from the early 1780s on, the Dutch realized that their previous role as intermediaries in the wider Atlantic world had only been possible as long as this suited the major European powers, particularly Great Britain. Without serious naval power and strong allies, the Dutch were at the mercy of their rivals. The demise of the Dutch Atlantic became evident during the Fourth Anglo-Dutch War (1780–84) and was sealed at the ending of the Napoleonic Wars and the final establishment of the Kingdom of the Netherlands (1815).

What might have seemed like a temporary crisis in 1780 turned out to be the beginning of a permanent territorial contraction and the economic and demographic decline of the Dutch Atlantic. Even if Dutch elites—including the newly appointed king Willem I, the first Dutch monarch ever—still nurtured high hopes for Suriname as a plantation economy and

Curaçao as a commercial hub, by 1830 such dreams were buried. The production of tropical staples was taken over by the Dutch East Indies, where all sorts of semi-bonded but non-slave labor arrangements proved to be immensely lucrative. Curaçao as well as St. Eustatius entered a long period of crisis as in the era of free trade and American ascent there was no longer any need for their services as intermediaries.

This period of transition witnessed massive, even revolutionary change. The Atlantic slave trade was abolished, and the institution of slavery was bound to follow. The United States attained independence, followed by Haiti and much of Latin America. This was an era of "Creole triumphalism," but the Dutch Atlantic remained an outsider to this phenomenon. The only revolutionary spirit in the colonies was expressed by revolting slaves, most dramatically in the 1795 Curaçao slave revolt. In the colonies as in the metropolis, there had been strong divides between pro-British ancient régime "Orangists" and pro-French "Patriots," but no Creole nationalism nor a questioning of the slave trade or slavery. Likewise, in the Netherlands, there was broad consensus that the sole function of the colonies was to benefit the metropolis, and that in the Atlantic, this implied a continuation of slavery. The abolition of the slave trade was simply imposed by the British; slavery would continue until 1863. The Dutch Atlantic simply imploded in the process.

CONCLUSION

A Heterogeneous and Creolized Interimperial Realm

Huge ambitions, large-scale deployment of troops and warships, and rapid colonial expansion and contraction had characterized the First Dutch Atlantic (1600–1680). But the Dutch moment in Atlantic history did not last long, and the Second Dutch Atlantic (1680–1815) was an era with a distinct character. Dutch Brazil and New Netherland had been lost and the earlier high ambitions abandoned. The Dutch Republic acquired no new colonies or trading posts in the long eighteenth century, but was able to cling to its remaining possessions until the Napoleonic period. After 1680, the Dutch Atlantic was largely left alone by foreign naval forces, though brief French and British raids and occupations were a reminder of the vulnerability of the Dutch colonies. Moreover, during European wars spilling over into the Atlantic Ocean, privateers, especially Britons, did much damage to the Dutch Atlantic.

Peaceful relations between the Dutch realm and the Atlantic empires were partly predicated on the small size of the Dutch Atlantic. In Europe itself, the Dutch Republic was no longer a major state, and after their rule in North America and Brazil had come to an end, the Atlantic presence of the Dutch was confined to West Africa, the Guianas, and six Caribbean islands. But the Dutch Atlantic did matter. In no foreign empire were the Guianas demographically and economically as important to the metropolis as in the Dutch case. And again in contrast to the other Atlantic powers, the insular Dutch Caribbean may have only had a commercial function, but it was one of great importance not only to the metropolis but to the entire Atlantic system.

Migrations, predominantly from Africa and secondarily from Europe, defined the early modern Atlantic world. The Dutch Americas fitted this mold. The inhabitants of the Dutch Guianas and the insular Dutch Caribbean were overwhelmingly black and enslaved—enslaved Africans and their descendants making up the vast majority in the Guianas but dominating even in Curaçao, despite that island's primary function as a commercial entrepôt. Slavery brought slave resistance, and the black majorities in the Dutch Americas produced several slave revolts, including those in Berbice (1763–64) and Curaçao (1795), which were among the largest slave uprisings anywhere in the Americas. Although no sustained large-scale revolts broke out in Suriname, marronage was rampant in that colony, and the Maroon Wars threatened the colony's existence to an extent unknown anywhere else in plantation America.

Slave revolts, but also Amerindian resistance and Maroon defiance, required a military answer, as did occasional external threats in times of international war. Slaves bought from planters for this purpose as well as free blacks and coloreds had a prominent role in this warfare. More generally, free men and women of African descent were increasingly visible in the Dutch military forces, both in the Caribbean and in Elmina, where whites were outnumbered in the mid-eighteenth century by Eurafrican soldiers, the children of European males and Akan women. Free people of color were especially conspicuous in colonial port cities, where they worked side by side with slaves, both groups performing tasks essential to the functioning of the ports. Slaves and free people of color were employed as domestic servants and artisans, and contributed to the maritime economy as sailors, fishermen, caulkers, dock-hands, warehouse workers, and sailmakers. This trend was in keeping with other parts of Atlantic America, from Boston and New York via the Danish islands to Brazil.[1] At the same time, however, the vast majority of slaves in the Dutch Atlantic worked in the Guianas, on plantations widely removed not only geographically but also culturally and demographically from the small urban enclaves.

Among themselves, the Dutch American colonies were anything but homogeneous, nor did they form a political unity. This was not exceptional from an Atlantic perspective. While France's American colonies may have relied on the imperial state for protection, funding, and cultural standards, each still pursued its own political and economic agenda.[2] Britain's overseas empire in 1760, Jack P. Greene has written, "continued to be a collection of self-contained and . . . largely self-governing polities tied to a metropolis that had proven itself incapable of marshaling and deploying the fiscal and administrative resources necessary to fuse the overseas empire into a tidily organized whole under the direction of an effective bureaucracy."[3] In the Dutch case, heterogeneity was a product not only of the widely diverging geographic and economic characteristics of the various colonies, but also of the political organization of the Dutch Republic, a federal state that was ruled by representatives of the seven constitutive provinces and that lacked powerful central institutions. In such a climate, diverse arrangements for colonial governance were allowed to thrive: if the West India Company ruled most colonies, Suriname and Berbice were governed by companies of their own.

Decentralization affected the knowledge infrastructure of the Dutch colonial realm, which remained underdeveloped on account of the colonies' religious scene and because state initiatives were virtually absent. The lack of an overarching authority and policy for all colonies was reflected in religious privileges that differed from colony to colony—Jews being barred from Demerara and Essequibo, but nowhere else, Methodism being allowed only on St. Eustatius, and Catholicism being legalized for most of the eighteenth century only on Curaçao.

The great diversity of European backgrounds of the settlers was a serious obstacle to the transmission of Dutchness in the colonies in Guiana and the insular Caribbean. White culture in Suriname developed from a mixture of northwestern European as well as Ashkenazi and Sephardi origins, while European migration to the other Guiana colonies was increasingly British. The colonies on the Caribbean islands, home to many different groups of European immigrants among whom the Dutch were not dominant, assumed traits of their immediate foreign environments, with Curaçao, Aruba, and Bonaire importing many elements from the

Spanish Main, and the English Windward Islands influencing Saba, St. Maarten, and St. Eustatius, where English became the main language. But of course cultural development was not exclusively and, for most inhabitants of the Dutch Atlantic, not even primarily about intra-European acculturation. Particularly in the Guianas, creolization marked the birth not only of new Afro-Caribbean cultures, but also of new cultural forms deriving from the asymmetrical "encounters" between Africans, Europeans, and to a much lesser degree Amerindians. The most telling illustration of this process in the Dutch Atlantic was the rise of new languages, in particular Papiamentu and Sranantongo.

Metropolitan aloofness enabled (frequently illegal) initiatives by local officials and residents to proliferate. Over time, a whole corpus of unwritten laws came about that deviated from those upheld in the republic, such as the practice in Curaçao of performing marriage services in private houses in order to accommodate the island's poor. Nor did metropolitan officials guide the colonies' economic development, which instead depended on the initiatives of local merchants and planters. That was evident in the elaboration of rules and regulations pertaining to slavery, which were devised locally and therefore differed from place to place. Local initiatives were also paramount in the colonies' commercial development. Settlers made specific choices for trading partners in the Americas, frequently challenging metropolitan ordinances. This was standard practice throughout the New World, where officials tended to side with colonial elites and modify metropolitan instructions. They also assisted settlers in their interimperial contraband trade. The Dutch officials on Curaçao who exempted products brought in from the Spanish colonies from customs duties were not alone, nor those in Suriname who condoned trade with North America. Likewise, customs officers in British North America and the British West Indies enabled ship captains to export colonial produce to non-British colonies such as Suriname by issuing fake clearance papers that stated British colonies as the destination.[4]

Legal or illegal, interimperial trade was indispensable to the development of the Dutch Atlantic, just as the development of the Dutch Atlantic was an important element in the expansion of interimperial commercial ties in the wider Atlantic world. The commercial entanglement between the metropolitan and colonial Dutch, on the one hand, and the foreign colonies in the New World, on the other, was manifold. Scores of vessels from British North America arrived each year in almost every Dutch colony with foodstuffs and horses, which were exchanged for rum, molasses, cacao, cash, or whatever else the Americans were looking for. Trade with the French West Indies involved the Dutch purchase of cash crops and sale of provisions, manufactures, or slaves, while the Spanish (circum-) Caribbean was a major supplier to Dutch vessels of cacao, hides, tobacco, mules, annatto, and balsam in payment for textiles, guns, and ironware. The only major site of interimperial Dutch trade in the eastern Atlantic was the Gold Coast, where merchants from Brazil offered low-grade Bahian tobacco and gold dust from Minas Gerais in their quest for slaves and textiles. Apart from the numerous forms of bilateral interimperial commerce, the Dutch colonies also functioned as bridges between other empires, Curaçaoans shipping mules from the Spanish Main to the French Caribbean and St. Eustatius connecting merchants from British and French America. If such connections were the *raison d'être* of the two Dutch entrepôts, they were also indispensable to the Dutch colonies that specialized in cash crop production. The horses on Suriname's sugar plantations came off British ships, just like the enslaved Africans arriving in the lesser Guianas during their period of expansion in the late eighteenth century. Without these foreign linkages, none of Dutch America could have been developed for colonial purposes.

Cash crop production, especially in Suriname, was the other pillar of the Dutch Atlantic economy. St. Eustatius had its own, albeit modest, sugar industry, while Berbice, Demerara, and Essequibo produced a variety of tropical crops that grew in volume and value mainly in the latter half of the eighteenth century. Their rise occurred largely after the collapse of an artificial investment boom in Suriname had created havoc, not so much in its production capacity but certainly in its financial situation and hence access to credit. The ensuing crisis of the most important Dutch Atlantic colony in turn accelerated the demise of the West India Company, which had long ceased to turn a profit after it had become merely a governing body with no commercial monopoly whatsoever.

The company's dissolution in 1791 and the subsequent assumption by the Dutch government of colonial governance were therefore long overdue, but the new construction did not usher in an era of profitability. The interruption of transatlantic trade in the two decades on either side of 1800, coupled with the British conquest of the economically most promising parts of Dutch America—the three western Guiana colonies—finally reduced the Dutch Atlantic to economic insignificance. By the time the Napoleonic era ended, the Dutch slave trade had been abolished (1814), the two Caribbean entrepôts had lost their interimperial function, cash crop exports had withered, and the colonial populations had shrunk. The Second Dutch Atlantic was over.

The end came during the Age of Revolutions, but the ideas underlying this age hardly affected the Dutch Atlantic. Nowhere did the colonial elites consider severing the ties with the metropolis. Nor did antislavery make any headway in the Dutch Republic and its successor states. While abolitionist treatises did appear in print, no movement emerged to put the end of the slave trade on the political agenda. The Haitian Revolution, if noticed at all in the metropolis, was mainly interpreted as a warning of what might happen if blacks were to attain their freedom. In the end, the Dutch slave trade was abolished under British pressure, not as the outcome of a domestic debate, and the demise of slavery had to wait for another half-century. The one episode in which the Dutch Atlantic did feature in the Age of Revolutions was the 1795 slave revolt in Curaçao, which echoed the symbols and slogans of the French and Haitian Revolutions. This revolt was, however, quickly and brutally suppressed and did not have any impact in the Netherlands. The story of the Dutch, then, suggests an alternative to the dominant reading of Atlantic history, in which the displacement of native residents of the Americas and colonial revolts during the Age of Revolutions are crucial watersheds.

And yet the demise of the Second Dutch Atlantic did coincide with the revolutionary era, since the events that marked that juncture put an end to the special role the Dutch had always played as go-betweens. In this role, the Dutch had left their mark on the wider Atlantic world. They provided a reliable alternative source of European consumer goods to any potential customers and a market for any sort of New World products, wherever produced. The high quality and low prices of the European manufactures (especially textiles), Asian spices, and New World rum they offered for sale to foreign settlers both in the Dutch colonies and on foreign soil made the Dutch popular trading partners. The trade they conducted was frequently at odds with mercantilist laws that were, at least formally, upheld in rival empires. And yet, such breaches did not challenge mercantilism—if anything, Dutch imports and exports allowed the various mercantilist systems to function better, plugging holes and adding lubricants wherever possible. The occasional confiscation of their ships and goods by vigilant officials was the price the Dutch were willing to pay, albeit grudgingly.

In keeping with the notion that the Dutch developed the first modern economy—as suggested by Jan de Vries and Ad van der Woude—one could argue that the Dutch were ahead of their time by using Curaçao, St. Eustatius, and to some extent St. Maarten as virtual free trade zones. After all, only after the Seven Years' War did Britain, France, and Spain assign a free trade status to numerous islands they held in the Caribbean. In the British case, it is clear that increased slave demand in foreign colonies provided an important rationale for opening up trade—just like Curaçao's heavy involvement in the *asiento* slave trade had prompted the Dutch decision to make the island a free port a century earlier.[5]

The Dutch adopted only a watered-down version of mercantilism, less encompassing than that of their competitors. This made sense in light of the modest size of their own Atlantic realm and the lack of sufficient naval support. The absence of full-blown mercantilist policies was reflected in the Dutch home market's receptivity to transatlantic products that did not arrive directly from Dutch colonies, but were reexported by rival European countries. Planters in Dutch America lacked the protection that their colleagues in other parts of the New World could count on at home. The state was, then, not prominently present in the eighteenth-century Dutch Atlantic, which differed conspicuously from the major Atlantic powers, which all aspired to develop the financial means to wage war, protect trade, acquire territories overseas, and secure access to transatlantic markets. The Dutch Republic lacked both a strong state and the financial and demographic means to maintain a powerful navy.[6]

The easy access to products from foreign Atlantic colonies enjoyed in the Dutch home market was paralleled by the openness of the Dutch colonies in the Greater Caribbean, not just to produce from elsewhere in the New World, but equally to residents of foreign empires. Compared to the strict rules that applied in Spanish, French, and British America, the prevailing regulations were lenient, enabling many foreign merchants to establish themselves in the Dutch islands, taking their business along with them and adding to the colonies' commercial prosperity. This was especially true for St. Eustatius. Such openness also helped Germans and Britons to move as planters to Suriname and the Guianas.

The involvement of the Dutch in the (other) Atlantic empires also extended to finance. If foreign mercantilist policies frequently hurt Dutch commercial interests, protectionism could not damage such financial involvement in other parts of the Americas. Dutch investors poured money not only into the Danish Caribbean and the infant United States, but also into England. England's adoption of the Navigation Acts actually helped spur on Dutch investments in English trade in the wake of the Glorious Revolution, as the two neighbors became close political and military allies. During the following three decades, Dutch capital was invested in England's reexport trade with the European mainland. The role of Dutch intermediary merchants was almost reduced to insignificance in these years, as merchants in one country established direct ties with producers in the other. These developments allowed English merchants to abandon active trade and engage in the commission business, providing service to producers and merchants in various locales, in particular North America and the Caribbean. Dutch investments thus helped English merchants focus their resources and energies on the Atlantic world.[7] Time and again, then, the Dutch provided the lubricants that helped oil the Atlantic machine, in the process making contraband trade one of their Atlantic pillars in a way not even replicated by the equally active Danes.

Nonetheless, the Dutch are often overlooked in mainstream histories of the Atlantic. They are usually permitted a brief appearance on the political Atlantic scene in the second and third quarters of the seventeenth century, when they took their war of independence against Habsburg Spain to Africa and the Americas. As European forerunners in New York, they are also given some attention, but no longer do the Dutch feature in mainstream Atlantic narratives after their mainland presence in Brazil and New Netherland had come to an end. Students of slavery may occasionally refer to the Dutch slave trade or slavery and marronage in Suriname, and historians of West Africa cannot avoid the Dutch presence there, while some economic historians of the Thirteen Colonies have pointed to the presence of Dutch smugglers both on North America's eastern seaboard and in Caribbean waters. In general, however, the Dutch are conspicuously absent from histories of the Atlantic world. The small size of the Second Dutch Atlantic and the traditional focus of Dutch historians on the Dutch *East* India Company are obvious reasons for this neglect. Other explanations stem from the U.S. background of most practitioners of

Atlantic history, whose vantage point is usually British North America. In their narratives, the Dutch disappear from view once New Netherland is incorporated into the English domain, and certainly once England and the Dutch Republic overcome their political rivalry. That the Dutch play no more than a supporting role in general Atlantic histories derives also from linguistic limitations. Although their number is on the rise, few Atlanticists have mastered the Dutch language, which means that they rely on publications that are often outdated or resort to hyperbole or understatement of Dutch contributions.

And yet, much is gained by including the Dutch, in the first place because our knowledge of the Atlantic world at large would benefit from a discussion of commonalities and differences between the Dutch realm and the Atlantic empires. Thus far, comparative history seems to have had a limited appeal among Atlantic historians—and when comparisons are made, they tend to be between the English and the Spanish Atlantic.[8] An analysis of the Second Dutch Atlantic, however, reveals interesting parallels to the British Atlantic. Both were religiously and administratively decentralized but racially and ethnically fairly homogeneous. Both differed fundamentally from the religiously and politically unified but polyglot and ethnically complex Spanish colonial world. This raises questions about the strength of the respective imperial governments and about the influence of religion—did Protestantism, with its tendency to produce what J. H. Elliot has called a "plurality of creeds," foster theological heterogeneity as well as ethnic exclusivity?[9]

Integrating the Dutch also makes sense from another vantage point. As seen above, the Dutch structural commercial linkages with other parts of the Atlantic basin enabled foreign mercantilism to function better. Dutch smuggling also offers further proof of what an increasing body of studies has shown: the power of the metropolis to lay down the law in the colonies was limited throughout the Atlantic world. Metropolitan laws were often modified or rejected by elites who knew they were operating from a position of strength. Likewise, the ubiquity of Dutch contraband trade, condoned or encouraged by foreign economic and political elites, confirms the interconnectedness of the Atlantic world, in which the Dutch frequently served as intermediaries between subjects of other empires. As Alison Games has argued, "any study of the Dutch is one of entanglement."[10]

By highlighting the role of entanglement in the Dutch Atlantic, we have sought to contribute to the study of interimperial connectivity in the Atlantic world.[11] Further study is required to investigate the cultural and social dimensions of this phenomenon. Here, a trail has been blazed by students of the (non-Dutch) Atlantic empires, who have provided much insight into hybridization in the interactions between whites, natives, and people of African origin in discrete colonies.[12] A more conspicuous lacuna is the study of the Atlantic's impact on the Dutch Republic itself, economically or otherwise. Whereas scholars such as Marcy Norton and Catherine Molineux have shown the potential of researching the ways in which the Atlantic influenced Europe, few students of Dutch history have taken up the challenge of reversing the focus.[13] Some excellent works have been published on the seventeenth-century Dutch empire, but the Second Dutch Atlantic still lacks such an examination.[14]

Our book ends in 1815. If the First Dutch Atlantic projected political might that was based on conquests from the Iberians, and the Second Dutch Atlantic exuded economic strength founded on enslaved labor and illicit trade, the early nineteenth century did not see a new beginning. Dutch colonialism, from a metropolitan point of view, became a spectacular success in the Indonesian archipelago, but the Dutch Atlantic slowly faded into the background—in an economic sense, at least. Paradoxically, Dutch involvement with the remaining Caribbean colonies increased, if only because they lost their appeal to outsiders. After 1815, therefore, and particularly over the past century, as the wider Dutch Atlantic fell apart, the Dutch Caribbean, devoid of its interimperial framework, became more exclusively *Dutch* colonial than ever before.

NOTES

Introduction

1. For a succinct overview of Dutch decolonization, see Van den Doel, *Afscheid*, and De Jong, *Avondschot*.

2. On postcolonial migrations and their significance for Dutch ideas about national identity and colonial history, see Oostindie, *Postcolonial Netherlands*.

3. See for a more detailed historiographical essay Oostindie and Roitman, "Repositioning."

4. See, e.g., De Vries, "Dutch Atlantic Economies," 2; De Vries and Van der Woude, *First Modern Economy*, 476; Emmer, *Dutch in the Atlantic Economy*, 1.

5. Postma and Enthoven, *Riches from Atlantic Commerce*; Enthoven and Den Heijer, "Nederland."

6. Klooster, "Inter-Imperial Smuggling"; Klooster, "Curaçao as a Transit Center"; Oostindie, "Modernity," and particularly Oostindie and Roitman, "Repositioning the Dutch"; and Oostindie and Rotman, "Introduction."

7. Klooster, *Illicit Riches*; Oostindie and Roitman, *Dutch Atlantic Connections*.

8. Klooster, *Dutch Moment*.

9. De Vries, "Limits of Globalization," 729.

10. Cruz, "For Richer or Poorer."

11. Price, *First-Time* and *Alabi's World*; see also the work of Richard and Sally Price on John Gabriel Stedman's *Narrative* (Price and Price, "Introduction").

12. See, e.g., Dewulf, "Emulating a Portuguese Model"; Fatah-Black, "Suriname and the Atlantic World"; Van Groesen, *Legacy of Dutch Brazil*; and *Amsterdam's Atlantic*; Haefeli, *New Netherland*; Jordaan, *Slavernij en vrijheid*; Romney, *New Netherland Connections*; Rupert, *Creolization and Contraband*; Vink, *Creole Jews*, and the various contributions to Klooster and Oostindie, *Curaçao*, and Oostindie and Roitman, *Dutch Atlantic Connections*.

13. Israel, *Dutch Primacy*; Wallerstein, *Modern World-System*, II, 36–71.

14. The one previous attempt to discuss "all" Dutch Atlantic history that comes to mind is Cornelis Goslinga's valiant but flawed and outdated trilogy on *The Dutch in the Caribbean*.

15. Emmer and Gommans, *Rijk aan de rand van de wereld*, 455.

16. Murrin, "English Rights," 58.

17. Voorhees, "In the Republic's Tradition," 50–51; Mouw, "Moederkerk and Vaderland." For the language battle in New York City, see Goodfriend, "Archibald Laidlie," 244. For New Netherland and its aftermath, see also Jacobs, *Colony of New Netherland*; Goodfriend, *Before the Melting Pot*; and *Revisiting New Netherland*.

18. Hackett, *Rude Hand of Innovation*, 57–58, 75, 154.

19. See Schnurmann, *Atlantische Welten*; and Koot, *Empire at the Periphery*.

20. Quotation taken from Worden, *Cape Town*, xiii. For a more elaborate discussion of geography, see Oostindie and Roitman, "Introduction," 5–6. On the Cape Colony, Worden, *Cape Town*; and Ward, *Networks of Empire*.

1. Entanglements

1. Klooster, *Dutch Moment*, 33–112.

2. Den Heijer, *Geschiedenis van de WIC*, 17–18; Vogt, *Portuguese Rule*, 166.

3. Lesger, *Rise of the Amsterdam Market*, 46, 129–30, 135–37; Gelderblom, *Zuid-Nederlandse kooplieden*, 158, 178–82, 224.

4. Mauro, *Le Portugal*, 538.

5. Ratelband, *Nederlanders in West-Afrika*, 36.

6. Moerbeeck, *Redenen*.

7. De Laet, *Jaerlyck Verhael*, 4:282–87.

8. Hartog, *Bovenwindse eilanden*, 107; Goslinga, *Dutch in Caribbean and Wild Coast*, 446.

9. Jean-Baptiste Colbert, "Propositions sur les avantages que l'on pourrait tirer des Etats de Hollande pour l'augmentation du commerce du royaume," in Clément, Lettres, 2:658–60; Ly, *Compagnie du Sénégal*, 104; Pritchard, *In Search of Empire*, 270; Mims, *Colbert's West India Policy*, 195–99.

10. Goslinga, *Dutch in Caribbean and Wild Coast*, 447–56, 478–81; Pritchard, "Franco-Dutch War," 11–15.

11. Schwartz and Postma, "Dutch Republic and Brazil," 174–76. The WIC minutes show that the first Portuguese ship admitted to sell its cargo of tobacco to the Dutch in West Africa arrived in 1689. Nationaal Archief, the Netherlands (NAN), Verspreide West-Indische Stukken 37, "Memorie betreffende de geschillen met Portugal over het vertollen van Portugese schepen ter Kuste van Guinea gedurende de 17e en 18 eeuw," undated.

12. Fatah-Black, *White Lies*, 42–43; Zeeuws Archief (ZA), Archief van de Staten van Zeeland (SZ), 2035/22, Johan Tressy to the States of Zeeland, ca. June 1668.

13. Schnurmann, *Atlantische Welten*, 252.

14. Fatah-Black, *White Lies*, 57–58.

15. Pitman, *Development of the British West Indies*, 197; Schnurmann, *Atlantische Welten*, 294–301.

16. Schnurmann, *Atlantische Welten*, 302–3.

17. Ibid., 304–5.

18. This was reported by Captain Philip Aubin of the Betsy, which sailed to Paramaribo in 1756. Duncan, *Mariner's Chronicle*, 1: 106.

19. Enthoven, "That Abominable Nest of Pirates," 252.

20. Knappert, *Geschiedenis*, 221; Abenon, *Guadeloupe*, 2:12.

21. Klooster, *Illicit Riches*, 119.

22. Israel, "Dutch Role," 109.

23. Gauci, *Politics of Trade*, 178.

24. Hattendorf, "To Aid and Assist," 177–78; Israel, *Dutch Primacy*, 340–44.

25. Bromley, "French Privateering War," 217.

26. Crouse, *French Struggle*, 149.

27. Ibid., 149–52.

28. Hartsinck, *Beschryving van Guiana*, 297.

29. Curaçao's ties were particularly close with nearby Coro, the recipient of most vessels based on the Dutch island. Joseph de Anieto, the main merchant in Coro around 1690, received weekly letters from Curaçao. Archivo General de Indias (AGI, Seville), Santo Domingo 198 R1 N7f, Governor Marquis de Cassal to the King, Caracas, May 31, 1690.

30. Klooster, *Illicit Riches*, 55, 73.

31. Ibid., 59; Rupert, *Creolization and Contraband*, 74; Hartog, *Curaçao*, I: 365.

32. Goslinga, "Curaçao as Slave-Trading Center," 1–50.

33. Jordaan, *Slavernij en vrijheid*, 47; Schnurmann, *Atlantische Welten*, 165–70, 273.

34. Perera, *Provincia fantasma*, 199.

35. Araúz Monfante, *Contrabando holandés*, 1:114.

36. Hemming, "How Brazil Acquired Roraima," 302.

37. Thompson, *Colonialism and Underdevelopment*, 184; Hemming, "How Brazil Acquired Roraima," 305–6. For mining expeditions in Suriname, see: Bijlsma, "Mijnwerk der societeit," 335–38.

38. Commander Abraham Beekman to the West India Company, October 20, 1679, April 16, 1680, and March 2, 1682, in *Report and Accompanying Papers*, 144–48, 153–54.

39. WIC, Chamber of Zeeland, to Abraham Beekman, commander of Essequibo, August 21, 1684, in ibid., 164.

40. Whitehead, *Lords of the Tiger Spirit*, 161.

41. Crespo Solana, *Mercaderes atlánticos*, 42.

42. Israel, *Dutch Republic*, 959–68. The first stadholderless period had lasted from 1650 until 1672.

43. Olivas, "Global Politics," 92–93; Israel, *Dutch Primacy*, 361–62, 368.

44. Goslinga, *Dutch in Caribbean and Guianas*, 130.

45. Netscher, *Geschiedenis*, 100–101; De Goeje, "Verslag," 33–41.

46. Ransoming was a device frequently used by the French during this war. They also resorted to it at Fort Gambia in 1702 and 1704, in Nevis in 1706, and in Rio de Janeiro in 1711. Bromley, "French Privateering War," 223.

47. Hrodej, *Cassard*, 172–75; Hartsinck, *Beschryving van Guiana,* 62.

48. Netscher, *Geschiedenis*, 155–57; Hrodej, *Cassard*, 181–82.

49. Netscher, *Geschiedenis*, 158–59.

50. Hrodej, *Cassard*, 187; Goslinga, *Dutch in Caribbean and Guianas*, 131; Knappert, *Geschiedenis*, 36.

51. AGI, Santo Domingo 696, Governor Joseph Francisco de Cañas to the King, Caracas, June 16, 1713.

52. Goslinga, *Dutch in Caribbean and Guianas*, 98–99; Hrodej, *Cassard*, 202.

53. Den Heijer, *Goud, ivoor en slaven*, 347.

54. Wolbers, *Geschiedenis van Suriname*, 90–93; Van der Meiden, *Betwist bestuur*, 74–75; Goslinga, *Dutch in Caribbean and Guianas*, 99, 282–83.

55. NAN, Nieuwe West-Indische Compagnie (NWIC) 607, fols. 556–57, read in the WIC meeting of June 12, 1770.

56. Verhees-Van Meer, *Zeeuwse kaapvaart*, 56.

57. Ibid., 142; Bromley, "French Privateering War," 241. The Zeeland privateers captured 80 percent of enemy ships in the North Sea or the Atlantic and 20 percent in the Mediterranean. Calculated on the basis of Verhees-Van Meer, *Zeeuwse kaapvaart*, 138–39.

58. NAN, NWIC 567, fol. 551, deposition of Johan Goetvrint, Juan Moyaart, Philippo Henrix, Becker, Bastiaan Fredrix, and Davit Senior, Curaçao, August 22, 1703.

59. J. de Wildt to Anthonie Heinsius, December 20, 1703, in Veenendaal, *Briefwisseling*, 584–85.

60. Klooster, "Between Habsburg Neglect," 708–10. See also Borges, *Casa de Austria*, 66, 76–77; and Olivas, "Global Politics," 94–96.

61. Klooster, "Between Habsburg Neglect," 710. During the Nine Years' War, it was the Dutch who had proposed sending a joint fleet to the Americas in addition to those bound for the Channel and the Mediterranean. The English refused to go along, since they feared that the Dutch would use such an expedition to usurp Anglo-American trade or possessions. Clark, *Dutch Alliance*, 39.

62. Satsuma, *Britain and Colonial Maritime War*, 43, 50, 58–62, 105–110, 124. Israel, *Dutch Primacy*, 373–74.

63. NAN, NWIC 907A, WIC, Chamber of Amsterdam to unknown, January 19, 1712; meetings of the WIC, Chamber of Amsterdam, April 12 and 19, 1712. The company originally floated the plan to obtain Puerto Rico through negotiations, but ultimately the slave trade was prioritized.

64. Israel, *Dutch Republic*, 971, 985.

65. Crespo Solana and Klooster, "República Holandesa."

66. NAN, Verspreide West-Indische Stukken 40, the Marquis de St. Gil to the States General, The Hague, December 28, 1741.

67. Klooster, *Illicit Riches*, 124–27.

68. Bruijn, "Protection of Dutch Shipping," 127–28; Den Heijer, "Public and Private West India Interest," 165–66. Although the actions of the Compañía led to resentment among the Dutch, just as Britain condemned the numerous Spanish captures of its vessels in the Caribbean, the States General never considered joining Britain in the War of Jenkins' Ear. Dunthorne, *Maritime Powers*, 313–17.

69. Felice Cardot, *Rebelión de Andresote*, 19–23.

70. NAN, Oud Archief Curaçao 1548, fol. 60, statement by Joseph Gotar, Curaçao, January 14, 1739.

71. Feliciano Ramos, *Contrabando inglés*, 171.

72. Zahedieh, "Merchants of Port Royal," 592–93.

73. Araúz Monfante, *Contrabando holandés*, 1:97, 99, 2:137–42; Robles, *América a fines del siglo XVII*, 81.

74. Klooster, *Illicit Riches*, 76; Grahn, *Political Economy of Smuggling*, 41.

75. Araúz Monfante, *Contrabando holandés*, 2:84–85.

76. Klooster, *Illicit Riches*, 77–78.

77. AGI, Santo Domingo 602, Gabriel de Zuloaga, Governor of Caracas, to Gregorio de Espinosa de los Monteros, Caracas, November 13, 1744, Gregorio Espinosa, Governor of Cumaná, to Gabriel de Zuloaga, Cumaná, January 15, 1745.

78. Enthoven, "Suriname and Zeeland," 249–60, 256; Van der Linde, *Surinaamse suikerheren*, 89–90.

79. AGI, Santo Domingo 713, Phelipe Ricardos (Governor of Caracas), "Noticias del methodo, que deve practicarse para extinguir el comercio Ylicito en la Provincia de Venezuela," ca. 1751.

80. Netscher, *Geschiedenis*, 91–92.

81. Den Heijer, *Goud, ivoor en slaven*, 347n48.

82. Father Bartolomé de San Miguel, prefect of the Capuchin order, to the king, Caracas, March 9, 1728, in Carrocera, *Misiones de los capuchinos*, 175–76. Nonetheless, a ban existed in mid-century Essequibo on selling arms to indigenous groups, since these could be used against the Dutch. Hoonhout, "West Indian Web," 47.

83. Whitehead, *Lords of the Tiger Spirit*, 154.

84. Thompson, *Colonialism and Underdevelopment*, 177.

85. Den Heijer, *Goud, ivoor en slaven*, 284. See also Paesie, *Lorrendrayen op Africa*, 289–92.

86. Schwartz and Postma, "Dutch Republic and Brazil," 181 (table 7.4).

87. Ibid., 186, 192–93, 195 (table 7.8).

88. In the years 1713–17, more than fifty vessels returned to Boston from Suriname, and probably more from Rhode Island. Bernstein, *Origins of Inter-American Interest*, 17.

89. Postma, "Breaching the Mercantile Barriers," 114–15; Postma, "Suriname and its Atlantic Connections," 300–304; Fatah-Black, *White Lies*, 47–48.

90. Douglass, *Summary*, 108.

91. Postma, "Suriname and its Atlantic Connections," 301, 303.

92. Representation of the Lt. Governor Edw. Byam, Council and Assembly of Antigua, to the Council of Trade and Plantations, November 17, 1731, in Headlam and Newton, *Calendar of State Papers, 1731*, 348–50.

93. Lovejoy, *Rhode Island Politics*, 19.

94. These entries were registered in the period December 1729–December 4, 1730. Pares, *Yankees and Creoles*, 48–49.

95. Ostrander, "Colonial Molasses Trade," 79.

96. Pitman, *Development of British West Indies*, 281–82; Pares, *War and Trade*, 396–97; Anderson, *Crucible of War*, 578.

97. Fatah-Black, *White Lies*, 60–61.

98. In the 1730s, for example, some families from New York moved to Curaçao. NAN, NWIC 315, council of Curaçao to WIC, Chamber of Amsterdam, Curaçao, May 29, 1737.

99. Robert Quary to the Commissioners of Customs, Philadelphia, March 6, 1700, in Headlam, *Calendar of State Papers, 1700*, 106.

100. Schnurmann, *Atlantische Welten*, 278–81; Matson, *Merchants and Empire*, 76–78. Twenty-nine vessels steered to Curaçao in the period December 1729–December 1730. Pares, *Yankees and Creoles*, 49.

101. Klooster, *Illicit Riches*, 98–101; Koot, *Empire at the Periphery*, 174–75.

102. Klooster, *Illicit Riches*, 98.

103. White, *Beekmans of New York*, 320.

104. NAN, NWIC 1154, fol. 34, Governor Jan Noach du Fay to the WIC, Chamber of Zeeland, October 20, 1724.

105. Araúz Monfante, *Contrabando holandés*, 1:60–61.

106. Enthoven, "That Abominable Nest of Pirates," 260.

107. NAN, NWIC 622, fols. 209ff, dagregisters St. Eustatius, July 1, 1743–December 24, 1744.

108. Enthoven, "That Abominable Nest of Pirates," 267–69.

109. William Mathew, Governor of St. Christopher, to the Council of Trade and Plantations, May 26, 1737, in Davies, *Calendar of State Papers, 1737*, 170.

110. Paesie, *Lorrendrayen op Africa*, 250–51, 253–54; Postma, *Dutch in the Atlantic Slave Trade*, 197–99.

111. Leebeek, "Caraïbische stapelmarkt," 19. During a five-month period in late 1752 and early 1753, almost all of the 640 enslaved Africans reexported from Barbados were shipped to St. Eustatius. O'Malley, *Final Passages*, 368.

112. In 1752, ten vessels from St. Christopher, Montserrat, St. Croix, Guadeloupe, St. Eustatius, and Saba disembarked a total of fifty-six enslaved Africans at St. Maarten. Another vessel introduced an unknown number. NAN, NWIC 1188, "Lijst van alle de ingekoomen vaartuygen met haare laadingen in de bay Philipsburg van den 1 January 1752 tot den 1 January 1753."

113. NAN, NWIC 1183, slaves sold from the ships Goude Put, Phenix, Duynvliet, and Rusthoff. Residents of St. Eustatius made up most of the buyers from the Dutch Caribbean. Unlike foreign customers, who purchased one or more dozen Africans, residents of St. Eustatius typically bought a single slave, suggesting that their captives would be employed on the island itself and not resold.

114. Knappert, *Geschiedenis*, 218–19.

115. Enthoven, "That Abominable Nest of Pirates," 272–74.

116. Quoted in ibid., 273.

117. Pérotin-Dumon, *Ville aux îles*, 153, 181.

118. Klooster, *Illicit Riches*, 119–20.

119. NAN, NWIC 622, fol. 209ff. These Africans were imported in the period July 1, 1643–June 30, 1644.

120. Armytage, *Free Port System*, 36–37, 45–46; Menkman, "Statiaansche toestanden," 111–12.

121. Jarvis, *In the Eye of All Trade*, 170, 173, 354.

122. Knappert, *Geschiedenis*, 224.

123. Of the 146 vessels arriving in St. Eustatius in 1733, only 24 hailed from the Thirteen Colonies (Rhode Island: 13; Boston: 5; New York: 3; Maryland, North Carolina, and Virginia: each 1). Likewise, only 12 out of 175 vessels coming to St. Maarten in 1735–36 had departed from North America (Rhode Island: 10, Boston: 1, Salem: 1). Ibid., 219, 224.

124. Truxes, *Defying Empire*, 59; Avitable, "Colonial Connecticut," 167, 297–98.

125. Tapley, *Early Coastwise Shipping*, 99, 166. Rarely did the Salem merchants—and those from Marblehead, Ipswich, Gloucester, Newburyport, and Beverly who were listed as based in Salem—venture to other ports outside the British empire, apart from voyages to Guadeloupe and Martinique at the end of the Seven Years' War (when these islands were under British occupation).

126. Ahn, "Anglo-French Treaty," 169, 175, 180. See also Coombs, *Conduct of the Dutch*, 281–83, 301–08, 369–72.

127. Wilson, *French Foreign Policy*, 130. Black, *Trade, Empire*, 122.

128. Wilson, *French Foreign Policy*, 134.

129. Israel, *Dutch Republic*, 997.

130. Carter, *Neutrality or Commitment*, 41.

131. A British admiral wrote from Jamaica in 1758 that Sainte-Domingue received goods "either from the islands of Saint Eustatius or Curaçao in small sloops and brigantines, or from Holland in very large ships," which carried back French-produced sugar, indigo, and coffee. Truxes, *Defying Empire*, 95. See also Chassaigne, "L'économie des îles sucrières," 101.

132. Carter, *Neutrality or Commitment*, 86; Klooster, *Illicit Riches*, 103. See also Pares, *War and Trade*, 384.

133. Lydon, *Pirates, Privateers, and Profits*, 118–19; Rogge, *Handelshuis Van Eeghen*, 52–53.

134. Stadsarchief Amsterdam (SAA), Archief Brants 1397, Anthony Beaujon to Jn. Is. de Neufville and I. de Neufville van der Hoop, St. Eustatius, April 3, 1760.

135. Baugh, "Withdrawing from Europe," 3–4.

136. Ibid., 22, 28.

137. Pares, *War and Trade*, 391.

138. Villiers, *Marine royale*, 477; Enthoven, "That Abominable Nest of Pirates," 280;2 Leebeek, "Caraïbische stapelmarkt," 24–5.

139. Klooster, *Illicit Riches*, 103.

140. Ibid., 97–98; Garrigus, "Blue and Brown," 244–46, 250, 253–55.

141. NAN, NWIC 1174, fols. 91–112, 213–29, 1461–70, dagregisters Curaçao, July 1, 1785–June 30, 1786. In 1775, even an entire human cargo from Africa was sent for sale to Saint-Domingue, after Curaçao's traders had bought all 238 Africans disembarked from a Dutch slaver. NAN, NWIC 1166, fol. 17, Governor Jean Rodier to the WIC, Chamber of Zeeland, Curaçao, January 10, 1775.

142. NAN, WIC, 609, fol. 556, Governor Jean Rodier and Council to the WIC, March 14, 1774.

143. López Cantos, *Francisco de Saavedra*, 102.

144. Tarrade, "Commerce," 30, 36.

145. Araúz Monfante, *Contrabando holandés*, 1:105.

146. Izard, *Miedo a la revolución*, 85.

147. Aizpurua A., "Mulas venezolanas," 13; Amézaga Aresti, *Vicente Antonio de Icuza*, 50; Chabert, Flandrin, and Huzard, *Instructions et observations*, 3:292.

148. Duviols, "Côtes du Venezuela," 11 ; Araúz Monfante, *Contrabando holandés*, 1:110.

149. NAN, NWIC, 209, fol. 454, placard issued by Governor Jan Gales, January 15, 1739.

150. NAN, NWIC, 612, fol. 645, C. A. Roelans, customs collector, and Michiel Römer, bookkeeper, to the WIC, Curaçao, April 4, 1783.

151. Izard, "Contrabandistas," 73.

152. Miguel de Araujo from Coro bought the schooner Nra. Sa. del Carmen y la Soledad in Curaçao, sending it to Jacmel in the early 1780s to sell mules. A few years later, Francisco Manzano from Coro counted on a license from the Intendencia to introduce a sloop from Curaçao and sail to the colonies with two hundred mules. González Batista, *Archivo Histórico de Coro*, 137, 139.

153. Klooster, *Illicit Riches*, 74.

154. Vivas Piñeda, "Botín a bordo," 358. See also Klooster, *Illicit Riches*, 147–53.

155. Whitehead, *Lords of the Tiger Spirit*, 164–65. *Venezuela–British Guiana Boundary Arbitration*, 1:134.

156. Proceedings of the States General, July 31, 1759, in Report and Accompanying Papers, 383; Whitehead, *Lords of the Tiger Spirit*, 156. Contraband trade between the Spanish Main and Essequibo and Demerara did not come to a complete halt in the last quarter of the eighteenth century. Izard, "Contrabandistas," 52n82.

157. *Venezuela-British Guiana Boundary Arbitration*, 146–47; Hoonhout, "West Indian Web," 31–32.

158. Fatah-Black, *White Lies*, 65.

159. Pares, *Yankees and Creoles*, 37.

160. Weeden, *Early Rhode Island*, 322.

161. Carpenter, *Arts and Crafts*, 9.

162. Proceedings of the General Assembly of Rhode Island, South Kingstown, January 24, 1764, in Bartlett, *Records of Rhode Island*, 380; Pares, *Yankees and Creoles*, 154. At times

the shipments of molasses traveled on Surinamese ships, with merchants and planters sailing to Boston to ensure the sale and organize return cargoes, but this remained illegal until a new bylaw was adopted by the Sociëteit van Suriname in 1783 allowing such trade. North American ships, therefore, controlled this business, their captains negotiating purchases with local merchants or sending "agents" to buy molasses at the plantations. Fatah-Black, *White Lies*, 177–78; Pares, *Yankees and Creoles*, 106–7.

163. He carried out his plan nonetheless, shipping thirteen captives to the Dutch island. NAN, Sociëteit van Suriname 415, Governor's journal, April 23 and May 11, 1776.

164. Hardesty, *Unfreedom*, 21–22.

165. Grant, "Black Immigrants," 256n14. In the second half of the 1780s, a regular U.S. slave trade began to be conducted in Paramaribo that soon eclipsed the Dutch trade, initially in the form of an intra-Caribbean commerce but by the early 1790s with slaves arriving directly from Africa on board North American ships. Fatah-Black, "Suriname and the Atlantic World," 234.

166. John Adams to Robert R. Livingstone, The Hague, July 30, 1783, Founders Online, National Archives, http://founders.archives.gov/documents/Adams/06-15-02-0080, accessed on March 5, 2017.

167. Van der Oest, "Forgotten Colonies," 357.

168. Evans, "Plantation Hoe," 86.

169. Van de Kreeke, "Essequebo en Demerary," 27–28.

170. Hoonhout, "Noodzaak van smokkelhandel," 65; O'Malley, *Final Passages*, 370.

171. Van Winter, *Aandeel*, 15n5.

172. Netscher, *Geschiedenis*, 138.

173. *Hollandsche Historische Courant*, June 11, 1785; Hoonhout, "Noodzaak van smokkelhandel," 63, 66.

174. Oostindie, "British Capital," 42; Van de Kreeke, "Essequebo en Demerary," 43.

175. Cf. Hoonhout, "West Indian Web," 239–46.

176. Oostindie, "British Capital," 36; Van de Kreeke, "Essequebo en Demerary," 57.

177. McGowan, "French Revolutionary Period," 10–11.

178. Farley, "Economic Circumstances," 27.

179. Among the eighty-eight plantations in Berbice at the time of the slave revolt of 1763–64, for example, one out of four owners had a French name, while four estates had distinctly Swiss names: "De dertien cantons" (The thirteen cantons), "Zwitserlandt," "Helvetia," and "Altenklingen." *Kortbondige beschryvinge*, inlay after p. 4.

180. Farley, "Economic Circumstances," 25.

181. Oostindie, "British Capital," 37.

182. Barrow, *Trade and Empire*, 142; Proceedings of the General Assembly of Rhode Island, South Kingstown, January 24, 1764, in Bartlett, *Records of Rhode Island*, 381.

183. Enthoven, "That Abominable Nest of Pirates," 271–72; Klooster, "Inter-Imperial Smuggling," 171; Klooster, *Illicit Riches*, 95.

184. Jarvis, *In the Eye of All Trade*, 169; Enthoven, "That Abominable Nest of Pirates," 261.

185. Leebeek, "Caraïbische stapelmarkt," 33, 46; Knappert, *Geschiedenis*, 219.

186. Morgan and Rushton, *Banishment in the Early Atlantic World*, 215; O'Shaughnessy, *Men Who Lost America*, 297–98.

187. Spooner, *Risks at Sea*, 100–101; Klooster, *Illicit Riches*, 95–96; Enthoven, "That Abominable Nest of Pirates," 288–93.

188. Hartog, *Bovenwindse eilanden*, 191; Goslinga, *Dutch in Caribbean and Guianas*, 455.

189. Fatah-Black, *White Lies*, 191.

190. Villiers, *Commerce colonial atlantique*, 242; Goslinga, *Dutch in Caribbean and Guianas*, 456.

191. Baesjou, "Juffrouw Elisabeth," 53–58; Everts, "Krijgsvolk," 96–99.

2. Institutions, Finance, Trade

1. Schneeloch, *Aktionäre*, 62–67, 70–71, 74–78; Den Heijer, *Geschiedenis van de WIC*, 31, 102, 104–5, 107–8.

2. Schneeloch, *Aktionäre*, 347–49.

3. Goslinga, *Dutch in Caribbean and Guianas*, 5; Van der Bijl, *Idee en Interest*, 212; Schotanus, *Van der Spiegel*, 3:928.

4. Van der Bijl, *Idee en Interest*, 225; Goslinga, *Dutch in Caribbean and Guianas*, 26; Den Heijer, *Geoctrooieerde compagnie*, 94–95; De Vries and Van der Woude, *Nederland, 1500–1815*, 536–37.

5. Den Heijer, *Geschiedenis van de WIC*, 112–16.

6. Ibid., 111.

7. Den Heijer, *Goud, ivoor en slaven*, 299–314.

8. Emmer, "West India Company," 76.

9. Van der Meiden, *Betwist bestuur*, 31–35.

10. Like Berbice, the Dutch Leeward Islands had originated as patroonships, but these had ended in the latter days of the first company or during the new company's startup years.

11. Netscher, *Geschiedenis*, 152–53.

12. Ibid., 158–62.

13. Ibid., 119, 121–22. Two hundred personnel were maintained in Curaçao and an equal number in Africa (at least after 1729), while soldiers and corporals alone made up 232 men in Demerara and Essequibo in 1794. Goslinga, *Dutch in Caribbean and Guianas*, 107; Den Heijer, *Geschiedenis van de WIC*, 180; NAN, Raad van Koloniën 118, "Twee maande-lijkse lijste van de sterkte van de zeven compagnien van het corps troupen van Haar Hoog-mogende garnisoen houdende binnen Stabroek in Rio Demerary Essequebo en onderhoorige posten," September 1, 1794.

14. Schneeloch, "Bewindhebber," 15–19; Goslinga, *Dutch in Caribbean and Guianas*, 10–12; Van Winter, *Kamer Stad en Lande*, 93.

15. NAN, Verspreide West-Indische Stukken 932, "Op de kust van Guinea. Ontfangen voor de vrije inhandeling der particulieren a f20,- per slaaf" (1741–46) and "Guinea, slaven recognitie" (1771–1780). It can be deduced from the tax income from the slave trade that the total number of 15,666 slaves was sold to the Brazilians in the latter decade. We are indebted to Henk den Heijer for this reference. Schwartz and Postma erroneously assumed that the slave trade between the WIC and Brazilian ships diminished or stopped entirely after 1730. Schwartz and Postma, "Dutch Republic and Brazil," 196.

16. Den Heijer, *Goud, ivoor en slaven*, 369–70.

17. NAN, Raad van Koloniën 96, fols. 909–10, advice from O. A. Duin at Fort Sebas-tiaan in Chama for Jacobus de Veer, May 8, 1793.

18. Schotanus, *Van der Spiegel*, 3:942.

19. *Memorie welke de Planters en Ingezeetenen*, 34.

20. Netscher, *Geschiedenis*, 149–50.

21. Van de Kreeke, "Essequebo en Demerary," 29.

22. Ibid., 30, 43.

23. Den Heijer, *Goud, ivoor en slaven*, 308.

24. Goslinga, *Dutch in Caribbean and Guianas*, 31–32.

25. Whereas the first issue in that year of the South Sea Bubble yielded 3,765,000 guil-ders, the second offering was much less successful, earning only 7,500 guilders.

26. Den Heijer, *Geschiedenis van de WIC*, 175, 179–80.

27. Van der Meiden, *Betwist bestuur*, 125.

28. Ibid., 78, 84, 100.

29. NAN, Staten-Generaal 5782, WIC directors J. van Loon and P. Backer to the States General, Amsterdam, January 9, 1748. Den Heijer, "Public and Private West India Interest," 165.

30. Den Heijer, "Public and Private West India Interest," 165–66; Fatah-Black, *White Lies and Black Markets*, 192–93.

31. Leebeek, "Caraïbische stapelmarkt," 14. See also chapter 1 of this book.

32. Roitman and Jordaan, "Fighting a Foregone Conclusion," 85–95.

33. Van de Voort, "Westindische plantages," 91–117, 153–96; Van Stipriaan, "Debunking Debts," 74–83; De Vries and Van der Woude, *Nederland, 1500–1815*, 178–79; Den Heijer, *Geschiedenis van de WIC*, 186–87.

34. Emmer, "Het zwarte gat," 114–15; Schotanus, *Van der Spiegel*, 3:920, 932.

35. Hall, *Slave Society*, 20; Van de Voort, "Westindische plantages," 106–7.

36. Van de Voort, "Westindische plantages," 157–58; Hall, *Slave Society*, 20.

37. Schotanus, *Van der Spiegel*, 3:931, table 17. The losses in the thriving colonies of Demerara and Essequibo can be explained by the close connections to British and North American traders (see chapter 1 of this book).

38. Schotanus, *Van der Spiegel*, 3:945; Goslinga, *Dutch in Caribbean and Guianas*, 585–86.

39. Schutte, *Nederlandse Patriotten en de koloniën*, 90–95, 110.

40. Van Winter, *Kamer Stad en Lande*, 103.

41. Goslinga, *Dutch in Caribbean and Guianas*, 605–8.

42. Goslinga, *Dutch in Caribbean and Surinam*, 163.

43. Enthoven, "Assessment," 433.

44. De Vries, "Netherlands in the New World," 132–33; De Jong, *Krimpende horizon*.

45. Enthoven, "Assessment," 423.

46. Veluwenkamp, "Ondernemersgedrag," 78.

47. Rogge, *Handelshuis Van Eeghen*, 48.

48. NAN, Sociëteit van Suriname 564, fol. 37, report of the directors of the Sociëteit van Suriname, submitted October 6, 1707; Postma, *Dutch in the Atlantic Slave Trade*, 171.

49. Fatah-Black, *White Lies and Black Markets*, 80–81.

50. Postma, "Suriname and its Atlantic Connections," 317 (table 11.7).

51. De Hullu, "Memorie," 394–95. The effect of the slave revolt is visible in the diminished imports from the colony in the 1760s.

52. Van der Oest, "Forgotten Colonies," 351 (table 12.7).

53. Fatah-Black, *White Lies and Black Markets*, 99.

54. De Vries and Van der Woude, *Nederland, 1500–1815*, 549.

55. Klooster, "Curaçao and the Caribbean Transit Trade," 215–17; Klooster, *Illicit Riches*, 191.

56. Klooster, "Curaçao and the Caribbean Transit Trade," 207.

57. See NAN, NWIC 621–24 for the trade between the republic and St. Eustatius.

58. Klooster, *Illicit Riches*, 84–86.

59. The merchant house of Thomas and Adrian Hope, which was originally based in Rotterdam but later moved to Amsterdam, obtained dyewood from these camps in Belize in exchange for their supplies of sugar, brandy, salted beef from Ireland, and cloth. Araúz Monfante, *Contrabando holandés*, 1:84–87.

60. Klooster, *Illicit Riches*, 177–78.

61. Ibid., 93.
62. Pares, *War and Trade*, 380–81.
63. Koot, *Empire at the Periphery*, 121.
64. Schnurmann, *Atlantische Welten*, 350–53; Koot, *Empire at the Periphery*, 153, 203.
65. Governor the Earl of Bellomont to Council of Trade and Plantations, New York, November 7, 1698, in Fortescue, *Calendar of State Papers, 1697–1698*, 531; Harrington, *New York Merchant*, 255, 268; Matson, *Merchants and Empire*, 207.
66. Truxes, *Letterbook of Greg & Cunningham*, 91.
67. Matson, *Merchants and Empire*, 146–49, 208–11.
68. Merritt, "Tea Trade," 126–27.
69. Harrington, *New York Merchant*, 344–46.
70. Tyler, *Smugglers and Patriots*, 187, 192, 198–99, 209; Enthoven, "Going Dutch," 43–44.
71. Klooster, "Overview of Dutch Trade," 365–84, 378–79.
72. Ormrod, *Rise of Commercial Empires*, 200–201.
73. Wokeck, *Trade in Strangers*, 73–74, 80–86; Enthoven, "Going Dutch," 36–37.
74. Johnson, "Fair Traders and Smugglers," 139.
75. Schnurmann, *Atlantische Welten*, 355–64.
76. Baxter, *House of Hancock*, 83–86, 93–95, 114–18. In 1759–60, the Hope firm bought large quantities of tea from the Dutch East India Company. Enthoven, "Going Dutch," 43.
77. Barrow, *Trade and Empire*, 150.
78. Wood, *William Shirley*, 143.
79. Enthoven, "Going Dutch," 44.
80. Chu, "Debt and Taxes," 135–36; Van Winter, *Aandeel*, 1:90, 112–13, 117.
81. Welling, "Prize of Neutrality," 194, 221; Van Winter, *Aandeel*, 2: 67. In the years 1804–7, U.S. exports to the Netherlands of foreign produce amounted to 83.9 percent of the value of all exports. Calculated on the basis of Pitkin, *Statistical View*, 203.
82. Den Heijer, *Goud, ivoor en slaven*, 96 (table 5.1).
83. Reinders Folmer-Van Prooijen, *Van goederenhandel naar slavenhandel*, 149. In contrast to the MCC, the WIC lost more than 10 percent of the ships it fitted out in 1674–1740, including one-third of the vessels that were its own property. Den Heijer, *Goud, ivoor en slaven*. 108.
84. Harteveld, "Op Africa Gevaaren," 38.
85. Den Heijer, *Goud, ivoor en slaven*, 127–35; Reinders Folmer-Van Prooijen, *Van goederenhandel naar slavenhandel*, 145.
86. Annual averages in guilders: 1701–10: 312,923; 1711–20: 306,357; 1721–30: 314,686. Derived from Den Heijer, *Goud, ivoor en slaven*, 129 (table 5.8) and 136 (table 5.9).
87. Cf. Feinberg, "Africans and Europeans," 54, 59.
88. Den Heijer, *Goud, ivoor en slaven*, 114, 116–17, 119, 121–23, 163; Den Heijer, "West African Trade," 151–56; Paesie, *Lorrendrayen op Africa*, 209 (table 4.2); Reinders Folmer-Van Prooijen, *Van goederenhandel naar slavenhandel*, 145.
89. Postma, *Dutch in the Atlantic Slave Trade*, 113–14; Paesie, *Lorrendrayen op Africa*, 245–46.
90. Vos, "Slave Trade," 33–34.
91. http://slavevoyages.org/assessment/estimates, Voyages: The Transatlantic Slave Trade Database, accessed on September 14, 2017. Postma, "Reassessment," 122–23; Paesie, "Zeeuwen," 2–3, 9.

92. Figures calculated by Gerhard de Kok, based on the Trans-Atlantic Slave Trade Database and Paesie, "Zeeuwen," 2–3, 9.

93. Postma, "Reassessment," 123, 129; Postma, *Dutch in the Atlantic Slave Trade,* 209. Postma assumed that interlopers were responsible for some 10,000 slaves embarked in the years 1700–1730, a number revised upwards to 40,000–43,000 by Paesie, *Lorrendrayen op Africa,* 257–58.

94. Hernæs, *Slaves,* 239–40; Green-Pedersen, "Scope," 149–97; Jordaan and Wilson, "Eighteenth-Century Free Ports,"

95. The overall number of Africans disembarked by Britain in the New World was 3,259,441 (Voyages "The Trans-Atlantic Slave Trade Database, http://slavevoyages.org/assessment/estimates, accessed on September 14, 2017), whereas the number of Africans carried from British to non-British colonies was 257,590 or 7.9 percent. See O'Malley, *Final Passages,* 151 (table 7), 222 (table 13), 308 (table 14), 309 (table 15), and 312 (table 16). We have avoided counting those Africans twice who are listed in both of O'Malley's tables 7 and 13 (i.e., those exported from Jamaica and Barbados in 1711–15). The number of slaves sent directly from Africa to non-British colonies must have been small.

96. Calculated on the basis of Postma, "Reassessment," 134, table 5.5. We have not included unknown destinations in our calculation.

97. Paesie, *Lorrendrayen op Africa,* 248–50.

98. Calculated on the basis of Postma, "Reassessment," 134, table 5.6. We have not included unknown destinations in our calculation.

99. Reinders Folmer-Van Prooijen, *Van goederenhandel naar slavenhandel,* 148–51.

100. Calculated at 1.4 percent, although this rises to 5.4 percent when 7 of the 59 ships that failed to complete the voyage are not taken into account. Reinders Folmer-Van Prooijen, *Van goederenhandel naar slavenhandel,* 148.

101. The exact numbers were 50,688,435 and 64,239,435 guilders. Calculated on the basis of Van Rossum and Fatah-Black, "Wat is winst?," 18 (table 4).

102. Eltis, Emmer, and Lewis, "More than Profits?"; Den Heijer, *Goud, ivoor en slaven,* 165; Fatah-Black and Van Rossum, "A Profitable Debate?"

103. Visser, "Verkeersindustrieën," 30; De Vries and Van der Woude, *Nederland, 1500–1815,* 388.

104. Clark, *La Rochelle,* 162.

105. Reesse, *Suikerhandel van Amsterdam,* 47–56; Visser, "Verkeersindustrieën," 31.

106. Koot, *Empire at the Periphery,* 131.

107. Posthumus, *Nederlandsche prijsgeschiedenis,* 1:122–25, 129.

108. Huetz de Lemps, *Géographie,* 476–77; Butel, *Négociants bordelais,* 64; Cavignac, *Jean Pellet,* 212. Only in 1774–76 were Dutch imports larger than those of the "North."

109. Other sugar came by way of Scandinavia.

110. Van Dillen, "Memorie Suriname," 187–89, 199–202, 206–7.

111. Van Dillen, "Memorie Suriname," 355–57, 415–18, 420–23, 443–46.

112. Chesapeake tobacco had been important for the Dutch industry since the mid-seventeenth century, when imports generally arrived directly on Dutch ships. By 1700, when Dutch ports received almost 40 percent of England's colonial tobacco, Amsterdam and Rotterdam merchants rarely dealt directly with the Chesapeake, usually importing tobacco from London or from Scottish ports. The Dutch share of England's reexports declined after 1730, when France became the main customer.

113. Klooster, *Illicit Riches,* 188–91; De Vries and Van der Woude, *Nederland, 1500–1815,* 383–84. Ormrod, *Rise of Commercial Empires,* 199–201. The Amsterdam tobacco industry came to an end in the early nineteenth century, when French competition gave it the

deathblow. The number of workers declined from 1800 in 1806 to 50 in 1811 and 2 in 1816. H.B., "Amsterdamsche nijverheid," 20.

114. Murray, "Rotterdamsche toeback-coopers," 59–61; 67. Klooster, *Illicit Riches*, 189.

115. Klooster, *Illicit Riches*, 183.

116. Van Wijk, "Chocolademolens," 4–7; Van den Hoek Ostende, "Chocolaadmolens," 65.

117. Paesie, *Geschiedenis van de MCC*, 145, 148.

118. De Kok, "Cursed Capital," 10–11, 19.

119. Van Dillen, "Memorie Suriname," 164–65.

120. Sánchez Belén, "Comercio holandés," 192–95.

121. Crespo Solana, *Comercio marítimo*, 80.

122. Ibid., 81–88.

123. Klooster, *Illicit Riches*, 178–79.

124. The breakdown for selected years, based on table 16 in this chapter, is as follows: 1750: 67.7%, 1775: 64.1%, 1780: 62.0%, 17886: 75.2%, and 1790: 82.8%.

125. De Vries and Van der Woude, *Nederland, 1500–1815*, 533 (table 10.8).

126. Butel, "France, the Antilles, and Europe," 170.

127. The 157 million livres tournois at which Butel values France's American imports in 1772 equate to 72 million guilders (1 livre tournois = 0.46 guilders). British imports were valued at £5.246 million, which would have translated to a sales value (x 1.5) of £7.869 million or 94.428 million guilders. For the British figures, see Price, "Imperial Economy," 101.

3. West Africa

1. Feinberg, "Africans and Europeans," 35. Feinberg, "Africans and Europeans," and Den Heijer's *Goud, ivoor en slaven* are the best scholarly introductions to the early modern history of Dutch West Africa. See also Van der Ham, *Dof goud*, and Van Engelen, *Kasteel van Elmina*.

2. NAN, NWIC 119, surgeon major J. G. Schneider to the Heren X, Elmina, November 11, 1774. Postma, *Dutch in the Atlantic Slave Trade*, 66.

3. Indigo and cotton were cultivated on Curaçao in the last two decades of the seventeenth century. The production of indigo was abandoned around the turn of the century, but small-scale cotton production continued. Klooster, *Illicit Riches*, 62–63.

4. NAN, NWIC 919, Henrico van Wezel, Abrah. Pantser, C. G. Beindorp, Hendrik de Schepper, and Willem Butler to the Heren X [undated, received November 21, 1709]; director general Adriaan Schoonheit to the Heren X, February 28, 1710.

5. Daaku, *Trade and Politics*, 44–45. New attempts at cash crop production were made in the early nineteenth century. Yarak, *Asante and the Dutch*, 104–5.

6. Van Dantzig, *Hollandais sur la côte de Guinée*, 99–102, 141–43. Based on Willem Bosman's *Nauwkeurige beschryving*, Daaku and Den Heijer have argued that the WIC's attempts to mine gold contributed to the outbreak of war with Komenda in 1694. Daaku, *Trade and Politics*, 26–27, 83; Den Heijer, *Goud, ivoor en slaven*, 131. Although Komenda did attack Dutch gold miners and capture some of them, setting off Dutch retaliation, these events did not mark the start of the war. The hostilities had broken out prior to the attack on the gold miners. Law, "Komenda Wars," 142–43.

7. NAN, NWIC 55B, Heren X to director general Jan Pranger and council in Guinea, Amsterdam, May 30, 1731. NAN, NWIC 109, fols. 291–93, director general Jan Pranger, G. Ockers, B. Overbeke, and J. Elet to the Heren X, Elmina, April 3, 1732.

8. Bosman, *Nauwkeurige beschryving*, 90.

9. Den Heijer, *Goud, ivoor en slaven*, 127 (table 5.7), 134; Bosman, *Nauwkeurige beschryving*, 88.

10. Daaku, *Trade and Politics*, 68, 70.

11. Ibid., 38–39; Feinberg, "Africans and Europeans," 51; Den Heijer, *Goud, ivoor en slaven*, 216, 218.

12. Shumway, *Fante and the Transatlantic Slave Trade*, 45–46; Law, "Komenda Wars."

13. Newton, "Slavery, Sea Power and the State," 180–83.

14. Feinberg, "Africans and Europeans," 145–50.

15. Baesjou, "Trade Conflicts," 30–33; Van den Assum, "WIC-Appolonia War," 7–8, 16–17.

16. Baesjou, "Trade Conflicts," 34–37; Van den Assum, "WIC-Appolonia War," 20–34.

17. Postma, *Dutch in the Atlantic Slave Trade*, 99–101, 114–16, 122–25; Den Heijer, "West African Trade," 149. See also Den Heijer, *Naar de koning van Dahomey*.

18. Feinberg, "Africans and Europeans," 34–36, 65–66, 84; Den Heijer, *Goud, ivoor en slaven*, 82.

19. In both 1709 and 1736, a total of 142 military men were listed. The number dropped to 117 by 1749. NAN, NWIC 919, General muster roll, Elmina, May 16, 1709; NAN, NWIC 923, Martinus François de Bordes to the WIC, Elmina, August 20, 1736; NAN, NWIC 113, fols. 573–74, Jan van Voorst to the Heren X, Elmina, July 15, 1749.

20. Bosman, *Nauwkeurige beschryving*, 91.

21. NAN, NWIC 119, fiscal W. Suljard van Leefdael to the Heren X, Elmina November 7, 1773; J. C. Fennekol to the Heren X, Axim, February 28, 1777; NAN, NWIC 936, P. Volkmar, Thomas van den Berg, J. v.d. Penije, G.J. Gallé, and H. Heijcoop to the Heren X, Elmina, February 8, 1781.

22. Feinberg, "Africans and Europeans," 36–38; Kruijtzer, "European Migration," 101; Curtin, "White Man's Grave," 95; Davies, "Living and Dead," 89–94.

23. NAN, NWIC 97, director general Joan van Sevenhuijsen to the Heren X, May 8, 1699; NAN, NWIC 106, director general Pieter Valckenier to the Heren X, Elmina, June 15, 1725. In 1755, many clerks died, along with the director and his family. NAN, NWIC 926, director general N. M. van der Noot de Gietere to the WIC, Elmina, April 30, 1755. The director general would himself pass away on October 24 of the same year.

24. Van Dantzig, *Hollandais sur la Côte de Guinée*, 111; NAN, NWIC 97, agreement between Joan van Sevenhuijsen on behalf of the WIC and Edward Necote, Gerard Gone, and Howsy Freeman on behalf of the Royal African Company at Cape Coast, Elmina, February 21, 1701.

25. NAN, NWIC 97, director general Joan van Sevenhuijsen to the Heren X, July 31, 1700; NAN, NWIC 919, H. Haring and council to the Heren X, Elmina, undated [received September 21, 1713]; NAN, NWIC 923, director general Jan Pranger to the WIC, Elmina, December 14, 1732. Up to three times per year, the wife or relatives of company personnel could claim their monthly wages. Van den Heuvel, *Bij uijtlandigheijt van haar man*, 20–22, 32–40. One low-ranking official in Elmina dutifully transferred fifty guilders each year to his wife back home. NAN, NWIC 113, fol. 377r, Jacob de Petersen to the WIC, Chamber of Zeeland, Elmina, July 1, 1745.

26. *Vaderlandsche historie*, 142–43; Van Winter, *Kamer Stad en Lande*, 232.

27. Van Gelder, *Zeepost*, 161.

28. NAN, NWIC 929, minister Gerardus Verbeet to the WIC Chamber of Amsterdam, Elmina, October 20, 1764.

29. NAN, NWIC 923, director general Jan Pranger and council to the WIC, Elmina, May 3, 1733. Marriages were so rarely contracted in Elmina that one minister who was eager to get married with an arriving widow whose original destination had been Suriname had to comb the archives to prove to the director that there were precedents. See NAN, NWIC 919, H. Haring and council to the Heren X, Elmina, undated [read July 11, 1715].

30. De Kok, "Forten," 13, 17.
31. Doortmont, Everts, and Vrij, "Tussen de Goudkust," 313–19.
32. Ibid., 183–85.
33. Universiteitsbibliotheek Leiden, Stukken met betrekking tot de Verenigde Oostindische Compagnie (VOC) en de Westindische Compagnie (WIC), request to the States General, received January 28, 1744.
34. NAN, Verspreide West-Indische Stukken 41, examination of Gideon Bonrepas, Jacob vcan Hellen, and Jan Conel by the provincial court of Holland, Zeeland, and West-Friesland, Vlissingen, October 2, 1743; examination of David Jol, Maarten Stam and Jan Decker, Vlissingen, October 25, 1743, examination of Jan Ridder, Vlissingen, November 9, 1743, in "Requeste van verscheide Hollandsche en Zeeuwsche Geinteresseerden in de vaart op de Kust van Africa," undated, pp. 10–4; examination of Anthonij Beevers and Jacobus de Nijssen, Vlissingen, November 6, 1743; examination of Adriaan Schoor, Vlissingen, February 27, 1744, in appendix to directors of the Middelburgse Commercie Compagnie to the States of Zeeland, September 29, 1744, p. 22.
35. NAN, NWIC 97, director general Joan van Sevenhuijsen to the Heren X, April 15, 1700; Feinberg, "Africans and Europeans," 87.
36. NAN, NWIC 936, fol. 803, director general Pieter Volkmar to the WIC Chamber of Amsterdam, Elmina, January 9, 1783; De Marrée, *Reizen op en beschrijving*, 2:9.
37. NAN, NWIC 929, J. P. Huijdecoper to te WIC, Axim, September 14, 1763, p. 55; Krabbendam, "Reading in Elmina."
38. NAN, NWIC 97, minister Eduard Jorck van Slangenburgh to the Heren X, May 6, 1699; NAN, NWIC 55A, Heren X to director general Pieter Nuijts and council, The Hague, July 23, 1706; NAN, NWIC 923, A. van Overbeke, Jan de Winter, F.W. Gawron, J. Elet, Dl. Guichert, M. de Bordes, and F. Barovius to the WIC, Elmina, May 21, 1734; Bosman, *Nauwkeurige beschrijving*, 96; Schwartz and Postma, "Dutch Republic and Brazil," 187.
39. Daaku, *Trade and Politics*, 84, 87, 105; Feinberg, "Africans and Europeans," 121–26; Doortmont, Everts, and Vrij, "Tussen de Goudkust"; Van der Ham, *Dof goud*, 125, 131.
40. Balai, *Slavenschip*, 109–13.
41. NAN, NWIC 926, director general Jan van Voorst and council to the WIC, Elmina, May 12, 1751.
42. Balai, *Slavenschip*, 114.
43. Feinberg, "Africans and Europeans," 65–67.
44. Law, *Ouidah*, 4–6; Feinberg, "Africans and Europeans," passim.
45. Newman, *New World of Labor*, 114–24, 132.
46. The word *tapoeyer* probably derives from the Brazilian Tapuya, who had helped the Dutch capture Elmina in 1637.
47. Feinberg, "Africans and Europeans," 86–92.
48. Postma, *Dutch in the Atlantic Slave Trade*, 165–68. Extrapolating from the records of MCC slave voyages, Postma suggests that the total may have been as high as 300, but this latter estimate is far too high, taking into account the most recent figures from the Transatlantic Slave Trade Database. Balai, *Slavenschip*, 81.
49. Balai, *Slavenschip*, 196–200.
50. Postma, *Dutch in the Atlantic Slave Trade*, 72–73.
51. NAN, NWIC 926, director general Jan van Voorst and council to the WIC, Elmina, May 12, 1751; NAN, NWIC 929, Hendrik Walmbeeke to the Heren X, Elmina, July 15, 1764; NAN, NWIC 119, fiscal W. Suljard van Leefdael to the Heren X, Elmina, November 7, 1773.
52. Feinberg, "Africans and Europeans," 10–16, 25–30, 41, 126–32; Den Heijer, *Goud, ivoor en slaven*, 166, 220–24, 240–50.

53. Everts, "Krijgsvolk," 79.

54. Ibid., 96–98; Everts, "Social Outcomes," 160.

55. Bosman, *Nauwkeurige beschryving*, 176.

56. Postma, *Dutch in the Atlantic Slave Trade*, 87; Everts, "Social Outcomes," 158.

57. Feinberg, "Africans and Europeans," vi–viii, xiii, 65, 71, 80–84, 136, 155–58.

58. Ibid., 99–111, 117–20, 136–51, 157; Everts, "Social Outcomes," 159–60. Although the Dutch initially identified Elmina's leadership with various strongmen, by the second quarter of the eighteenth century their correspondence began to refer consistently to a king. His position seems to have gained in strength in the eighteenth century. Feinberg, "Africans and Europeans," 100–103.

59. Bosman, *Nauwkeurige beschryving*, 67; NAN, NWIC 919, director general Adriaan Schoonheit to the Heren X, February 28, 1710.

60. De Marrée, *Reizen op en beschrijving*, 1:182, 2:126; Feinberg, "Africans and Europeans," 144; Postma, *Dutch in the Atlantic Slave Trade*, 70. Dutchmen found guilty of sleeping with married African women were bound to pay tobacco and brandy, the amounts depending on their rank. Throughout the eighteenth century, the Dutch also regularly donated gifts to the Ashante, Fante, and other trading partners. See Boone, "Nederlandse relaties met Ashanti," 57.

61. Yarak, *Asante and the Dutch*, 174–76.

62. De Marrée, *Reizen op en beschrijving*, 2:16–25.

63. NAN, NWIC 113, minister Jacobus Elisa Joannes Capitein to the Heren X, Elmina, February 14, 1743, appendix; NAN, NWIC 926, minister Michael Beckering to the WIC, Elmina, January 2, 1756.

64. Postma, *Dutch in the Atlantic Slave Trade*, 69; NAN, NWIC 113, memorandum of fiscal Huijbert van Rijk for the Heren X, Elmina, November 15, 1743.

65. NAN, NWIC 113, fol. 320r, Jacob de Petersen to the Heren X, Elmina, July 1, 1745.

66. Capitein, *Dissertatio*; Eekhof, *Negerpredikant*; Kpobi, *Mission*. For similar English attempts to "civilize" West African boys and return them as missionaries to their native soil, see Glasson, *Mastering Christianity*, 174–75.

67. Brentjes, *Anton Wilhelm Amo*; Firla, "Anton Wilhelm Amo," 56–78; Abraham, "Life and Times," 60–81.

68. See, e.g., Kolfin et al., *Black is Beautiful*, 241–71, and, much earlier, Blakely, *Blacks in the Dutch World*, 104–15.

69. Feinberg, "Africans and Europeans," 92; Postma, *Dutch in the Atlantic Slave Trade*, 70; "Hoe heette Christian?," http://www.vandervegt.be/samenvatting/, and "De Oranjes an Zwart verbeeld: Stdthouder Willem V met 'zijn' Cupido en Sideron," by Esther Schreuder, https://estherschreuder.wordpress.com/2011/09/19/de-oranjes-en-zwart-verbeeld-stadhouder-willem-v-en-cupido-en-cedron/, both accessed on October 31, 2014.

70. Doortmont, Everts, and Vrij, "Tussen de Goudkust," 195–205.

71. Ibid., 492–95, 518–25.

72. Van der Ham, *Dof goud*, 128.

73. Everts, "Krijgsvolk," 87; Everts, "Cherchez la femme," 50–52.

74. Lever, "Mulatto Influence," 253; Feinberg, "Africans and Europeans," 90.

75. Blanchard, "Language of Liberation," 507.

76. Everts, "Krijgsvolk," 87–90.

77. NAN, NWIC 936, fol. 123–24, P. Woortman and council to the Heren X, Elmina, December 11, 1779; P. Volkmar, Thomas van den Berg, J. v.d. Penije, G. J. Gallé, and H. Heijcoop to the Heren X, Elmina, February 8, 1781.

78. NAN, Raad der Amerikaanse Bezittingen 113H, "Eenige vraagen, betrekkelyk de kuste van Guinea, ter beantwoordinge voorgesteld aan de heeren Jongbloed magazijn meester en Koch tweede resident aldaar."

79. Feinberg, "Africans and Europeans," 92.

80. Everts, "Social Outcomes," 159; Everts, "Krijgsvolk," 86. For a similar arrangement in Danish West Africa, see Ipsen, *Daughters of the Trade*, 64–65.

81. Everts, "Cherchez la femme," 54; NAN, NWIC 929, minister Gerardus Verbeet to the WIC Chamber of Amsterdam, Elmina, October 20, 1764.

4. The Guianas

1. In fiction, Raleigh's exploits were immortalized in V. S. Naipaul's *The Loss of Eldorado*.

2. Keye, *Waere onderscheyt*, 3; Herlein, *Beschryvinge*, preface (no page).

3. McCusker and Menard, "Sugar Industry," 295–97. The Dutch contribution to the emergence of plantation agriculture in the French Caribbean was much more significant than in the English West Indies. Klooster, *Dutch Moment*, 167–70, 172–74.

4. Ellis, *Coffee House*, 144–45; *Le commerce de l'Amérique par Marseille* (1764) referred to in *Encyclopaedie*, 412.

5. The following paragraphs are based on Oostindie, "Modernity," 115–18.

6. Van Stipriaan, "Suriname Rat Race," 97.

7. Raynal, *Histoire*, 4:336 (my translation); Oostindie, *Roosenburg*, 128; Van Stipriaan, *Surinaams contrast*, 139; Oostindie and Van Stipriaan, "Hydraulic Society," 79–86; Oostindie, "British Capital," 35–55.

8. Davids, "Sources"; Van Stipriaan, "Suriname Rat Race."

9. Van Stipriaan, *Surinaams contrast*, 128–34.

10. Ibid., 35, 128, 135; Van de Oest, "Forgotten Colonies," 350.

11. Oostindie, *Roosenburg*, 155–56; Van Stipriaan, *Surinaams contrast*, 350–57.

12. Placard for the management of plantations, 1757, in Schiltkamp and De Smidt, *West-Indisch Plakaatboek* 1973, 1:673–74.

13. Oostindie, *Roosenburg*, 131–39, 251–59, and particularly Van Stipriaan, *Surinaams contrast*, 318.

14. Van Stipriaan, *Surinaams contrast*, 316–19; Oostindie, *Roosenburg*, 131–33.

15. Lommerse, "Population Figures," 325–56; Oostindie, "British Capital," 35.

16. Hoefte and Vrij, "Free Black and Colored Women," 145–68, 147.

17. Enthoven, "Dutch Crossings," 160; Van Stipriaan, *Surinaams contrast*, 311, 314. In 1795, the total free population of Suriname was put at 4,953. A minority of unknown size among this legal category was of mixed origins.

18. Quoted in Van Lier, *Frontier Society*, 38–39.

19. Fatah-Black, "Suriname," 53–58; Fatah-Black, "Paramaribo," 58–59; Zijlstra, "Anglo-Dutch Suriname"; Games, "Cohabitation, Surinam-Style."

20. Klooster, *Dutch Moment*, 225.

21. Cohen, *Jews*; Davis, "Regaining Jerusalem." The all-time peak of the Jewish population was 1,411, in 1787. The number of plantations owned by Jews was 40 in 1694 and 115 in 1760, but sharply fell to some 40 again in 1788. Vink, *Creole Jews*, 56; Kruijtzer, "European Migration," 119; Van Lier, *Frontier Society*, 85–86, 90–92.

22. Klooster, "Curaçao as a Transit Center," 44–45.

23. Van Stipriaan, *Surinaams contrast*, 293–94.

24. Schalkwijk, *Colonial State*, 158–59, 268–69, 302.

25. Oostindie, *Roosenburg*, 423; Schalkwijk, *Colonial State*, 158–59, 268–69; Van Stipriaan, *Surinaams contrast*, 293–94.

26. Nettelbeck, *Lebensgeschichte*, 25.

27. Oostindie, *Roosenburg*, 341–48; Van Stipriaan, *Surinaams contrast*, 205–31.

28. Cohen, *Jews*, 126; Kruijtzer, "European Migration," 118; Fatah-Black, "Paramaribo," 60–63.

29. Fatah-Black, "Paramaribo," 70–71.

30. Fatah-Black, "Suriname," 152; Oostindie and Maduro, *In het land*, 7.

31. Oostindie and Maduro, *In het land*, 13–17, 153–64.

32. Fatah-Black, "Suriname," 152.

33. Rodway, *History*, 165, 248. Zvi Loker, *Jews in the Caribbean*, 140–63; Koulen, "Slavenhouders," 50–51.

34. De Villiers, *Storm*, 137–38 (4-8-1752), 138 (31-8-1752), 172 (31-5-1755).

35. Oostindie, "British Capital," 53.

36. See "Estimates," Trans-Atlantic Slave Trade Database, http://www.slavevoyages.org/assessment/estimates, accessed on March 5, 2017.

37. Cf. Drescher, "Long Goodbye," and the various reactions to Drescher's essay in Oostindie, *Fifty Years Later*. See also chapter 9, this book.

38. Oostindie, "Same Old Song," 151–52.

39. For Suriname, see, e.g., Kals, *Neerlands hoofd- en wortelzonde*; for Curaçao, Jordaan, "Free Blacks."

40. McNeill, *Mosquito Empires*, 3–5, 60–62.

41. Oostindie, *Roosenburg*, 131–39, 251–59; Van Stipriaan, *Surinaams contrast*, 310–46, in particular 318. Cf. Ortiz, *Contrapunteo cubano*; Berlin, *Many Thousands Gone*; Morgan, *Slave Counterpoint*.

42. Oostindie, *Roosenburg*, 169–76. As the number of Amerindians was low and they mostly kept a distance from colonial society, the number of mixed relations and offspring with part Amerindian roots remained low throughout.

43. Price and Price, "Introduction"; Oostindie, "Voltaire"; and "British Capital," 52.

44. Buve, "Gouverneur"; Roitman, "Portuguese Jews."

45. De Villiers, *Storm*, 390 (August 29, 1772). Amerindian support in 1763 was "much to the advantage of the colony," according to the revolt's first historian, J. J. Hartsinck, in 1770 (Hartsinck, *Beschryving*, 1:488). See also Bolingbroke, *Voyage*, 191, 195; Swaving, *Swaving's reizen*, 199; Whitehead, *Lords of the Tiger Spirit*, 151–71; Thompson, *Colonialism and Underdevelopment*, 191–213.

46. Hoonhout, "West Indian Web," 46–47.

47. Hartsinck, *Geschiedenis*, 1:374, 381, 404.

48. Kars, "Slavenopstand"; Kars, "Policing"; Hartsinck, *Geschiedenis*, 1:488; *Coffy-Van Hoogenheim Correspondence*, 18.

49. All general histories of Suriname devote ample space to marronage and the Maroon wars. Specific studies include Dragtenstein, *Ondraaglijke stoutheid*; Hoogbergen, *Bosnegers*; and *Boni Maroon Wars*; Price, *First-Time*; Thoden van Velzen and Hoogbergen, *Zwarte vrijstaat*.

50. Stedman's *Narrative* was first published in 1796, followed within a few years by various translations, including a Dutch one (1799–1800). The original text was only discovered and published two centuries later. Price and Price, "Introduction."

51. Hoonhout, "West Indian Web," 116–23.

52. Oostindie and Van Stipriaan, "Hydraulic Society," 92–95; Van der Pijl, *Levende-doden*; Wooding, *Evolving Culture*.

53. Benjamins, "Treef," 685–87; Vink, *Creole Jews*, 65.

54. Ben-Ur, "Purim in the Public Eye," 57–58.

55. Arends, "History," 122–25.

56. Smith, "History," 139–41.

57. Price, *First-Time*; and *Alabi's World*; Price and Price, *Afro-American Arts*; and *Maroon Arts*; Thoden van Velzen and Van Wetering, *Great Father*.

58. See, e.g., Schiltkamp and De Smidt, *West-Indisch Plakaatboek*, 1:672–3. See Van Lier, *Frontier Society*, 145–46, 150.

59. Price and Price, *Stedman's Surinam*, 186.

60. Van Stipriaan, *Surinaams contrast*, 285–95; Oostindie, *Roosenburg*, 92–93.

61. Hoogbergen, "Binnenlandse oorlogen," 160–61.

62. NAN NWIC 537, fols. 745–6 and NWIC 534, fols. 1368–70.

63. Van Stipriaan, *Surinaams contrast*, 283–85; Oostindie, *Roosenburg*, 93–94.

64. Kuniss, *Surinam und seine Bewohner*, 105–13.

65. Fermin, *Nieuwe algemeene beschryving*, 94.

66. Buddingh', *Van Punt en Snoa*, 153.

67. Hoefte and Vrij, "Free Black and Colored Women," 152; Von Sack, *Narrative*, 114.

68. Fatah-Black, "Slaves."

69. Bosman, *Nieuw Amsterdam*, 28.

70. Kuniss, *Surinam und seine Bewohner*, 185–88.

71. *Voyageur François*, 356.

72. Knappert, "Labadists in Suriname," 259–61.

73. For instance, in Suriname between 1760 and 1800 there were outbreaks of smallpox in 1763–65, 1780, 1785, 1789, 1792, and 1800; yellow fever in 1760–66, 1793, 1795–96, and 1800; typhoid in 1779, and tetany in 1786. Cohen, *Jews*, 38.

74. Cohen, *Jews*, 62–65.

75. NAN, Archieven Raad van Politie 2/3 bls., fols. 133–134, ordinance of Governor J. van Scharphuijsen and the Council of Policy, Paramaribo, July 10, 1694.

76. Van Sijpesteijn, *Mauricius*, 68n1. Cf. Stedman, *Narrative*; Van Stipriaan, *Surinaams contrast*, 289. Van Stipriaan has calculated that the average alcohol intake per free person in 1827 came to 141 liters (289n30).

77. Bosman, *Nieuw Amsterdam*, 20; Candlin, *Last Caribbean Frontier*, 38.

78. Oostindie, *Roosenburg*, 83; Van Stipriaan, *Surinaams contrast*, 289–91.

79. Kuniss, *Surinam und seine Bewohner*, 115. Manuscript diary of Michaël Alexius Schabel, Curaçao, 1707–8, translated by Jaime Koos Visker and Antoon Stikvoort, entry of November 19, 1707. See for the original Latin version Schunck, "Schabel."

80. Bolingbroke, *Voyage*, 46–47.

81. Price and Price, *Stedman's Surinam*, 131; Von Sack, *Narrative*, 112..

82. McLeod, *Elisabeth Samson*.

83. Hoefte and Vrij, "Free Black and Colored Women," 160.

84. Vrij, "Wapenvolk," 60–62.

85. Stanwood, "Between Eden and Empire," 1342, 1344. An example of strong Dutch Reformed-Huguenot family and friendship relations may be found in Oostindie, *Roosenburg*, 310–23.

86. De Gaay Fortman, "Luthersche gemeente in Berbice," 1:24, 3:78.

87. Van der Linde, *Visioen van Herrnhut*, 133.

88. Ibid., 142–43, 150.

89. Ibid., 161.

90. Wolbers, *Geschiedenis van Suriname*, 407.

91. Oostindie, "Same Old Song?" 154–58.

92. For a quantitative assessment of the Jewish presence in Dutch colonies, see Kruijtzer, "European Migration," 119.

93. Frijhoff and Spies, *Bevochten eendracht*, 121, 124; Cohen, *Jews*, 19.

94. New Christian was a legal and social category in Spain and Portugal and their colonies, referring to Jewish (and Muslim) converts to Christianity and their descendants.

95. Klooster, "Jews in the Early Modern Caribbean and the Atlantic World," 974–75.

96. Between 1759 and 1814, 135 out of 430 migrant *despachados* ended up in Suriname, 73 in Curaçao, 56 in London, and 40 in France. The rest arrived in a wide range of destinations in the Americas as well as Europe (Cohen, *Jews*, 25).

97. Netscher, *Geschiedenis*, 131.

98. Ibid., 184–85.

99. Klooster, "Essequibo Liberties." Jews were unable to serve on a colonial council until 1836 in Suriname and 1844 on Curaçao.

100. Ben-Ur with Frankel, *Remnant Stones*.

101. Cohen, *Jews*, 54.

102. NAN, Sociëteit van Suriname 500, memorandum of the regents and deputies of the Portuguese Jewish nation, Jacob Henriques Barrios Jessurun, David Nunes Monsanto, and Samuel Hoheb Brandon, for J. G. Wichers, governor general of Suriname and the Courts of Policy and Criminal Justice, Paramaribo, January 5, 1785.

103. NAN, Archieven Raad van Politie 2/3 bls, fols. 165, 176, meetings of the Council of Policy of Suriname, May 6 and July 8, 1695.

104. Goslinga, *Dutch in Caribbean and Guianas*, 363–64.

105. Lenders, *Strijders voor het Lam*, 75.

106. NAN, Sociëteit van Suriname 564, fol. 37, report of the directors of the Society of Suriname, submitted October 6, 1707.

107. Oudschans Dentz, "Grepen uit de geschiedenis," 175.

108. Ibid., 177–79.

109. Nassy et al., *Geschiedenis*, 1:3; Davis, "Regaining Jerusalem," 13.

110. Thompson, *Colonialism and Underdevelopment*, 75.

5. The Insular Caribbean

1. Smith, *Wealth of Nations*, 442.

2. Goslinga, *Dutch in Caribbean and Guianas*, 141; Klooster, *Illicit Riches*, 62–63.

3. Around 1800, the population of Bonaire was just below 1,000, that of St. Maarten 5,571, and that of Saba 1,301. Lommerse, "Population Figures," 331–34.

4. Philipsburg in St. Maarten and Oranjestad in St. Eustatius never outgrew their small size.

5. Klooster, *Illicit Riches*, 61.

6. "Extract uit het trouwboek"; "Huwelijken uit Notariële Akten (1783–1803)," online at http://www.archiefvriend.com/index.php/bronnen/60-huwelijkenprotocollen, accessed May 23, 2016. In 1783–1803, 276 bridegrooms were Curaçaoan natives and 139 were European born. Another 21 were born in the Americas outside Curaçao.

7. Three families were English, three Swiss, two Danish, and one each originated in Belgium, Portugal, Poland, and Sweden. Krafft, *Historie*, 57.

8. Rutten, *Dutch Transatlantic Medicine Trade*, 52.

9. Enthoven and Van der Maas, "Zorrug dat je erbij komt," 529. Curaçao's armed forces were smaller in number than those of Suriname, averaging 262 in the period 1722–57. NAN, NWIC 602, fol. 741, extract from the garrison files by Gijsbert Vos Jansz, 1759. As the garrison in St. Eustatius was even smaller yet, it is not surprising that Admiral Rodney's 1781 attack on the "Golden Rock" met with no significant resistance whatsoever.

10. Malaria did not occur on Curaçao. Rutten, *Dutch Transatlantic Medicine Trade*, 109.

11. Krafft, *Historie*, 44–56; Klooster, *Illicit Riches*, 65–67.

12. Krafft, *Historie*, 46; Goslinga, *Dutch in Caribbean and Guianas*, 239.

13. Goslinga, *Dutch in Caribbean and Guianas*, 115.

14. Claus van Laar, "Memorie van geheime consideration," in Coomans-Eustatia, Coomans, and van der Lee, *Breekbare Banden*, 53–99, 86.

15. Klooster, "Curaçao as a Transit Center," 46.

16. For Curaçao, see Klooster, *Ilicit Riches*, 61; for Bonaire, NAN, NWIC 246, inventory of slaves, Bonaire, November 10, 1789; for Aruba, NAN, NWIC 246, inventory of slaves, Aruba, October 12, 1789.

17. Jordaan, *Slavernij en vrijheid*, 134–36.

18. Only the number for 1789 includes free people of color. Sources: 1700: Goslinga, *Dutch in Caribbean and Guianas*, 129; 1715: Klooster, *Illicit Riches*, 89; 1738: NAN, Nieuwe West-Indische Compagnie 250, fols. 164–66, "Lijste van alle duijtes hoofden & famillien die op 't eijland St. Eustatius woonagtigh sijn beschreeven den 11 februarij A.o 1738"; 1747: Goslinga, *Dutch in Caribbean and Guianas*, 138; 1762 and 1779: Goslinga, *Dutch in Caribbean and Guianas*, 152; 1789: Lommerse. "Population Figures," 333.

19. Goslinga, *Dutch in Caribbean and Guianas*, 265.

20. Jarvis, *In the Eye of All Trade*, 165, 173.

21. Goslinga, *Dutch in Caribbean and Guianas*, 127; Barka, "Citizens," 230–36; Enthoven, "That Abominable Nest of Pirates," 250–551, 274, 296–97.

22. Macpherson, *Annals of Commerce*, 3:677; Goslinga, *Dutch in Caribbean and Guianas*, 138, 150; Barka, "Citizens," 230.

23. Klooster, "Curaçao as a Transit Center," 39.

24. Rupert, *Creolization and Contraband*, 95–97, 162–64, 196–208.

25. Jordaan, *Slavernij en vrijheid*, 193–218.

26. Oostindie, "Slave Resistance," 5.

27. Scott, "Crisscrossing Empires," 133; Bosch, *Reizen*, 2:366–7.

28. Knight and Prime, *St. Thomas 1803*, 163. For 522 out of a total of 1,521 free coloreds, no place of birth was given. This was not the first wave of migrants that arrived on St. Thomas from Curaçao. The 1690s had seen a similar movement: "A list of the names of inhabitants. The Danish Westindian Islands (The Virgin Islands) from 1650–ca. 1825," http://www.dkconsulateusvi.com/inhabitants/inhabitants07052002.pdf, accessed on March 5, 2017.

29. Wilson, *Commerce in Disguise*, 73, 83, 92.

30. The Beaujon family firm was established in St. Eustatius in March 1780, moved to Amsterdam one year later after the conquest by Rodney, then resumed its operations in October 1782 on Curaçao before appearing in the Guianas. NAN, Oud-Archief van St. Eustatius, inv. no. 123; Oostindie, "British Capital," 47–49.

31. Fatah-Black, "Suriname," 152–53; Oostindie, "British Capital," 36.

32. Archivo General de Indias [AGI, Seville], Santo Domingo 792, Deposition of "Adrian Molinero," "Federico Blanco" [Frederik de Witt], and Lucas Hansz, May 31, 1753.

33. Lommerse, "Population Figures," 331–34.

34. Goslinga, *Dutch in Caribbean and Guianas*, 127–55; Enthoven, "Abominable Nest," 242–95; Jordaan and Wilson, "Eighteenth-Century Free Ports," 276–80, 284–92.

35. Hoetink, *Patroon*; and *Caribbean Race Relations*.

36. Klooster, "Subordinate but Proud," 285–95; Rupert, *Creolization and Contraband*, 103–243; Jordaan, *Slavernij en vrijheid*.

37. Klooster, "Subordinate but Proud," 289.

38. Jordaan, *Slavernij en vrijheid*, 30–33; Rupert, *Creolization and Contraband*, 93–94, 135.

39. Jordaan, *Slavernij en vrijheid*, 27, 263, 272.

40. Renkema, *Het Curaçaose plantagebedrijf*; Allen, *Di ki manera?*

41. Jordaan, *Slavernij en vrijheid*, 52–54; Rupert, *Creolization and Contraband*, 141–45, 155–62.

42. Jordaan, *Slavernij en vrijheid*, 66–73.

43. Ibid., 272–86.

44. Ibid., 92.

45. Ibid., 97–98.

46. Council meeting, Curaçao, March 20, 1713, in "Notulen gehouden by de Ed. Raadt," 134.

47. Goslinga, *Dutch in Caribbean and Guianas*, 248; Klooster, "Rising Expectations," 68; Rupert, "Inter-colonial Networks," 81–84.

48. Jordaan, "Veranderde situatie," 490–95; De Hoog, *Van rebellie tot revolutie*; Klooster, "Curaçao as a Transit Center," 47.

49. Paula, *1795*, 268.

50. Genovese, *From Rebellion to Revolution*, 91–94; Rodway, *History*, 2:77.

51. Instruction for Jacob Pietersz. Tolck, director of Curaçao, 1638, and instruction for Mathias Beck, vice-director of Curaçao, Bonaire, and Aruba, June 8, 1655, in Schiltkamp and De Smidt, *Publikaties Curaçao, Aruba, Bonaire*, 6, 55.

52. The States General upheld this decision. Jordaan, "Slavernij en vrijheid," 173–74.

53. AGI, Santo Domingo 697, Governor Marcos de Betancourt to King Philip V, Caracas, August 30, 1716.

54. Jordaan, "Slavernij en vrijheid," 181; Klooster, *Illicit Riches*, 61.

55. NAN, Verspreide West-Indische Stukken 978, report of W.A.S. van Grovestins and W.C Boeij; Goslinga, *Dutch in Caribbean and Guianas*, 152. Goslinga's numbers for St. Eustatius, which differ from those in the report, add up to a 9:2 ratio.

56. Jordaan, *Slavernij en vrijheid*, 126–31.

57. *Bijlagen tot de Post van den Neder-Rhijn* (1784), 43. NAN, NWIC 607, fol. 344, Governor Jean Rodier to the WIC, September 27, 1769.

58. Jordaan, *Slavernij en vrijheid*, 119–20. Henricus, who was already active as a trader in 1743, died at a ripe old age in 1802. "Aktes uit het notariële archief Curaçao (OAC tot 1828) in chronologische volgorde. Deel 1: 1800–1809," *De Archiefvriend*, online at http://www.archiefvriend.com/index.php/bronnen/82-notarieel-archief-1800-1809, accessed on May 26, 2016.

59. Rupert, *Creolization and Contraband*, 147; Jordaan, *Slavernij en vrijheid*, 134, 141, 288.

60. Klooster, "Subordinate but Proud," 287. For the slaves Beltran owned, see Buddingh', *Otrobanda*, 223; and Mongui Maduro Library, Curaçao, Mikvé Israel Archief, 1.2, 58, affidavit of Anthony Beltran, 1775. He owned two small vessels: first the schooner *La Flora* and later the sloop *St. Anthonij*. Jordaan, *Slavernij en vrijheid*, 141–42. Antonio's father was the free black Francisco Bertran or Beltran, who was appointed by Governor du Fay as factor of the WIC's "Ceru Fortuna" plantation before the governor sold him that plantation in 1731. Four years later, Francisco Beltran sold it himself. Visman, "Van slaaf tot plantagehouder," 44–45. In 1748, Francisco Beltran sold a house and a piece of land to Antonio, who also bought an adjacent plot from another free black man. Buddingh', *Otrobanda*, 223; Jordaan, *Slavernij en vrijheid*, 127.

61. NAN, NWIC 317, Antonio Beltran, captain of the free blacks, to the WIC, Chamber of Amsterdam, Curaçao, August 17, 1750.

62. Cf. Borucki, From Shipmates to Soldiers, 112.

63. NAN, NWIC 1191, declaration of Andres Claassen, Guan Francisco Tambour, Hendrik Albertus Pietersz, Thomas Britto, Pedro Bastian, and Bentura Zogaso, St. Eustatius, November 7, 1760.

64. Van der Lee, *Curaçaose vrijbrieven*, 124, 127.

65. By 1710, there were three regiments of free blacks. Jordaan, "Free Blacks and Coloreds," 81.

66. NAN, NWIC 318, Gerret Specht, captain of the citizens, to the WIC, Curaçao, January 21, 1767.

67. Jordaan, "De vrijen en de Curaçaose defensie," 126, 129.

68. NAN, NWIC 611, fol. 485, governor Jean Rodier and council to the WIC, Curaçao, February 15, 1780, NAN, NWIC 1176, fols. 420–21, minutes of the council of Curaçao, undated [1789].

69. Julien Raimond to "my dear fellow citizens and brothers," Paris, November 9, 1792, in *Correspondence de Julien Raimond*, 104.

70. Klooster, "Subordinate but Proud," 289; Han Jordaan, "Free Blacks and Coloreds," 82.

71. NAN, NWIC 1168, fol. 706, Governor Jean Rodier to the WIC, Chamber of Amsterdam, Curaçao, February 4, 1779. NAN, NWIC 1162, fol. 63, Governor Isaac Faesch to the WIC, Chamber of Amsterdam, Curaçao, September 22, 1758.

72. Emmanuel and Emmanuel, *Jews of the Netherlands Antilles*, 240.

73. NAN, NWIC 599, fols. 912–13, Jan Gerard Pax and Nathaniel Ellis, delegates of the Council of Curaçao, to Governor Isaac Faesch and councilors, Curaçao, September 24, 1753.

74. NAN, NWIC 608, fol. 68, Governor Jean Rodier to the WIC, February 20, 1771.

75. NAN, NWIC 324, Governor Johannes de Veer Abz. to the WIC, Chamber of Amsterdam, Curaçao, July 13, 1789.

76. NAN, NWIC 611, fol. 328, Governor Jean Rodier to the WIC, Curaçao, May 3, 1779.

77. Rupert, *Creolization and Contraband*, 234-43.

78. Jacobs, "Upper Guinea Origins," 351–70; Heywood and Thornton, *Central Africans*, 241, 267.

79. Rupert, *Creolization and Contraband*, 214–47, 228–33; Klooster, "Between Habsburg Neglect," 712–13.

80. Van Putte, *Dede piquiña*, 19, 41.

81. Grovestins and Boey, "Rapport," 123. Bonaire was still home to 284 Amerindians in 1806. Goslinga, *Dutch in Caribbean and Surinam*, 130.

82. Knappert, *Geschiedenis*, 213. For a similar process in the Danish West Indies, see Mulich, "Microregionalism," 83.

83. Knappert, *Geschiedenis*, 186; Van Winter, *Kamer Stad en Lande*, 242–43. The colony's public records were kept in English, starting in 1751. Jarvis, *In the Eye of All Trade*, 355.

84. De Jong, *Reize naar de Caribische eilanden*, 108. See also de Hullu, "Leven op St. Eustatius," 147–48.

85. Hartog, *Mogen de eilanden zich verheugen*, 125.

86. Highfield, "Patterns," 149.

87. Frijhoff and Spies, *Bevochten eendracht*, 179–80, 354.

88. Knappert, *Geschiedenis*, 166–69; Larsen, "Negro Dutch Creole Dialect," 119–24, 123; Carstens, *St. Thomas in Early Danish Times*, 39–40.

89. NAN, NWIC 1191, minister Barach Houwink to the Heren X, St. Maarten, October 22, 1763.

90. Hartog, *Mogen de eilanden zich verheugen*, 44, 48.

91. NAN, NWIC 607, fol. 498, Church Council of Curaçao to the WIC, January 25, 1770.

92. SAA, Archief Classis Amsterdam (ACA) 225, fol. 203, pastor Rudolphus Wildrik to the classis Amsterdam, Curaçao, June 22, 1759.

93. NAN, NWIC 318, Council of Curaçao to the WIC Chamber of Amsterdam, July 31, 1766. Governor Jean Rodier to the WIC Chamber of Amsterdam, Curaçao, August 8, 1765 and September 29, 1766. Hamelberg, *Nederlanders op de West-Indische eilanden*, 1:182–84.

94. Emmanuel and Emmanuel, *Jews of the Netherlands Antilles*, 152.

95. Hartog, *History of Saba*, 31, 34.

96. "A List of the Names of Inhabitants: The Danish Westindian Islands (The Virgin Islands) from 1650—ca. 1825," http://www.dkconsulateusvi.com/inhabitants/inhabitants 07052002.pdf, p. 277, accessed on March 5, 2017.

97. Goslinga, *Dutch in Caribbean and Guianas*, 256–57.

98. NAN, NWIC 1161, fols. 95 and 99, Governor Isaac Faesch to the WIC Chamber of Amsterdam, November 22, 1754, and undated petition of Albert Urdaal, Pieter Beek, Gebhard Lupke, Dirk van der Meer, J.W. Bouman, Marten Hempel, Pieter Redoch, and Christian Zelting. A minor factor in the subsequent growth of the Lutheran congregation may have been the tendency of white male residents to convert to Lutheranism in order to avoid the exercise of "honorific functions," for which only members of the Dutch Reformed Church were eligible. Hamelberg, *Nederlanders op de West-Indische eilanden*, 1:156n2.

99. Hartog, *Mogen de eilanden zich verheugen*, 59.

100. De Gaay Fortman, "Lutherschen op St. Eustatius en in Essequibo," 346–49.

101. NAN, NWIC 318, Reformed Church council to the WIC, Chamber of Amsterdam, Curaçao, February 28, 1766; Wolbers, *Geschiedenis van Suriname*, 382.

102. SAA, ACA, 226, fol. 126, Church Council of Curaçao to the stadholder's representative and the WIC, October 2, 1786. NAN NWIC 324, J. de Veer Abz, I. O. van Brandt, Michiel Römer, Coenraad Visser, I. N. van Starkenborgh, C. F. G. Serz, and R. I. Brands to the WIC, Chamber of Amsterdam, May 18, 1787. SAA, ACA, 226, fol. 303, pastor R. Wildrik to the classis Amsterdam, Curaçao, November 15, 1790. Church Council of Curaçao to the classis Amsterdam, October 11, 1791; Hartog, *Mogen de eilanden zich verheugen*, 63, 65.

103. Hartog, *Mogen de eilanden zich verheugen*, 76–79.

104. Drew, *Life of Thomas Coke*, 169, 174, 199–204, 247, 263; Goslinga, *Dutch in Caribbean and Guianas*, 264. By 1830, 300 slaves, 120 free persons of color, and 39 whites made up the Methodist congregation. Knappert, *Geschiedenis*, 113–15, 206.

105. Van Luijk, "Caicedo," 125.

106. Ibid., 118, 120; AGI, Santo Domingo 744, Diego de Bañas y Sotomayor, Bishop of Caracas, to King Charles II, Caracas, May 3, 1686; NAN, NWIC 569, fol. 492, pastor Nic. Verkuijl to the WIC, Curaçao, June 1, 1707; Rupert, *Creolization and Contraband*, 86–88.

107. Rupert, *Creolization and Contraband*, 148.

108. Brada, *Paters Jezuieten op Curaçao*, 28–29.

109. Rupert, *Creolization and Contraband*, 153; Brada, *Kerkgeschiedenis Curaçao*, 33.

110. Brada, *Kerkgeschiedenis Curaçao*, 14 Governor Faesch believed their number to be just ten or twelve. NAN, NWIC 1157, fol. 144, Governor Isaac Faesch to the WIC, Chamber of Amsterdam, Curaçao, September 12, 1741.

111. Rutgers, *Schabel*, Part 2: 24 (entry of February 2, 1708).

112. Van Luijk, "Caicedo," 132.

113. NAN, SG 5775, resolutions of the WIC, Chamber of Amsterdam, October 16, 1720.

114. Perhaps Catholicism also prospered publicly in the sparsely inhabited islands of Bonaire and Aruba as well, but virtually nothing is known about their religious life in this early period. Catholics would dominate the islands' population in the nineteenth century.

115. During the French invasion of 1747, for instance, this concern led to the pillaging of Catholic-owned houses in Delft and Amsterdam. Dekker, "Oproeren in Holland," 311.

116. NAN, NWIC 596, fol. 98, complaints and grievances presented to the WIC by Joan Wilhem Claus van Laar, Curaçao, December 31, 1747.

117. NAN, NWIC 588, fol. 251, Governor Isaac Faesch to the WIC, Chamber of Amsterdam, Curaçao, September 22, 1740; NAN NWIC 588, fol. 6, pastor Wigboldus Rasvelt to the WIC, Curaçao, January 29, 1742.

118. NAN, Raad van Koloniën 77, Johannes de Veer Abz. to the Council of Colonies in the West Indies, Curaçao, January 30, 1795.

119. Bosch, *Reizen*, 1:220, 226.

120. Emmanuel and Emmanuel, *Jews of the Netherlands Antilles*, 528–29.

121. NAN, NWIC 617, fol. 63, deposition of Jossiyahu Pardo, David Aboab, Elias de Crasto, David Carillo, David Abendana, Isaq de Marchena, Josua Enriques, Ishac Per.a [Pereira], and Mordochay Enriques, Curaçao, October 9, 1680.

122. Rutgers, *Schabel*, Part 1: 90–91.

123. Buddingh', *Otrobanda*, 103–4.

124. Frijhoff, "Threshold of Toleration," 40–42. For the roots of religious toleration in the Dutch colonies, see Haefeli, *New Netherland*, 279–87.

125. Block, *Ordinary Lives*, 203–4.

6. The Circulation of Knowledge

1. Lewis, *Main Currents*, 109, 327; Davis, *Slavery and Human Progress*, 80; Van Kempen, *Geschiedenis*, 1:221.

2. Nassy et al., *Geschiedenis*, 1:3.

3. See *Caribbean Newspapers, Series 1, 1718–1876*, available through Newsbank.com, http://www.readex.com/content/caribbean-newspapers-series-1-1718-1876-american-antiquarian-society, accessed on October 6, 2017. The *Antigua Gazette* of December 9, 1799, reported on news about the surrender circulating in St. Pierre on September 4.

4. ZA, Middelburgse Commercie Compagnie (20), 58.1, local representative Adriaan Spoors to the directors of the MCC, April 30, 1763; De Villiers, *Storm*, 21, 225 (Storm, May 2, 1763, Clarke June 6, 1763), 238 (February 28, 1764); Bankroft, *Beschryving*, 290–91; Oostindie, "British Capital," 43–44.

5. Oostindie, "Slave Resistance," 8–9. See Klooster and Oostindie, *Curaçao*, for more detailed analyses of the transfer and suppression of revolutionary ideas in Curaçao and the wider Caribbean.

6. See http://www.nationaalarchief.nl/trefwoord/sailing-letters, accessed on October 6, 2017.

7. Citations and translations taken from "Brieven als buit," http://www.brievenalsbuit.nl/, accessed on October 6, 2017.

8. See, e.g., Delbourgo and Dew, "Introduction"; and Roberts, "Situation Science."

9. The following two sections are mainly based on Oostindie, "Intellectual Wastelands," where a fuller analysis and complete references may be found.

10. Delbourgo and Dew, "Introduction," 21.

11. Zandvliet, *Mapping*, 78, 183–86, 263; Den Heijer, *Grote Atlas*.

12. Cook, *Matters,* 332–38; Lack, "Maria Sibylla Merian"; and Reitsma, *Maria Sibylla Merian*.

13. Hance, "Carl Linnaeus's Forgotten Apostle"; Pain, "Forgotten Apostle"; Van Andel, Maas, and Dobreff, "Ethnobotanical Notes."

14. Schelling, "Verhandeling," 74–75; Benjamins and Snelleman, *Encyclopaedie, 595*; Van der Kuyp, *Surinaamse medische en paramedische kroniek*, 15; Oostindie and Maduro, *In het land*, 109–10; Dragtenstein, *Trouw*; Snelders, *Vrijbuiters*, 193–212.

15. Stoffers, "Botanisch onderzoek."

16. Koehler, Finger, and Piccolini, "'Eels' of South America."

17. Higman, *Slave Populations*, 272; Craton, *Searching*, 128–31; Oostindie, *Roosenburg*, 139–49; Rutten, *Apothekers*, 59; Rutten, *Dutch Transatlantic Medicine Trade*, 105–10; Snelders, *Vrijbuiters*, 213–6.

18. Higman, *Slave Populations*, 27; Van der Kuyp, *Surinaamse medische en paramedische kroniek*, 24–8; Rutten, *Apothekers*, 117–20; Rutten, *Dutch Transatlantic Medicine Trade*, 23, 50, 101.

19. Davids, "Scholarly Atlantic."

20. See chapter 3.

21. Van Kempen, *Geschiedenis*, 1:236.

22. Oostindie and Maduro, *In het land*, 29–30, 171–72.

23. De Palm, *Encyclopedie*, 497–99; Rutgers, "Schrijven," 74–75.

24. Bruijning and Voorhoeve, *Encyclopedie*, 656–58; Gobardhan-Rambocus, *Onderwijs*, 45–46; Van Kempen, *Geschiedenis*, 1:255, 268–69 and 2:338–39; De Palm, *Encyclopedie*, 498.

25. Quotation from Van Kempen, *Geschiedenis*, 2:339. The Dutch mother institution of the Maatschappij was founded in 1784 and soon had departments throughout the country. See Benjamins and Snelleman, *Encyclopaedie*, 455–56; Van Kempen, *Geschiedenis*, 5:39–43, and *Geschiedenis*, 2:339–41.

26. Cohen, *Jews*, 73, 95–123, 175; Lewis, *Main Currents*, 97; Nassy et al., *Geschiedenis*; Van Kempen, *Geschiedenis*, 1:261–3.

27. Eensgezindheid, *Verzameling*.

28. Medical doctor Voegen van Engelen, cited in Van Kempen, *Geschiedenis*, 1:256; Bruijning and Voorhoeve, *Encyclopedie*, 67, 235, 473; Davids, "Sources," 665; Gobardhan-Rambocus, *Onderwijs*, 45; Van Kempen, *Geschiedenis*, 1:267, 269, 274 and 2:331; Voegen van Engelen, *De Surinaamsche artz*.

29. Groot, *Batavia*, 151; Gobardhan-Rambocus, *Onderwijs*, 38, 41, 43; Van Kempen, *Geschiedenis*, 5:35–8.

30. Van Groesen, "Recht door zee," 70; University Libraries Leiden, Baesjou collection; Krabbendam, "Reading in Elmina."

31. NAN NWIC 585, fols. 924–64, inventory of possessions of former governor Juan Pedro van Collen, December 19, 20, and 22, 1738.

32. Rutgers, *Schrijven*, 66–67, 81.

33. Alberts-Luijdjens, "Historical Development," 78–81, 84; Rutgers, *Schrijven*, 66–67, 81.

34. Benjamins and Snelleman, *Encyclopaedie*, 139; Cohen, *Jews*, 97; 106–23, 181–251; Gobardhan-Rambocus, *Onderwijs*, 44, 47; Van Kempen, *Geschiedenis*, 1:255, 262–64 and 2:325–29; Nassy et al., *Geschiedenis*, 2:69.

35. Davids, "Scholarly Atlantic."

36. Cohen, *Jews*, 45, 102, 119; Davis, "David Nassy"; Gobardhan-Rambocus, *Onderwijs*, 42–43; Van Kempen, *Geschiedenis*, 1:261–63; Nassy et al., *Geschiedenis*; Phaf-Rheinberger, *Air of Liberty*, 66–67.

37. Lammens, *Bijdragen*, 72, 94–95.

38. Davids, "Dutch and Spanish Global Networks," 35, 49 (quote); Boomgaard, "Introduction." Huigen, "Introduction," 8, 11; Van Meerkerk, "Colonial Objects," 415–35; Zandvliet, *Mapping*, 227–9; Rutten, *Dutch Transatlantic Medicine Trade*, 98. For example, in 1640, the inventory of the WIC's Amsterdam office included not only objects pertaining to Atlantic exploits, but also Chinese paintings (Van Wijhe, "Amsterdam," 32). On the other hand, around 1700 the office inventory of the Groningen Chamber of the WIC included a precious little ivory sculpture of a woman with an offer plate probably acquired

in Benin. See Stichting Volkenkundige Collectie Nederland, http://www.svcn.nl/collection. aspx?oid=1415-1, accessed on October 6, 2017.

39. McClellan, *Colonialism and Science*, 289. On the Spanish Americas, see Engstrand, *Spanish Scientists*, and, particularly on the Spanish Caribbean, McCook, *States of Nature*. On Saint-Domingue, see McClellan, *Colonialism and Science*. On the British empire and particularly the West Indies, see Cobley, "Historical Development"; Drayton, *Nature's Government*; and Grove, *Green Imperialism*.

40. Davids, "Dutch and Spanish Global Networks"; "Scholarly Atlantic."

41. Van Kempen, *Geschiedenis*, 1:264–68; Rutgers, *Schrijven*, 66–67.

42. Schmidt, *Inventing Exoticism*; Van den Boogaart, "Books," 116; Davids, *Rise*, 539, 542–43.

43. Law, "Problems of Plagiarism."

44. Van den Boogaart, "Books," 117, 121–24.

45. Contemporary works on New Netherland include Van den Enden, *Kort verhael*; Megapolensis, *Kort ontwerp*; Plockhoy, *Kort en klaer ontwerp*; and De Vries, *Korte historiael*.

46. Rochefort, *Histoire*; *Le tableau de l'isle de Tabago*.

47. Hering, *Beschryving*, 57; Smith, *Wealth of Nations*, 442.

48. Price and Price, "Introduction," lxxiii–lxxx.

49. Emmer and Gommans, *Rijk aan de rand*, 68–124; Landwehr, *VOC*; Sens, *Mensaap*, 7.

50. See, e.g., Wagenaar, *Hedendaagse historie* (1739) and the cumulative series *Vaderlandsche historie* compiled by the 18th-century historian Jan Wagenaar.

51. Den Heijer, "Public and Private West India Interest."

52. Dutch pamphlets 1486–1853: The Knuttel and van Alphen Collections, https://www.kb.nl/ (accessed October 6, 2017).

53. Van den Bel, Hulsman, and Wagenaar, *Reizen van Adriaan van Berkel*, 13–16.

54. Schneider and Hemels, *De Nederlandse krant*; Van Driel, *Alom te bekomen*, 288.

55. Price and Price, "Introduction," lxxii–lxxxiii; Oostindie, "Stedman."

56. Paasman, *Reinhart*, 128–32.

57. *Brief van eenen Utrechtschen heer*, 19.

58. Israel, *Dutch Republic*, 1001; McCants, "Exotic Goods."

59. Schama, *Embarrassment*, 172; Wijsenbeek, "Ernst en Luim."

60. Boswell cited in Pottle, *Boswell*, 281; Luzac, *Hollands rijkdom* 4:119; Van Koolbergen, "Materiële cultuur," 145; Dibbits, *Vertrouwd bezit*, 160, 321–26; Wijsenbeek-Olthuis, *Achter de gevels*, 453–54; Rudé, *Crowd*, 114–19; Jones and Spang, "Sans-culottes"; Blondé and Van Damme, "Consumer and Retail 'Revolutions,'" 5, 12; Ellis, *Coffee House*, 259.

61. De Vries and Van der Woude, *Nederland, 1500–1850*, 383–89; Davids, *Rise*, 188–98, 225–27.

62. De Jong and Zondervan, *Kleine Geschiedenis*. See also Blakely, *Blacks in the Dutch World*; and Van Stipriaan, Heilbron, Bijnaar, and Smeulders , *Op zoek*.

63. Oostindie and Maduro, *In het land*, 6–19, 140–64; Fatah-Black, "Suriname," 152.

64. Oostindie, *Roosenburg*, 311–28. Will deposited by Jan van Sandick, The Hague, February 23, 1745.

65. Haarnack and Hondius, "'Swart' in Nederland"; Blakely, *Blacks in the Dutch World*, 78–170; Kolfin, *Slavenzweep*, 11, 23–29 and passim; Price and Price, "Introduction," xxxviii–xlviii.

7. Contraction

1. *English Review*, December 1786, "National Affairs" section, "Holland."

2. Smith, *Wealth of Nations*, 442.

3. Parts of this chapter are based verbatim on Oostindie, "Dutch Decline."

4. *English Review*, December 1786, "National Affairs" section, "Holland."

5. Emmer, *Dutch in the Atlantic Economy*, 219–20.

6. For the Atlantic, this was first the Council of American Possessions and Settlements (1791–95), next the West India Committee (1795–1800), and finally the Council of American Possessions (1801–6).

7. Hoonhout, "Noodzaak van smokkelhandel," 62; Van der Oest, "Forgotten Colonies," 353; N.N., "Amsteldam," 1319.

8. In 1807–12, the U.S. share of the trade of La Guiara in Venezuela was 53.4 percent, while that of Curaçao had shrunk to 15.4 percent. Lucena Salmoral, *Características*, 222, 227.

9. Letter of 76 British settlers in Essequibo and Demerara to George III [early 1781], NAN, NWIC 1.05.01.02, no. 533, 441–49.

10. Quoted in *Rechtsgeleerd advis*, 11–12 (University of Leiden Special Collections).

11. Voyages: The Trans-Atlantic Slave Trade Database, http://slavevoyages.org/assessment/estimates (accessed October 6, 2017).

12. Mijnhardt, "Dutch Enlightenment," 212–13; Popkin, "Print Culture," 282.

13. Quoted in Les, *Van Indië*, 2, 51.

14. Schutte, *Nederlandse Patriotten en de koloniën*, 15–16, 58–59, 144–49; Klooster, *Revolutions*, 98.

15. Oostindie, "Same Old Song."

16. Debate in the Zeeland Chamber of the WIC, 1677, quoted in Van der Bijl, *Idee en interest*, 216. A comprehensive overview of Dutch views on slavery in this period is presented by Paasman, *Reinhart*, 98–165.

17. Gallandat, *Noodige onderrichtingen*, 6–7.

18. Aristodemos and Sincerus, *Brieven*, e.g. 1:45–46; Barrau, "Waare staat."

19. Oostindie, "Same Old Song," 145–53.

20. Raynal, *Histoire*, 344, 350, 364, and likewise in his *Suppléments*, 3:84–85. A Dutch edition of his work was published shortly after (*Tafreel*, 1784), but certainly the Dutch educated classes were competent to read the French originals, all published in the Republic as well. Raynal, *Tafreel*, 334–47.

21. Luzac, *Hollands rijkdom*, 4:467, 471. These books were adaptions of the French study *La richesse de la Hollande* (1778) by Jacques Accarias de Sérionne, for which Luzac had acted as publisher (Van Vliet, *Elie Luzac*, 328). Stedman, *Narrative*; Riemer, *Missions-Reise*, 90–94; Malouet, *Collection*, 3:13–14, 114–17.

22. Paasman, *Reinhart*, 110–16, 121–28.

23. De Vreede in *Nationaale Vergadering*, volume 7 (1797), 10–14.

24. Schutte, *Nederlandse Patriotten*, 15–16, 58–59, 144–49; Sens, "Dutch Anti-Slavery Attitudes," 96–98; Klooster, *Revolutions*, 98.

25. For analyses of Dutch abolitionism and the decision process leading to the 1863 Emancipation, see Drescher, "Long Goodbye"; Janse, *De Afschaffers*; Oostindie, *Fifty Years Later*; and Siwpersad, *Nederlandse regering*.

26. Schutte, *Nederlandse Patriotten*, 3, 55–56, 90–105, 115, 141.

27. On a more personal level, he expressed anger because a private slave had been taken away from him during his travels to Europe. See Bom, *Verslag*, 2–4, 17, 38–39.

28. Cited in Renkema, "A. Kikkert," 27–32, 27; cf. Lok, *Windvanen*, 403.

29. Oostindie, "British Capital," 48.

30. Wolbers, *Geschiedenis van Suriname*, 445, 455–57, 476, 484–85.

31. Ibid., 463–64; Goslinga, *Dutch in Caribbean and Surinam*, 164.

32. Nassy et al., *Geschiedenis*, 1:1, 2:32–34; Lammens, *Bijdragen*, 56; cf. Van der Meiden, *Betwist bestuur*.

33. Goslinga, *Dutch in Caribbean and Surinam*, 180.

34. Letter of 76 British settlers in Essequibo and Demerara to George III [early 1781]; NAN, NWIC 533, fols 441–49.

35. Bolingbroke, *Voyage*, 176–77, 209–10, 370; NAN, NWIC 915, fols. 38–41, 96, "Rapport aan zyn Doorlugtigste Hoogheid den Heere Prince van Orange & Nassau [. . .] naar de Colonien van den Staat in de West-Indien," by W. A. van Sirtema van Grovestins and W. C. Boeij, July 27, 1790.

36. Wagenaar, *Vaderlandsche historie*, 33:220–28.

37. Bolingbroke, *Voyage*, 50 (figures c. 1800), 277–78, 312–13.

38. Bom, *Verslag*, 1, 5, 7–10, 17–18, 22–23, 46–48.

39. Delacoste, *Geschiedkundig en waar verhaal*, 91–93.

40. Oostindie, "British Capital," 48.

41. Netscher, *Geschiedenis*, 285–87.

42. Delacoste, *Geschiedkundig en waar verhaal*, v. 41.

43. Swaving, *Swaving's reizen*, 191–93; Koulen, "Slavenhouders"; Schomburgk, *Description*, 42.

44. Goslinga, *Dutch in Caribbean and Surinam*, 154. The population of St. Eustatius declined from 7,830 to 2,591, St. Maarten from 5,571 to 3,559, and Saba from 1,301 to 1,145, hence in total from 14,702 to 7,295. In 1960, the combined population stood at 4,722. See Lommerse, "Population Figures," 334.

45. See Klooster and Oostindie, *Curaçao*, for detailed analyses. The following is also based on Fatah-Black, "Patriot Coup d'État"; and Jordaan, "Patriots."

46. Fatah-Black, "Patriot Coup d'État," 137.

47. Jordaan, "Patriots," 166–67.

48. Bailyn, *Atlantic History*, 101, 104–5. See also Elliott, *Empires*, 329.

49. Klooster, *Revolutions*, 37–38, 146.

50. For a comparative perspective, see Geggus, "Slave Rebellion."

51. Jordaan, "Patriots," 144, 166.

52. J. W. Hudig, Rotterdam, November 10, 1791, quoted in Oostindie, *Roosenburg*, 362; Wolbers, *Geschiedenis van Suriname*, 464, 547–51; Goslinga, *Dutch in Caribbean and Surinam*, 175–76.

53. Curaçao: 3,714 (17.6 percent) in 1789 to 4,549 (32.3 percent) in 1816. Suriname: from 2,671 (17.6 percent) in 1789 to 6,104 (12.2) in 1816. See Lommerse, "Population Figures," 315–42, 326, 331–32.

54. Jordaan, *Slavernij en vrijheid*, 278–79, 260–61; Klooster, "Subordinate but Proud," 294; Oostindie, "Slave Resistance," 15–18.

55. Van der Veen, *Groot-Nederland*, 44–47.

56. Oostindie, *Roosenburg*, 137–38, 188–92, and "Same Old Song?," 153–58, Van Stipriaan, *Surinaams contrast*, 369–407.

57. For a broader perspective on culture-making in the "Black Atlantic," see Mintz and Price, *Birth*; and Thornton, *Cultural History*.

58. Emmer, "Myth"; cf. Elliott, "Afterword," 246–49. Part of this closing section is based on Oostindie, "Modernity."

59. Ormrod, *Rise of Commercial Empires*, 43. See also O'Brien, "Mercantilism"; and Emmer, "Jesus Christ," 219–20.

60. De Vries, "Dutch Atlantic Economies," 21. See De Vries, "Limits of Globalization," 714–15 and 732 for the distinction between "hard" and "soft" globalization.

61. Quoted in Koot, "Anglo-Dutch Trade," 97.

62. Quoted in De Jong, *Krimpende horizon,* 124.

63. Memorandums written by civil servant J.C. van der Kemp, September 2, 1806, quoted in de Hullu, "1786. Mémoire," and "Algemeene toestand," 413, 419.

64. De Jong, *Krimpende horizon,* 129, 136; Van der Veen, *Groot-Nederland,* 97–110.

65. "Uit de pers," 496–500.

66. Van Zanden and Van Riel, *Nederland,* 223.

67. Reesse, *Suikerhandel van Amsterdam,* xxxiii, xli.

Conclusion

1. Bernand, *Negros esclavos y libres,* 38–39; Hall, *Slave Society,* 87–93; Foy, "Ports of Slavery," 66–89.

2. Banks, *Chasing Empire,* 42.

3. Greene, *Creating the British Atlantic,* 133–34; See also Mancke, "Negotiating an Empire," 251–57.

4. Pitman, *Development of the British West Indies,* 206.

5. Cf. O'Malley, *Final Passages,* 295.

6. O'Brien, "Inseparable Connections," 63–65.

7. Ormrod, *Rise of Commercial Empires,* 322–30.

8. Schmidt, "Dutch Atlantic," 174–75; Klooster, "Atlantic and Caribbean Perspectives," 70–72.

9. Elliott, *Empires,* 140, 207.

10. Games, "Conclusion," 359.

11. Recent publications on this topic include Prado, *Edge of Empire*; Finucane, *Temptations of Trade*; and Dillon and Drexler, "Haiti." See Gould, "Entangled Histories," 764–86, for a discussion of interimperial entanglement.

12. Cf. for the First Dutch Atlantic: Merwick, *Shame and Sorrow*; Otto, *Dutch-Munsee Encounter*; Meuwese, *Brothers in Arms*; Hulsman, "Nederlands Amazonia"; and Romney, *New Netherland Connections.*

13. Norton, *Sacred Gifts*; Molineux, *Faces of Perfect Ebony.*

14. The publications of Benjamin Schmidt and Michiel van Groesen are examples of works on the First Dutch Atlantic. See for instance Schmidt, *Innocence Abroad,* and Van Groesen, *Amsterdam's Atlantic.* See Klooster, "Atlantic and Caribbean Perspectives" for the preference of Atlantic historians to tackle cultural phenomena.

BIBLIOGRAPHY

Unpublished Sources

Archivo General de Indias (AGI), Seville
Audiencia de Santo Domingo

Mongui Maduro Library, Curaçao
Mikvé Israel Archief

Nationaal Archief, the Netherlands (NAN), The Hague
Nieuwe West-Indische Compagnie
Oud Archief Curaçao
Oud Archief van St. Eustatius

Raad van Koloniën
Sociëteit van Suriname
Staten-Generaal
Verspreide West-Indische Stukken

Stadsarchief Amsterdam (SAA), Amsterdam

Archief Brants
Archief Classis Amsterdam

Universiteitsbibliotheek Leiden

Baesjou Collection
Stukken met betrekking tot de Verenigde Oostindische Compagnie (VOC)
en de Westindische Compagnie (WIC)

Zeeuws Archief (ZA), Middelburg

Archief van de Staten van Zeeland
Middelburgse Commercie Compagnie

Published Sources

Abenon, Lucien René. *La Guadeloupe de 1671 à 1759: Étude politique, économique et sociale.* 2 vols. Paris: Editions l'Harmattan, 1987.

Abraham, William E. "The Life and Times of Wilhelm Anton Amo." *Transactions of the Historical Society of Ghana*, 7 (1964): 60–81.

Ahn, Doohwan. "The Anglo-French Treaty of Commerce of 1713: Tory Trade Politics and the Question of Dutch Decline." *History of European Ideas* 36, no. 2 (2010): 167–80.

Aizpurua A., Ramón. "Las mulas venezolanas y el Caribe Oriental del siglo XVIII: datos para una historia olvidada." *Boletín Americanista* 30, no. 38 (1998): 5–15.

Alberts-Luijdjens, Monique. "Historical Development of Libraries in the Netherlands Antilles and Aruba." In *Caribbean Libraries in the 21st Century: Changes, Challenges, and Choices*, edited by Cheryl Peltier-Davis and Shamin Renwick, 31–40. Medford, NJ: Information Today, 2007.

Allen, Rose Mary. *Di ki manera? A Social History of Afro-Curaçaoans, 1863–1917.* Amsterdam: SWP, 2007.

Amézaga Aresti, Vicente de. *Vicente Antonio de Icuza, comandante de corsarios.* Caracas: Comisión Nacional de Cuatricentenario de Caracas, 1966.

Anderson, Fred. *Crucible of War: The Seven Years' War and the Fate of Empire, 1754–1766*. New York: Alfred A. Knopf, 2000.

Andel, Tinde van, Paul Maas, and James Dobreff, "Ethnobotanical Notes from Daniel Rolander's *Diarium Surinamicum* (1754–1756): Are These Plants Still Used in Suriname Today?" *Taxon* 61 (2012): 852–53.

Araúz Monfante, Celestino Andrés. *El contrabando holandés en el Caribe durante la primera mitad del siglo XVIII*. 2 vols. Caracas: Academia Nacional de la Historia, 1984.

Arends, Jacques. "The History of the Surinamese Creoles I. A Sociohistorical Survey." In *Atlas*, edited by Carlin and Arends, 115–30.

Aristodemus and Sincerus. *Brieven over het bestuur der colonien Essequebo en Demerary, gewisseld tusschen de heeren . . .* 12 vols. Amsterdam: W. Holtrop, 1785–88.

Armytage, Frances. *The Free Port System in the British West Indies: A Study in Commercial Policy, 1766–1822*. London: Longmans, Green and Co, 1953.

Assum, Pim van den. "The WIC-Appolonia War of 1761–1764: A Detailed Inquiry how the Dutch Lost and the Consequences of this Loss." MA thesis, University of Leiden, 2012.

Avitable, Joseph. "The Atlantic World Economy and Colonial Connecticut." PhD diss., University of Rochester, 2009.

Baesjou, René. "De Juffrouw Elisabeth op de Kust van Guinea ten tijde van de Vierde Engelse Oorlog." In *Ik ben eigendom van . . . Slavenhandel en plantageleven*, edited by Bea Brommer, 49–61. Wijk en Aalburg: Pictures Publishers, 1993.

——. "Trade Conflicts in Eighteenth-Century Western Gold Coast, and the Formation of the Nzema State." In *Prospettive di studi Akan: Saggi in memoria di Vinigi L. Grottanelli*, edited by Mariano Pavanello, 23–55. Roma: CISU, 1998.

Bailyn, Bernard. *Atlantic History: Concept and Contours*. Cambridge, MA: Harvard University Press, 2005.

Balai, Leo. *Het slavenschip Leusden. Slavenschepen en de West-Indische Comapgnie, 1720–1738*. Zutphen: Walburg Pers, 2011.

Bankroft, Edward. *Beschryving van Guiana, en een bericht van de rivieren Berbice, Essequebo en Demerary: In brieven. Uit het Engelsch vertaald en verrykt met de Aanmerkingen van den Hoogduitschen, en enige van den Nederduitschen Vertaaler*. Amsterdam: Gerbrand Roos, 1794.

Banks, Kenneth J. *Chasing Empire across the Sea: Communications and the State in the French Atlantic, 1713–1763*. Montreal: McGill-Queen's University Press, 2002.

Barka, N. "Citizens of Sint Eustatius, 1781." In *Lesser Antilles*, edited by Pacquette and Engerman, 223–38.

Barrau, A. "De waare staat van den slaaven-handel in onze Nederlandsche colonien." *Bijdragen tot het menschelijk geluk* 3 (1790): 341–88.

Barrow, Thomas C. *Trade and Empire: The British Customs Service in Colonial America, 1660–1775*. Cambridge, MA: Harvard University Press, 1967.

Bartlett, John Russell, ed., *Records of the Colony of Rhode Island and Providence Plantations, in New England, Vol. VI*. Providence: Knowles, Anthony, 1861.

Baugh, Daniel A. "Withdrawing from Europe: Anglo-French Maritime Geopolitics, 1750–1800." *The International History Review*, 20 (1998): 1–32.

Baxter, William T. *The House of Hancock: Business in Boston, 1724–1775.* Cambridge, MA: Harvard University Press, 1945.

Bel, Martijn van den, Lodewijk Hulsman, and Lodewijk Wagenaar, eds. *De reizen van Adriaan van Berkel naar Guiana: Indianen en planters in de 17e eeuw.* Leiden: Sidestone Press, 2014.

Ben-Ur, Aviva. "Purim in the Public Eye: Leisure, Violence, and Cultural Convergence in the Dutch Atlantic." *Jewish Social Studies* 20, no. 1 (2013): 32–76.

Ben-Ur, Aviva, with Rachel Frankel. *Remnant Stones: The Jewish Cemeteries of Suriname.* 2 vols. Cincinnati: Hebrew Union College Press, 2009–12.

Benjamins, Herman Daniel "Treef en lepra in Suriname," *West-Indische Gids* 11 (1930), 187–218.

Benjamins, Herman Daniel, and Joh. F. Snelleman, eds. *Encyclopaedie van Nederlandsch West-Indië.* The Hague: Nijhoff, 1914.

Berlin, Ira. *Many Thousands Gone: The First Two Centuries of Slavery in North America.* Cambridge, MA: Harvard University Press, 2000.

Bernand, Carmen. *Negros esclavos y libres en las ciudades hispanoamericanas.* Madrid: Fundación Histórica Tavera, 2001.

Bernstein, Harry. *Origins of Inter-American Interest, 1700–1812.* Philadelphia: University of Pennsylvania Press, 1945.

Bijl, M. van der. *Idee en Interest: Voorgeschiedenis, verloop en achtergronden van de politieke twisten in Zeeland en vooral in Middelburg tussen 1702 en 1715.* Groningen: Wolters-Noordhoff/Bouma's Boekhuis, 1981.

Black, Jeremy. *Trade, Empire and British Foreign Policy, 1689–1815.* London: Routledge, 2007.

Blakely, Allison. *Blacks in the Dutch World: The Evolution of Racial Imagery in a Modern Society.* Bloomington: Indiana University Press, 1993.

Blanchard, Peter. "The Language of Liberation: Slave Voices in the Wars of Independence." *Hispanic American Historical Review* 82, no. 3 (2002): 499–523.

Block, Kristen. *Ordinary Lives in the Early Caribbean: Religion, Colonial Competition, and the Politics of Profit.* Athens: University of Georgia Press, 2012.

Blondé, Bruno, and Ilja van Damme. "Consumer and Retail 'Revolutions': Perspectives from a Declining Urban Economy; Antwerp in the Seventeenth and Eighteenth Centuries." *XIV International Economic History Congress.* Helsinki, 2006.

Bolingbroke, Henry. *A Voyage to the Demerary, Containing a Statistical Account of the Settlements There, and of those on the Essequebo, the Berbice, and other Contiguous Rivers of Guyana.* London: Richard Phillips, 1807.

Bom, Jan. *Verslag van Mr. Jan Bom, voorheen secretaris van t gouvernement der colonie Essequebo en Demerary, enz. Wegens syne en verscheidene burgers . . . doormengd met eenige reflectien, over de oorzaak der overgave van die colonie aan Groot-Brittanje.* Amsterdam, 1799.

Boogaart, Ernst van den. "Books on Black Africa: The Dutch Publications and Their Owners in the Seventeenth and Eighteenth Centuries." *Paideuma, Mitteilungen zur Kulturkunde* 33 (1987): 115–26.

Boomgaard, Peter, "Introduction: From the Mundane to the Sublime: Science, Empire, and the Enlightenment (1760s–1820s)." In *Empire and Science in the Making: Dutch*

Colonial Scholarship in Comparative Global Perspective, 1760–1830, edited by Peter Boomgaard, 1–37, New York: Palgrave Macmillan, 2013.

Boone, Dave. "Nederlandse relaties met Ashanti: Het perspectief van de Tweede West-Indische Compagnie, 1750–1772." MA thesis, Leiden University, 2005.

Borges, Analola. *La Casa de Austria en Venezuela durante la Guerra de Sucesión Española (1702–1715)*. Salzburg, Santa Cruz de Tenerife, 1963.

Borucki, Alex. *From Shipmates to Soldiers: Emerging Black Identities in the Rio de la Plata*. Albuquerque: University of New Mexico Press, 2015.

Bosch, Gerardus Balthazar. *Reizen in West-Indië*. Amsterdam: S. Emmering, 1985.

Bosman, L. *Nieuw Amsterdam in Berbice: De planning en bouw van een koloniale stad, 1764–1800*. Hilversum: Verloren, 1994.

Bosman, Willem. *Nauwkeurige beschryving van de Guinese Goud- Tand- en Slave-kust* . . . Utrecht: Anthony Schouten, 1704.

Brada, Willibrordus Menno Jan. *Kerkgeschiedenis Curaçao (1742–1776)*. Willemstad, 1951.

———. *Paters Jezuieten op Curaçao*. Willemstad, 1950.

Brentjes, Burchard. *Anton Wilhelm Amo: der schwarze Philosoph in Halle*. Leipzig: Koehler & Amelang, 1976.

Brief van eenen Utrechtschen heer . . . Utrecht: Schoonhoven & Van den Brink, 1777.

Bromley, John Selwyn. "The French Privateering War, 1702–13," in *Corsairs and Navies, 1660–1760*, 213–41. London: The Hambledon Press, 1987.

Bruijn, Jacobus Ruurd. "Protection of Dutch Shipping: The Beginning of Dutch Naval Presence in the Caribbean, 1737–c. 1775." In *Global Crossroads and the American Seas*, edited by Clark G. Reynolds, 127–33. Missoula: Pictorial Histories Publishing, 1988.

Bruijning, Conrad Friederich Albert., and J. Voorhoeve, eds. *Encyclopedie van Suriname*. Amsterdam: Elsevier, 1977.

Buddingh', Bernard R. *Otrobanda: 'Aen de Oversijde van deese haven': De geschiedenis van Otrobanda, stadsdeel van Willemstad, Curaçao van 1696 tot 1755*. Curaçao: Drukkerij "De Curaçaosche Courant" N.V., 2006.

———. *Van Punt en Snoa: Ontstaan en groei van Willemstad, Curacao vanaf 1634: De Willemstad tussen 1700 en 1732 en de bouwgeschiedenis van de synagoge Mikvé-Israël 1730–1732*. 's-Hertogenbosch: Aldus Uitgevers, 1994.

Butel, Paul. "France, the Antilles, and Europe in the Seventeenth and Eighteenth Centuries: Renewals of Foreign Trade." In *The Rise of Merchant Empires: Long-Distance Trade in the Early Modern World, 1350–1750*, edited by James D. Tracy, 153–73. Cambridge: Cambridge University Press, 1990.

———. *Les négociants bordelais, l'Europe et les îles au XVIIIe siècle*. Paris: Aubier, 1974.

Buve, Raymond. "Gouverneur Johannes Heinsius: De rol van Van Aerssen's voorganger in de Surinaamse Indianenoorlog, 1678–1680." *West-Indische Gids* 45 (1966): 14–26.

Candlin, Kit. *The Last Caribbean Frontier, 1795–1815*. New York: Palgrave Mac-Millan, 2012.

Capitein, Jacobus Elisa Joannes. *Dissertatio politico-theologica de servitute, libertati christianae non contraria* . . . Leiden: S. Luchtmans, 1742.

Carpenter, Ralph E. *The Arts and Crafts of Newport, Rhode Island, 1640–1820.* Newport, RI: Preservation Society of Newport County, 1954.

Carrocera, Buenaventura de. *Misiones de los capuchinos en los Llanos de Caracas: Documentos (1700–1750).* Caracas: Academia Nacional de la Historia, 1972.

Carstens, Johan L. *St. Thomas in Early Danish Times: A General Description of all the Danish, American or West Indian Islands.* Edited and translated by Arnold R. Highfield. St. Thomas, United States Virgin Islands: The Virgin Islands Humanities Council, 1997.

Carter, Alice Clare. *Neutrality or Commitment: The Evolution of Dutch Foreign Policy, 1667–1795.* London: Edward Arnold, 1975.

Cavignac, Jean. *Jean Pellet, commerçant de gros, 1694–1772: Contribution à l'étude du négoce bordelaise du XVIIIe siècle.* Paris: S.E.V.P.E.N., 1967.

Chabert, Philibert, Pierre Flandrin, and Jean-Baptiste Huzard. *Instructions et observations sur les maladies des animaux domestiques.* 6 vols. 3rd ed. Paris: De L'Imprimerie et dans le Librairie Vétérinaire de Madame Huzard, 1808.

Chassaigne, Philippe. "L'économie des îles sucrières dans les conflits maritimes de la seconde moitié du XVIIIème siècle." *Histoire, économie et société* 7, no. 1 (1988): 93–105.

Chu, Jonathan M. "Debt and Taxes: Public Finance and Private Economic Behavior in Postrevolutionary Massachusetts." In *Entrepreneurs: The Boston Business Community, 1700–1850,* edited by Conrad Edick Wright and Katheryn P. Viens, 121–49. Boston: Massachusetts Historical Society, 1997.

Clark, George Norman. *The Dutch Alliance and the War against French Trade, 1688–1697.* Manchester: Manchester University Press, 1923.

Clark, John G. *La Rochelle and the Atlantic Economy during the Eighteenth Century.* Baltimore: Johns Hopkins University Press, 1981.

Clément, Pierre, ed. *Lettres, instructions et mémoires de Colbert.* 2 vols. Paris: Imprimerie impériale, 1863.

Cobley, Alan G. "The Historical Development of Higher Education in the Anglophone Caribbean." In *Higher Education in the Caribbean: Past, Present and Future Directions,* edited by Glenford D. Howe, 1–23. Barbados: The University of the West Indies Press, 2000.

Cohen, Robert. *Jews in Another Environment: Surinam in the Second Half of the Eighteenth Century.* Leiden: E. J. Brill, 1991.

Cook, Harold J. *Matters of Exchange: Commerce, Medicine, and Science in the Dutch Golden Age.* New Haven: Yale University Press, 2007.

Coomans-Eustatia, Maritza, Henny E. Coomans, and To van der Lee, eds. *Breekbare Banden: Feiten en visies over Aruba, Bonaire en Curaçao na de Vrede van Munster, 1648–1998.* Bloemendaal: Stichting Libri Antilliani, 1998.

Coombs, Douglas. *The Conduct of the Dutch: British Opinion and the Dutch Alliance during the War of the Spanish Succession.* The Hague: Martinus Nijhoff, 1953.

Correspondence de Julien Raimond avec ses frères, de Saint-Domingue, et les pieces qui lui ont été adressées par eux. Paris: De l'Imprimerie du Cercle Social, l'an deuxième de la Republique Française, n.d.

Craton, Michael. *Searching for the Invisible Man: Slaves and Plantation Life in Jamaica.* Cambridge, MA: Harvard University Press, 1978.

Crespo Solana, Ana. *El comercio marítimo entre Amsterdam y Cádiz (1713–1778)*. Madrid: Banco de España, 2000.

——. *Mercaderes atlánticos: Redes del comercio flamenco y holandés entre Europa y el Caribe*. Córdoba: Universidad de Córdoba, 2009.

Crespo Solana, Ana, and Wim Klooster. "La República Holandesa y su posición en el contexto colonial americano después de 1713." *Anuario de Estudios Americanos* 72 (2015): 125–48.

Crouse, Nellis M. *The French Struggle for the West Indies, 1665–1713*. London: Frank Cass, 1966 [1943].

Cruz, Laura E. "For Richer or for Poorer: The Promise and Limitations of Dutch Atlantic History." Review of *Riches from Atlantic Commerce: Dutch Transatlantic Trade and Shipping, 1585–1817*, edited by Johannes Postma and Victor Enthoven, *H-Atlantic* (April 2005), http://www.h-net.org/reviews//showpdf.php?id=10429.

Curtin, Philip D. "The White Man's Grave: Image and Reality, 1780–1850." *Journal of British Studies* 1 (1961): 94–110.

Daaku, Kwame Yeboa. *Trade and Politics on the Gold Coast, 1600 to 1720*. Oxford: Clarendon Press, 1970.

Dantzig, Albert van. *Les hollandais sur la Côte de Guinée à l'époque de l'essor de l'Ashanti et du Dahomey, 1680–1740*. Paris: Société française d'histoire d'outre-mer, 1980.

Davids, Karel. "Dutch and Spanish Global Networks of Knowledge in the Early Modern Period: Structures, Connections, Changes." In *Centres and Cycles of Accumulation in and Around the Netherlands during the Early Modern Period*, edited by Lissa Roberts, 29–52. Vienna: Lit Verlag 2011.

——. *The Rise and Decline of Dutch Technological Leadership: Technology, Economy and Culture in the Netherlands, 1350–1800*. Leiden: Brill, 2008.

——. "The Scholarly Atlantic: Circuits of Knowledge between Britain, the Dutch Republic and the Americas in the Eighteenth Century." In *Dutch Atlantic Connections*, edited by Oostindie and Roitman, 224–48.

——. "Sources of Technological Change in the Dutch Guiana, c. 1670–1860." In *Mundialización de la Ciencia y Cultura Nacional*, edited by Antonio Lafuente and Alberto Elena, 659–72. Madrid: Universidad Autónoma de Madrid, 1993.

Davies, K. G., ed. *Calendar of State Papers, Colonial Series, America and West Indies, 1737*. London: Her Majesty's Stationery Office, 1963.

——. "The Living and the Dead: White Mortality in West Africa, 1684–1732." In *Race and Slavery in the Western Hemisphere: Quantitative Studies*, edited by Stanley L. Engerman and Eugene D. Genovese, 83–98. Princeton, NJ: Princeton University Press, 1975.

Davis, David Brion. *Slavery and Human Progress*. New York: Oxford University Press, 1984.

Davis, Natalie Zemon. "David Nassy's 'Furlough' and the Slave Matthaeus." In *New Essays in American Jewish History Commemorating the Sixtieth Anniversary of the Founding of the American Jewish Archives*, edited by Pamela S. Nadell, Jonathan D. Sarna, and Lance J. Sussman, 79–94. Cincinnati: The American Jewish Archives, 2010.

——. "Regaining Jerusalem: Eschatology and Slavery in Jewish Colonization in Seventeeth-Century Suriname." *Cambridge Journal of Postcolonial Literary Inquiry* 3, no. 1 (2016): 11–38.

Dekker, Rudolf M. "Oproeren in de provincie Holland 1600–1775: Frequentie en karakter, relatie met de conjunctuur en repressie." *Tijdschrift voor Sociale Geschiedenis* 7 (1977): 299–329.

Delacoste, J. C. *Geschiedkundig en waar verhaal der gebeurtenissen, welke in de colonie Demerary by en zedert het vertrek van den baron van Grovestins hebben plaats gehad.* The Hague: H. C. Susan, 1798.

Delbourgo, James, and Nicholas Dew. "Introduction: The Far Side of the Ocean." In *Science and Empire in the Atlantic World*, edited by James Delbourgo and Nicholas Dew, 1–28. Oxford: Routledge, 2008.

Dewulf, Jeroen. "Emulating a Portuguese Model: The Slave Policy of the West India Company and the Dutch Reformed Church in Dutch Brazil (1630–1654) and New Netherland (1614–1664) in Comparative Perspective." *Journal of Early American History*, 4 (2014): 3–36.

Dibbits, Hester. *Vertrouwd bezit: Materiële cultuur in Doesburg en Maassluis, 1650–1800.* Nijmegen: SUN, 2001.

Dillen, Johannes Gerard van. "Memorie betreffende de kolonie Suriname." *Economisch-Historisch Jaarboek* 24 (1950): 162–7.

Dillon, Elizabeth Maddock, and Michael Drexler. "Haiti and the Early United States, Entwined." In *The Haitian Revolution and the Early United States: Histories, Textualities, Geographies*, edited by Elizabeth Maddock Dillon and Michael Drexler, 1–16. Philadelphia: University of Pennsylvania Press, 2016.

Doel, Wim van den. *Afscheid van Indië: De val het het Nederlandse imperium in Azië.* Amsterdam: Prometheus, 2001.

Doortmont, Michiel R., Natalie Everts, and Jean-Jacques Vrij. "Tussen de Goudkust, Nederland en Suriname: De Euro-Afrikaanse families Van Bakergem, Woortman, Rühle en Huydecoper." *De Nederlandsche Leeuw: Tijdschrift van het Koninklijk Nederlandsch Genootschap voor Geslacht- en Wapenkunde* 117 (2000): 170–212, 310–44, 490–577.

Douglass, William. *A Summary, Historical and Political, of the First Planting, Progressive Improvements, and Present State of the British Settlements in North-America.* Boston, 1755.

Dragtenstein, Frank. *"De ondraaglijke stoutheid der wegloopers": Marronage en koloniaal beleid in Suriname, 1667–1768.* Utrecht: Culturele Antropologie, Universiteit Utrecht, 2002.

——. *"Trouw aan de blanken": Quassie van Nieuw Timotibo, twist en strijd in de 18de eeuw in Suriname.* Amsterdam: KIT Publishers, 2004.

Drayton, Richard. *Nature's Government: Science, Imperial Britain, and the "Improvement" of the World.* New Haven: Yale University Press, 2000.

Drescher, Seymour. "The Long Goodbye: Dutch Capitalism and Antislavery in Comparative Pespective." In *Fifty Years Later*, edited by Oostindie, 25–66.

Drew, Samuel. *The Life of the Rev. Thomas Coke, LL. D. Including in Detail his Various Travels and Extraordinary Missionary Exertions, in England, Ireland, America, and the West Indies.* London: Thomas Cordeux, 1817.

Driel, Johanna van. *Alom te bekomen: Veranderingen in de boekdistributie in de Republiek 1720–1800.* Amsterdam: De Buitenkant, 1999.

Duncan, Archibald. *The Mariner's Chronicle; Being A Collection of the Most Interesting Narratives of Shipwrecks, Fires, Famines, and Other Calamities Incident to a Life of Maritime Enterprise.* 2nd ed. 2 vols. London: James Cundee, 1804.

Dunthorne, Hugh. *The Maritime Powers 1721–1740: A Study of Anglo-Dutch Relations in the Age of Walpole.* New York: Garland Publishing, 1986.

Duviols, Jean-Paul. "Les côtes du Venezuela au XVIIIe siècle: témoignage d'un contrebandier." *Cahiers du monde hispanique et luso-brésilien* 32 (1979): 5–17.

Eekhof, Albert. *De negerpredikant Jacobus Elisa Joannes Capitein, 1717–1747.* The Hague: Nijhoff, 1917.

Eensgezindheid. *Verzameling van uitgezochte verhandelingen, betreffende den landbouw in de kolonie Suriname: Opgesteld door het Landbouwkundig Genootschap: De Eensgezindheid, gevestigd in de devisie Matappika, binnen dezelve kolonie.* Amsterdam: Gartman & Uylenbroek, 1804.

Elliott, John Huxtable. *Empires of the Atlantic World: Britain and Spain in America, 1492–1830.* New Haven: Yale University Press, 2006.

Ellis, Markman. *The Coffee House. A Cultural History.* London: Weidenfeld & Nicolson, 2004.

Eltis, David, Pieter C. Emmer, and Frank D. Lewis. "More than Profits? The Contribution of the Slave Trade to the Dutch Economy: Assessing Fatah-Black and van Rossum." *Slavery & Abolition* 37, no. 4 (2016): 724–35.

Emmanuel, Isaac S., and Suzanne A. Emmanuel. *History of the Jews of the Netherlands Antilles.* Cincinatti: American Jewish Archives, 1970.

Emmer, Piet, and Jos Gommans. *Rijk aan de rand van de wereld: De geschiedenis van Nederland overzee.* Amsterdam: Bert Bakker, 2012.

Emmer, Pieter. *The Dutch in the Atlantic Economy, 1580–1880: Trade, Slavery and Emancipation.* Aldershot: Ashgate, 1998.

Emmer, Pieter Cornelis. "Het zwarte gat: investeren in Suriname. De Westindische plantageleningen, 1751–1774." In *In het verleden behaalde resultaten: Bijdragen tot de Nederlandse beleggingsgeschiedenis*, edited by Hubrecht Willem van den Doel and Gerton van Boom, 103–21. Amsterdam: Bert Bakker, 2002.

——. "'Jesus Christ Was Good, but Trade Was Better': An Overview of the Transit Trade of the Dutch Antilles, 1634–1795." In *Lesser Antilles*, edited by Paquette and Engerman, 206–22.

——. "The Myth of Early Modern Globalisation: The Atlantic Economy, 1500–1800," *European Review* 11 (2003), 37–47.

——. "The West India Company, 1621–1791: Dutch or Atlantic." In *Companies and Trade: Essays on Overseas Trading Companies during the Ancien Régime*, edited by Leonard Blussé and Femme Gaastra, 71–95, The Hague: Martinus Nijhoff, 1981.

Enden, Franciscus van den. *Kort verhael van Nieuw-Nederlants gelegenheit, deughden, natuerlycke voorrechten en byzondere bequamheidt ter bevolking.* N.p., 1662.

Engelen, Marcel van. *Het kasteel van Elmina: In het spoor van de Nederlandse slavenhandel in Afrika.* Amsterdam: De Bezige Bij, 2013.

Engerman, Stanley L., and Barry W. Higman. "The Demographic Structures of the Caribbean Slave Societies in the Eighteenth and Nineteenth Centuries." In *General*

History of the Caribbean. Vol. 3, *The Slave Societies of the Caribbean*, edited by Franklin W. Knight, 45–104. London: Macmillan/UNESCO, 1997.

Engstrand, Iris H. W. *Spanish Scientists in the New World: The Eighteenth-Century Expeditions.* Seattle: University of Washington Press, 1981.

Enthoven, Victor. "'That Abominable Nest of Pirates': St. Eustatius and the North Americans, 1680–1780." *Early American Studies: An Interdisciplinary Journal* 10 (2012): 239–301.

——. "An Assessment of Dutch Transatlantic Commerce, 1585–1817." In *Riches from Atlantic Commerce*, edited by Postma and Enthoven, 385–445.

——. "Dutch Crossings. Migration between the Netherlands and the New World, 1600–1800." *Atlantic Studies* 2 (2005): 153–76.

——. "Going Dutch: Interloping in the Dutch Atlantic World," In *Small is Beautiful? Interlopers and Smaller Trading Nations in the Pre-Industrial Period*, edited by Markus A. Denzel, Jan de Vries, and Philipp Robinson Rossner, 21–48. Steiner: Stuttgart, 2011.

——. "Suriname and Zeeland: Fifteen Years of Dutch Misery on the Wild Coast, 1667–1682." In *International Conference on Shipping, Factories and Colonization*, edited by J. Everaert and J. Parmentier, 249–60. Brussels: Académie Royale des Sciences d'Outre-Mer, 1996.

Enthoven, Victor and Henk den Heijer. "Nederland en de Atlantische wereld, 1600–1800: Een historiografisch overzicht." *Tijdschrift voor Zeegeschiedenis* 24 (2005): 147–66.

Enthoven, Victor, and H. J. van der Maas, "Zorrug dat je erbij komt: Rekrutering over de grens," *Militaire Spectator* 177 (2008), 524–34

Evans, Chris. "The Plantation Hoe: The Rise and Fall of an Atlantic Commodity, 1650–1850." *William and Mary Quarterly* 69, no. 1 (2012): 71–100.

Everts, Natalie. "Cherchez la Femme: Gender-Related Issues in Eighteenth-Century Elmina." *Itinerario: European Journal of Overseas History* 20, no. 1 (1996): 45–57.

——. "Krijgsvolk in Elmina: Asafo, garnizoen en Tapoeyerkwartier, 1700–1815." In *Geweld in de West*, edited by Victor Enthoven, Henk de Heijer, and Han Jordaan, 75–107. Leiden: KITLV Uitgeverij.

——. "Social Outcomes of Trade Relations: Encounters between Africans and Europeans in the Hubs of the Slave Trade on the Guinea Coast." In *Migration, Trade, and Slavery in an Expanding World: Essays in Honor of Pieter Emmer*, edited by Wim Klooster, 141–62. Leiden: Brill, 2009.

"Extract uit het trouwboek der Gereformeerde Gemeente op het eiland Curaçao van de jaren 1714 tot en met 1722." In *Vijfde Jaarlijksch verslag van het Geschied-, Taal-, Land- en Volkenkundig Genootschap, gevestigd te Willemstad, Curaçao.* Amsterdam: J. H. de Bussy, 1901.

Farley, Rawle. "The Economic Circumstances of the British Annexation of British Guiana (1795–1815)." *Revista de Historia de América* 39 (1955): 21–59.

Fatah-Black, Karwan, "Paramaribo as Dutch and Atlantic Nodal Point, 1640–1795." In *Dutch Atlantic Connections*, edited by Oostindie and Roitman, 52–71.

——. "The Patriot Coup d'État in Curaçao, 1796." In *Curaçao in the Age of Revolutions*, edited by Klooster and Oostindie, 123–40.

——. "Slaves and Sailors on Suriname's Rivers," *Itinerario* 36, no. 3, 61–82.

——. "Suriname and the Atlantic World, 1650–1800." PhD diss., University of Leiden, 2013.

——. *White Lies and Black Markets: Evading Metropolitan Authority in Colonial Suriname, 1650–1800*. Leiden: Brill, 2015.

Fatah-Black, Karwan, and Matthias van Rossum. "Beyond Profitability: The Dutch Transatlantic Slave Trade and its Economic Impact." *Slavery & Abolition* 31, no. 1 (2015): 63–83.

——. "A Profitable Debate?" *Slavery & Abolition* 37, no. 4 (2016): 736–43.

Feinberg, Harvey M. "Africans and Europeans in West Africa: Elminans and Dutchmen on the Gold Coast during the Eighteenth Century." *Transactions of the American Philosophical Society*, n.s., 79 (1989): 1–186.

Felice Cardot, Carlos. *La rebelión de Andresote (Valles del Yaracuy, 1730–1733): Discurso de recepción como individuo de número de la Academia Nacional de la Historia* (Caracas: Impr. Nacional, 1952).

Fermin, Philip. *Nieuwe algemeene beschryving van de colonie van Suriname. Behelzende al het merkwaardige van dezelve, met betrekkinge tot de historie, aardryks- en natuurkunde*. Harlingen: V. van der Plaats junior, 1770.

Finucane, Adrian. *The Temptations of Trade: Britain, Spain, and the Struggle for Empire*. Philadelphia: University of Pennsylvania Press, 2016.

Firla, Monika. "Anton Wilhelm Amo (Nzema, Rep. Ghana). Kammermohr—Privatdozent für Philosophie—Wahrsager." *Tribus* 51 (2002): 55–90.

Fortescue, John William, ed. *Calendar of State Papers, Colonial Series, America and West Indies*. Volume 16: 1697–1698. London: Her Majesty's Stationery Office, 1905.

Foy, Charles R. "Ports of Slavery, Ports of Freedom: How Slaves Used Northern Seaports' Maritime Industry to Escape and Create Trans-Atlantic Identities." PhD diss., Rutgers University, 2008.

Frijhoff, Willem. "The Threshold of Toleration: Interconfessional Conviviality in Holland during the Early Modern Period." In *Embodied Belief: Ten Essays on Religious Culture in Dutch History*, edited by Willem Frijhoff, 39–65. Hilversum: Verloren, 2002.

Frijhoff, Willem, and Marijke Spies. *1650: bevochten eendracht*. The Hague: Sdu Uitgevers, 1999.

Gaay Fortman, B. de. "De geschiedenis der Luthersche gemeente in Berbice I." *West-Indische Gids* 25 (1942): 20–27.

——. "De geschiedenis der Luthersche gemeente in Berbice III." *West-Indische Gids* 25 (1942): 65–89.

——. "Lutherschen op St. Eustatius en in Essequibo." *West-Indische Gids* 23, no. 1 (1940): 346–52.

Gallandat, David Henri. *Noodige onderrichtingen voor de slavenhandelaaren*. Middelburg: Gillissen, 1769.

Games, Alison. "Cohabitation, Suriname-Style: English Inhabitants in Dutch Suriname after 1667." *The William and Mary Quarterly* 72, no. 2 (2015): 195–242.

——. "Conclusion: A Dutch Moment in Atlantic Historiography." In *Dutch Atlantic Connections*, edited by Oostindie and Roitman, 357–73.

Garrigus, John D. "Blue and Brown: Contraband Indigo and the Rise of a Free Colored Planter Class in French Saint-Domingue." *The Americas* 50, no. 2 (October 1993): 233–63.

Gauci, Perry. *The Politics of Trade: The Overseas Merchant in State and Society, 1660–1720.* Oxford: Oxford University Press, 2001.

Geggus, David. "Slave Rebellion during the Age of Revolution." In *Curaçao in the Age of Revolutions*, edited by Klooster and Oostindie, 23–56.

Gelderblom, Oscar. *Zuid-Nederlandse kooplieden en de opkomst van de Amsterdamse stapelmarkt (1578–1630).* Hilversum: Verloren, 2000.

Genovese, Eugene D. *From Rebellion to Revolution: Afro-American Slave Revolts in the Making of the New World.* Baton Rouge: Louisiana State University Press, 1979.

Glasson, Travis. *Mastering Christianity: Missionary Anglicanism and Slavery in the Atlantic World.* New York: Oxford University Press, 2012.

Gobardhan-Rambocus, Lila. *Onderwijs als sleutel tot maatschappelijke vooruitgang: Een taal- en onderwijsgeschiedenis van Suriname, 1651–1975.* Zutphen: Walburg Pers, 2001.

Goeje, Claudius Henricus de. "Een verslag van den commandeur der kolonie Essequebo Pieter van der Heijden Rezen aan de Kamer van Zeeland der West-Indische Compagnie over den aanval van Fransche kapers in februari 1709." *West-Indische Gids* 30 (1949): 33–41.

González Batista, Carlos. *Archivo Histórico de Coro, documentos para la historia de las Antillas neerlandesas, Fondo Registro Principal I.* Coro: Centro de Investigaciones Históricas "Pedro Manuel Arcaya," 1997.

Goodfriend, Joyce D. "Archibald Laidlie (1727–1779): The Scot Who Revitalized New York City's Dutch Reformed Church." In *Transatlantic Pieties: Dutch Clergy in Colonial America*, edited by Leon van den Broeke, Hans Krabbendam, and Dirk Mouw, 239–57. Holland, MI, and Grand Rapids, MI: Van Raalte Press and William B. Eerdmans Publishing Company, 2012.

——. *Before the Melting Pot: Society and Culture in Colonial New York City, 1664–1730.* Princeton, NJ: Princeton University Press, 1992.

——. ed., *Revisiting New Netherland: Perspectives on Early Dutch America.* Leiden: Brill, 2005.

Goslinga, Cornelis Ch. "Curaçao as a Slave-Trading Center during the War of the Spanish Succession (1702–1714)." *Nieuwe West-Indische Gids* 52 (1977): 1–50.

——. *The Dutch in the Caribbean and on the Wild Coast, 1580–1680.* Assen: Van Gorcum, 1971.

——. *The Dutch in the Caribbean and in the Guianas 1680–1791.* Assen: Van Gorcum, 1985.

——. *The Dutch in the Caribbean and in Surinam 1791/5–1942.* Assen: Van Gorcum, 1990.

Gould, Eliga H. "Entangled Histories, Entangled Worlds: The English-Speaking Atlantic as a Spanish Periphery." *The American Historical Review* 112, no. 3 (2007): 764–86.

Grahn, Lance. *The Political Economy of Smuggling: Regional Informal Economies in Early Bourbon New Granada.* Boulder: Westview Press, 1997.

Grant, John N. "Black Immigrants into Nova Scotia, 1776–1815." *The Journal of Negro History* 58 (1973): 253–70.

Green-Pedersen, Svend E. "The Scope and Structure of the Danish Negro Slave Trade." *The Scandinavian Economic History Review* 19 (1971): 149–97.

Greene, Jack P. *Creating the British Atlantic: Essays on Transplantation, Adaptation, and Continuity.* Charlottesville: University of Virginia Press, 2013.

Groesen, Michiel van. *Amsterdam's Atlantic: Print Culture and the Making of Dutch Brazil.* Philadelphia: University of Pennsylvania Press, 2016.

——, ed. *The Legacy of Dutch Brazil.* Cambridge: Cambridge University Press, 2014.

——. "Recht door zee: Ontvoering, muiterij en slavenhandel in Arguin, 1633–1634." In *Het gelijk van de Gouden Eeuw: Recht, onrecht en reputatie in de vroegmoderne Nederlanden,* edited by Michiel van Groesen, Judith Pollman, and Hans Cools, 57–71. Hilversum: Verloren, 2014.

Groot, Hans. *Van Batavia naar Weltevreden. Het Bataviaasch Genootschap van Kunsten en Wetenschappen 1778–1867.* Leiden: KITLV Uitgeverij, 2009.

Grove, Richard H. *Green Imperialism: Colonial Expansion, Tropical Island Edens and the Origins of Environmentalism, 1600–1860.* Cambridge: Cambridge University Press, 1995.

Grovestins, Willem August Sirtama and Willem Cornelis Boey, "Rapport . . . betreffende het eiland Curaçao [1791]." In *Breekbare banden,* edited by Coomans-Estatia et al., 109–26.

H. B. "De Amsterdamsche nijverheid in 1816." *Amstelodamum: Maandblad voor de kennis van Amsterdam* 13, no. 1 (1926): 18–21.

Haarnack, Carl and Dienke Hondius, with Elmer Kolfin, "'Swart' in Nederland—Afrikanen en Creolen in de Noordelijke Nederlanden vanaf de middeleeuwen tot de twintigste eeuw," in *Black is beautiful: Rubens tot Damas,* 88–107. Amsterdam: De Nieuwe Kerk/Zwolle: Waanders, 2008.

Hackett, David G. *The Rude Hand of Innovation: Religion and Social Order in Albany, New York 1652–1836.* New York: Oxford University Press, 1991.

Haefeli, Evan. *New Netherland and the Dutch Origins of American Religious Liberty.* Philadelphia: University of Pennsylvania Press, 2012.

Hall, Neville A. T. *Slave Society in the Danish West Indies: St. Thomas, St. John, and St. Croix.* Edited by Barry W. Higman. Baltimore: Johns Hopkins University Press, 1992.

Ham, Gijs van der. *Dof goud: Nederland en Ghana, 1593–1872.* Amsterdam/Nijmegen: Rijksmuseum/Vantilt, 2013.

Hamelberg, Johannes Hermanus Jacobus. *De Nederlanders op de West-Indische eilanden.* 2 vols. Amsterdam: J. H. de Bussy, 1901.

Hance, Jeremy. "Carl Linnaeus's Forgotten Apostle Rediscovered: An Ecological Account of 18th Century Suriname." *Mongabay.com,* August 11, 2008. https://news.mongabay.com/2008/08/account-of-18th-century-amazon-adventurer-to-be-published-for-the-first-time.

Hardesty, Jared. *Unfreedom: Slavery and Dependence in Eighteenth-Century Boston.* New York: New York University Press, 2016.

Harrington, Virginia D. *The New York Merchant on the Eve of the Revolution.* New York: Columbia University Press, 1935.

Harteveld, Geoffrey. "'Op Africa Gevaaren': Een verkenning van de Nederlandse scheepvaart op Guinea voor de tweede helft van de achttiende eeuw, 1756–1791." MA thesis, University of Leiden, 2013.

Hartog, Johan. *De Bovenwindse eilanden Sint Maarten, Saba, Sint Eustatius: Eens gouden rots, nu zilveren dollars.* Aruba: De Wit, 1964.

——. *Curaçao: Van kolonie tot autonomie.* 2 vols. Aruba: De Wit, 1961.

——. *History of Saba.* Saba, Netherlands Antilles: Van Guilder N.V., 1975.

——. *Mogen de eilanden zich verheugen: Geschiedenis van het Protestantisme op de Nederlandse Antillen.* [Willemstad:] Kerkeraad van de Verenigde Protestantse Gemeente van Curaçao, 1969.

Hartsinck, Jan Jacob. *Beschryving van Guiana, of de wilde kust in Zuid-America.* Amsterdam: Gerrit Tielenburg, 1770.

Hattendorf, John B. "'To Aid and Assist the Other': Anglo-Dutch Cooperation in Coalition Warfare at Sea, 1689–1714." In *Anthonie Heinsius and the Dutch Republic, 1688–1720: Politics, War, and Finance,* edited by Jan A. F. de Jongste and Augustus J. Veenendaal, Jr., 177–98. The Hague: Institute of Netherlands History, 2002.

Headlam, Cecil, ed. *Calendar of State Papers, Colonial Series, America and West Indies, 1700. Preserved in the Public Record Office.* London: His Majesty's Stationery Office, 1910.

Headlam, Cecil and Arthur Percival Newton, eds. *Calendar of State Papers, Colonial Series, America and West Indies.* Volume 38: 1731. London: His Majesty's Stationery Office, 1938.

Heijer, Henk den. *De geoctrooieerde compagnie: De VOC en de WIC als voorlopers van de naamloze vennootschap.* Amsterdam: Stichting tot bevordering der notariële wetenschap, Deventer: Kluwer, 2005.

——. *Geschiedenis van de WIC.* Zutphen: Walburg Pers, 1994.

——. *Goud, ivoor en slaven: Scheepvaart en handel van de Tweede Westindische Compagnie op Afrika, 1674–1740.* Zutphen: Walburg Pers, 1997.

——. *Naar de koning van Dahomey: het journaal van de gezantschapsreis van Jacobus Elet naar het West-Afrikaanse koninkrijk Dahomey in 1733.* Zutphen: Walburg Pers, 2000.

——. "A Public and Private Dutch West India Interest." In *Dutch Atlantic Connections,* edited by Oostindie and Roitman, 159–82.

——. "The West African Trade of the Dutch West India Company, 1674–1740." In *Riches from Atlantic Commerce,* edited by Postma and Enthoven, 139–69.

Heijer, Henk den, Piet Emmer, Gijs Boink, Paul van den Brink, Karwan Fatah-Black, Johan van Langen, Jean-Jacques Vrij, and Rob van Diessen. *Grote Atlas van de West-Indische Compagnie, II. De Nieuwe WIC, 1674–1791.* Voorburg: Uitgeverij Asia Maior/Atlas Maior, 2011.

Hemming, John. "How Brazil Acquired Roraima." *Hispanic American Historical Review* 70 (1990): 295–325.

Hering, Johannes Hermanus. *Beschryving van het eiland Curaçao en de daar onder hoorende eilanden, Bon-aire, Oroba en Klein Curaçao. Benevens een kort bericht, wegens het gesprongen schip Alphen.* Amsterdam: J. v. Selm, 1779.

Herlein, J. D. *Beschryvinge van de volk-plantinge Zuriname* [. . .]. Leeuwarden: Injema, 1718.

Hernæs, Per O. *Slaves, Danes, and African Coast Society: The Danish Slave Trade from West Africa and Afro-Danish Relations on the Eighteenth-Century Gold Coast.* Trondheim: University of Trondheim, 1995.

Heywood, Linda M. and John K. Thornton. *Central Africans, African Creoles, and the Foundation of the Americas, 1585–1660*. Cambridge: Cambridge University Press, 2007.

Heuvel, Danielle van den. *"Bij uijtlandigheijt van haar man": echtgenotes van VOC-zeelieden, aangemonsterd voor de kamer Enkhuizen (1700–1750)*. Amsterdam: Aksant, 2005.

Highfield, Arnold R. "Patterns of Accommodation and Resistance." In *Bondmen and Freedmen in the Danish West Indies: Scholarly Perspectives*, edited by George F. Tyson, 142–59. St. Thomas, United States Virgin Islands: Virgin Islands Humanities Council, 1996.

Higman, Barry W. *Slave Populations of the British Caribbean 1807–1834*. Baltimore: Johns Hopkins University Press, 1984.

Hoefte, Rosemarijn, and Jean Jacques Vrij. "Free Black and Colored Women in Early-Nineteenth-Century Paramaribo, Suriname." In *Beyond Bondage: Free Women of Color in the Americas*, edited by David Barry Gaspar and Darlene Clark Hine, 145–68. Urbana: University of Illinois Press, 2004.

Hoek Ostende, J. H. van den. "Chocolaadmolens." *Jaarboek van het Genootschap Amstelodamum* 71 (1979): 65–78.

Hoetink, Harry. *Caribbean Race Relations. A Study of Two Variants*. London: Oxford University Press, 1967.

——. *Het patroon van de oude Curaçaose samenleving. Een sociologische studie*. Assen: Van Gorcum: 1958.

Hoog, Levina de. *Van rebellie tot revolutie: Oorzaken en achtergronden van de Curaçaose slavenopstanden in 1750 en 1795*. Willemstad and Leiden: UNA, KITLV, STICUSA, 1983.

Hoogbergen, Wim. "De binnenlandse oorlogen in Suriname in de achttiende eeuw." In *Geweld in de West*, edited by Enthoven, Den Heijer, and Jordaan, 147–82.

——. *The Boni Maroon Wars In Suriname*. Leiden: Brill, 1990.

——. *"De bosnegers zijn gekomen!" Slavernij en rebellie in Suriname*. Amsterdam: Prometheus, 1992.

Hoonhout, Bram. "De noodzaak van smokkelhandel in Essequebo and Demerary, 1750–1800." *Tijdschrift voor Zeegeschiedenis* 32 (2013): 54–70.

——. "The West Indian Web: Improvising Colonial Survival in Essequibo and Demerara, 1750–1800." PhD diss., European University Institute, 2017.

Hrodej, Philippe. *Jacques Cassard: Armateur et corsaire du Roi-Soleil*. Rennes: Presses Universitaires de Rennes, 2002.

Huetz de Lemps, Christian. *Géographie du commerce de Bordeaux à la fin du règne de Louis XIV*. Paris: Mouton, 1975.

Huigen, Siegfried. "Introduction." In *The Dutch Trading Companies as Knowledge Networks*, edited by Siegfried Huigen, Jan de Jong, and Elmer Kolfin, 1–16. Leiden: Brill, 2010.

Hullu, Johannes de. "De algemeene toestand onzer West-Indische bezittingen in 1806." *West-Indische Gids* 2 (1921): 407–21.

——. "Het leven op St. Eustatius omstreeks 1792." *West-Indische Gids* 1 (1919): 144–50.

——. "Memorie van den Amerikaanschen raad over de Hollandsche bezittingen in West-Indië in Juli 1806." *West-Indische Gids* 4, no. 1 (1923): 387–98.

Hulsman, Lodewijk Augustinus Henri Christiaan. "Nederlands Amazonia: Handel met indianen tussen 1580 en 1680. PhD diss., University of Amsterdam, 2009.

Ipsen, Pernille. *Daughters of the Trade: Atlantic Slavers and Interracial Marriage on the Gold Coast.* Philadelphia: University of Pennsylvania Press, 2015.

Israel, Jonathan I. *Dutch Primacy in World Trade, 1585–1740.* Oxford: Clarendon Press, 1989.

——. "The Dutch Role in the Glorious Revolution," in *The Anglo-Dutch Moment: Essays on the Glorious Revolution and its World Impact.* Cambridge: Cambridge University Press, 1991.

——. *The Dutch Republic: Its Rise, Greatness, and Fall 1477–1806.* Oxford: Clarendon Press, 1995.

Izard, Miguel. "Contrabandistas, comerciantes e ilustrados." *Boletín Americanista* 20, no. 28 (1978): 23–86.

——. *El miedo a la revolución: La lucha por la libertad en Venezuela (1777–1830).* Madrid: Editorial Tecnos, 1979.

Jacobs, Bart. "The Upper Guinea Origins of Papiamentu. Linguistic and Historical Evidence." *Diachronica* 26 (2009): 319–79.

Jacobs, Jaap. *The Colony of New Netherland: A Dutch Settlement in Seventeenth-Century America.* Ithaca, NY: Cornell University Press, 2009.

Janse, Maartje. *De afschaffers: Pubieke opinie, organisatie en politiek in Nederland 1840–1880.* Amsterdam: Wereldbibliotheek, 2007.

Jarvis, Michael J. *In the Eye of All Trade: Bermuda, Bermudians, and the Maritime Atlantic World, 1680–1783.* Chapel Hill: University of North Carolina Press for the Omohundro Institute of Early American History and Culture, 2010.

Johnson, Victor L. "Fair Traders and Smugglers in Philadelphia, 1754–1763." *The Pennsylvania Magazine of History and Biography* 83, no. 2 (1959): 125–49.

Jones, Colin, and Rebecca Spang. "Sans-culottes, sans café, sans tabac: Shifting Realms of Necessity and Luxury in Eighteenth-Century France." In *Consumers and Luxury: Consumer Culture in Europe, 1650–1850*, edited by Maxine Berg and Helen Clifford, 37–62. Manchester: Manchester University Press, 1999.

Jong, Cornelius de. *Reize naar de Caribische eilanden in de jaren 1780 en 1781.* Haarlem: François Bohn, 1807.

Jong, Johannes Joseph Petrus, de *Avondschot: Hoe Nederland zich terugtrok uit zijn Aziatische imperium.* Meppel: Boom, 2011.

Jong, Theo Petrus Maria de. *De krimpende horizon van de Hollandse kooplieden: Hollands welvaren in het Caribisch Zeegebied (1780–1930).* Assen: Van Gorcum, 1966.

Jordaan, Han. "Free Blacks and Coloreds and the Administration of Justice in Eighteenth-Century Curaçao." *New West Indian Guide* 84 (2010): 63–86.

——. "Slavernij en vrijheid op Curaçao: De dynamiek van een achttiende-eeuws Atlantisch handelsknooppunt." PhD diss., University of Leiden, 2012.

——. *Slavernij en vrijheid op Curaçao: De dynamiek van een achttiende-eeuws Atlantisch handelsknooppunt.* Zutphen: Walburg Pers, 2013.

——. "De veranderde situatie op de Curaçaose slavenmarkt en de mislukte slavenopstand op de plantage Santa Maria in 1716." In *Veranderend Curaçao: Collectie essays opgedragen aan Lionel Capriles ter gelegenheid van zijn 45-jarig jubileum bij de Maduro & Curiel Bank N.V.*, edited by Henny E. Coomans, Maritza Coomans-Eustatia, and Johan van 't Leven, 473–501. Bloemendaal: Stichting Libri Antilliani, 1999.

——. "De vrijen en de Curaçaose defensie, 1791–1800." In *Geweld in de West*, edited by Enthoven, Den Heijer, and Jordaan, 109–43.

Jordaan, Han, and Victor Wilson. "The Eighteenth-Century Danish, Dutch and Swedish Free Ports in the Northeastern Caribbean: Continuity and Change." In *Dutch Atlantic Connections*, edited by Oostindie and Roitman, 275–308.

Kals, Joannes Guiljelmus. *Neerlands hooft- en wortel-sonde , het verzuym van de bekeringe der heydenen* [. . .]. Leeuwarden: Koumans, 1756.

Kars, Marjoleine. "Policing and Transgressing Borders: Soldiers, Slave Rebels, and the Early Modern Atlantic." *New West Indian Guide* 83 (2009): 191–217.

——. "De slavenopstand van Berbice." *Geschiedenis Magazine* 6 (2012): 45–49.

Kempen, Michiel van. *Een geschiedenis van de Surinaamse literatuur. V: Bijlagen, lijst van geraadpleegde archieven, bibliografie, summary, résumé*. Paramaribo: Okopipi, 2002.

——. *Een geschiedenis van de Surinaamse literatuur.* 4 vols. Breda: De Geus, 2003.

Keye, Otto. *Het waere onderscheyt, tussen koude en warme landen . . .* 's-Gravenshage: Henricus Hondius, 1659.

Klooster, Wim. "Atlantic and Caribbean Perspectives: Analyzing a Hybrid and Entangled World." In *Peoples & the Sea: Thalassography and Historiography in the Twenty-First Century*, edited by Peter N. Miller, 60–83. Ann Arbor: University of Michigan Press, 2013.

——. "Between Habsburg Neglect and Bourbon Assertiveness: Hispano-Dutch Relations in the New World, 1650–1750." In *España y los diecisiete Países Bajos, siglos XVI–XVIII: Una revisión historiográfica*, edited by Ana Crespo Solana and Manuel Herrero Sánchez, 703–18. Córdoba: Universidad de Córdoba, 2002.

——. "Curaçao and the Caribbean Transit Trade." In *Riches from Atlantic Commerce*, edited by Postma and Enthoven, 203–18.

——. "Curaçao as a Transit Center to the Spanish Main and the French West Indies." In *Dutch Atlantic Connections*, edited by Oostindie and Roitman, 25–51.

——. *The Dutch Moment: War, Trade, and Settlement in the Seventeenth-Century Atlantic World*. Ithaca, NY: Cornell University Press, 2016.

——. "The Greater Caribbean in 1795: The Rising Expectations of Free and Enslaved Blacks." In *Curaçao in the Age of Revolutions*, edited by Klooster and Oostindie, 57–74.

——. "The Essequibo Liberties: The Link between Jewish Brazil and Jewish Suriname," *Studia Rosenthaliana* 42–43 (2010–2011): 77–82.

——. *Illicit Riches: Dutch Trade in the Caribbean, 1648–1795*. Leiden: KITLV Press, 1998.

——. "Inter-Imperial Smuggling in the Americas, 1600–1800." In *Soundings in Atlantic History: Latent Structures and Intellectual Currents, 1500–1825*, edited by Bernard Bailyn and Patricia L. Denault, 141–80, 505–28. Cambridge, MA: Harvard University Press, 2009.

——. "Jews in the Early Modern Caribbean and the Atlantic World." In *The Cambridge History of Judaism*. Vol. 7: *The Early Modern Period, c.1500–c.1815*, edited by Adam Sutcliffe and Jonathan Karp, 972–96. Cambridge: Cambridge University Press, 2017.

——. "An Overview of Dutch Trade with the Americas, 1600–1800." In *Riches from Atlantic Commerce*, edited by Postma and Enthoven, 365–84.

——. *Revolutions in the Atlantic World: A Comparative History.* New York: New York University Press, 2009.

Klooster, Wim, and Gert Oostindie, eds. *Curaçao in the Age of Revolutions, 1795–1800.* Leiden: KITLV Press, 2011.

Knappert, Laurentius. *Geschiedenis van de Nederlandsche Bovenwindsche eilanden in de 18de eeuw.* The Hague: Martinus Nijhoff, 1932.

——. "The Labadists in Suriname." In *Dutch Authors on West Indian History: A Historiographical Selection*, edited by Marie Antoinette Petronella Meilink Roelofsz, 255–79. The Hague: Martinus Nijhoff, 1982.

Knight, David W., and Laurette de T. Prime. *St. Thomas 1803: Crossroads of the Diaspora (The 1803 Proceedings and Register of the Free Colored).* St. Thomas, United States Virgin Islands: Little Nordside Press, 1999.

Koehler, Peter J., Stanley Finger, and Marco Piccolini. "The 'Eels' of South America: Mid-18th-Century Dutch Contributions to the Theory of Animal Electricity." *Journal of the History of Biology* 42 (2009): 715–63.

Kok, Gerhard de. "Cursed Capital: The Economic Impact of the Transatlantic Slave Trade on Walcheren around 1770." *Tijdschrift voor Sociale en Economische Geschiedenis* 13, no. 3 (2016): 1–27.

——. "Forten, factorijen en fraude." MA thesis, University of Leiden, 2012.

Kolfin, Elmer. *Van de slavenzweep en de muze: Twee eeuwen verbeelding van slavernij in Suriname.* Leiden: KITLV Uitgeverij, 1997.

Kolfin, Elmer, Arnoud Bijl, Vincent Boele, and Nicolette Sluijter-Seijffert, *Black is Beautiful: Rubens tot Dumas.* Amsterdam/Zwolle: De Nieuwe Kerk/Waanders, 2008.

Koolbergen, Hans van. "De materiële cultuur van Weesp en Weesperkarspel in de zeventiende en achttiende eeuw." *Volkskundig Bulletin* 9 (1983): 3–52.

Koot, Christian. "Anglo-Dutch Trade in the Chesapeake and the British Caribbean 1621–1733." In Oostindie and Roitman, *Dutch Atlantic Connections*, edited by Oostindie and Roitman, 72–99.

——. *Empire at the Periphery: British Colonists, Anglo-Dutch Trade, and the Development of the British Atlantic, 1621–1713.* New York: New York University Press, 2011.

Kortbondige beschryvinge van de colonie de Berbice. Amsterdam: S. J. Baalde, 1763.

Koulen, Paul. "Slavenhouders en Geldschieters: Nederlandse belangen in Berbice, Demerara en Essequebo, 1815–1819." *Gen: Tijdschrift voor familiegeschiedenis* 21, no. 1 (2015): 46–52.

Kpobi, David Nii Anum. *Mission in Chains: The Life, Theology and Ministry of the Ex-Slave Jacobus E.J. Capitein (1717–1747) with a Translation of his Major Publications.* Zoetermeer: Boekencentrum, 1993.

Krabbendam, Rob. "Reading in Elmina: The Private Library of Jan Pieter Theodoor Huydecoper in West Africa, 1757–1767." MA thesis, University of Leiden, 2012.

Krafft, Arnoldus Johannes Cornelius. *Historie en oude families van de Nederlandse Antillen: Het Antilliaans patriciaat.* The Hague: Nijhoff, 1951.

Kramer, Klaas. "Plantation development in Berbice from 1753 to 1779: the shift from the interior to the coast." *New West Indian Guide/Nieuwe West-Indische Gids* 65:1/2 (1991): 51–65.

Kreeke, Frank van de. "Essequebo en Demerary, 1741–1781: Beginfase van de Britse overname." MA thesis, University of Leiden, 2013.

Kruijtzer, Gijs. "European Migration in the Dutch Sphere." In *Dutch Colonialism*, edited by Oostindie, 97–154.

Kuniss, J. D. *Surinam und seine Bewohner oder Nachrichten über die geographischen, physischen, statistischen, moralischen und politischen Verhältsnisse dieses Landes während eines zwanzigjährigen Aufenthalts daselbst.* Erfurt: Beyer und Maring, 1805.

Kuyp, E. van der. "Surinaamse medische en paramedische kroniek, tijdvak 1494–1899." *Surinaams Medisch Bulletin/Surinam Medical Bulletin* 9:2 (1985), 1–67.

Lack, Walter H. "Maria Sibylla Merian: The Metamorphosis of Insects." In *The Great Naturalists*, edited by Robert Huxley, 118–23. London: Thames & Hudson, 2007.

Laet, Johannes de. *Jaerlyck Verhael van de Verrichtinghen der Gheoctroyeerde West-Indische Compagnie in derthien Boecken.* Edited by Samuel Pierre l'Honoré Naber and Johan Carel Marinus Warnsinck. 4 vols. The Hague: Martinus Nijhoff, 1931–37.

Lammens, Adriaan François. *Bijdragen tot de kennis van de kolonie Suriname: dat gedeelte van Guiana hetwelk bij tractaat ten jare 1815 aan het Koningrijk Holland is verbleven, tijdvak 1816 tot 1822: eerste afdeling Geographie, statistica, zeden en gewoonten: vierde afdeling Voorname belangen der kolonie.* Amsterdam: Vrije Universiteit, 1982.

Landwehr, John. *VOC: A Bibliography of Publications Relating to the Dutch East India Company 1602–1800.* Utrecht: Hes Publishers, 1991.

Larsen, Jens. "The Negro Dutch Creole Dialect." In *Bondmen and Freedmen in the Danish West Indies: Scholarly Perspectives*, edited by George F. Tyson, 119–24. St. Thomas, United States Virgin Islands: The Virgin Islands Humanities Council, 1996.

Law, Robin. *Ouidah: The Social History of a West-African Slaving Port, 1727–1892.* Athens: Ohio University Press, 2005.

——. "The Komenda Wars, 1694–1700: A Revised Narrative." *History in Africa* 34 (2007): 133–68.

——. "Problems of Plagiarism: Harmonization and Misunderstanding in Contemporary European Sources; Early (Pre-1860s) Sources for the "Slave Coast" of West Africa." *Paideuma, Mitteilungen zur Kulturkunde* 33 (1987): 337–58.

Le Voyageur François, ou la connoissance de l'Ancien et du Nouveau Monde, vol. XI. Paris: L. Cellot, 1750.

Lee, To van der. *Curaçaose vrijbrieven 1722–1863: Met indices op namen van vrijgelatenen en hun voormalige eigenaren.* The Hague: Algemeen Rijksarchief, 1998.

Leebeek, C. D. M. J. "Sint Eustatius als Caraïbische stapelmarkt: Handel en scheepvaart tijdens de zevenjarige oorlog, 1756–1763." MA thesis, University of Leiden, 2006.

Lenders, Maria. *Strijders voor het Lam: Leven en Werk van Herrnhutter Broeders en Zusters in Suriname, 1735–1900.* Leiden: KITLV Uitgeverij, 1996.

Les, Lubbertus. *Van Indië onder de Compagnie tot Indië onder de Staat: De koloniale titel in de staatsregeling van 1798.* Utrecht: Oosthoek, 1948.

Lesger, Clé. *The Rise of the Amsterdam Market and Information Exchange: Merchants, Commercial Expansion and Change in the Spatial Economy of the Low Countries, c. 1550–1630.* Aldershot: Ashgate, 2006.

Lever, J. T. "Mulatto Influence on the Gold Coast in the Early Nineteenth Century: Jan Nieser of Elmina." *African Historical Studies* 3 (1970): 253–61.

Lewis, Gordon K. *Main Currents in Caribbean Thought: The Historical Evolution of Caribbean Society in its Ideological Aspects 1492–1900.* Baltimore: Johns Hopkins University Press, 1983.

Lier, Rudolf Asueer Jacob van. *Frontier Society: A Social Analysis of the History of Surinam.* The Hague: M. Nijhoff, 1971.

Linde, Jan Marinus van der. *Het visioen van Herrnhut en het apostolaat der Moravische broeders in het Suriname, 1735–1863.* Paramaribo: C. Kersten, 1956.

——. *Surinaamse suikerheren en hun kerk: Plantagekolonie en handelskerk ten tijde van Johannes Basseliers, predikant en planter in Suriname, 1667–1689.* Wageningen: Veenman, 1966.

Lok, Matthijs. *Windvanen: Napoleontische bestuurders in de Nederlandse en Franse Restauratie (1813–1820).* Amsterdam: Bakker, 2009.

Loker, Zvi, *Jews in the Caribbean: Evidence on the History of the Jews in the Caribbean Zone in Colonial Times.* Jerusalem: Misgav Yerushalayim, 1991.

Lommerse, Hanneke. "Population Figures." In *Dutch Colonialism*, edited by Oostindie, 315–42.

López Cantos, Ángel. *Don Francisco de Saavedra: Segundo intendente de Caracas.* Sevilla: Escuela de Estudios Hispano-Americanos de Sevilla, 1973.

Lovejoy, David S. *Rhode Island Politics and the American Revolution, 1760–1776.* Providence, RI: Brown University Press, 1958.

Lucena Salmoral, Manuel. *Características del comercio exterior de la provincial de Caracas durante el sexenio revolucionario (1807–1812).* Madrid: Instituto de Estudios Fiscales, 1990.

Luijk, J. Benigno van. "El P. Agustín Caicedo y Velasco, prefecto apostólico de Curaçao (1715–1738)." *Missionalia Hispánica* 17 (1960): 119–34.

Luzac, Elias. *Hollands rijkdom, behelzende den oorsprong van den koophandel, en van de magt van dezen Staat; de toeneemende vermeerdering van deszelfs koophandel en scheepvaart; de oorzaaken, welke tot derzelver aanwas medegewerkt hebben; die, welke tegenwoordig tot derzelver verval strekken; mitsgaders de middelen, welke dezelven wederom zouden kunnen opbeuren, en tot hunnen voorigen bloei brengen.* Vols. 2–3. Leyden: Luzac en Van Damme, 1780–83.

Ly, Abdoulaye. *La Compagnie du Sénégal.* N.p.: Présence Africaine, 1958.

Lydon, James G. *Pirates, Privateers, and Profits.* Upper Saddle River: The Gregg Press, 1970.

Macpherson, David. *Annals of Commerce, Manufactures, Fisheries, and Navigation, with Brief Notices of the Arts and Sciences Connected with Them.* 4 vols. London: Nichols, 1805.

Malouet, Pière-Victor. *Collection de mémoires et correspondences officielles sur l'administration des colonies et notamment sur la Guiane française et hollandaise.* Paris: Baudouin.

Mancke, Elizabeth. "Negotiating an Empire: Britain and Its Overseas Peripheries, c. 1550–1780." In *Negotiated Empires*, edited by Daniels and Kennedy, 235–65.

Marrée, J. A. de. *Reizen op en beschrijving van de Goudkust van Guinea, voorzien met de noodige ophelderingen, journalen, kaart, platen en bewijzen.* 2 vols. The Hague and Amsterdam: Gebroeders van Cleef, 1817–18.

Matson, Cathy. *Merchants and Empire: Trading in Colonial New York.* Baltimore: Johns Hopkins University Press, 1998.

Mauro, Frédéric. *Le Portugal, le Brésil et l'Atlantique au XVIIe siècle (1570–1670): Étude économique.* Paris: Fondation Calouste Gulbenkian, 1983.

McCants, Anne E. C. "Exotic Goods, Popular Consumption, and the Standard of Living: Thinking about Globalization in the Early Modern World." *Journal of World History* 18 (2007): 433–62.

McClellan, James E. *Colonialism and Science: Saint Domingue in the Old Regime.* Baltimore: Johns Hopkins University Press, 1992.

McCook, Stuart. *States of Nature: Science, Agriculture, and Environment in the Spanish Caribbean, 1760–1940.* Austin: University of Texas Press, 2002.

McCusker, John J., and Russell R. Menard. "The Sugar Industry in the Seventeenth Century." In *Tropical Babylons: Sugar and the Making of the Atlantic World, 1450–1680*, edited by Stuart B. Schwartz, 289–330. Chapel Hill: University of North Carolina Press, 2004.

McGowan, Winston F. "The French Revolutionary Period in Demerara-Essequibo, 1793–1802." *History Gazette* [Guyana] 55 (1993): 1–18.

McLeod, Cynthia. *Elisabeth Samson: Een vrije zwarte vrouw in het achttiende-eeuwse Suriname.* Utrecht: Vakgroep Culturele Antropologie, Universiteit Utrecht, 1993.

McNeill, John Robert. *Mosquito Empires. Ecology and War in the Greater Caribbean, 1620–1914.* Cambridge: Cambridge University Press, 2010.

Meerkerk, Edwin van. "Colonial Objects and the Display of Power: The Curious Case of the Cabinet of William and the Dutch India Companies." In *The Dutch Trading Companies as Knowledge Networks*, edited by Siegfried Huigen, Jan de Jong, and Elmer Kolkin, 415–36. Leiden: Brill, 2010.

Megapolensis, Johannes. *Een kort ontwerp van de Mahakuase Indianen, haer landt, tale, statuere, dracht, godes-dienst ende magistrature. Aldus beschreven ende nu kortelijck den 26. Augusti 1644 opgesonden uyt nieuwe Nederlant.* Alkmaar: ca. 1644.

Meiden, Gerard Willem van der. *Betwist bestuur: Een eeuw strijd om de macht in Suriname 1651–1753.* Amsterdam: De Bataafsche Leeuw, 1987.

Memorie welke de Planters en Ingezeetenen van de Colonie Essequebo en Demerary respectievelyk aan Haar Hoog Mog. de Heeren Staaten Generaal der Vereenigde Nederlanden, presenteeren over de belangen derzelve Colonie. 1785.

Menkman, Willem Rudolf. "Sint Eustatius' gouden tijd." *West-Indische Gids* 14 (1932–33): 369–96.

——. "Statiaansche toestanden in de XVIIIe eeuw." *West-Indische Gids* 15 (1934): 105–23.

Merritt, Jane T. "Tea Trade, Consumption, and the Republican Paradox in Prerevolutionary Philadelphia." *Pennsylvania Magazine of History and Biography* 128, no. 2 (2004): 117–48.

Merwick, Donna. *The Shame and the Sorrow: Dutch-Amerindian Encounters in New Netherland*. Philadelphia: University of Pennsylvania Press, 2006.

Meuwese, Mark. *Brothers in Arms, Partners in Trade: Dutch-Indigenous Alliances in the Atlantic World, 1595–1674*. Leiden: Brill, 2012.

Mijnhardt, Wijnand W. "The Dutch Enlightenment: Humanism, Nationalism, and Decline." In *Dutch Republic*, edited by Jacob and Mijnhardt, 197–223.

Mims, Stewart L. *Colbert's West India Policy*. New Haven: Yale University Press, 1912.

Mintz, Sidney W., and Richard Price. *The Birth of African-American Culture: An Anthropological Perspective*. Boston: Beacon Press, 1976.

Moerbeeck, Jan Andriesz. *Redenen waarom de West-Indische Compagnie dient te trachten het Landt van Brasilia den Coninck van Spangien te ontmachtigen*. Amsterdam: Cornelis Lodewijcksz, 1624.

Molineux, Catherine A. *Faces of Perfect Ebony: Encountering Atlantic Slavery in Imperial Britain*. Cambridge, MA: Harvard University Press, 2012.

Morgan, Gwenda, and Peter Rushton. *Banishment in the Early Atlantic World: Convicts, Rebels and Slaves*. London: Bloomsbury, 2013.

Morgan, Philip D. *Slave Counterpoint: Black Culture in the Eighteenth-Century Chesapeake and Lowcountry*. Williamsburg, VA: The Omohundro Institute of Early American History and Culture, 1998.

Mouw, Dirk Edward. "Moederkerk and Vaderland: Religion and Ethnic Identity in the Middle Colonies, 1690–1772." PhD diss., University of Iowa, 2009.

Mulich, Jeppe. "Microregionalism and Intercolonial Relations: The Case of the Danish West Indies, 1730–1830." *Journal of Global History* 8 (2013): 72–94.

Murray, W. G. D. "De Rotterdamsche toeback-coopers." *Rotterdamsch jaarboekje*, 5th ser., 1 (1943): 18–83.

Murrin, John M. "English Rights as Ethnic Aggression: The English Conquest, the Charter of Liberties of 1682, and Leisler's Rebellion in New York." In *Authority and Resistance in Early New York*, edited by William Pencak and Conrad E. Wright, 56–94. New York: New-York Historical Society, 1988.

Naipaul, Vidiadhar Surajprasad. *The Loss of Eldorado. A History*. London: André Deutsch, 1969.

[Nassy, David, et al.] *Geschiedenis der kolonie van Suriname: behelzende derzelver opkomst, voortgang, burgerlyke en staatkundige gesteldheid, tegenwoordigen staat van koophandel, en eene volledige en naauwkeurige beschryving van het land, de zeden en gebruiken der ingezetenen*. Amsterdam: Allart en Van der Plaats, 1791.

Nationaale Vergadering representeerende het Volk van Nederland, Dagverhaal der handelingen van de Nationaale Vergadering representeerende het Volk van Nederland. De Haage: Van Schelle en comp, 1796–98.

Netscher, Pieter Marinus. *Geschiedenis van de koloniën Essequebo, Demerary en Berbice, van de vestiging der Nederlanders aldaar tot op onzen tijd*. The Hague: Martinus Nijhoff, 1888.

Nettelbeck, Joachim. *Des Seefahrers und aufrechten Bürgers Joachim Nettelbeck wundersame Lebensgeschichte von ihm selbst erzählt*. Ebenhausen: Wilhelm Langewiesche-Brandt, 1910.

Newman, Simon P. *A New World of Labor: The Development of Plantation Slavery in the British Atlantic.* Philadelphia: University of Pennsylvania Press, 2013.

Newton, Joshua D. "Slavery, Sea Power and the State: The Royal Navy and the British West African Settlements, 1748–1756." *The Journal of Imperial and Commonwealth History* 41 (2013): 171–93.

N. N., "Amsteldam," in *Nieuwe Nederlandsche Jaarboeken* 27 (1792), 1315–23.

Norton, Marcy. *Sacred Gifts, Profane Pleasures: A History of Tobacco and Chocolate in the Atlantic World.* Ithaca, NY: Cornell University Press, 2008.

"Notulen gehouden by de Ed. Raadt, sedert den 16 February 1713." *Eerste Jaarlijksch verslag van het Geschied-, Taal-, Land- en Volkenkundig Genootschap, gevestigd te Willemstad, Curaçao.* Amsterdam: J. H. de Bussy, 1897.

O'Brien, Patrick K. "Inseparable Connections: Trade, Economy, Fiscal State, and the Expansion of Empire, 1688–1815." In *The Oxford History of the British Empire II: The Eighteenth Century*, edited by Peter J. Marshall, 53–77. Oxford: Oxford University Press, 1998.

———. "Mercantilism and Imperialism in the Rise and Decline of the Dutch and British Economies 1585–1815." *De Economist* 148 (2000): 469–501.

Oest, Eric Willem van der. "The Forgotten Colonies of Essequibo and Demerara, 1700–1814." In *Riches from Atlantic Commerce*, edited by Postma and Enthoven, 323–61.

Olivas, Aaron Alejandro. "The Global Politics of the Transatlantic Slave Trade during the War of the Spanish Succession, 1700–1715." In *Early Bourbon Spanish America: Politics and Society in a Forgotten Era (1700–1759)*, edited by Francisco A. Eissa-Barroso and Ainara Vázquez Varela, 85–109. Leiden: Brill, 2013.

O'Malley, Gregory E. *Final Passages: The Intercolonial Slave Trade of British America, 1619–1807.* Chapel Hill: University of North Carolina Press for the Omohundro Institute of Early American History and Civilization, 2014.

Oostindie, Gert. "'British Capital, Industry and Perseverance' versus Dutch 'Old School'? The Dutch Atlantic and the Takeover of Berbice, Demerara and Essequibo, 1750–1815." *BMGN—Low Countries Historical Review* 127 (2012): 28–55.

———, ed. *Dutch Colonialism, Migration and Cultural Heritage.* Leiden: KITLV Press, 2008.

———. "Dutch Decline during the 'Age of Revolutions.'" In *Dutch Atlantic Connections*, edited by Oostindie and Roitman, 309–35.

———, ed. *Fifty Years Later: Antislavery, Capitalism and Modernity in the Dutch Orbit.* Pittsburgh: University of Pittsburgh Press, 1996.

———. "Intellectual Wastelands? Scholarship in and for the Dutch West Indies up to ca. 1800." In *Empire and Science*, edited by Boomgaard, 253–80.

———. "Modernity and Demise of the Dutch Atlantic, 1650–1914." In *The Caribbean and the Atlantic World Economy*, edited by Adrian Leonard and David Pretel, 108–36. New York: Palgrave, 2015.

———. *Postcolonial Netherlands: Sixty-Five Years of Forgetting, Commemorating, Silencing.* Amsterdam: Amsterdam University Press, 2011.

———. *Roosenburg en Mon Bijou: Twee Surinaamse plantages, 1720–1870.* Dordrecht: Foris, 1989.

———. "Same Old Song? Perspectives on Slavery and Slaves in Suriname and Curaçao." In *Fifty Years Later*, edited by Oostindie, 143–78.

——. "Slave Resistance, Colour Lines, and the Impact of the French and Haitian Revolutions in Curaçao." In *Curaçao in the Age of Revolutions*, edited by Klooster and Oostindie, 1–22.

——. "Voltaire, Stedman, and Surinam Slavery." *Slavery and Abolition* 14, no. 2 (1993): 1–34.

Oostindie, Gert, and Emy Maduro. *In het land van de overheerser II: Antillianen en Surinamers in Nederland 1634/1667–1954*. Dordrecht: Foris, 1986.

Oostindie, Gert, and Jessica Vance Roitman, eds. *Dutch Atlantic Connections, 1680–1800: Linking Empires, Bridging Borders*. Leiden: Brill 2014.

——. "Introduction." In *Dutch Atlantic Connections*, edited by Oostindie and Roitman, 1–21.

——. "Repositioning the Dutch in the Atlantic, 1680–1800." *Itinerario* 36 (2012): 129–60.

Oostindie, Gert, and Alex van Stipriaan. "Slavery and Slave Cultures in a Hydraulic Society: Suriname." In *Slavery and Slave Cultures in the Americas*, edited by Stephan Palmié, 78–99. Knoxville: University of Tennessee Press, 1995.

Ormrod, David. *The Rise of Commercial Empires: England and the Netherlands in the Age of Mercantilism, 1650–1770*. Cambridge: Cambridge University Press, 2003.

Ortiz, Fernando. *Contrapunteo cubano del tabaco y del azúcar*. La Habana: Jesus Montero, 1940.

O'Shaughnessy, Andrew Jackson. *The Men Who Lost America: British Leadership, the American Revolution, and the Fate of the Empire*. New Haven: Yale University Press, 2013.

Ostrander, Gilman M. "The Colonial Molasses Trade." *Agricultural History* 30 (1956): 77–84.

Otto, Paul. *The Dutch-Munsee Encounter in America: The Struggle for Sovereignty in the Hudson Valley*. New York: Berghahn Books, 2006.

Oudermeulen, C. van der. "Iets dat to voordeel der deelgenoten van de Oost-Indische Compagnie en tot nut van ieder ingezeten van dit gemeenebest kan strekken." In *Stukken, raakende den tegenwoordigen toestand der Bataafsche bezittingen in Oost-Indiën den handel op dezelve*, edited by Dirk van Hogendorp. The Hague: M. C. Leeuwestyn; Delft: M. Roelofswaert, 1801.

Oudschans Dentz, Fred. "Grepen uit de geschiedenis van het onderwijs in Suriname in de 17e en 18e eeuw." *West-Indische Gids* (1956): 174–82.

Paasman, Albertus Nicolaas. *Reinhart: Nederlandse literatuur en slavernij ten tijde van de verlichting*. Leiden: Nijhoff, 1984.

Paesie, Rudolf. *Lorrendrayen op Africa: De illegale goederen- en slavenhandel op West-Afrika tijdens het achttiende-eeuwse handelsmonopolie van de West-Indische Compagnie, 1700–1734*. Amsterdam: De Bataafsche Leeuw, 2008.

Paesie, Ruud. *Geschiedenis van de MCC: Opkomst, bloei en ondergang*. Zutphen: Walburg Pers, 2014.

——. "Zeeuwen en de slavenhandel: een kwantitatieve analyse." *Zeeland* 19 (2010): 2–13.

Pain, Stephanie. "The Forgotten Apostle." *New Scientist* 195 (August 4, 2007): 41–45.

Palm, Julius Philip de, ed. *Encyclopedie van de Nederlandse Antillen*. Zutphen: Walburg Pers, 1985.

Pares, Richard. *War and Trade in the West Indies, 1739–1763.* Oxford: Clarendon Press, 1936.

——. *Yankees and Creoles: The Trade between North America and the West Indies before the American Revolution.* Cambridge, MA: Harvard University Press, 1956.

Paula, Alejandro F., ed. *1795: De slavenopstand op Curaçao: Een bronnenuitgave van de originele overheidsdocu-menten.* Curaçao: s.n., 1974.

Perera, Miguel Ángel. *La provincia fantasma: Guyana siglo XVII: Ecología cultural y antropología histórica de una rapiña, 1598–1704.* Caracas: Universidad Central de Venezuela, Consejo de Desarrollo Científico y Humanistico, 2003.

Pérotin-Dumon, Anne. *La ville aux îles, la ville dans l'île: Basse-Terre et Pointe-à-Pitre, Guadeloupe, 1650–1820.* Paris: Éditions Karthala, 2000.

Phaf-Rheinberger, Ineke. *The "Air of Liberty": Narratives of the South Atlantic Past.* Amsterdam: Rodopi, 2008.

Pijl, Yvon van der. *Levende-doden: Afrikaans-Surinaamse percepties, praktijken en rit-uelen rondom dood en rouw.* Amsterdam: IBS/Rozenburg, 2007.

Pistorius, Thomas. *Korte en zakelyke beschryvinge van de Colonie van Zuriname [. . .].* Amsterdam: Crajenschot, 1763.

Pitman, Frank Wesley. *The Development of the British West Indies, 1700–1763.* New Haven: Yale University Press, 1917.

Plockhoy, Pieter Cornelisz. *Kort en klaer ontwerp, diendende tot een onderling accoort, om den arbeyd, onrust en moeyeleyckheyt van alderley handwerckluyden te verlich-ten door een onderlinge Compagnie ofte Volckplanting aan de Zuyt-revier in Nieuw-Nederland op te rechten* Amsterdam: Otto Barentsz. Smient, 1662.

Popkin, Jeremy D. "Print Culture in the Netherlands on the Eve of the Revolution." In *Dutch Republic*, edited by Jacob and Mijnhardt, 273–91.

Posthumus, Nicolaas Wilhelmus. *Inquiry into the History of Prices of Holland.* 2 vols. Leiden: E. J. Brill, 1946.

——. *Nederlandsche prijsgeschiedenis.* 2 vols. Leiden: E. J. Brill, 1943.

Postma, Johannes. "Breaching the Mercantile Barriers of the Dutch Colonial Empire: North American Trade with Surinam during the Eighteenth Century." In *Merchant Organization and Maritime Trade in the North Atlantic, 1660–1815*, edited by Olaf Uwe Janzen, 107–31. St. John's, Newfoundland: International Maritime Economic History Association, 1998.

——. *The Dutch in the Atlantic Slave Trade.* New York: Cambridge University Press, 1990.

——. "A Reassessment of the Dutch Atlantic Slave Trade." In *Riches from Atlantic Commerce*, edited by Postma and Enthoven, 115–38.

——. "Suriname and its Atlantic Connections, 1667–1795." In *Riches from Atlantic Commerce*, edited by Postma and Enthoven, 287–322.

Postma, Johannes, and Victor Enthoven, eds. *Riches from Atlantic Commerce: Dutch Transatlantic Trade and Shipping, 1585–1817.* Leiden: Brill, 2003.

Pottle, Frederick A., ed. *Boswell in Holland 1763–1764.* New Haven: Yale University Press, 1928.

Prado, Fabrício. *Edge of Empire: Atlantic Networks and Revolution in Bourbon Río de la Plata.* Berkeley: University of California Press, 2015.

Price, Jacob M. "The Imperial Economy, 1700–1776." In *The Oxford History of the British Empire*. Vol. 2, *The Eighteenth Century*, edited by Peter J. Marshall, Alaine Low, and William Roger Louis. Oxford: Oxford University Press, 1998.

Price, Richard. *Alabi's World*. Baltimore: Johns Hopkins University Press, 1990.

———. *First-Time: The Historical Vision of an Afro-American People*. Baltimore: John Hopkins University Press, 1983.

Price, Richard, and Sally Price. "Introduction." In John Gabriel Stedman, *Narrative of a Five Years Expedition against the Revolted Negroes of Surinam . . .* , by John Gabriel Stedman, xiii–xcvii. Baltimore: Johns Hopkins University Press, 1988.

———, eds., *Stedman's Surinam: Life in an Eighteenth-Century Slave Society*. Baltimore and London: Johns Hopkins University Press, 1992.

Price, Sally, and Richard Price. *Afro-American Arts of the Suriname Rain Forest*. Berkeley: University of California Press, 1980.

———. *Maroon Arts. Cultural Vitality in the African Diaspora*. Boston: Beacon Press, 1999.

Pritchard, James. "The Franco-Dutch War in the West Indies, 1672–1678: An Early 'Lesson' in Imperial Defense." In *New Interpretations in Naval History: Selected Papers from the Thirteenth Naval History Symposium held at Annapolis, Maryland, 2–4 October 1997*, edited by William M. McBride and Eric P. Reed. Annapolis: Naval Institute Press, 1998.

———. *In Search of Empire: The French in the Americas, 1670–1730*. Cambridge: Cambridge University Press, 2004.

Putte, Florimon van. *Dede piquiña ku su bisiña: Papiamentu-Nederlands en de onverwerkt verleden tijd*. Zutphen: Walburg Pers, 1999.

Ratelband, Klaas. *Nederlanders in West-Afrika 1600–1650: Angola, Kongo en São Tomé*. Zutphen: Walburg Pers, 2000.

Raynal, Guillaume-Thomas. *Histoire philosophique et politique des établissements et du commerce des Européens dans les deux Indes*. Amsterdam: 1774.

———. *Tafreel van de bezittingen en den koophandel der Europeänen in de beide Indiën, getrokken uit de wysgerige en staatkundige geschiedenis van de bezittingen en den koophandel der Europeänen in de beide Indiën*. Amsterdam: M. Schalekamp, 1784.

———. *Suppléments a l'histoire philosophique et politique des établissements et du commerce des Européens dans les deux Indes*. The Hague: 1781.

Rechtsgeleerd advis in de zaak van den gewezen Stadhouder, en over deszelfs schryven aan de gouverneurs van de Oost- en West-Indische bezittingen van den Staat. Door de burgers mr. B.[avius] Voorda en mr. J[ohan] Valckenaer. Ingelevert ter Vergadering der Provisioneele Representanten van het Volk van Holland. op den 7 January 1796 en in 't licht gegeven op last derzelve Vergadering. The Hague: ter 's Lands Drukkerye van Holland, 1796.

Reesse, Jan Jacob. *De suikerhandel van Amsterdam van 1813 tot 1894: Een bijdrage tot de handelsgeschiedenis des vaderlands hoofdzakelijk uit de archieven verzameld en samengesteld door J.J. Reesse*. The Hague: Nijhoff, 1911.

Reinders Folmer-Van Prooijen, C. *Van goederenhandel naar slavenhandel: De Middelburgse Commercie Compagnie, 1720–1755*. Middelburg: Koninklijk Zeeuwsch Genootschap der Wetenschappen, 2000.

Reitsma, Ella. *Maria Sibylla Merian & dochters: Vrouwenlevens tussen kunst en wetenschap.* Zwolle: Waanders, 2008.

Renkema, Wim. "'Slavernij en koloniale experimenten, 1815–1866: A. Kikkert." In *De gouverneurs van de Nederlandse Antillen sinds 1815,* edited by Gert Oostindie, 27–31. Leiden: KITLV Uitgeverij, 2011.

——. *Het Curaçaose plantagebedrijf in de negentiende eeuw.* Zutphen: Walburg Pers, 1981.

Report and Accompanying Papers of the Commission appointed by the President of the United States to investigate and report on the divisional line between the Republic of Venezuela and British Guiana. Washington, DC: Government Printing Office, 1897.

Riemer, Johann Andreas. *Missions-Reise nach Suriname und Berbice: Zu einer am Surinamfluss im dritten Grad der Linie wohnende Freynegernation, nebst einige Bemerkungen über die Missionsanstalten der Brüderunität zu Paramaribo.* Zittau/ Leipzig: Schöpfische Buchhandlung, 1810.

Roberts, Lissa. "Situation Science: Local Exchanges and Networks of Circulation." *Itinerario* 33 (2009): 9–30.

Robles, Gregorio de. *América a fines del siglo XVII: Noticias de los lugares de contrabando.* Valladolid: Casa-Museo de Colón, Seminario americanista de la Universidad de Valladolid, 1980.

Rochefort, Charles de. *Histoire naturelle et morale des iles Antilles de l'Amérique.* Rotterdam: Arnout Leers, 1658.

——. *Le tableau de l'isle de Tabago, ou de la Nouvelle Oüalchre, l'une des Isles Antilles de l'Amerique, Dependante de la souverainité des Hauts & Puissans Seigneurs les Estats Generaus des Provinces Unies des Pais-bas.* Leyde: Jean le Carpentier, 1665.

Rodway, James. *History of British Guiana from the Year 1668 to the Present Time.* Georgetown: J. Thompson, 1891.

Rogge, J. *Het handelshuis Van Eeghen: Proeve eener geschiedenis van een Amsterdamsch handelshuis.* Amsterdam: Van Ditmar, 1948.

Roitman, Jessica Vance. "Portuguese Jews, Amerindians, and the Frontiers of Encounter in Colonial Suriname." *New West Indian Guide* 88 (2014): 18–52.

Roitman, Jessica Vance, and Han Jordaan. "Fighting a Foregone Conclusion: Local Interest Groups, West Indian Merchants, and St. Eustatius, 1780–1810." *Tijdschrift voor Sociale en Economische Geschiedenis* 12 (2015): 79–100.

Romney, Susanah Shaw. *New Netherland Connections: Intimate Networks and Atlantic Ties in Seventeenth-Century America.* Chapel Hill: University of North Carolina Press for the Omohundro Institute of Early American History and Culture, 2014.

Rossum, Matthias van, and Karwan Fatah-Black. "Wat is winst? De economische impact van de Nederlandse trans-atlantische slavenhandel," *Tijdschrift voor Sociale en Economische Geschiedenis* 9 (2012): 3–29.

Rudé, George. *The Crowd in History. A Study of Popular Disturbances in France and England, 1730–1848.* New York: Wiley & Sons, 1964.

Rupert, Linda M. *Creolization and Contraband: Curaçao in the Early Modern Atlantic World.* Athens and London: The University of Georgia Press, 2012.

——. "Inter-colonial Networks and Revolutionary Ferment in Eighteenth-Century Curaçao and Tierra Firme." In *Curaçao in the Age of Revolutions*, edited by Klooster and Oostindie, 75–96.

Rutgers, Wim, ed. *Michael Joannes Schabel: missionaris op Curaçao (1704–1713)*. Willemstad: University of Curaçao; Fundashon pa Planifikashon di Idioma, 2016.

——. "Schrijven is zilver, spreken is goud: Oratuur, auratuur en literatuur van de Nederlandse Antillen en Aruba." PhD diss., Utrecht University, 1994.

Rutten, A. M. G. *Apothekers en chirurgijns: Gezondheidszorg op de Benedenwindse eilanden van de Nederlandse Antillen in de negentiende eeuw*. Assen: Van Gorcum, 1989.

——. *Dutch Transatlantic Medicine Trade in the Eighteenth Century Under the Cover of the West India Company*. Rotterdam: Erasmus Publishing, 2000.

Sack, Albert von. *A narrative of a voyage to Surinam: of a residence there during 1805, 1806, and 1807; and of the author's return to Europe by way of North America*. London: W. Bulmer, 1810.

Sánchez Belén, Juan Antonio. "El comercio holandés en la bahía de Cádiz en 1684." In *El Sistema Atlántico español (siglos XVII–XIX)*, edited by Carlos Martinez Shaw and José María Oliva Melgar, 163–202. Madrid: Marcial Pons, 2005.

Satsuma, Shinsuke. *Britain and Colonial Maritime War in the Early Eighteenth Century: Silver, Seapower and the Atlantic*. Woodbridge: Boydell Press, 2013.

Schalkwijk, Marten. *The Colonial State in the Caribbean: Structural Analysis and Changing Elite Networks in Suriname, 1650–1920*. The Hague: Amrit/NiNsee, 2010.

Schama, Simon. *The Embarrassment of Riches: An Interpretation of Dutch Culture in the Golden Age*. Berkeley: University of California Press, 1988.

Schelling, G. W. "Verhandeling over den melaatschheid." PhD diss., University of Utrecht, 1769.

Schiltkamp, Jacob A. and Jacobus Thomas de Smidt, eds. *West Indisch Plakaatboek: Plakaten, ordonnantiën en andere wetten, uitgevaardigd in Suriname, 1667–1816*. Amsterdam: S. Emmering, 1973.

——, eds. *West Indisch Plakaatboek: Publikaties en andere wetten alsmede de oudste resoluties betrekking hebbende op Curaçao, Aruba, Bonaire*. Amsterdam: S. Emmering, 1978.

Schmidt, Benjamin. "The Dutch Atlantic: From Provincialism to Globalism." In *Atlantic History: A Critical Appraisal*, edited by Jack P. Greene and Philip D. Morgan, 163–87. Oxford: Oxford University Press, 2009.

——. *Innocence Abroad: The Dutch Imagination and the New World, 1570–1670*. Cambridge: Cambridge University Press, 2001.

——. *Inventing Exoticism: Geography, Globalism, and Europe's Early Modern World*. Philadelphia: University of Pennsylvania Press, 2015.

Schneeloch, Norbert H. *Aktionäre der Westindischen Compagnie von 1674: die Verschmelzung der alten Kapitalgebergruppen zu einer neuen Aktiengesellschaft*. Stuttgart: Klett-Cotta, 1982.

——. "Die Bewindhebber der Westindischen Compagnie in der Kammer Amsterdam 1674–1700." *Economisch- en Sociaal-Historisch Jaarboek* 36 (1973): 1–52.

Schneider, Maarten, and Joan Hemels. *De Nederlandse krant 1618–1978: Van 'nieuwstydinghe' tot dagblad*. Baarn: Wereldvenster, 1979.

Schnurmann, Claudia. *Atlantische Welten: Engländer und Niederländer im amerikanisch-atlantischen Raum 1648–1713.* Köln: Böhlau Verlag, 1998.

Schomburgk, Robert Hermann. *A Description of British Guiana, Geographical and Statistical: Exhibiting its Resources and Capabilities, Together with the Present and Future Condition and Prospects of the Colony.* London: Cass, 1970 [1840].

Schotanus, F. B. *Raadpensionaris L.P. van der Spiegel: Tussen twee republieken.* Amstelveen: Schotanus Boeken, 2002.

Schunck, Christine W. M. "Michael Joannes Alexius Schabel S. J., "Notitia de Coraçao, Bonayre, Oruba" 1705 and "Diurnum" (1707–1708)." *Archivum Historicum Societatis Iesu* 66 (1997): 89–162.

Schutte, Gerrit Jan. *De Nederlandse Patriotten en de kolonien: Een onderzoek naar hun denkbeelden en optreden, 1770–1800.* Groningen: Wolters, 1974.

Schwartz, Stuart B., and Johannes Postma. "The Dutch Republic and Brazil as Commercial Partners on the West African Coast during the Eighteenth Century." In *Riches from Atlantic Commerce*, edited by Postma and Enthoven, 171–99.

Scott, Julius S. "Crisscrossing Empires: Ships, Sailors and Resistance in the Lesser Antilles in the Eighteenth Century." In *Lesser Antilles*, edited by Paquette and Engerman, 128–43.

Sens, Angelie. "Dutch Anti-Slavery Attitudes in a Decline-Ridden Society, 1750–1815." In *Fifty Years Later*, edited by Oostindie, 89–104.

——. *"Mensaap, heiden, slaaf"*: *Nederlandse visies op de wereld rond 1800.* The Hague: SDU Uitgevers, 2001.

Shumway, Rebecca. *The Fante and the Transatlantic Slave Trade.* Rochester, NY: University of Rochester Press, 2011.

Sijpesteijn, Cornelius Ascanius van. *Mr. Jan Jacob Mauricius, gouverneur-generaal van Suriname, van 1742 tot 1751.* The Hague: de gebroeders van Cleef, 1858.

Siwpersad, Jozef Pranhudass. *De Nederlandse regering en de afschaffing van de Surinaamse slavernij (1833–1863).* Groningen: Bouma, 1979.

Smith, Adam. *An Inquiry into the Nature and Causes of the Wealth of Nations.* Amsterdam: MetaLibri, 2007.

Smith, Norval S. H. "The History of the Surinamese Creoles II: Origin and Differentiation." In *Atlas*, edited by Carlin and Arends, 131–51.

Smith, Simon D. "Gedney Clarke of Salem and Barbados: Transatlantic Super-Merchant." *New England Quarterly* 76 (2003): 499–549.

Snelders, Stephen. *Vrijbuiters van de heelkunde: Op zoek naar medische kennis in de tropen 1600–1800.* Amsterdam: Atlas, 2012.

Spooner, Frank C. *Risks at Sea: Amsterdam Insurance and Maritime Europe, 1766–1780.* Cambridge: Cambridge University Press, 1983.

Stanwood, Owen. "Between Eden and Empire: Huguenot Refugees and the Promise of New Worlds." *American Historical Review* 118, no. 5 (2013): 1319–44.

Stedman, John Gabriel. *Narrative, of a Five Years Expedition against the Revolted Negroes of Surinam.* London: J. Johnson and J. Edwards, 1796.

Stipriaan, Alex van. "Debunking Debts: Image and Reality of a Colonial Crisis: Suriname at the End of the 18th Century." *Itinerario: European Journal of Overseas History* 19 (1995): 69–84.

——. *Surinaams contrast: Roofbouw en overleven in een Caraïbische plantagekolonie, 1750–1863.* Leiden: KITLV Uitgeverij, 1993.

——. "The Suriname Rat Race: Labour and Technology on Sugar Plantations, 1750–1900." *New West Indian Guide* 63 (1989): 94–117.

Stipriaan, Alex van, Waldo Heilbron, Aspha Bijnaar, and Valika Smeulders. *Op zoek naar de stilte: Sporen van het slavernijverleden in Nederland.* Leiden/Amsterdam: KITLV Uitgeverij/NiNsee, 2007.

Stoffers, Antonius Lambertus. "Botanisch onderzoek van de Nederlandse Antillen," *Nieuwe West-Indische Gids* 46 (1968): 73–89.

Swaving, Justus Gerardus. *Swaving's reizen en lotgevallen; Door hemzelve beschreven.* Dordrecht: Blussé & Van Braam, 1827.

Tapley, Harriet Silvester, ed. *Early Coastwise and Foreign Shipping of Salem: A Record of the Entrances and Clearances of the Port of Salem, 1750–1769.* Salem, MA: The Essex Institute, 1934.

Tarrade, Jean. "Le commerce entre les Antilles françaises et les possessions espagnoles d'Amérique à la fin du XVIIIe siècle." In *Commerce et plantation dans la Caraïbe XVIIIe et XIXe siècles: Actes du Colloque de Bordeaux, 15–16 mars 1991,* edited by Paul Butel, 27–43. Bordeaux: Maison des Pays Ibériques, 1992.

Thoden van Velzen, Hendrik Ulbo Erik, and Wim Hoogbergen. *Een zwarte vrijstaat: De Okaanse samenleving in de 18e eeuw.* Leiden: KITLV Uitgeverij, 2011.

Thoden van Velzen, Hendrik Ulbo Erik, and W. van Wetering. *The Great Father and the Danger: Religious Cults, Material Forces, and Collective Fantasies in the World of the Surinamese Maroons.* Dordrecht: Foris, 1988.

Thompson, Alvin O. *Colonialism and Underdevelopment in Guyana, 1580–1803.* Bridgetown, Barbados: Carib Research & Publications, 1987.

Thornton, John. *A Cultural History of the Atlantic World, 1250–1820.* Cambridge: Cambridge University Press, 2012.

Truxes, Thomas M. *Defying Empire: Trading with the Enemy in Colonial New York.* New Haven: Yale University Press, 2008.

——, ed. *Letterbook of Greg & Cunningham, 1756–1757: Merchants of New York and Belfast.* Oxford: Oxford University Press for the British Academy, 2001.

Tyler, John W. *Smugglers and Patriots: Boston Merchants and the Advent of the American Revolution.* Boston: Northeastern University Press, 1986.

"Uit de pers." *West-Indische Gids* 1 (1919): 496–500.

Veen, Sytze van der. *Groot-Nederland & Groot-Colombia, 1815–1830: De droom van Willem I.* Hilversum: Uitgeverij Verloren, 2015.

Veenendaal, Augustus Johannes, Jr. *De briefwisseling van Anthonie Heinsius 1702–1720.* Vol. 2. The Hague: Martinus Nijhoff, 1978.

Veluwenkamp, Jan Willem. "Ondernemersgedrag op de Hollandse stapelmarkt in de tijd van de Republiek: De Amsterdamse handelsfirma Jan Isaac de Neufville & Comp., 1730–1764." PhD diss., University of Leiden, 1981.

Venezuela-British Guiana Boundary Arbitration: The Case of the United States of Venezuela before the Tribunal of Arbitration to Convene at Paris. 3 vols. New York: Evening Post, 1898.

Verhees-Van Meer, J. Th. J. *De Zeeuwse kaapvaart tijdens de Spaanse Successieoorlog 1702–1713.* Middelburg: Koninklijk Zeeuwsch Genootschap der Wetenschappen, 1986.

Villiers, Patrick. *Le commerce colonial atlantique et la guerre d'indépendance des États Unis d'Amérique 1778–1783.* New York: Arno Press, 1977.

——. *Marine royale, corsaires et trafic dans l'Atlantique de Louis XIV à Louis XVI.* Dunkerque: Société Dunkerquoise d'Histoire et d'Archéologie, 1991.

Villiers, John A. J. de. *Storm van 's Gravesande; Zijn werk en zijn leven uit zijne brieven opgebouwd.* The Hague: Nijhoff, 1920.

Vink, Wieke. *Creole Jews: Negotiating Community in Colonial Suriname.* Leiden: KITLV Press, 2010.

Visman, M. A. "Van slaaf tot plantagehouder: Een aspect van het 18e eeuws plantagewezen op Curaçao," *Nieuwe West-Indische Gids 55*, no. 1 (1981): 39–51.

Visser, Cornelis. "Verkeersindustrieën te Rotterdam in de tweede helft der achttiende eeuw." PhD diss., Nederlandsche Handels-Hoogeschool, 1927.

Vivas Piñedo, Gerardo. "Botín a bordo: Enriquecimiento ilícito en el corso guipuzcoano de Venezuela durante el siglo XVIII." *Itsas Memoria. Revista de Estudios Marítimos del País Vasco 5* (2006): 357–77.

Vliet, Rietje van. *Elie Luzac (1721–1796): Boekverkoper van de Verlichting.* Nijmegen: Vantilt, 2009.

Voegen van Engelen, J. *De Surinaamsche artz 1786–1788: Facsimile met een inleiding van Prof. Dr. G.A. Lindeboom.* Utrecht: Natuurwetenschappelijke Studiekring voor Suriname en de Nederlandse Antillen, 1981 [1788].

Vogt, John. *Portuguese Rule on the Gold Coast, 1469–1682.* Athens: University of Georgia Press, 1979.

Voorhees, David William. "In the Republic's Tradition: The Persistence of Dutch Culture in the Mid-Atlantic Colonies after the 1664 English Conquest." *De Halve Maen* 74, no. 3 (2001), 49–54.

Voort, Johannes Petrus van de. "De Westindische plantages van 1720 tot 1795: financiën en handel." PhD diss., University of Nijmegen, 1973.

Vos, Jelmer. "The Slave Trade from the Windward Coast: The Case of the Dutch, 1740–1805." *African Economic History* 38 (2010): 29–51.

Vries, David Pietersz de. *Korte Historiael ende Journaels Aenteykeninge van verscheyden voyagiens in de vier delen des werelts-ronde, als Europa, Africa, Asia ende America gedaen.* Edited by Herman Theodoor Colenbrander. The Hague: Martinus Nijhoff, 1911.

Vries, Jan de. "The Dutch Atlantic Economies," in *The Atlantic Economy during the Seventeenth and Eighteenth Centuries: Organization, Operation, Practice, and Personnel,* edited by Peter A. Coclanis, 1–29. Columbia, South Carolina: University of South Carolina Press, 2005.

——. "The Limits of Globalization in the Early Modern World." *The Economic History Review* 63:3 (2010): 710–33.

——. "The Netherlands in the New World: The Legacy of European Fiscal, Monetary, and Trading Institutions for New World Development from the Seventeenth to the Nineteenth Centuries." In *Transferring Wealth and Power from the Old World to the New: Monetary and Fiscal Institutions in the 17th through the 19th Centuries,* edited by Michael D. Bordo and Roberto Cortés-Conde, 100–139. Cambridge: Cambridge University Press, 2001.

Vries, Jan de, and Ad van der Woude. *Nederland 1500–1815: De eerste ronde van moderne economisch groei.* Amsterdam: Balans, 1995.

——. *The First Modern Economy: Success, Failure, and Perseverance of the Dutch Economy, 1500–1815.* Cambridge: Cambridge University Press, 1997.

Vrij, Jean Jacques. "Wapenvolk in een wingewest: de slavenkolonie Suriname, 1667–1799." In *Geweld in de West*, edited by Enthoven, Den Heijer, and Jordaan, 45–74.

Wagenaar, Jan. *Hedendaagse historie, of Tegenwoordige staat der Vereenigde Nederlanden.* Amsterdam: Isaak Tirion, 1739.

——. *Vaderlandsche historie, vervattende de geschiedenissen der nu Vereenigde Nederlanden, inzonderheid die van Holland, van de vroegste tyden af.* Amsterdam: Isaak Tirion, 1751.

Wallerstein, Immanuel. *The Modern World-System.* Vol. 2, *Mercantilism and the Consolidation of the European World-Economy, 1600–1750.* New York: Academic Press, 1980.

Ward, Kerry. *Networks of Empire: Forced Migration in the Dutch East India Company.* Cambridge: Cambridge University Press, 2008.

Weeden, William B. *Early Rhode Island: A Social History of the People.* New York: Grafton Press, 1910.

Welling, George M. "The Prize of Neutrality: Trade Relations between Amsterdam and North America 1771–1817; A Study in Computational History." PhD diss., University of Groningen, 1998.

White, Philip L. *The Beekmans of New York in Politics and Commerce, 1647–1877.* New York: New York Historical Society, 1956.

Whitehead, Neil L. *Lords of the Tiger Spirit: A History of the Caribs in Colonial Venezuela and Guyana 1498–1820.* Dordrecht: Foris, 1988.

Wijhe, J. M. "Amsterdam in het begin der 17e eeuw: Aanteekeningen van Ernst Brinck," *Amstelodamum* 20 (1923): 25–33.

Wijk, E. van. "Chocolademolens en de Fak Brouwers." *De Wete* 27, no. 2 (1998): 2–11.

Wijsenbeek, Thera. "Ernst en Luim. Koffiehuizen in de Republiek." In *Koffie in Nederland: Vier eeuwen cultuurgeschiedenis*, edited by Pim Reinders, Thera Wijsebeek, and S. Braat, 32–54. Zutphen: Walburg Pers, 1994.

Wijsenbeek-Olthuis, Thera. *Achter de gevels van Delft: Bezit en bestaan van rijk en arm in een periode van achteruitgang (1700–1800).* Hilversum: Verloren, 1987.

Wilson, Arthur McCandless. *French Foreign Policy during the Administration of Cardinal Fleury, 1726–1743: A Study in Diplomacy and Commercial Development.* Cambridge, MA: Harvard University Press, 1936.

Wilson, Victor. *Commerce in Disguise: War and Trade in the Caribbean Free Port of Gustavia, 1793–1815.* Åbo: Åbo Akademi University Press, 2015.

Winter, Pieter Jan van. *Het aandeel van den Amsterdamschen handel aan den opbouw van het Amerikaansche Gemeenebest.* The Hague: Martinus Nijhoff, 1927.

——. *De Westindische Compagnie ter kamer Stad en Lande.* The Hague: Martinus Nijhoff, 1978.

Wokeck, Marianne S. *Trade in Strangers: The Beginnings of Mass Migration to North America.* University Park: The Pennsylvania State University Press, 1999.

Wolbers, Julien. *Geschiedenis van Suriname.* Amsterdam: S. Emmering, 1970 [1861].

Wood, George Arthur. *William Shirley, Governor of Massachusetts, 1741–1756: A History.* New York: Columbia University, Longmans, Greene & Co., and London: P. S. King & Son, 1920.

Wooding, Charles Johan. *Evolving Culture: A Cross-Cultural Study of Suriname, West-Africa and the Caribbean.* Washington, DC: University Press of America, 1981.

Worden, Nigel, ed. *Cape Town between East and West: Cultural Identities in a Dutch Colonial Town.* Johannesburg: Jacana, and Hilversum: Verloren, 2012.

Yarak, Larry W. *Asante and the Dutch, 1744–1873.* Oxford: Clarendon Press, 1990.

Zanden, Jan Luiten van, and Arthur van Riel. *Nederland 1780–1914: Staat, instituties en economische ontwikkeling.* Amsterdam: Balans, 2000.

Zandvliet, Kees. *Mapping for Money: Maps, Plans and Topographic Paintings and their Role in Dutch Overseas Expansion during the 16th and 17th centuries.* Amsterdam: De Bataafsche Leeuw, 1998.

Zijlstra, Suze, "Anglo-Dutch Suriname: Ethnic Interaction and Colonial Transition in the Caribbean, 1651–1682," PhD thesis, University of Amsterdam, 2015.

INDEX

Adams, John, 51
Ahanta people, 101, 103
Akan people, 114, 118–19, 251
Allen, Thomas, 44
Amanahyia, 103
American Revolutionary War, 55–56, 69,
    77, 182, 186, 227, 246, 249
Amerikaansche voyagien, 214
Amerindians, 10, 21, 29–31, 37–38, 50,
    121–23, 128–29, 131, 143–50, 162,
    182, 184, 221, 251
Amo, Anton Wilhelm, 117
Amsterdam: Abraham ter Borch & Sons,
    68; Berbice, role in, 32, 61, 136; cacao
    market, 36, 92; coffee cultivation,
    126, 218; commercial links, 12, 36,
    71, 73, 75–76, 89–93, 126, 130, 219;
    Curaçao, role in, 73; de Neufville trade
    house, 69; ecclesiastical authority,

12, 187–88; Jewish population,
159–60; labor environment, 92–93;
mercantilist policies, 26, 30, 75–76,
134; National Slavery Monument,
2; New York, trade with, 76; planter
loans, 67–68, 71; political dominance,
7, 9; publishing industry, 215–16;
slave trade, impact on, 80, 107; sugar
industry, 89, 91, 218; Suriname, role
in, 71, 134; tobacco industry, 91–92,
218; West India Company (WIC)
chamber, 9, 52, 58, 60–62, 66, 107
Andresote, 36
Angola, 24, 80, 84, 148
Angostura, 29
Anguilla, 43–44
annatto, 29–30, 254
Antigua, 31, 39, 43–44, 48, 52
Antwerp, 20–21, 218

Lightning Source UK Ltd.
Milton Keynes UK
UKHW010716070820
367846UK00002B/452/J